Southern Living
COOK-OFF
COOKBOOK

Lucky 7 Coconut-
Lemon Cake

Southern Living®

COOK-OFF

COOKBOOK

Oxmoor House®

Cover: Southern-Fried Stuffed Chicken With Roasted Red
Pepper-and-Vidalia Onion Gravy, page 23
Back Cover: Cream Cheese Flan, page 284; Tex-Mex Egg Rolls
With Creamy Cilantro Dipping Sauce, page 230; Spicy Tex-Mex
Chicken Cobbler, page 166; Melt-in-Your-Mouth Braised and
Barbecued Chicken, page 95

Southern Living®

Executive Editor: Susan Dosier
Foods Editors: Scott Jones, Andria Scott Hurst
Senior Writer: Donna Florio
Associate Foods Editors: Shirley Harrington, John McMillan,
    Kate Nicholson, Mary Allen Perry, Shannon Sliter Satterwhite,
    Joy E. Zacharia
Assistant Foods Editor: Vicki Poellnitz
Assistant Recipe Editor: John McMillan
Test Kitchens Director: Lyda H. Jones
Assistant Test Kitchens Director: James Schend
Test Kitchens Specialist/Food Styling: Vanessa A. McNeil
Test Kitchens Staff: Rebecca Kracke Gordon, Pam Lolley,
    Alyssa Porubcan, Angela Sellers, Vie Warshaw
Senior Photographers: Ralph Anderson, Charles Walton IV
Photographers: Tina Cornett, Mary Margaret Chambliss,
    William Dickey, Beth Dreiling
Senior Photo Stylist: Buffy Hargett
Assistant Photo Stylist: Rose Nguyen, Lisa Powell, Cari South
Photo Services Director: Ann Nathews Griffin
Photo Librarian: Tracy Duncan
Photo Services: Amanda Leigh Abbett, Ginny P. Allen,
    Catherine Carr, Lisa Dawn Love

Oxmoor House, Inc.

Editor in Chief: Nancy Fitzpatrick Wyatt
Executive Editor: Susan Carlisle Payne
Art Director: Cynthia R. Cooper
Copy Chief: Allison Long Lowery

Southern Living® *Cook-Off Cookbook*

Editor: Alyson Moreland Haynes
Senior Writer: Patricia Wilens
Copy Editors: Donna Baldone, Jacqueline B. Giovanelli
Editorial Assistant: Dawn Russell
Senior Photographer: Jim Bathie
Photographer: Brit Huckabay
Senior Photo Stylist: Kay E. Clarke
Photo Stylist: Amy Wilson, Ashley Wyatt
Director, Test Kitchens: Elizabeth Tyler Luckett
Assistant Director, Test Kitchens: Julie Christopher
Test Kitchens Staff: Kristi Carter, Nicole Lee Faber, Kathleen
    Royal Phillips, Jan A. Smith, Elise Weis, Kelley Wilton
Color Specialist: Rick Tucker
Director of Production: Phillip Lee
Associate Production Manager: Leslie Wells Johnson
Production Assistant: Faye Porter Bonner

Contributors

Designer: Nancy C. Johnson
Indexer: Mary Ann Laurens
Editorial Consultant: Jean Wickstrom Liles
Photographers: Adam Barnes, Lee Harrelson
Interns: Amber Ballew, Tamara Goldis, Julie Perno

Contents

Dear Friends,

Our *Southern Living* Cook-Off is the largest annual Cook-Off in the country, and with almost 34,000 entries in the 2003 competition, you can imagine how difficult it was to select the finalists. But what a mouthwatering experience! And what wonderful recipes were leftover to fill our files and to share with you through the pages of our magazines and cookbooks.

In addition to all the prizewinning recipes from the 2003 contest, this all-new cookbook is packed full of some of the most irresistible contest submissions from all over the country. In these 434 recipes and over 150 color photos, you'll definitely detect a Southern accent with a fresh, contemporary twist. You're sure to find just the right recipe for next weekend's supper club or tonight's pasta dinner.

To qualify as a contest finalist, entrants had to include every essential detail and instruction in his or her recipe. We didn't make any changes to the finalists' recipes; however, we did occasionally make changes to the recipes in this book to adjust salt or flavor levels or to alter the preparation method to give the dish broader appeal. The result is a top-notch collection of all-new recipes you'll prize in your kitchen. We certainly loved tasting and photographing them.

So grab your mixer, heat up your skillet, and step up to the grill. A grand taste of *Southern Living* Cook-Off 2003 awaits you.

Susan Dosier

Susan Dosier
Executive Foods Editor
Southern Living

P.S. Consider this letter a personal invitation to enter the next *Southern Living* Cook-Off. We'd love to see *your* recipe win $100,000—just like first-time entrant Susan Rotter did in 2003. To enter, your recipe needs to include at least one sponsor product—a product made by one of the advertisers in our magazine. Some of the finest companies in the United States are sponsors, so our entrants found this easy to do. We're grateful to each of the sponsors who helped make this contest possible. The contest categories and sponsors change a little each year, so visit **www.southernlivingcookoff.com** for the latest information and rules—or call and ask us to mail them to you (1-800-366-4712). We add sponsors throughout the year, so be sure to check the list occasionally.

2003 Cook-Off Highlights

Take a ringside seat as the nation's most inventive
cooks bake, fry, grill, and sauté their way to the
pinnacle of cooking fame and fortune. Here's a taste
of the fun and excitement that leads up to the
presentation of the $100,000 grand prize!

Take a behind-the-scenes look at our $100,000 recipe contest!

In a weekend of friendly competition, one finalist wins bragging rights to the title "Best Cook in the South."

The *Southern Living* Cook-Off is 48 hours of food, fun, and suspense, a weekend of friendly competition and culinary finesse. When the crumbs settle, one lucky contestant goes home with $100,000 and a claim to the title "Best Cook in the South."

Southern Living staff prejudges contest entries in the Test Kitchen.

For nearly a year before the autumn weekend when the finalists face off, the magazine's staff wades through nearly 40,000 entries to narrow the field. (See *How to Create a Prize-winning Recipe*, page 355.)

Between January and June, recipes pour in via mail, fax, and the Internet, even Special Delivery. Foods Staff teams assess entries for taste potential, ease of preparation, creative use of sponsor products, and appeal to readers as they skim off the top contenders in each of five categories. Hundreds of recipes are tested and tasted during the summer until the staff chooses the best three in each category.

By the end of August, calls go out coast to coast to give the 15 lucky finalists the exciting news: 'Your recipe is tops, we'll see you at the Cook-Off.' Each finalist is guaranteed prizes of $1,000, a *Southern Living* cookbook library, and an all-expense paid trip to the Cook-Off for themselves and a guest.

Hugs and laughter that begin Thursday at the airport

Onstage at the Cook-Off

last through the weekend. Each arriving contestant is greeted by a *Southern Living* foods editor or Test Kitchens' specialist who is their individual host. "I felt like a celebrity for a few days, starting with being greeted at the airport with cameras and ribbons," says finalist **Karen Peters**. **Nancy Fazakerley** agrees, "The *Southern Living* family went all out to make us feel like VIPs."

At orientation Thursday afternoon, *Southern Living* Foods Editor Scott Jones explains the rules and schedule, then the contestants get to know one another. Teachers, homemakers,

"I didn't think I had a snowball's chance in a Viking oven until I got the call. Short of cooking with Julia Child, it doesn't get any better than this!"—Jeremy Bazata

Finalists wait to hear the *Signature Desserts* prize winner.

computer wiz, professional chef, designer, and business owners—they all love to cook and love to *talk* about cooking. "I learned a lot of great tips from the other finalists and feel privileged to be among them," says Nancy. Karen and **Jeremy Bazata** also praise the cordial atmosphere. "It isn't a competition as much as a sharing of friendship, inspiration, and culinary insights," says Jeremy. "It's not about winning—although that would be very exciting—it's about the inventive process."

Before Thursday's buffet dinner, the finalists tour the competition kitchens to check the facilities and supplies provided for the next day's cooking. Everything is ready . . . a year in the planning, the 2003 *Southern Living* Cook-Off is about to begin.

> "What made the event so special was the camaraderie among us."
> —Nancy Fazakerley

The History of the *Southern Living* Cook-Off

For 25 years, the *Southern Living* Cooking School's annual special section in the magazine showcased the best recipes we could create from sponsor products. In 2001, we decided to find out how our readers use these products and to reward the best recipes.

After a year of planning, the first *Southern Living* Cook-Off took place in September 2002 at Orlando's Gaylord Palms Resort. Ginnie Prater of Anniston, Alabama, took home the $100,000 grand prize for her Pecan Pie Cheesecake.

The 2003 Cook-Off took place in Nashville at the Gaylord Opryland Resort and Convention Center. (Meet Grand Prize Winner Susan Rotter and the other 14 finalists in profiles at the front of chapters 1–5.) The 2004 Cook-Off is set for Birmingham.

First Grand Prize Winner!

Ginnie Prater

Cooking gets under way Friday morning, each contestant working at an assigned station. Contestants have 90 minutes to prepare their dish—30 minutes for preparation and one hour of cooking time. (For recipes that take longer, contestants are allowed a head start on preparation the previous evening.) Finalists' recipes will be served to the judges by categories in 30-minute intervals. Ready, set, cook!

First up is the *Signature Desserts* category. **Lynda Sarkisian** is first ready to bake—her Sweet Potato Cake With Coconut Filling and Caramel Frosting is a multistep recipe, and the clock is ticking. Once the cake layers are out of the oven, Lynda puts them in a freezer to hasten the cooling process. Slices of her

Jeremy assembles the ingredients for her bread pudding.

Lynda Sarkisian   Jo Gonzalez-Hastings   Jeremy Bazata

cake join the Cream Cheese Flan made by **Jo Gonzalez-Hastings** and Jeremy's Layered Almond-Cream Cheese Bread Pudding With Amaretto Cream Sauce. A *Southern Living* staffer whisks all three dishes to the judges' room (see *Meet the Judges,* page 20) where one recipe will be awarded the $10,000 category prize, putting it in the running for the grand prize. (See chapters 1–5 for more about each finalist as well as their recipes.)

Lynda spreads the Caramel Frosting on her Sweet Potato Cake to present to the judges.

Karen Peters

Nancy Fazakerley

Ruth Kendrick

Karen, Nancy, and **Ruth Kendrick** keep the mood light as they prepare their recipes in the *One-Dish Wonders* category. "We had a blast preparing our dishes for judging," says Karen. "We joked, we laughed, we even sang while we cooked. We felt more like friends than contestants out to beat each other." Each finalist plates a serving of her cooked dish—Karen's Quick-and-Spicy Chicken 'n' Dumplings, Nancy's Tomato-Leek-Bacon Tart, and Ruth's Spicy Tex-Mex Chicken Cobbler.

Benjamin Chapin

John Mills

Susan Rotter

Benjamin Chapin and **John Mills** are the Cook-Off's two male contestants, joining **Susan Rotter** in the *Taste of the South* category. Susan is surprised by the convention center's unconventional kitchen setups. "Cooking without a sink was both frightening and enlightening," she says. "I didn't realize how dependent I am on running water."

Susan fries the chicken for what will become the grand prize winning dish.

Ben plates a serving of his Down-South Crab Cakes With Collard Greens and Roasted Garlic Beurre Blanc, while John puts the finishing touches on Sautéed Smoked Gouda Cheese Grits With Black Bean Salsa. Susan makes the deadline with Southern-Fried Stuffed Chicken With Roasted Red Pepper-and-Vidalia Onion Gravy.

Lynne Milliron

Gloria Bradley

Carol Daggers

Over at *Simple and Scrumptious Entrées*, **Lynne Milliron** drops shrimp into a sizzling skillet as fellow contestant **Gloria Bradley** prepares steaks for grilling. In a few minutes, Lynne's Texas Pesto Shrimp Over Rice is heading for the judges' room with Gloria's Grilled Chile-Rubbed Rib Eyes With Herb Cheese and Asparagus Bundles and Melt-in-Your-Mouth Braised and Barbecued Chicken made by **Carol Daggers**.

Frances Benthin and **Kathy Specht** are veteran contesters, so they share pointers with first-timer **Stacy Lamons** as they prepare their *Kids Love It!* recipes. "I know my recipe, so making it comes naturally," says Kathy. "I leave worrying about winning at home so I can take in all the fun and excitement."

Frances and Stacy are making finger-food recipes with Latino influences: Tex-Mex Chicken Crunchies and Tex-Mex Egg Rolls With Creamy Cilantro Dipping Sauce, respectively. Kathy serves up a sweet and gooey twist on an old favorite, French toast, with her Caramel-Pecan French Toast.

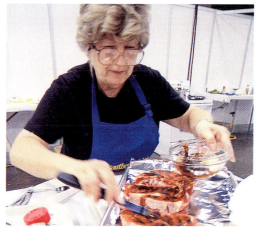
Gloria works backstage on the rib eye steaks that will be presented to the judges.

Frances Benthin

Kathy Specht

Stacy Lamons

Kathy works diligently to make her French toast the best it can be for the judges to taste.

"I'm here to do my best and have fun."
—Frances Benthin

Frances demonstrates her winning recipe onstage with Shirley Harrington from *Southern Living*.

The cooking done, finalists rehearse for the next day's demonstrations, which will be filmed for a cable television show. They try out the rock star–style microphone headsets they'll wear on stage. Later that evening, the contestants meet the judges at a gala dinner at the elegant Hermitage Suite Hotel hosted by *Southern Living* Editor in Chief John Floyd and Publisher Rich Smyth.

Before the Saturday taping, the finalists enjoy the royal treatment at the hotel's salon, followed by a photo session. At showtime, the

Lynne gets her make up applied at the hotel spa.

OUR CONTESTANTS' NUMBER ONE INSPIRATION: MOM

Nearly every Cook-Off finalist credits his or her cooking skills to a supportive mother or grandmother. Many recall early experiences that set them on the path to culinary excellence.

"My mom welcomed me in the kitchen, let me help, and had an abundance of patience," says Jeremy Bazata. "She made cooking fun for me and created culinary traditions that our family still celebrates today."

Susan Rotter remembers spending summer days in her grandmother's kitchen making biscuits, pies, cakes, and other wonderful things. "She was the first to show me that cooking could be an art," says Susan. Karen Peters credits her grandmother and great-grandmother for demonstrating that cooking can be a labor of love.

Ruth Kendrick's mother set an example. "She wasn't fancy, just a good, basic farm cook," says Ruth. "She cooked for the family and hired hands, and she always had a dessert, usually chocolate cake."

Mothers taught our contestants good habits. "My mom let me try anything as long as I cleaned up my mess," says Stacy Lamons. "She said a good chef always cleans up after herself." Waste not, want not was the credo of Kathy Specht's mother—whatever bizarre concoction Kathy made, the family ate it. "She also inspired me to be creative and to have a great time in the kitchen," says Kathy.

Many tales of toy ovens make us think that it may really be best to learn young. So take to heart this advice from grand-prize winner Susan Rotter: "Mothers, let your children make a mess in the kitchen. Learning to cook and succeeding at cooking instills self-esteem and teaches analytical skills —why didn't this rise, why is it different from last time. My mom let me cook and made me think I could do whatever I wanted, no matter what. That confidence has carried over into nearly every aspect of my life."

contestants are backstage watching on closed-circuit television as host Al Roker welcomes the audience. He introduces three *Southern Living* food experts who will present the recipes with the finalists: Test Kitchens Professional Rebecca Kracke Gordon, Assistant Test Kitchens Director James Schend, and Associate Foods Editor Shirley Harrington.

> "I was so busy enjoying everything that I can honestly say I was never nervous."
> —Karen Peters

The ladies of *Simple and Scrumptious Entrées* are first to take the stage. Al asks questions as an abbreviated version of each recipe is prepared. Suspense builds as Carol, Lynne, and Gloria await the judges' decision. Al announces the winner of the $10,000 category prize: Carol Daggers for Melt-in-Your-Mouth Braised and Barbecued Chicken.

Jeremy, Lynda, and Jo demonstrate their luscious *Signature Desserts* recipes. "We were calming each other down and cheering each other on," says Jeremy. Jo shrieks with delight when Al announces that her Cream Cheese Flan wins the category.

The remaining finalists demonstrate their recipes and then hear the announcement of each category winner. "For one thrilling moment, I felt like the star of my own cooking show," says Susan, who is named the winner of the *Taste of the South* category.

Ruth (center) is congratulated by Nancy and Karen as her chicken cobbler wins in the *One-Dish Wonders* category.

Finally, the five category winners gather onstage for the big moment. Carol, Susan, and Jo, are joined by *Kids Love It!* winner Stacy and *One-Dish Wonders* winner Ruth.

Everyone holds their breath as Al tears open the envelope. The grand prize goes to—ta da!—**Susan Rotter** for her Southern-Fried Chicken Stuffed With Roasted Red Pepper-and-Vidalia Onion Gravy. Amid cheers, applause, and a downpour of streamers, Carol, Ruth, Jo, and Stacy surround a shaken Susan with hugs and congratulations. "I was absolutely flattened when Al called my name," says Susan. "I was sure Jo's flan was going to win, so I was watching *her*."

As Susan happily accepts a giant check for $100,000, she says, "I never thought I'd win. In fact, when I met (head judge) Andria Hurst the evening

Susan accepts the check for $100,000.

before, her reaction made me worry that she hadn't even been able to stomach my recipe. Boy, did she have me fooled!"

Al closes the show, announcing that Susan's $10,000 category prize will be donated to the charity of her choice, the National Multiple Sclerosis Society, as contest rules require of the grand prize winner.

Dinner that evening is fun and informal at the Country Music Hall of Fame, where contestants let off steam and cut a rug. They are guests of honor at a *Southern Living* farewell brunch Sunday morning.

As they head home, these new friends vow to meet again at next year's Cook-Off. "I hope to come up with something great next year because I want to defend my title," says Jo. Lynne agrees, "This was my first Cook-Off and I'm hooked! I really want to come back."

For Ruth, winning a category is icing on the cake. "No matter what the outcome, you go home a winner," she says. "It's such an honor to be invited. I came with the intention of having a good time and meeting wonderful people—and I did."

"I came home with so much more than I had when I went."
—Lynda Sarkisian

Dancing the night away at the Country Music Hall of Fame.

Top 10
food trends
in our 2003 Cook-Off

Sifting through nearly 40,000 Cook-Off entries gives us a chance to assess what Southern Living readers most like to cook. Executive Editor and Cook-Off judge Susan Dosier shares her thoughts about food trends evident in this year's contest. Recipes based on seven of these trends were selected as finalists.

Spicy Tex-Mex Chicken Cobbler

1 Southwestern cuisine is very trendy. (For us, Southwestern includes Mexican and Tex-Mex flavors.) We know from reader surveys that Southwestern is a close second to Italian in the category of favorite ethnic foods. Our contesters embraced full-flavored Southwestern fare, and you see its success among our finalists.

2 Italian remains our readers' top ethnic cuisine, which we saw in many casserole and one-dish entries. Canned tomatoes and tomato sauces are a convenience product of choice.

Tomato-Leek-Bacon Tart

3 Asian cuisine is sweeping the South, reflecting a national trend. Coconut milk was the surprise ingredient of the Cook-Off entries, showing up creatively in all sorts of recipes. We also saw typical Asian ingredients and flavor variations, such as curry paste, and interesting combinations of fresh ginger, green onions, and cilantro.

Down South Crab Cakes With Collard Greens and Roasted Garlic Beurre Blanc

4 Southern food and cooking are hot, hot, hot. Readers played the Southern card even in categories other than *Taste of the South*. We love this. It reflects an increased national awareness of what Southern food is and what makes a good Southern recipe. Our contest entries and finalists clearly reflect the "tradition with a twist" trend in our magazine's pages.

Sautéed Smoked Gouda Cheese Grits With Black Bean Salsa

5 Spice levels are getting bolder and more complex, whether the heat is from hot sauce, peppers, or combinations of fresh and/or dried herbs and spices. Contesters relied on herbs and spices to infuse recipes with flavor and give them more *oomph*, frequently combining multiple spices to achieve desired flavors. Spice blends often were used effectively to keep ingredient lists short.

6 Many readers value a complex recipe. Some of the submitted recipes required extensive preparation and cooking, making it a challenge for the judges to find simple, streamlined recipes that tasted great. For an involved recipe to be chosen as a finalist, it has to really be worth the time.

Southern-Fried Stuffed Chicken With Roasted Red Pepper-and-Vidalia Onion Gravy

7 Cheesecake remains one of our readers' most prized desserts. We saw many cheesecake entries, but none made it to the final round.

Melt-in-Your-Mouth Braised and Barbecued Chicken

8 We see a real nod to chicken thighs in our entries. The *Southern Living* Test Kitchens applaud this, as we like the flavor, versatility, and inexpensive price of thigh meat. Chicken is the top protein choice in reader surveys.

9 Tropical and fresh fruits turn our readers' heads. Mango and citrus fruits were the most popular. Of course, having Sunkist as a sponsor influenced citrus usage.

10 Our readers love all kinds of cheese, and our contestants used it shredded, melted, grated, baked in a casserole, sprinkled on a pizza, as a garnish—you name it.

Four-Meat Hearty Pasta Bake

Meet our 2003 Cook-Off judges

It's a tough job, but someone has to do it. *Southern Living* Foods Editor **Andria Scott Hurst** heads a panel that faces the enviable task of sampling the foods that are the cream of our contest's rather large crop. That's the easy part.

Selecting winners is not so easy, even for seasoned professionals. Andria's fellow judges are Test Kitchens' Specialist **Vanessa McNeil;** Executive Editor **Susan Dosier; Susan Leathers,** Nashville *Tennessean* assistant features editor; and **Peter D'Andrea,** executive chef at Gaylord's Opryland Resort and Convention Center. Using score cards, the judges evaluate each recipe for taste, texture, visual appeal, and originality. And they do it all in one morning. "We taste only, we don't eat a whole serving," says Susan Dosier. "Still, I figure I ate my total caloric intake for the day before noon."

Judges know nothing about the recipes or contestants prior to the Cook-Off. Magazine staffers who are judges are isolated from selection of finalists.

"The grand prize winner, Southern-Fried Stuffed Chicken With Roasted Red Pepper-and-Vidalia Onion Gravy, is the epitome of creativity," says Andria. "All the winners are tops, but this one has it all—great flavor and appearance, and it makes good use of sponsor products."

> "Choosing a winner is not an easy job, but it is a delicious one."—Judge Andria Hurst

Taste of the South

These unique recipes showcase our
readers' creativity and offer
new twists on Southern classics.

Southern-Fried Stuffed Chicken With Roasted
Red Pepper-and-Vidalia Onion Gravy

Susan Rotter was looking online for home decorating ideas when she came across the cook-off information on **southernliving.com.** For the first time in her life, Susan entered a contest. Lucky for her she did, considering her triumph.

Nathan Rotter is now proud to call himself "Mr. Fried Chicken." He deserves some credit because Susan invented the dish—stuffed with his favorite things—to get him to stop saying that her fried chicken wasn't as good as his grandmother's.

Susan has 140 eager taste-testers at the Nashville firm where she is a software developer—it's standing room only to sample her specialty shaped, or sculpted, cakes.

Susan learned to cook from her mother and maternal grandmother, who was known as the best cook in the county. "My mother encouraged me in the kitchen, which led me to be an achiever in other ways," says Susan. "She told me I could do anything I wanted, no matter what. I believed her. And I still do."

$100,000 Grand Prize Winner!

Southern-Fried Stuffed Chicken With Roasted Red Pepper-and-Vidalia Onion Gravy

4   **ounces cream cheese, softened**
1   **cup dry chicken-flavored stuffing mix**
½   **cup (2 ounces) finely shredded Romano cheese**
½   **cup chopped Vidalia onion**
¼   **cup minced fresh basil**
4   **large boned chicken breast halves with skin**
4   **ready to serve bacon slices**
1   **large egg**
1   **cup milk**
1   **cup all-purpose baking mix** *
2   **teaspoons Creole seasoning**
1   **teaspoon black pepper**
Canola oil
Roasted Red Pepper-and-Vidalia Onion Gravy

Stir together first 5 ingredients in a medium bowl. Set aside.

Place chicken, skin side down, between 2 sheets of heavy-duty plastic wrap; flatten to ¼-inch thickness using a mallet or rolling pin.

Spread one-fourth cream cheese mixture on skinless side of each chicken breast half; top with 1 piece of bacon. Roll up chicken, jellyroll fashion, lifting skin and tucking roll under skin.

Whisk together egg and milk in a bowl. Combine baking mix, Creole seasoning, and pepper in a shallow dish. Dip chicken rolls in egg mixture; dredge in baking mix mixture.

Pour oil to depth of 2 inches into a large skillet; heat to 350°. Fry chicken rolls, in batches, 10 to 12 minutes or until dark brown and done, turning

chicken rolls often. Drain on a wire rack over paper towels.

Spoon ¼ cup Roasted Red Pepper-and-Vidalia Onion Gravy on each of 4 individual serving plates; top with 1 chicken roll. Drizzle with remaining gravy. **Makes:** 4 servings.
Prep: 25 min., **Cook:** 12 min. per batch

Roasted Red Pepper-and-Vidalia Onion Gravy:

1   **large Vidalia onion, halved vertically**
1   **large red bell pepper, halved and seeded**
Non-stick foil
1   **tablespoon olive oil**
¼   **teaspoon kosher salt**
3   **tablespoons butter**
3   **tablespoons all-purpose flour**
2   **cups chicken broth**
2   **teaspoons Creole seasoning**
2   **tablespoons minced fresh basil**
Black pepper to taste

Dice 1 onion half; set aside.

Cut remaining onion half into slices. Place onion slices and bell pepper halves, cut sides down, on a baking sheet lined with nonstick aluminum foil; drizzle with oil, and sprinkle with salt.

Broil 5 inches from heat about 10 minutes or until bell pepper looks blistered. Place bell pepper halves in a zip-top freezer bag; seal and let stand 10 minutes to loosen skin. Peel bell pepper halves, and dice one half. Reserve diced bell pepper and remaining half. Dice roasted onion, and set aside.

Melt butter in a large skillet over medium-high heat. Add reserved diced raw onion, and sauté 10 minutes or until onion begins to brown. Stir in flour; cook, stirring constantly, 5 minutes, or until flour mixture is caramel-colored. Stir in chicken broth and Creole seasoning. Reduce heat to medium, and cook, stirring constantly, until thickened.

Process gravy mixture and reserved bell pepper half in a blender until smooth, stopping to scrape down sides.

Combine gravy mixture, reserved diced roasted bell pepper, diced roasted onion, basil, and black pepper. **Makes:** 3 cups.
Prep: 20 min., **Cook:** 35 min., **Other:** 10 min.

＊For testing purposes only, we used Bisquick Original All-Purpose Baking Mix.

Susan Rotter
Nolensville, Tennessee

Susan created her $100,000 dish trying to prepare something her husband would like as much as his grandmother's fried chicken.

Necessity is the mother of invention when you want to spice up leftovers, but John and Greta Barbour Mills finessed a batch of leftover grits into a winning recipe.

John grew up loving the foods of his native Louisiana. He was a wiz at French toast before he was 10 years old. By age 13, he was making court-bouillon.

John now shares daily cooking chores with his wife, Greta Barbour. They toyed with adding a variety of ingredients that might complement the grits, which were chilled, then cut into squares for frying. Black beans and gouda worked well, but a roux was less successful and subsequently dropped from the recipe.

When the couple served the dish to friends, beer was the beverage of choice for its yeasty flavor. Then John had the idea to wet the squares in beer, rather than water, to give the batter more flavor. The crisp-crusted result was so good that a cousin, who was familiar with the cook-off, urged the Millses to enter.

Sautéed Smoked Gouda Cheese Grits With Black Bean Salsa

Sautéed Smoked Gouda Cheese Grits With Black Bean Salsa

2   cups milk
¾   cup water
¾   cup quick-cooking grits, uncooked
¾   cup chopped smoked Gouda cheese
½   teaspoon salt
2   tablespoons butter
2   cups all-purpose flour
2   tablespoons salt
2   teaspoons black pepper
1   cup beer
Butter
Olive oil
Black Bean Salsa
½   cup sour cream
1   medium tomato, seeded and diced
2   tablespoons chopped fresh parsley
2   tablespoons chopped green onions
12 fresh chives, cut into 1-inch pieces

Stir together milk and ¾ cup water in a 1½-quart saucepan over medium-high heat; bring to a boil. Stir in grits, cheese, and ½ teaspoon salt; cook, stirring constantly, 9 minutes or until thickened. Stir in 2 tablespoons butter. Pour grits into a lightly greased 11- x 7-inch baking dish. Cover and chill 3 hours or until firm.

Combine flour, 2 tablespoons salt, and pepper in a shallow dish. Pour beer into a small bowl.

Cut grits into 2-inch squares. Dip grits squares into beer, and dredge in flour mixture, repeating procedure twice.

Melt 1 tablespoon butter in a large skillet over medium heat; stir in 1 tablespoon oil.

Cook grits squares, in batches, in hot butter mixture 5 minutes on each side or until golden, adding butter and oil as needed.

Arrange 3 grits squares in center of 6 individual serving plates.

Spoon Black Bean Salsa evenly over grits squares. Top evenly with sour cream. Sprinkle evenly with tomato, parsley, green onions, and chives. **Makes:** about 6 servings.

Prep: 35 min., **Cook:** 10 min. per batch, **Other:** 3 hrs.

Black Bean Salsa:
2   tablespoons butter
1   medium onion, diced
2   garlic cloves, minced
2   (15-ounce) cans black beans, drained
⅔   cup picante sauce
2   medium tomatoes, seeded and diced
2   teaspoons chili powder
1   teaspoon salt
½   teaspoon black pepper
¼   teaspoon ground cumin
3   tablespoons chopped fresh parsley
3   tablespoons chopped green onions

Melt butter in a medium saucepan over medium heat; add onion and garlic, and sauté until tender. Stir in beans and next 6 ingredients; cook, stirring occasionally, 3 minutes or until thoroughly heated. Stir in parsley and green onions. **Makes:** about 4½ cups.

Prep: 15 min., **Cook:** 5 min.

John and Greta Barbour Mills
Jackson, Mississippi

The grits will lose a lot of "character" if you dip them in water, instead of beer, before frying. **John** says beer seems to absorb flour better, making a dense crust that isn't likely to stick while it cooks. And, he says, it provides "a nice 'back note' of flavor."

"Italian is my favorite cuisine, and I like to dabble in all kinds of cooking—French, Asian, Creole—but seafood is really my specialty," says Benjamin Chapin.

Ben started in the restaurant business in high school, washing dishes. Little by little, he worked his way through the kitchen, and now is the sous chef at the Charlotte Harbor Yacht Club in Port Charlotte, Florida.

Ben grew up cooking with his mother and grandmother in nearby Punta Gorda. Even after training in restaurants with skilled master chefs, he still loves to cook down-home Southern favorites. A veteran of the annual Iron Fish cooking competition at Charlotte Harbor, Ben blends prime elements of Southern haute cuisine, such as crab cakes, in this recipe that's truly a taste of the South.

$2,000 Finalist & Brand Winner!

PAM® Brand Winner

Down-South Crab Cakes With Collard Greens and Roasted Garlic Beurre Blanc

2 cups cornbread crumbs
¼ cup diced red bell pepper
¼ cup chopped fresh chives
¼ cup Creole mustard
½ cup mayonnaise
2 large eggs
1 teaspoon chipotle pepper sauce
1 teaspoon Worcestershire sauce
¼ cup chopped ready to serve bacon
1 pound fresh jumbo lump crabmeat
Vegetable cooking spray
Collard Greens
Roasted Garlic Beurre Blanc
Garnishes: chopped fresh chives, diced red bell pepper

Preheat oven to 375°.
Combine cornbread crumbs and next 8 ingredients in a large bowl. Gently stir in crabmeat. Shape mixture into 10 (3- to 3½-inch) patties. Place on a baking sheet coated with cooking spray.
Bake at 375° for 12 minutes.
Spoon Collard Greens onto individual serving plates, using a slotted spoon; top each serving with 2 crab cakes.
Drizzle with Roasted Garlic Beurre Blanc. Garnish, if desired. **Makes:** 5 servings.
Prep: 30 min., **Cook:** 12 min.

Collard Greens:

½ cup diced prosciutto
3 tablespoons butter
½ cup diced onion
2 tablespoons minced garlic
2 pounds fresh collard greens
3 cups chicken broth

Heat a large Dutch oven over medium-high heat; add prosciutto, and sauté 2 minutes. Add butter, onion, and garlic; sauté until onion is tender. Add greens and broth. Bring to a boil; reduce heat, and simmer 30 to 45 minutes or until greens are tender. **Makes:** 10 cups.
Prep: 10 min., **Cook:** 55 min.

Ben folds the crabmeat into the other ingredients carefully to avoid breaking up the lumps. His baked cakes offer big crab taste in every bite.

Roasted Garlic Beurre Blanc:

6 garlic cloves
Olive oil
Salt and black pepper to taste
½ cup fresh lemon juice (2 lemons)
½ cup dry white wine
1 cup whipping cream
¼ cup cold butter, cut into pieces
1 teaspoon kosher salt
½ teaspoon ground red pepper

Place garlic in center of an aluminum foil sheet. Drizzle garlic lightly with oil; sprinkle with salt and black pepper to taste.
Bake garlic at 350° for 20 to 25 minutes or until golden.
Squeeze out pulp from each garlic clove into a medium saucepan. Add lemon juice and white wine to garlic. Cook, uncovered, over medium-high heat about 20 minutes or until reduced by three-fourths. Stir in whipping cream; reduce heat and simmer, uncovered, 10 to 15 minutes or until reduced by half. Remove from heat; gradually whisk in butter, a few pieces at a time, until sauce is slightly thickened and smooth. Stir in 1 teaspoon salt and ground red pepper. **Makes:** 2 cups.
Prep: 40 min., **Cook:** 1 hr.

Benjamin Chapin
Punta Gorda, Florida

Down-South Crab Cakes With Collard Greens
and Roasted Garlic Beurre Blanc

DOLE® Brand Winner

Praline-Filled Carrot Cake

1   (16-ounce) bag baby carrots
3   cups all-purpose flour
2⅔ cups sugar
1½ teaspoons baking powder
1½ teaspoons baking soda
1   teaspoon salt
2   teaspoons ground cinnamon
1⅓ cups vegetable oil
6   large eggs
1   (11-ounce) can mandarin
    oranges, drained
1   tablespoon vanilla extract
¾   cup chopped pecans
½   cup sweetened flaked coconut
Cinnamon-Cream Cheese Frosting
Praline Cream Filling
Spiced Pecans

Grease and flour 3 (9-inch) round cakepans; set aside.

Cook baby carrots in boiling water to cover 20 to 30 minutes or until tender. Drain carrots, and let cool slightly. Coarsely mash carrots, using a potato masher, in a pan or in a food processor until smooth (you will need 1½ cups).

Combine flour and next 5 ingredients in a large bowl. Make a well in center of mixture. Add oil and next 3 ingredients. Beat 1 minute at low speed with an electric mixer; increase speed to medium, and beat 30 seconds. Stir in mashed carrots, pecans, and coconut. Pour batter evenly into prepared pans.

Bake at 350° for 23 minutes or until a wooden pick inserted in center comes out clean. (Do not overbake.) Cool in pans on wire racks 10 minutes; remove and cool completely on wire racks.

Spoon 2 tablespoons Cinnamon-Cream Cheese Frosting in center of a cake plate; top with 1 cake layer. Pipe or spread a 1-inch wide border of Cinnamon-Cream Cheese Frosting around outside top edge of cake layer. Spread a 2-inch circle of frosting in center of cake layer. Spread about half of Praline Cream Filling around unfrosted portion on top of cake layer.

Top with 1 cake layer, and repeat procedure on top of second layer with frosting and filling. Top with remaining cake layer, and spread remaining frosting on top and sides of cake. Garnish with Spiced Pecans. Store in refrigerator.

Makes: 12 servings.
Prep: 1 hr., **Cook:** 53 min., **Other:** 10 min.

Cinnamon-Cream Cheese Frosting:

1   (8-ounce) package cream
    cheese, softened
½   cup butter, softened
2   teaspoons ground cinnamon
1   teaspoon vanilla extract
4½ cups sifted powdered sugar

Beat first 4 ingredients in a large mixing bowl at medium speed with an electric mixer until fluffy. Gradually add powdered sugar, beating to spreading consistency. **Makes:** about 5 cups.
Prep: 10 min.

Praline Cream Filling:

6   tablespoons butter
6   tablespoons light brown sugar
¼   cup whipping cream
1   teaspoon vanilla extract
1   teaspoon bourbon

Melt butter in a small saucepan over medium heat. Stir in brown sugar and cream; cook, stirring constantly, until mixture comes to a boil. Reduce heat, and boil gently, uncovered, 3 minutes, stirring occasionally. Remove from heat. Stir in vanilla and bourbon. Let cool to spreading consistency, stirring occasionally.
Makes: ½ cup.
Prep: 5 min., **Cook:** 5 min.

Spiced Pecans:

¼   cup firmly packed brown sugar
1   tablespoon orange juice
1   teaspoon ground cinnamon
½   cup pecan halves
Non-stick foil

Whisk together first 3 ingredients in a small bowl. Add pecans; toss to coat.

Spread pecan mixture in a lightly greased 8-inch-square pan.

Bake at 350° for 10 to 12 minutes or until pecans are toasted and syrup is bubbly, stirring once.

Pour pecan mixture out onto a wire rack lined with nonstick aluminum foil. Gently separate pecans with a fork, and let cool completely. **Makes:** about ½ cup.
Prep: 5 min., **Cook:** 12 min.

Jennifer Owen
Marion, Indiana

Jennifer's carrot cake has it all—mandarin oranges, pecans, and coconut, a touch of cinnamon, a splash of bourbon, and a garnish of sugary pecans.

Potato-Crusted Catfish With
Warm Pinto Bean-and-Bacon Salsa

ROTEL® Brand Winner

Potato-Crusted Catfish With Warm Pinto Bean-and-Bacon Salsa

½   cup milk
1½ teaspoons fresh lemon juice
½   teaspoon kosher salt
½   teaspoon garlic powder
4   (6-ounce) catfish fillets
1   cup instant potato flakes
1   tablespoon vegetable oil
1   tablespoon butter
Warm Pinto Bean-and-Bacon Salsa

Stir together milk and lemon juice in a shallow bowl; let stand 5 minutes. Stir in salt and garlic powder. Dip catfish in milk mixture; dredge in potato flakes. **Heat** oil and butter in a large nonstick skillet over medium-high heat until butter melts.

Add catfish to skillet; cook 3 to 4 minutes on each side or until golden. Arrange catfish on individual serving plates and top with Warm Pinto Bean-and-Bacon Salsa. **Makes:** 4 servings.
Prep: 15 min., **Cook:** 8 min., **Other:** 5 min.

Mary Lou made great use of a few convenience products to create a quick and easy meal with outstanding flavor.

Warm Pinto Bean-and-Bacon Salsa:

1   (16-ounce) can pinto beans, rinsed and drained
1   (10-ounce) can diced tomatoes & green chilies
4   ready to serve bacon slices, cut crosswise into thin slices
¼   cup minced fresh cilantro

Stir together beans and tomatoes with chilies in a small saucepan over medium-low heat, and cook, stirring occasionally, until thoroughly heated. Stir in bacon and cilantro. Serve warm. **Makes:** 2 cups.
Prep: 5 min., **Cook:** 10 min.

Mary Lou Cook
Welches, Oregon

Southern Sunshine Fruit Dip

Substitute toasted pecans for walnuts to give this recipe a more Southern accent.

1   (8-ounce) package cream
    cheese, softened
1   (7-ounce) jar marshmallow
    cream
1   tablespoon grated orange rind
1   tablespoon orange juice
¼   cup ground walnuts
Strawberries, grapes, fresh
    pineapple

Beat cream cheese at medium speed with an electric mixer until creamy. Add marshmallow cream, orange rind, and orange juice; beat until smooth. Stir in walnuts. Cover and chill 30 minutes. Serve with fresh fruit. **Makes:** 2 cups.
Prep: 9 min., **Other:** 30 min.

Tip: This is an excellent make-ahead recipe to serve at parties. You can make and chill it several days in advance.
Marian Michael
Columbia, South Carolina

Marian serves this dip with strawberries, grapes, and melon. She says she's never served it without requests for the recipe.

Glenda's Bean Dip

Have plenty of tortilla chips or corn chips available to take the plunge into this hearty dip.

1   (16-ounce) can pinto beans,
    drained
1   (16-ounce) can chili beans,
    drained
2   tablespoons vegetable oil
½   cup chopped onion
⅔   cup chopped red bell pepper
2½ teaspoons chili powder
1   teaspoon salt
¼   teaspoon sugar
⅛   teaspoon garlic powder
⅛   teaspoon ground red pepper

Combine beans; mash with a potato masher or back of a spoon. Set aside. **Heat** oil in a medium skillet over medium-high heat. Sauté onion and red bell pepper 2 minutes.

Add reserved beans, chili powder, and remaining ingredients. Cook, stirring constantly, until thoroughly heated. Serve warm with chips. **Makes:** 3½ cups.
Prep: 10 min., **Cook:** 7 min.
Glenda Tatom
Stamps, Arkansas

Glenda always saves the liquid from the canned beans to thin the dip if necessary.

Crabmeat Dip

Keep these ingredients on hand for a quick and impressive dip for unexpected guests.

1   garlic clove, halved
1   (8-ounce) package cream
     cheese, softened
½   teaspoon salt
½   teaspoon pepper
2   teaspoons lemon juice
½   teaspoon hot sauce
1½   teaspoons Worcestershire
     sauce
1   (6-ounce) can crabmeat,
     drained
2   to 3 tablespoons milk

Rub sides of a medium bowl with cut sides of garlic; discard. Combine cream cheese and next 6 ingredients. Add milk, 1 tablespoon at a time, until desired consistency. Serve with assorted crackers or vegetables. **Makes:** 1½ cups.
Prep: 6 min.
Justin Castillo
Portland, Oregon

To provide a hint of garlic without overpowering the delicate crab flavor, **Justin** rubs the bowl with the cut sides of the garlic clove, and then discards it.

Bourbon Pecans

The bourbon flavor in these candied nuts is subtle.

½ cup firmly packed light brown sugar
½ cup granulated sugar
¼ cup water
¼ cup bourbon
1 teaspoon grated orange rind
¼ teaspoon ground cinnamon
¼ teaspoon salt
1 teaspoon vanilla extract
2 cups pecan halves, toasted

Combine first 7 ingredients in a 2-quart saucepan over medium heat; stir until sugar dissolves. Bring mixture to a boil, stirring constantly. Reduce heat to medium; cook to soft ball stage or until a candy thermometer registers 240°.
Remove from heat, and stir in vanilla and pecans. Working rapidly, pour pecans onto a jellyroll pan lined with nonstick aluminum foil; separate pecans using 2 forks. Cool completely; store in an airtight container. **Makes:** 3 cups.
Prep: 10 min., **Cook:** 30 min., **Other:** 1 hr.

Frances Rowell
Valdosta, Georgia

For **Frances**, this recipe truly represents the South. Every Christmas, she and her family exchange these nuts with friends in Alaska for their home-smoked and canned salmon.

Sweet Southern Pickles by Design

Homemade sweet pickles can take weeks to cure, but they're a snap to make because they get a jump start from store-bought hamburger dills. Although they improve with age, they're crisp and ready to eat after just 4 days.

1 (1-quart) jar hamburger dill pickle slices
½ cup cider vinegar
2¾ cups sugar
⅛ teaspoon salt
2 tablespoons pickling spice

Drain pickles, discarding liquid. Set pickle jar aside.
Combine pickles, vinegar, sugar, and salt in a large bowl, stirring well. Let stand 2 hours or until sugar dissolves, stirring often.

Place pickling spice in a double layer of cheesecloth. Gather edges of cheesecloth together; tie securely.
Spoon half of pickle mixture into reserved jar. Add cheese cloth bag; spoon remaining pickle mixture into jar. Cover with lid. Store in refrigerator at least 4 days before serving. Remove cheesecloth bag before serving. Store in refrigerator. **Makes:** 1 quart.
Prep: 9 min., **Other:** 2 hrs. plus 4 days

Candace Grantham
Dallas, Texas

Candace tells us that pickle juice sno-cones are a big hit with her kids and suggests serving the dill pickle juice over shaved ice.

Deviled Eggs With Cilantro Tuna Salad

Serve this unique rendition of deviled eggs at your next family reunion or neighborhood get-together.

12 large eggs
½ cup mayonnaise
4 (6-ounce) cans solid white tuna in spring water, drained and flaked
1 small onion, chopped
1 celery rib, chopped
½ cup finely chopped fresh cilantro
½ cup dill pickle relish
¼ teaspoon lemon juice
½ teaspoon celery seeds
¼ teaspoon pepper
Garnish: fresh cilantro sprigs

Place eggs in a single layer in a large saucepan; add water to cover eggs. Bring to a boil; cover, remove from heat, and let stand 15 minutes.

Drain immediately, and fill the pan with cold water and ice. Tap each egg firmly on a countertop until cracks form all over the shell. Peel eggs under cold running water.

Slice eggs in half lengthwise, and carefully remove yolks. Mash yolks with mayonnaise. Stir in tuna and next 7 ingredients. Spoon a heaping tablespoon tuna mixture into each egg white. Cover and chill 1 hour. Garnish, if desired. **Makes:** 12 servings.

Prep: 46 min., **Cook:** 3 min., **Other:** 1 hr., 15 min.

Tip: You will have extra tuna salad left. Store remaining tuna salad in the refrigerator and serve it on a sandwich, as a salad, or with crackers.

Leah Husk
Mechanicsville, Virginia

Leah discards the egg yolks when she makes this tuna salad, but we tossed them in. We like the flavor they add to the salad. What better Southern tradition than to add a new twist to deviled eggs? In fact, Southerners love them so much that there's a special plate on which to serve them.

Chicken Beignets With Lemon Aïoli

If you're looking for a new appetizer idea, we've got a winner. These crispy chicken fritters served with lemon mayonnaise will be the hit of your next party.

1 tablespoon vegetable oil
1½ cups diced boned and skinned chicken breast (about 1 large chicken breast)
¼ cup finely chopped red bell pepper
3 tablespoons finely chopped green onions
1 teaspoon lemon juice
1 teaspoon paprika
2 teaspoons minced fresh chives
Vegetable oil
1 large egg, lightly beaten
1 egg yolk, lightly beaten
¾ cup milk
1 teaspoon baking powder
¼ teaspoon hot sauce
2½ cups all-purpose baking mix *
Paprika (optional)
Lemon Aïoli

Heat 1 tablespoon oil in a skillet over medium-high heat. Add chicken and bell pepper; cook 3 to 4 minutes or until chicken is done. Add green onions, lemon juice, and paprika; cook 1 minute. Remove from heat, and stir in chives.

Pour oil to a depth of 3 inches into a Dutch oven; heat to 350°.

Combine egg and next 4 ingredients in a large bowl, stirring well. Add baking mix to egg mixture, stirring just until moistened. Fold in chicken mixture. Drop heaping tablespoonfuls of fritter batter into hot oil; fry 2 to 3 minutes or until golden, turning once. Sprinkle with paprika, if desired. Drain on paper towels. Serve immediately with Lemon Aïoli. **Makes:** about 2 dozen.

Prep: 15 min., **Cook:** 15 min.

Lemon Aïoli:
½ cup mayonnaise
2 tablespoons lemon juice
2 teaspoons Dijon mustard
1 garlic clove, minced
½ teaspoon hot sauce

Whisk together all ingredients. **Makes:** ⅔ cup.

Prep: 2 min.

*For testing purposes only, we used Bisquick Original All-Purpose Baking Mix.

Gloria Bradley
Naperville, Illinois

Here's another great entry from **Gloria,** who was a Finalist and Brand Winner in the Simple and Scrumptious Entrées category.

Banana Pepper Poppers

8 large banana peppers
16 bacon slices (about 1 pound)
2 (8-ounce) packages cream cheese, slightly softened

Cut peppers in half lengthwise. Remove seeds; set peppers aside.

Cook bacon in a large skillet 2 minutes on each side or until partially cooked; drain on paper towels, and set aside.

Cut each block of cream cheese lengthwise into 8 long strips. Place 1 strip cream cheese into each banana pepper half. Wrap each pepper with 1 bacon slice; secure with wooden picks. Place wrapped peppers onto a lightly greased baking sheet.

Bake at 425° for 7 minutes or until bacon is crisp. **Makes:** 16 servings.

Prep: 21 min., **Cook:** 11 min.

Ginny Emmerich
Jackson, Mississippi

Ginny knows from experience—men rave over these yummy treats. Many Southerners grow banana peppers and feel proud when they're eaten as a showcase appetizer instead of with the typical sandwich or as a salad condiment.

Mex'ed Up Potato-Stuffed Southern-Style Meat Loaf

6 small red potatoes (about 2- to 2½-inch diameter), peeled
2 pounds lean ground beef
1 pound Mexican chorizo, casings removed
1 large egg
1½ cups chicken-flavored stuffing mix
1 (10-ounce) can diced tomatoes with lime and cilantro, undrained
1 tablespoon Worcestershire sauce
1 tablespoon minced garlic
1 cup water
1 cup ketchup
½ cup firmly packed brown sugar
1¼ teaspoons dried oregano
1 teaspoon ground cumin
1 teaspoon ground red pepper
2 tablespoons chopped fresh cilantro

Place potatoes in a microwave-safe dish. Cover tightly with heavy-duty plastic wrap; fold back a small edge to allow steam to escape. Microwave at HIGH 3 minutes, turn potatoes, and cook 3 more minutes or until tender. Set aside.

Combine ground beef and next 7 ingredients in a large bowl until just blended (do not overmix).

Place half of meat mixture on a foil-lined, lightly greased 15- x 10-inch jellyroll pan. Shape meat into a 15- x 5-inch rectangle. Place cooked (whole) potatoes lengthwise down center of meat. Place remaining half of meat evenly over potatoes, pressing gently to seal edges and form a loaf. Set aside.

Combine ketchup and next 4 ingredients in a small bowl; mix well. Spread evenly over loaf.

Bake, uncovered, at 375° for 40 minutes; increase oven temperature to 400°, and cook 20 more minutes or until a meat thermometer registers 160°. Remove from oven; let stand 10 minutes before slicing. Sprinkle with chopped cilantro. **Makes:** 10 servings.

Prep: 25 min., **Cook:** 63 min., **Other:** 10 min.

Note: We tested with Mexican chorizo, which is a highly seasoned sausage made with fresh pork. Don't try to substitute Spanish chorizo, made with smoked pork, because it's much firmer in texture and will not incorporate in the meat loaf with the ground beef.

Susan Rotter
Nolensville, Tennessee

Tired of the same old meat loaf? Well, we've got a recipe for you. **Susan** created this unique combination of ground beef and chorizo, then spiced it up with Mexican seasonings. It's an explosion of flavors with tender little potatoes buried inside. See Susan's grand prizewinning recipe on page 23.

Classic Pimiento Cheese and Bacon Burger

Classic Pimiento Cheese and Bacon Burger

Word has it that none other then Elvis Presley liked pimiento cheese on his burger. We, too, sing the king's praises of pimiento cheese.

2   cups (8 ounces) shredded sharp
    Cheddar cheese
½   cup mayonnaise
1   (2-ounce) jar diced pimiento
⅛   teaspoon salt
⅛   teaspoon pepper
1   teaspoon chopped garlic
½   teaspoon hot sauce
2   pounds ground chuck
1   teaspoon chopped garlic
1   teaspoon salt
½   teaspoon pepper

6   kaiser rolls
12 bacon slices
    Lettuce leaves (optional)
    Tomato slices (optional)

Stir together first 7 ingredients in a small bowl. Cover and chill until ready to serve.

Combine ground chuck and next 3 ingredients in a medium bowl, blending well. Shape into 6 patties. Grill, covered with grill lid, over medium heat (300° to 350°) 15 minutes or until done, turning once.

To serve, place 1 hamburger patty on each roll; top each with about ⅓ cup pimiento cheese and 2 bacon slices. Serve with lettuce and tomato, if desired. **Makes:** 6 servings.

Prep: 14 min., **Cook:** 15 min.

Lynda Morgan
Memphis, Tennessee

Grilled Pork Tenderloin With Warm Pineapple Chutney

This sweet-and-sour fruit chutney is a perfect accompaniment with grilled pork. The chutney will keep up to 2 weeks in the refrigerator and can be served warm or cold.

⅓   cup fresh lemon juice
1   tablespoon barbecue
    seasoning*
2   (¾-pound) pork tenderloins
½   cup diced Vidalia onion
¼   cup diced red bell pepper
1   tablespoon minced fresh
    jalapeño
2   (8-ounce) cans pineapple
    tidbits, undrained
¼   cup raisins
⅓   cup orange juice
2   tablespoons light brown sugar
3   tablespoons rice wine vinegar
½   teaspoon salt
2   regular-size bags boil-in-bag
    brown rice

Combine lemon juice and barbecue seasoning in a large zip-top plastic bag; add pork. Seal bag, turning to coat pork; marinate in refrigerator 45 minutes.

Meanwhile, coat a 2-quart saucepan with cooking spray. Place pan over medium-high heat. Add onion, bell pepper, and jalapeño; sauté until onion is tender. Stir in pineapple, raisins, orange juice, brown sugar, and vinegar. **Bring** to a boil; reduce heat to low, and simmer, uncovered, 45 minutes, stirring occasionally, until liquid is reduced to ⅓ cup. Remove from heat. Stir in salt; keep warm.

Meanwhile, cook rice according to package directions; keep warm.

Grill pork, covered with grill lid, over medium-high heat (350° to 400°) about 20 minutes, turning once, or until a meat thermometer inserted into thickest portion registers 155°. Remove from grill; cover and let stand 5 minutes until temperature reaches 160°. Serve pork slices over rice. Top with pineapple chutney; serve immediately. **Makes:** 6 servings.

Prep: 17 min., **Cook:** 1 hr., 15 min., **Other:** 50 min.

*For testing purposes only, we used McCormick Barbecue Seasoning.

Tip: When using an instant-read thermometer to test the internal temperature of meat, be sure the indention on the stem of the thermometer is inserted well into the meat to get an accurate reading.

Jill Kucera
Raleigh, North Carolina

Jill keeps leftover Pineapple Chutney in the refrigerator up to 2 weeks and serves it warm or cold. Try it with grilled chicken, turkey, or tuna.

Peppered Pork Tenderloin on Smoky Chipotle Cornbread With Sweet Onion BBQ Sauce

Decrease the amount of pepper on the pork to 1½ teaspoons if you prefer a milder taste.

Smoky Chipotle Cornbread
Sweet Onion BBQ Sauce
- 2 (1¼-pound) pork tenderloins, trimmed
- 1 teaspoon butter, melted
- 1 teaspoon salt
- 2 teaspoons ground black pepper

Prepare Smoky Chipotle Cornbread. While it bakes, prepare Sweet Onion BBQ Sauce.

Rub pork with butter, salt, and pepper. Grill, covered with grill lid, over medium heat (300° to 350°) about 20 minutes or until a meat thermometer inserted into thickest portion registers 155°, turning once. Let pork stand, covered loosely with aluminum foil, 5 minutes until temperature reaches 160°. Slice into ¼-inch-thick slices. Serve with Smoky Chipotle Cornbread and Sweet Onion BBQ Sauce. **Makes:** 6 to 8 servings.
Prep: 5 min., **Cook:** 20 min.

Jim tops a slice of warm cornbread with several tenderloin medaillons, and drizzles plenty of sauce over the top.

Smoky Chipotle Cornbread:
- 1 cup all-purpose flour
- 1 cup stone-ground yellow cornmeal
- 2 tablespoons sugar
- 2 teaspoons baking powder
- 1 teaspoon salt
- 1 cup buttermilk
- 1 large egg, lightly beaten
- 6 tablespoons butter, melted
- 3 chipotle peppers in adobo sauce, chopped
- 1 tablespoon vegetable oil

Place a 9-inch cast-iron skillet in a 450° oven for 5 minutes.

Combine first 5 ingredients in a large bowl. Stir together buttermilk and next 3 ingredients; add to dry ingredients, stirring just until moistened. Add oil to hot iron skillet; tilt to coat evenly. Pour batter into prepared skillet. Bake at 450° for 18 to 20 minutes or until a wooden pick inserted in center comes out clean. **Makes:** 8 servings.
Prep: 8 min., **Cook:** 20 min.

Sweet Onion BBQ Sauce:
- 1 cup ketchup
- 1 cup cider vinegar
- 2 tablespoons lemon juice
- 1 cup firmly packed dark brown sugar
- 1 cup minced sweet onion
- 1 tablespoon Worcestershire sauce
- 1 tablespoon hot sauce
- 1 tablespoon freshly cracked black pepper
- 1 teaspoon garlic powder
- 5 drops mesquite liquid smoke (optional)
- 1 tablespoon whiskey (optional)

Combine all ingredients in a 2-quart saucepan; bring to a boil. Reduce heat to medium-low; simmer, uncovered, 20 minutes, stirring occasionally.
Makes: 3 cups.
Prep: 5 min., **Cook:** 20 min.

Jim Humphrey
Raleigh, North Carolina

Asian-Style Barbecue Sandwiches With Coleslaw

8 tablespoons hoisin sauce, divided
1 tablespoon olive oil
2 tablespoons rice vinegar
1 tablespoon fish sauce
1 teaspoon soy sauce
1 teaspoon ground pepper
2 teaspoons minced fresh ginger
4 garlic cloves, minced
2 (1-pound) pork tenderloins, trimmed
2 garlic cloves, sliced
Coleslaw
6 sesame seed buns or kaiser rolls, toasted

Stir together 6 tablespoons hoisin sauce and next 7 ingredients.

Cut 4 (½-inch-deep) slits in each tenderloin. Place a garlic slice into each opening. Place tenderloins in a large zip-top freezer bag. Pour in marinade; seal. Marinate in refrigerator 1 hour, turning once.

Meanwhile, prepare Coleslaw.

Transfer pork and marinade to a 13- x 9-inch pan lined with aluminum foil. Bake, covered, at 325° for 45 to 50 minutes or until a meat thermometer inserted in thickest portion registers 155°. Let stand 5 minutes until temperature reaches 160°.

Pour remaining juices from pan into a medium saucepan; bring to a boil. Add remaining 2 tablespoons hoisin sauce; reduce heat, and simmer 5 minutes. Pour over sliced pork.

Place pork on toasted buns; top with Coleslaw. **Makes:** 6 servings.

Prep: 29 min., **Cook:** 55 min.

Latrice uses toasted white loaf bread to make these sandwiches. We loved the Asian ingredients used in the barbecue and coleslaw, so we continued that theme by using sesame seed buns for these sandwiches. Kaiser rolls also work well.

Coleslaw:
4 cups thinly sliced green cabbage*
½ small red onion, thinly sliced
1 cup shredded carrot
1½ cups chopped fresh cilantro
¼ cup rice vinegar
3 tablespoons olive oil
½ teaspoon soy sauce
½ teaspoon sesame oil
½ teaspoon salt
½ teaspoon dried crushed red pepper
2½ teaspoons sugar

Combine first 4 ingredients in a large bowl; set aside.

Whisk together vinegar and next 6 ingredients. Pour over cabbage mixture, and toss. **Makes:** 5 cups.

Prep: 20 min.

*Try using 4 cups of prepackaged angel hair slaw for the green cabbage to save time.

Latrice Watkins
Lithonia, Georgia

Bourbon Street Pork Chops With Wilted Collard Greens

¼ cup firmly packed brown sugar
1 teaspoon salt
1 teaspoon coarsely ground black pepper
¼ cup bourbon
2 bone-in pork loin chops (about 1¾ pounds)
4 bacon slices, chopped
1 head collard greens, chopped (about 5 cups)*
½ cup thinly sliced red onion
2 tablespoons cider vinegar
½ teaspoon ground red pepper

Combine brown sugar, salt, and pepper in a small bowl.

Brush bourbon evenly over both sides of pork chops; sprinkle sugar mixture evenly over pork chops, pressing lightly to coat. Cover and let stand 30 minutes.

Grill chops, covered with grill lid, over medium-high heat (350° to 400°) 10 minutes on each side or until a meat thermometer inserted into thickest portion of chop registers 155°. Let stand 5 minutes until temperature reaches 160°. Keep warm until ready to serve.

Cook bacon in a large skillet over medium-high heat until crisp. Add chopped collard greens; cook 7 to 8 minutes, or until wilted. Add onion, vinegar, and red pepper; cook 1 more minute. To serve, spoon greens onto serving plates; top each serving with a pork chop. **Makes:** 2 servings.

Prep: 16 min., **Cook:** 33 min., **Other:** 30 min.

*If you're in a hurry, look for bags of already-chopped collard greens in the produce section of your grocery store.

Branden Saunders
Denver, Colorado

Stuffed Pork Chops With Pear Sauce

½ pound mild ground sausage
2 cups herb-seasoned stuffing *
1½ teaspoons salt
1 teaspoon pepper
1 teaspoon dried sage
½ teaspoon ground allspice
⅛ teaspoon ground ginger
1 (15¼-ounce) can pear halves in juice, undrained
¼ cup chopped onion
¼ cup chopped celery
6 tablespoons unsalted butter, melted
¾ cup plus 2 tablespoons chicken broth
2 large eggs, lightly beaten
6 (1½-inch-thick) large bone-in pork chops (10 to 12 ounces each)
1 teaspoon salt
½ teaspoon garlic powder
½ teaspoon pepper
Pear Sauce

Cook sausage in a medium skillet over medium heat, stirring until it crumbles and is no longer pink. Stir together sausage, stuffing mix, and next 5 ingredients in a large bowl.

Drain canned pears, reserving juice. Chop 3 pear halves, reserving remaining halves for Pear Sauce. Cook chopped pear, onion, and celery in butter in a medium skillet, stirring constantly, until tender; add to stuffing mixture.

Stir ¼ cup reserved pear juice, chicken broth, and eggs into stuffing mixture.

Cut slits in sides of pork chops to the bone, forming a pocket. Combine 1 teaspoon salt, garlic powder, and pepper; sprinkle evenly over both sides of pork chops. Spoon stuffing mixture generously into pockets. Place pork chops in a lightly greased roasting pan. Spoon any remaining stuffing mixture between pork chops in roasting pan. Pour ½ cup reserved canned pear juice over pork chops. Bake, covered, at 375° for 30 minutes. Uncover and cook 15 more minutes or until pork chops are done.

Prepare Pear Sauce while pork chops bake.

Remove pork chops to a serving platter. Top evenly with warm Pear Sauce.

Makes: 6 servings.
Prep: 44 min., **Cook:** 50 min.

Pear Sauce:

2 tablespoons unsalted butter
1 teaspoon brown sugar
2 teaspoons honey
¼ teaspoon ground allspice
2 canned pears halves, chopped
2 tablespoons pear juice
1 teaspoon cornstarch

Combine first 5 ingredients in a saucepan over medium heat until butter melts. Stir together pear juice and cornstarch, and add to pear mixture in pan. Bring mixture to a boil, and cook 1 minute or until sauce is thickened. **Makes:** 1 cup.
Prep: 10 min., **Cook:** 10 min.

***** For testing purposes only, we used Pepperidge Farm Herb-Seasoned Stuffing.

Helen McLain
Quinlan, Texas

We prepared this dish as **Helen** does with canned and fresh pears in the stuffing mixture and canned pears in the sauce. Then we tried it again using all canned pears in the stuffing. The canned pears decreased the prep time, and we liked the convenience.

Cola Ham

The cola provides the base for a sweet raisin glaze to spoon over the ham.

1 (8- to 10-pound) smoked fully cooked ham half (shank end)
1 (29-ounce) can sliced peaches in heavy syrup, drained
1 (20-ounce) can crushed pineapple in juice, drained
1½ teaspoons ground cinnamon
¾ teaspoon ground nutmeg
1 (16-ounce) package brown sugar, divided
1 (12-ounce) can cola soft drink
½ cup raisins

Score fat on ham in a diamond pattern; place ham, fat side up, in a shallow roasting pan.

Pulse peaches and next 3 ingredients in a blender or food processor until fruit is pureed.

Press three-fourths of brown sugar evenly over ham; pour peach mixture over ham. Pour cola into pan. Bake at 325° for 3 hours and 15 minutes or until a meat thermometer inserted into the thickest portion registers 140°,

basting occasionally. Remove from oven; skim fat from drippings, and pour drippings into a saucepan. Cover and let ham stand 30 minutes.

Add remaining brown sugar and raisins to drippings in saucepan. Bring to a boil; boil 25 minutes or until slightly thickened. Serve sauce over ham.

Makes: 16 servings.
Prep: 16 min., **Cook:** 3 hrs., 40 min.

William Muirhead
Cameron Park, California

Mesquite Country-Style Ribs

Cuban sofrito and recaito seasonings contribute tomato, bell pepper, onion, garlic, coriander, and oregano flavors to the sauce in this recipe.

6   pounds country-style pork ribs
Mesquite wood chips
1½ tablespoons pepper
1   tablespoon adobo seasoning
3   tablespoons spicy barbecue sauce
2   tablespoons Worcestershire sauce
2   tablespoons fresh lemon juice
3   tablespoons steak sauce
2   tablespoons prepared mustard
2   tablespoons sofrito seasoning *
2   tablespoons recaito seasoning *
2   packets sazón con azafrán *
½   teaspoon mesquite liquid smoke

Cook ribs in boiling water to cover in a large Dutch oven 1 hour; drain.
Meanwhile, soak mesquite chips in water at least 30 minutes; drain.
Stir together pepper and next 10 ingredients in a medium bowl.
Preheat grill to medium-high heat (350° to 400°) using both burners. After preheating, turn off 1 burner. Place mesquite chips in a disposable aluminum foil pan or an aluminum foil packet poked with holes on grill over briquettes covering lit burner. Coat food grate with cooking spray; place on grill. Place ribs on grate over unlit burner. Grill, covered with grill lid, 1 hour, turning and basting with sauce every 15 minutes. **Makes:** 4 to 6 servings.
Prep: 12 min., **Cook:** 2 hrs.

*For testing purposes only, we used Goya Sazón con Azafrán and Goya recaito, sofrito, and adobo seasonings. You can find these products in the Hispanic foods section of your grocery store.

Patrick Hall
Orlando, Florida

Mesquite Country-Style Ribs

Old-Timey Sausage-Tomato Gravy over Bacon Cornbread

Loaded with sausage, this tomato gravy is served over dressed-up cornbread. Prepare the cornbread while the gravy simmers so they'll be ready concurrently. Serve leftover gravy over cheese grits for another Southern treat.

1   **pound hot ground pork sausage**
3   **(28-ounce) cans whole tomatoes, undrained and coarsely chopped**
¼   **cup sugar**
1   **teaspoon salt**
½   **teaspoon pepper**
1   **teaspoon chopped garlic**
¼   **cup all-purpose flour**
¼   **cup water**
Bacon Cornbread

Cook sausage in a Dutch oven, stirring until it crumbles and is no longer pink. Drain. Add tomatoes and next 4 ingredients; simmer over medium heat 1 hour. Whisk together flour and water; add to tomato mixture. Cook 1 minute or until mixture begins to thicken. Serve over Bacon Cornbread. **Makes:** 8 servings.
Prep: 14 min., **Cook:** 1 hr.

Bacon Cornbread:
1   **pound bacon, chopped**
1   **cup yellow cornmeal**
1   **cup all-purpose flour**
1   **tablespoon baking powder**
1   **large egg, lightly beaten**
1½ **cups buttermilk**
¼   **cup shortening**

Cook bacon in a large skillet until crisp; set aside, reserving drippings.

Combine cornmeal and next 4 ingredients in a medium bowl; stir in bacon and reserved drippings.
Melt shortening in a 10-inch cast-iron skillet in a 425° oven. Pour batter into skillet; bake 25 minutes or until browned. **Makes:** 8 servings.
Prep: 12 min., **Cook:** 25 min.

Note: Use kitchen shears to quickly chop tomatoes while still in the can.

Wanda Bell
Ashburn, Georgia

After **Wanda** cooks the bacon, she adds the drippings to the gravy. We chose to put them in the cornbread to tenderize it and add lots of smoky flavor.

Stuffed Collard Rolls

8   **ounces hot ground pork sausage**
8   **ounces ground chuck**
1   **cup uncooked long-grain rice**
1   **teaspoon freshly ground black pepper**
1¼ **teaspoons salt**
¾   **cup water**
25 **fresh collard leaves (about 2 small bunches)**
4   **cups water**
¼   **pound smoked ham, cut into 1-inch chunks**
1   **medium onion, coarsely chopped**
½   **teaspoon freshly ground black pepper**
Liquid from hot peppers in vinegar

Combine first 6 ingredients in a medium bowl; set aside.
Remove stems from collards, and discard; wash leaves thoroughly. Blanch leaves in boiling water 2 minutes. Plunge into ice water to stop the cooking process; drain well.

Serve these delicious little bundles with black-eyed peas for an extra special New Year's Day dinner. Or **Lamont** suggests pairing them in the summertime with sliced vine-ripe tomatoes, garden fresh black-eyed peas, and hot cornbread.

Spoon 1 heaping tablespoon meat mixture into center of each collard leaf. For each roll, fold bottom side of leaf over filling, then fold left and right sides over filling. Fold remaining edge over to form a small bundle. Pour 4 cups water into a Dutch oven. Place bundles in a steamer basket in Dutch oven. Sprinkle evenly with ham, onion, and pepper. Cook, covered, over medium-low heat 1 hour or until rice is tender. Serve with pepper sauce. **Makes:** 5 to 6 servings.
Prep: 36 min., **Cook:** 1 hr., 10 min.

Lamont H. Pharmer
Ocala, Florida

Jambalaya Phyllo Parcels With Creole Cream Sauce

Filled with jambalaya, these pastry parcels make an elegant presentation. If you have leftover jambalaya, it can be refrigerated and reheated for a meal later in the week. It's wonderful drizzled with any remaining cream sauce and served with crusty bread and a salad.

1 **pound andouille sausage, diced**
1 **pound chicken tenderloins**
¼ **cup butter**
½ **cup chopped green onions**
½ **cup chopped celery**
2 **garlic cloves, minced**
2 **(14.5-ounce) can diced tomatoes, undrained**
¾ **teaspoon salt**
¼ **teaspoon freshly ground black pepper**
¼ **teaspoon cayenne pepper**
¼ **teaspoon dried crushed red pepper**
1½ **cups uncooked long-grain rice**
2½ **cups water**
Creole Cream Sauce
1 **cup butter, melted**
¼ **teaspoon ground red pepper**
1 **(16-ounce) package frozen phyllo pastry, thawed (9 x 14-inch sheets)**
Garnish: chopped parsley

Cook sausage in a large Dutch oven over medium-high heat, stirring occasionally, 5 minutes; drain and set aside, reserving drippings in pan. Add chicken to drippings in pan; cook 6 to 7 minutes, stirring occasionally, or until done. Remove chicken from pan. Melt ¼ cup butter in same pan over medium-high heat; add green onions, celery, and garlic. Cook 5 to 6 minutes, stirring occasionally, or until vegetables are tender. Add tomatoes and next 4 ingredients; cook 5 minutes, stirring occasionally. Add rice and water; bring to a boil. Reduce heat to low; cover and cook 30 to 35 minutes or until rice is tender and liquid is absorbed. Remove from heat, and cool slightly.

While rice mixture cooks, prepare Creole Cream Sauce.

Combine 1 cup melted butter and ground red pepper. Layer 5 sheets of phyllo, brushing each sheet lightly with butter mixture. Spoon ¾ cup rice mixture onto 1 shorter side of phyllo, leaving a 2-inch margin on the sides and top; drizzle with 2 tablespoons Creole Cream Sauce. Fold sides over towards center. Roll up dough, starting at the side with the filling to form a parcel. Place seam side down on an ungreased baking sheet. Repeat with remaining dough, rice mixture, and sauce. Bake at 375° for 15 to 20 minutes or until golden brown. Serve with remaining Creole Cream Sauce. Garnish, if desired. **Makes:** 8 servings.
Prep: 27 min., **Cook:** 1 hr., 8 min.

For an attractive presentation, **Lori** spreads about ¼ cup cream sauce on each plate, then places a phyllo parcel in the center of the sauce. She garnishes the plates with a scattering of fresh parsley.

Creole Cream Sauce:

¼ **cup butter**
¾ **cup chopped red bell pepper**
½ **cup chopped celery**
1 **garlic clove, minced**
1 **(6-ounce) can tomato paste**
1 **(14-ounce) can chicken broth**
¾ **teaspoon Worcestershire sauce**
½ **teaspoon hot paprika**
½ **teaspoon salt**
¼ **teaspoon freshly ground black pepper**
⅛ **teaspoon ground red pepper**
2 **teaspoons cornstarch**
2 **tablespoons water**
½ **cup heavy whipping cream**
3 **tablespoons butter, softened**

Melt ¼ cup butter in a medium saucepan over medium-high heat; add bell pepper, celery, and garlic. Cook, stirring occasionally, 5 minutes or until vegetable are tender. Whisk in tomato paste and next 6 ingredients; bring to a boil. Reduce heat, and simmer, uncovered, 10 minutes, stirring often.

Pour broth mixture into a blender; process until smooth. Return to saucepan. Whisk together cornstarch and water until smooth. Whisk cornstarch mixture into broth mixture; bring to a boil, whisking constantly. Add cream and 3 tablespoons butter, stirring until butter melts. Remove from heat.
Makes: about 3½ cups.
Prep: 8 min., **Cook:** 15 min.

Lori Laver
Sandy, Utah

Venison Tenderloin in
Wild Turkey Marinade

Venison Tenderloin in Wild Turkey Marinade

We cooked the venison directly on the grill rack and thought it was some of the best we have ever tasted. This cooking method adds a smoky dimension and tones down the bourbon.

1½ cups bourbon
1   cup vegetable oil
¼   cup fresh lime juice
1   medium onion, diced
4   bay leaves, crushed
4   garlic cloves, minced
2   teaspoons dried sage
1   teaspoon ground coriander
1   teaspoon salt
1   teaspoon pepper
2   teaspoons Worcestershire
    sauce
½   teaspoon fennel seeds
1   (1-ounce) envelope dry onion
    soup mix
2   (¾-pound) venison tenderloins

Combine first 13 ingredients in a large zip-top freezer bag. Add venison; seal bag. Marinate in refrigerator 5 hours, turning occasionally.

Remove tenderloins from marinade; discard marinade.

Grill tenderloins, covered with grill lid, over medium-high heat (350° to 400°) 16 minutes or until a meat thermometer inserted into thickest portion registers 155°. Cover and let stand 5 minutes until temperature reaches 160° before slicing. **Makes:** 4 to 6 servings.
Prep: 9 min., **Cook:** 16 min., **Other:** 5 hrs.

Note: If you'd rather not grill, place tenderloins on a lightly greased broiler pan and roast at 425° for 25 minutes or until a meat thermometer registers 155°. Cover and let stand 5 minutes until temperature reaches 160° before slicing.

Cheryl Anderson
Crittenden, Kentucky

Cheryl cooks the venison in a foil packet, which concentrates the bourbon flavor and steams the meat.

Hoppin' John's High Thighs

Green chiles add a pleasant bite to this sweet chicken dish.

1   cup chicken broth
1   (10-ounce) can diced tomatoes
    and green chiles, undrained
1   cup uncooked long-grain rice
1   (15.8-ounce) can black-eyed
    peas, rinsed and drained
¾   teaspoon salt
¼   teaspoon pepper
9   skinned chicken thighs
    (about 2¼ pounds)
2   tablespoons olive oil
1   cup bourbon
1   cup ketchup
1   tablespoon dark brown sugar
1   tablespoon cider vinegar
2   tablespoons Worcestershire
    sauce
3   green onions, sliced

Combine chicken broth and tomatoes in a 3-quart saucepan; bring to a boil. Add rice; reduce heat, and simmer, covered, 20 minutes or until rice is tender and liquid is absorbed. Stir in black-eyed peas; set aside.

Meanwhile, sprinkle salt and pepper over chicken thighs. Heat oil in a 12-inch skillet over medium-high heat. Add chicken; cook 10 minutes or until lightly browned. Remove from pan; discard drippings.

Combine bourbon and next 4 ingredients in a small bowl. Return chicken to skillet; pour sauce over chicken. Bring to a boil; boil, uncovered, 5 minutes. Reduce heat, and simmer, covered, 10 to 12 minutes or until chicken is done.

Serve chicken over rice mixture; spoon sauce over chicken. Sprinkle with green onions. **Makes:** 4 servings.
Prep: 4 min., **Cook:** 30 min.

Note: You can add more spice to this dish by adding chopped green chiles to the rice mixture or by using a spicier variety of diced tomatoes.

Geraldine Sale
Panama City, Florida

While the rice cooks, **Geraldine** prepares the chicken. While the chicken cooks, she prepares the sauce. She never wastes a minute of time and dinner is served in about 35 minutes.

Creole Chicken Fricassee

½   cup olive oil
10 skinned and boned chicken
    thighs
1   medium onion, chopped
1   green bell pepper, chopped
2   garlic cloves, minced
2   (10-ounce) cans diced tomatoes
    and green chiles, undrained
1   cup chicken broth
1   cup dry white wine
1   teaspoon dried thyme
½   teaspoon salt
4   small red potatoes, peeled and
    cubed (about 1 pound)
Hot cooked rice

Heat olive oil in a large Dutch oven until hot; add chicken thighs. Cook 5 minutes on each side or until browned. Remove chicken from pan; set aside, and keep warm.

Add onion, bell pepper, and garlic to Dutch oven; sauté over medium-high heat 4 minutes or until onion is crisp-tender. Add chicken, tomatoes and chiles, and next 4 ingredients, and cook 4 minutes, stirring often.

Add potato; bring to a boil. Reduce heat, and simmer, uncovered, 35 minutes, stirring often. Cook rice while chicken simmers. Serve fricassee over rice.
Makes: 5 servings.
Prep: 15 min., **Cook:** 55 min.

Carlos de Salazar
Miami, Florida

Carlos uses additional olive oil to sauté the vegetables. We omitted the extra oil and used the drippings from browning the chicken to impart extra flavor to the vegetables.

Mama Pearl's Southern Chicken and Dumplings Nuevo

Cotija cheese, a strongly flavored Hispanic crumbling cheese, can be found at large discount supercenters or Hispanic markets. Parmesan cheese is similar in flavor and could be used if cotija is not available in your local supermarket.

4 (6-ounce) skinned and boned chicken breasts
1 pound skinned and boned chicken thighs
4 (14-ounce) cans chicken broth (7 cups)
1 (10-ounce) package frozen chopped spinach, thawed
2½ cups all-purpose flour
¼ cup peanut oil
1 teaspoon salt
1 teaspoon bottled minced roasted garlic
1 to 3 tablespoons water
1 cup buttermilk
½ cup fresh lemon juice
1 tablespoon butter
4 poblano peppers
1 (4-ounce) can sliced mushrooms, drained
1 cup (4 ounces) crumbled cotija cheese
Fresh pico de gallo or salsa

Cut chicken into cubes. Bring chicken and chicken broth to a boil in a Dutch oven; cover, reduce heat, and simmer 30 minutes.

Meanwhile, drain spinach well, and press gently between paper towels to remove excess water.

Pulse spinach, flour, and next 3 ingredients in a food processor to blend. Add water through food chute, 1 tablespoon at a time, while processing, just until dough begins to form a ball. Roll dough out to ¼-inch thickness on a lightly floured surface. Cut into 2- x 1-inch rectangles.

After chicken mixture has simmered, uncover and bring to a boil; drop dumplings into boiling mixture, stirring gently. Cook dumplings, uncovered, 10 minutes. Stir in buttermilk, lemon juice, and butter. Cook over medium heat 20 minutes.

Meanwhile, broil poblano peppers on an aluminum foil-lined baking sheet 5 inches from heat about 15 minutes or until peppers look blistered, turning peppers over after 6 minutes. Place peppers in a zip-top plastic bag; seal and let stand 10 minutes to loosen skins. Peel peppers; remove and discard seeds. Chop peppers.

Stir peppers, mushrooms, and cheese into dumpling mixture, and cook 5 more minutes, stirring constantly. Serve with pico de gallo or salsa. **Makes:** 6 to 8 servings.
Prep: 39 min., **Cook:** 35 min., **Other:** 10 min.

Leah Lyon
Ada, Oklahoma

Leah's recipe got rave reviews from our taste-testing panel. She gives a Southern favorite a complete face-lift with the addition of spinach to the dumplings as well as snappy poblanos and sharp cotija cheese to the chicken mixture. The results are outstanding.

Spicy Southern Fried Chicken

Although its name implies otherwise, this fried chicken hides its spicy ingredients well. It's tame enough for kids, yet adults can spice it up with hot sauce.

2 cups buttermilk
1 tablespoon ground red pepper
1 teaspoon hot sauce
2 garlic cloves, minced
1 (3½-pound) cut up whole chicken
1 tablespoon seasoned salt
½ cup all-purpose flour
½ cup whole wheat flour
½ teaspoon ground red pepper
Vegetable oil
Hot sauce (optional)

Combine first 4 ingredients in a large zip-top freezer bag. Add chicken; seal and marinate in refrigerator 1 hour, turning once.

Remove chicken from marinade, discarding marinade. Sprinkle chicken with seasoned salt. Combine flours and ½ teaspoon red pepper. Dredge chicken in flour mixture.

Pour oil to a depth of ½ inch into a deep skillet; heat to 360°. Fry chicken, in batches, 19 to 23 minutes or until golden, turning once. Serve with hot sauce, if desired. **Makes:** 8 servings.
Prep: 9 min., **Cook:** 23 min. per batch, **Other:** 1 hr.

Tip: If you don't have a deep skillet, use a large Dutch oven.

Christina Chapman
Aurora, Colorado

Almond Chicken

We didn't want to miss a drop of the sweet onion-flavored sauce, so we served the chicken and sauce over a bed of rice to absorb every bit of the tasty juice.

⅓ cup peanut oil, divided
4 skinned and boned chicken breasts
¼ teaspoon salt
¼ teaspoon pepper
1 medium onion, sliced
3 tablespoons all-purpose flour
1 (14-ounce) can chicken broth
1 cup dry white wine
2 tablespoons Dijon mustard
⅔ cup sliced almonds, divided
¼ cup chopped fresh parsley, divided
Hot cooked rice

Heat 2 tablespoons oil in a large Dutch oven over medium-high heat. Sprinkle chicken breasts with salt and pepper; cook in hot oil 3 minutes each side or until browned. Remove chicken, reserving drippings in Dutch oven; set chicken aside. Saute onions in drippings 2 minutes or until onions are tender and slightly browned. Remove onions from Dutch oven; set aside.

Add remaining oil to Dutch oven. Add flour, and cook, whisking constantly, until mixture is peanut butter-colored, about 3 minutes. Remove from heat; whisk in chicken broth, wine, and mustard until smooth. Bring to a boil. Add half of almonds and half of parsley; top with chicken and onions. Reduce heat; cover and simmer 20 minutes, stirring occasionally. Uncover and simmer 10 more minutes.

Serve over hot cooked rice; top with remaining almonds and parsley. **Makes:** 4 servings.

Prep: 5 min., **Cook:** 45 min.

Vanessa Martin
New Orleans, Louisiana

Vanessa serves this easy, updated version of chicken fricassee over small roasted red potatoes.

Jerk Fried Chicken With Sweet Potatoes and Chipotle-Pineapple Sauce

1½ pounds sweet potatoes
2 tablespoons butter or margarine
½ teaspoon salt
¼ cup all-purpose flour
1½ teaspoons Jamaican jerk seasoning
1 teaspoon salt, divided
4 skinned and boned chicken breasts
2 tablespoons olive oil
1 tablespoon all-purpose flour
1 (20-ounce) can pineapple tidbits in juice, undrained
½ cup chopped red bell pepper
1 tablespoon honey
2 teaspoons spicy brown mustard
1 teaspoon minced chipotle pepper in adobo sauce
¼ cup sliced green onions
½ cup coarsely chopped pecans, toasted

Place sweet potatoes in a large saucepan; add water to cover. Bring to a boil; cover, reduce heat, and simmer 20 minutes or until tender; drain. Peel potatoes, and return to pan; add butter and ½ teaspoon salt. Mash potato in pan until smooth.

While potatoes simmer, stir together ¼ cup flour, jerk seasoning, and ½ teaspoon salt in a shallow dish. Dredge chicken in flour mixture.

Heat oil in large skillet over medium-high heat until hot. Add chicken; cook 5 minutes on each side or until done. Remove chicken to a serving platter, and keep warm, reserving drippings in skillet.

Add 1 tablespoon flour to drippings in skillet, stirring well. Stir in pineapple and juice, bell pepper, honey, mustard, chipotle pepper, and remaining ½ teaspoon salt. Cook over medium heat, stirring constantly, 4 to 5 minutes until sauce is slightly thickened. Serve chicken with mashed sweet potatoes, and pineapple sauce. Sprinkle with green onions and pecans. **Makes:** 4 servings.

Prep: 30 min., **Cook:** 25 min.

Priscilla Yee
Concord, California

Boiling the sweet potatoes as **Priscilla** does saves time because they're ready to mash in 20 minutes. But if you have a little time to spare, try baking the potatoes at 375° for an hour or until tender before mashing. Baked sweet potatoes add richness and depth to the flavor.

New and Nutty Fried Chicken

Creole-seasoned peanuts give a spicy, crunchy kick to this lightly fried chicken served over Asian-flavored slaw.

- 3 tablespoons fresh lime juice
- 2 tablespoons soy sauce
- 2 tablespoons creamy peanut butter
- 1 tablespoon sesame oil
- 1 tablespoon honey
- 1 tablespoon mayonnaise
- 1 teaspoon minced garlic
- ½ teaspoon hot sauce
- ¼ teaspoon Creole seasoning
- 2 cups finely shredded green cabbage
- 2 cups finely shredded red cabbage
- 2 carrots, shredded
- ½ cup raisins
- ½ cup thinly sliced red onion
- ½ cup chopped fresh cilantro
- ½ cup chopped dry-roasted peanuts
- 1 cup dry-roasted peanuts
- 1 teaspoon minced fresh ginger
- 1 teaspoon Creole seasoning
- 1 teaspoon Worcestershire sauce
- 1 teaspoon hot sauce
- 1 cup all-purpose flour
- 1 large egg, lightly beaten
- ½ cup milk
- 4 skinned and boned chicken breasts
- ¼ teaspoon salt
- ¼ teaspoon pepper
- 2 tablespoons vegetable oil

Garnish: fresh cilantro sprigs

Whisk together first 9 ingredients in a large bowl. Add cabbages, carrots, and next 4 ingredients, and toss well. Cover and chill at least 2 hours.

Place 1 cup peanuts and next 4 ingredients in a small bowl; toss well. Spoon nut mixture onto baking sheet, spreading evenly. Bake at 350° for 10 minutes or until nuts are lightly toasted. Cool slightly. (Do not turn off oven.)

Process nut mixture in a food processor until finely chopped; place in a shallow bowl. Place flour on a plate. Combine egg and milk in a shallow bowl. Sprinkle chicken with salt and pepper.

Dredge chicken in flour, dip in egg mixture; gently press chicken in peanut mixture.

Heat oil in a large ovenproof skillet over medium-high heat. Add chicken; fry 2 to 3 minutes on each side or until browned. Place skillet in oven; bake at 350° for 10 minutes or until chicken is done. Cut each breast into thin slices.

Mound slaw mixture evenly into shallow serving bowls or plates. Arrange chicken breast slices evenly over slaw mixture. Garnish, if desired. Serve immediately.

Makes: 4 servings.

Prep: 36 min., **Cook:** 26 min., **Other:** 2 hrs.

Tips: To shred cabbages, cut each head in half. Place cut side down on a cutting board. Slice downward into very thin slices. (Slice the onion the same way.) For easy cleanup, place flour and peanut dredging mixture on paper plates.

Melissa Kubala
Houston, Texas

If you prefer a chunkier coating on the chicken, **Melissa** suggests processing the peanut mixture less time.

New and Nutty Fried Chicken

Greek "Fried" Chicken With Salsa

In keeping with the Greek feel of this recipe, we suggest a steaming side of olive oil-tossed orzo.

1   (6-ounce) jar marinated artichoke hearts
2   cups seeded, diced plum tomatoes (about 6)
2   jalapeño peppers, seeded and minced
¼   cup sliced green onions
¼   cup chopped fresh cilantro
½   cup pitted, chopped kalamata olives
1   tablespoon fresh lemon juice
¼   teaspoon salt
½   cup crumbled feta cheese
4   skinned and boned chicken breasts
½   cup all-purpose flour
½   cup plain yogurt
½   teaspoon Greek seasoning
½   cup Italian-seasoned breadcrumbs
2   teaspoons chopped fresh rosemary

Drain artichoke hearts, reserving 1 tablespoon marinade. Coarsely chop artichokes. Combine artichokes, reserved marinade, and next 8 ingredients in a medium bowl; stir well. Set aside.

Place chicken between 2 sheets of heavy-duty plastic wrap; flatten to ½-inch thickness, using a mallet or rolling pin. Set aside.

Place flour in a shallow dish. Combine yogurt and Greek seasoning in a small bowl. Combine breadcrumbs and rosemary in another shallow dish.

Mary Lou goes all out in her presentation of this meal. She garnishes each serving with rosemary sprigs, lemon slices, and kalamata olives. Mary Lou serves this dish over rice.

Dredge chicken in flour, coating well; shake to remove excess flour. Spread a thin layer of yogurt mixture on each side of chicken breast, and coat with breadcrumb mixture. Repeat process with remaining chicken, flour, yogurt mixture, and breadcrumb mixture.

Place chicken on a lightly greased foil-lined baking sheet. Bake at 450° for 20 to 25 minutes or until done. Serve chicken with salsa. **Makes:** 4 servings.
Prep: 20 min., **Cook:** 25 min.

Mary Lou Cook
Welches, Oregon

Stuffed Chicken Breasts With Two-Cheese Grits

Use large chicken breasts (7 to 8 ounces each) for this recipe to hold all the delicious filling.

6   large skinned and boned chicken breasts
1¼ teaspoons salt, divided
1¼ teaspoons pepper, divided
1   (8-ounce) package cream cheese, softened
1   cup chopped ham
½   cup grated Parmesan cheese, divided
½   cup self-rising flour
1   teaspoon garlic powder
¼   cup butter
Two-Cheese Grits

Place chicken breasts between 2 sheets of heavy-duty plastic wrap; flatten to ½-inch thickness using a mallet or rolling pin. Sprinkle chicken with ¼ teaspoon each salt and pepper.

Combine cream cheese, ham, and ¼ cup Parmesan cheese, stirring well.

Spoon one-sixth of cream cheese mixture into center of each chicken breast. Roll up chicken breasts; secure with wooden picks. Combine flour, remaining 1 teaspoon each salt and pepper, remaining ¼ cup Parmesan cheese, and garlic powder; dredge chicken breasts in flour mixture, shaking off excess flour.

Melt butter in a large nonstick skillet over medium heat; add chicken breasts. Cook 6 to 7 minutes, turning often, or until well browned. Place chicken breasts on a baking sheet lined with aluminum foil. Bake at 375° for 20 to 23 minutes or until done.

Meanwhile, prepare Two-Cheese Grits. When chicken is done, remove wooden picks. Cut chicken into 1-inch-thick slices. Serve over grits. **Makes:** 6 servings.
Prep: 15 min., **Cook:** 30 min.

Two-Cheese Grits:
5   cups water
2   garlic cloves, minced
¼   cup butter
1   teaspoon salt
1   teaspoon pepper
1   cup uncooked quick-cooking grits
½   cup (2 ounces) shredded mozzarella cheese
¼   cup grated Parmesan cheese

Combine first 5 ingredients in a 3-quart saucepan; bring to a boil. Whisk in grits; return to a boil. Reduce heat to low; cook 2 to 5 minutes, stirring often, or until thickened and creamy. Stir in cheeses. **Makes:** about 5 cups.
Prep: 2 min., **Cook:** 5 min.

Rebecca Farrin
Loganville, Georgia

Scrumptious Sausage Stuffed Chicken

1   pound ground pork sausage
2   tablespoons olive oil, divided
2   tablespoons butter, divided
1   cup finely chopped onion
1½   cups finely chopped fresh
     mushrooms
2   (3-ounce) packages cream
     cheese, softened
3   tablespoons half-and-half
¼   teaspoon pepper
4   skinned and boned chicken
     breasts
½   teaspoon salt
1   cup half-and-half
⅛   teaspoon pepper

Denise serves this dish with sautéed cabbage and onions, and plenty of buttermilk biscuits for the gravy. Sometimes she serves mashed potatoes instead of biscuits.

Cook sausage in a large skillet over medium-high heat, stirring until it crumbles and is no longer pink; remove from skillet, and drain well. Wipe skillet with paper towels.

Heat 1 tablespoon oil and 1 tablespoon butter in skillet over medium-high heat. Add onion and mushrooms; cook 3 minutes or until tender. Add cooked sausage and cream cheese, stirring until cheese is melted. Stir in 3 tablespoons half-and-half and ¼ teaspoon pepper; cook 3 minutes, stirring constantly. Remove from heat; cool.

Place chicken between 2 sheets of heavy-duty plastic wrap. Flatten to ½-inch thickness using a mallet or rolling pin; sprinkle evenly with salt. Spoon about 2 tablespoons sausage mixture into center of each breast, reserving remaining sausage mixture. Roll up chicken breasts, and secure with wooden picks.

Heat remaining 1 tablespoon oil and remaining 1 tablespoon butter in a large nonstick skillet over medium-high heat. Brown chicken on all sides; remove from skillet, and place chicken in a roasting pan.

Bake at 375° for 40 minutes or until a meat thermometer inserted into thickest portion registers 160°; remove wooden picks, and place chicken on a serving platter, reserving drippings in pan. Cover chicken; keep warm.

Place pan with drippings on cooktop over high heat. Add 1 cup half-and-half and ⅛ teaspoon pepper; cook until mixture begins to thicken, stirring constantly. Stir in reserved sausage mixture, and cook 2 more minutes. Spoon gravy over chicken; serve immediately. **Makes:** 4 servings.
Prep: 25 min., **Cook:** 58 min.

Denise Nacinovich
Bellmore, New York

Rosemary Chicken Salad

Staples such as mayonnaise, Ranch dressing, and spicy mustard combine with fresh rosemary for a new twist on chicken salad.

1   tablespoon olive oil
1   teaspoon bottled minced
     roasted garlic
1   tablespoon minced fresh
     rosemary, divided
½   teaspoon salt, divided
1   pound chicken breast tenders
1½   tablespoons Ranch-style
     dressing
1   tablespoon mayonnaise
1   tablespoon spicy brown mustard
1   teaspoon minced fresh onion
¼   teaspoon pepper

Combine oil, garlic, 1½ teaspoons rosemary, and ¼ teaspoon salt in a medium bowl; add chicken tenders, and toss well. Brown chicken in a nonstick skillet over medium-high heat 8 to 9 minutes or until done. Cool slightly; dice chicken tenders.

Combine chicken, dressing, mayonnaise, mustard, onion, remaining 1½ teaspoons rosemary, remaining ¼ teaspoon salt, and pepper. Serve immediately, or cover and chill. **Makes:** 2½ cups.
Prep: 10 min., **Cook:** 9 min.

Tip: If you have boneless, skinless chicken breasts on hand, cut them into 1-inch strips and use in place of tenderloins.

Bev Chappell
Mableton, Georgia

Bev serves this herbed chicken salad on lettuce-lined plates or uses it to make sandwiches.

Taco Catfish With Black Bean Pico de Gallo

Taco Catfish With Black Bean Pico de Gallo

Black beans add interest to the pico de gallo that tops this taco-flavored catfish.

1   (15-ounce) can black beans, rinsed and drained
1   medium tomato, seeded and chopped
⅓   cup diced red onion
2   jalapeño peppers, seeded and minced
2   tablespoons chopped fresh cilantro
3   tablespoons lime juice
½   teaspoon kosher salt
½   cup cornmeal
2   tablespoons all-purpose flour
½   (1¼-ounce) envelope taco seasoning mix (2 tablespoons)
1   large egg, lightly beaten
2   tablespoons water
6   (6-ounce) catfish fillets
2   tablespoons vegetable oil
1   tablespoon butter, melted
¾   cup crumbled queso fresco cheese *
Garnishes: fresh cilantro sprigs, lemon slices

Combine first 7 ingredients in a medium bowl; set aside.

Combine cornmeal, flour, and taco seasoning in a shallow dish. Combine egg and water in a shallow dish; stir well. Dip fish in egg mixture; dredge in cornmeal mixture.

Heat oil and butter in a large nonstick skillet over medium-high heat. Add fish; cook in batches, 3 to 4 minutes on each side or until fish flakes with a fork. To serve, spoon bean mixture over fish; sprinkle with cheese. Garnish, if desired. **Makes:** 6 servings.
Prep: 8 min., **Cook:** 8 min. per batch

*You can substitute crumbled feta cheese for queso fresco.

Mary Lou Cook
Welches, Oregon

Mary Lou makes her pico de gallo with lemon juice, but we stuck with tradition and favored lime juice.

Fried Catfish With Tropical Salsa

6   (6-ounce) catfish fillets
1   tablespoon hot sauce
1   teaspoon seasoned salt
1   teaspoon garlic powder
1   teaspoon salt
½   teaspoon pepper
¼   cup olive oil, divided
2   tablespoons butter, divided
6   lemon wedges
Tropical Salsa

Rub catfish with hot sauce. Combine seasoned salt and next 3 ingredients; sprinkle over both sides of catfish. Heat 2 tablespoons oil and 1 tablespoon butter in a large nonstick skillet over medium heat. Add 3 fillets; cook 3 minutes on each side or until fish flakes with a fork. Repeat with remaining fillets, oil, and butter. Serve with lemon wedges and Tropical Salsa. **Makes:** 6 servings.
Prep: 5 min., **Cook:** 6 min. per batch

Kasey created a sweet fruit salsa to balance the picante flavor of the pan-seared catfish in this colorful dish.

Tropical Salsa:
1   (15-ounce) can tropical fruit salad, drained and chopped
2   tablespoons finely chopped sweet onion
2   tablespoons finely chopped roasted red bell pepper
½   teaspoon seeded and minced jalapeño pepper

Combine all ingredients in a bowl.
Makes: 1¼ cups.
Prep: 10 min.

Kasey Brooker
Murfreesboro, Tennessee

Miami Mahi With Mango Salsa

Juicy grilled fish and cool fresh salsa make a perfect South Floridian combination.

¼   cup olive oil
¼   cup fresh lime juice
¼   cup tequila
2   teaspoons Old Bay seasoning
1   teaspoon chopped fresh cilantro
6   mahi mahi fillets (¾ to 1 inch thick; about 2 pounds)
Mango Salsa

Place first 5 ingredients in a large zip-top freezer bag; add fish. Seal bag, and marinate in refrigerator 30 minutes to 1 hour, turning occasionally.
Meanwhile, prepare Mango Salsa.
Remove fish from marinade; discard marinade. Grill, covered with grill lid, over medium heat (300° to 350°) 5 minutes on each side or until fish flakes with a fork. Serve with Mango Salsa.
Makes: 6 servings.
Prep: 5 min., **Cook:** 10 min., **Other:** 30 min.

Mango Salsa:
2   ripe mangoes, peeled and diced
1   tablespoon grated orange rind
3   oranges, peeled, sectioned, and chopped
½   cup chopped green onions
1   jalapeño pepper, seeded and minced
1   teaspoon grated fresh ginger
½   teaspoon salt

Stir together all ingredients. Cover and let stand 30 minutes or up to 4 hours.
Makes: 3¼ cups.
Prep: 25 min., **Other:** 30 min.

Tip: To speed up the ripening process, place mangoes in a paper bag and let stand at room temperature for a few days.

Randolph Bush
Bridgeport, Connecticut

Randolph seeds the jalapeño before mincing it to reduce the level of heat in the salsa. If you prefer wild instead of mild, leave a few seeds in the jalapeño to spice things up a bit.

Southwestern Salmon Croquettes With Cilantro Cream Sauce

Crushed tortilla chips, corn, and roasted red bell pepper give these croquettes a Southwestern flair. Serve them on a pool of green chile-spiked cream sauce for the complete south-of-the-border experience.

1 cup heavy whipping cream
½ (4.5-ounce) can chopped green chiles, drained (about ¼ cup)
2 garlic cloves, minced
¾ cup chopped green onions
¼ cup chopped fresh cilantro
1 teaspoon salt
1 teaspoon pepper
3 (6-ounce) cans boneless, skinless pink salmon, drained
1½ cups finely crushed tortilla chips (about 5 ounces), divided
½ cup chopped onion
½ cup drained sliced bottled roasted red bell pepper
½ cup drained canned whole kernel corn
2 large eggs, lightly beaten

1 teaspoon lemon juice
¼ teaspoon pepper
⅛ teaspoon ground cumin
¼ cup vegetable oil

Combine first 3 ingredients in a saucepan; bring to a boil. Reduce heat, and simmer 5 minutes. Remove from heat, and stir in green onions, cilantro, 1 teaspoon salt, and 1 teaspoon pepper. Cover and keep warm.

Meanwhile, combine salmon, ½ cup crushed chips, onion, and next 6 ingredients. Shape mixture into 8 patties; dredge each patty in remaining crushed chips.

Heat oil in a large skillet over medium-high heat. Cook croquettes, in 2 batches, in hot oil 4 to 5 minutes on each side or until golden. Drain on paper towels. Serve immediately with cream sauce.

Makes: 4 servings.
Prep: 40 min., **Cook:** 25 min.

Tip: To easily crush chips, place in a zip-top plastic bag; seal bag, and gently crush with a rolling pin or mallet.

Mike Trantham
Allen, Texas

Mike adds cornmeal to the croquettes, but we omitted the cornmeal and increased the crushed tortilla chips to add more texture and flavor.

Tilapia With Warm Cajun Chutney

3 tablespoons olive oil
4 fresh tilapia or catfish fillets
1 medium onion, chopped
1 pound fresh okra, cut into ½-inch slices
2 (14.5-ounce) cans diced tomatoes and green chiles, undrained
⅛ teaspoon ground red pepper
1 teaspoon salt-free herb-and-spice seasoning*
½ teaspoon salt
2 cups hot cooked yellow rice

Heat oil in a large nonstick skillet over medium-high heat. Add fish, and cook 3 minutes on each side or until fish flakes with a fork. Remove fish from skillet; set aside, and keep warm.

Add onion and okra to skillet; sauté 5 minutes or until onion is tender. Add tomatoes and next 3 ingredients; simmer over medium-high heat 7 minutes or until okra is tender.

To serve, spoon rice onto individual serving plates; place a fish fillet over rice, and spoon 1 cup okra mixture over fish. **Makes:** 4 servings.
Prep: 12 min., **Cook:** 18 min.

*For testing purposes only, we used Mrs. Dash Seasoning Blend.

Shirley Murphy
West Palm Beach, Florida

Shirley serves this dish over black bean rice, but we thought yellow rice offered a burst of color and a subtle flavor perfectly matched to the Cajun chutney. When Shirley wants to make this meal extra special, she serves it with skillet cornbread.

Southern-Style Grits Topped With Shrimp and Andouille

1 pound unpeeled, large fresh shrimp
1 pound andouille sausage, cut in half lengthwise, then sliced into ½-inch-thick slices
1 tablespoon extra-virgin olive oil
½ cup finely chopped onion
½ cup finely chopped red bell pepper
½ cup finely chopped green bell pepper
1 teaspoon minced garlic
2 tablespoons chopped fresh thyme leaves
1½ cups heavy whipping cream
Southern-Style Grits
½ (8-ounce) package cream cheese, softened
½ teaspoon salt
¼ teaspoon white pepper
Garnishes: chopped green onions, fresh thyme sprigs

Peel shrimp, and devein, if desired. Set shrimp aside.

Heat a large skillet over medium-high heat; add sausage. Cook 3 to 4 minutes or until browned. Remove sausage from skillet; set aside. Add shrimp to skillet; cook 2 to 3 minutes or just until shrimp turn pink. Remove shrimp from skillet.

Heat oil in skillet; add onion and bell peppers. Cook 3 to 4 minutes or until tender. Add garlic and thyme; cook 1 minute. Add cream; bring to a boil. Reduce heat to medium-low; simmer, uncovered, 8 to 10 minutes or until slightly reduced and thickened, stirring occasionally.

Meanwhile, prepare Southern-Style Grits.

Spoon cream mixture into a blender; add cream cheese, salt, and pepper. Process until smooth. Return cream mixture to skillet; add sausage and shrimp. Cook 1 to 2 minutes or until thoroughly heated. Serve over grits; garnish, if desired. **Makes:** 4 to 6 servings.

Prep: 20 min., **Cook:** 24 min.

Southern-Style Grits:
2 cups chicken broth
2 cups milk
1 cup uncooked yellow grits
2 tablespoons butter
1½ teaspoons salt
½ teaspoon white pepper

Bring chicken broth and milk to a boil in a 3-quart saucepan; whisk in grits. Reduce heat to low; cover and cook 5 to 10 minutes, stirring occasionally, or until thickened and creamy. Stir in butter, salt, and pepper. Keep warm. **Makes:** about 4½ cups.

Prep: 5 min., **Cook:** 10 min.

Melissa Haun
Charlotte, North Carolina

Melissa makes this Southern favorite with stone-ground grits. However, we tested this recipe with regular grits since stone-ground are not available in all areas of the country. If you're fortunate enough to find stone-ground grits, Melissa recommends you simmer them, covered, for 30 to 45 minutes or until they're tender, smooth, and creamy. Put them on to cook as you start peeling the shrimp.

Southern-Style Grits Topped With
Shrimp and Andouille

Creole Shrimp Benedict

1   **pound medium-size, fresh shrimp**
3   **bacon slices, chopped**
1   **tablespoon balsamic vinegar**
1   **(10-ounce) package fresh spinach, trimmed and torn**
1   **tablespoon olive oil**
2   **teaspoons Cajun seasoning**
1   **(14.5-ounce) can diced tomatoes with green pepper, celery, and onion, drained**
½   **cup butter**
3   **egg yolks**
¼   **teaspoon salt**
2   **tablespoons lemon juice**
4   **English muffins, split and toasted**
    Lemon wedges

Peel shrimp and devein, if desired. Set aside.

Cook bacon in a large skillet until crisp; transfer bacon to a bowl, reserving drippings in skillet. Add vinegar and spinach to skillet; cook 2 minutes or until wilted, tossing often. Transfer spinach to a bowl; keep warm. Wipe skillet clean.

Heat oil in skillet until hot. Add shrimp and Cajun seasoning; cook 3 minutes or just until shrimp turn pink. Add tomatoes, and cook 2 minutes or until thoroughly heated. Transfer mixture to bowl.

Melt butter in top of a double boiler over barely simmering water; whisk in egg yolks, salt, and lemon juice. Cook, whisking constantly, 3 to 5 minutes or until thickened and a thermometer registers 160°.

To serve, place 2 muffin halves on a serving plate; top with spinach mixture, shrimp mixture, then top with sauce. Serve with lemon wedges. **Makes:** 4 servings.

Prep: 9 min., **Cook:** 19 min.

Beth Royals
Richmond, Virginia

Eggs With Crabmeat Rémoulade over Fried Green Tomatoes

Although this recipe takes a little time to prepare, the end result is well worth the effort. Plus, many of the steps can be done ahead. After tasting this dish, we all agreed it would be wonderful for brunch.

   Rémoulade Sauce
   Crabmeat Topping
1   **tablespoon Creole seasoning**
2   **large eggs**
¼   **cup milk**
4   **green tomatoes, cut into ½-inch slices**
1   **cup all-purpose flour**
1   **cup cornmeal**
½   **cup vegetable oil**
12   **large eggs**

Prepare Rémoulade Sauce; cover and chill.
Assemble ingredients for Crabmeat Topping, picking shell from crabmeat.
Combine Creole seasoning, 2 eggs, and milk in a shallow bowl; add tomato slices, and let stand 5 minutes. Combine flour and cornmeal; stir well. Dredge tomatoes in flour mixture.
Heat oil in a large skillet over medium heat. Fry tomatoes, in batches, 4 minutes or until browned, turning to brown both sides; drain on paper towels. Keep warm.
To poach eggs, lightly grease a large saucepan. Add water to a depth of 2 inches in pan. Bring water to a boil; reduce heat, and maintain at a light simmer. Break eggs, 1 at a time, into a measuring cup or saucer; slip eggs, 1 at a time, into water, holding cup as close as possible to surface of water. Simmer 5 minutes or until done. Remove eggs with a slotted spoon. Trim edges, if desired.
While eggs poach, sauté Crabmeat Topping.
To serve, arrange 2 tomato slices on each serving plate; top each tomato slice with a poached egg. Spoon Crabmeat Topping over eggs; drizzle with Rémoulade Sauce. **Makes:** 6 servings.
Prep: 20 min., **Cook:** 30 min.

Crabmeat Topping:
3   **tablespoons butter**
¼   **cup sliced green onions**
1   **garlic clove, minced**
2   **plum tomatoes, diced**
1   **pound fresh lump crabmeat, drained**

Melt butter in a medium saucepan over medium heat. Add green onions, garlic, and tomatoes; sauté 2 minutes. Add crabmeat; cook 3 minutes or until thoroughly heated, stirring occasionally.
Makes: 3 cups.
Prep: 15 min., **Cook:** 5 min.

Rémoulade Sauce:
1   **cup mayonnaise**
¼   **cup sliced green onions**
2   **tablespoons minced fresh parsley**
2   **tablespoons grated fresh horseradish**
2   **tablespoons lemon juice**
2   **tablespoons Dijon mustard**
2   **tablespoons Creole mustard**
1   **tablespoon minced fresh thyme**
1   **tablespoon minced fresh tarragon**
2   **teaspoons paprika**
2   **garlic cloves, minced**

Stir together all ingredients in a medium bowl. Cover and chill until ready to serve. **Makes:** 1¾ cups.
Prep: 10 min.

Judy Armstrong
Prairieville, Louisiana

Mexican Spoonbread Stuffed Peppers

4   bell peppers (green, red, yellow, orange, or any combination)
2   tablespoons butter
¾   cup diced red onion
¾   cup cornbread mix
1   large egg, lightly beaten
¼   cup milk
½   cup cream-style corn
⅛   teaspoon hot sauce
⅛   teaspoon salt
⅛   teaspoon black pepper
½   cup sour cream
½   cup (2 ounces) shredded sharp Cheddar cheese
2   tablespoons canned chopped green chiles

Remove stem portion from peppers (being careful not to make a hole in the top). Cut peppers in half horizontally, and place cut side up on an aluminum foil-lined 15- x 10-inch jellyroll pan coated with cooking spray.

Melt butter in a skillet over medium heat; add onion, and sauté until tender. Remove from heat.

Combine cornbread mix and next 9 ingredients in a medium bowl; stir in sautéed onion.

Divide mixture evenly among 8 pepper halves, filling about three-fourths full. Bake, uncovered, at 425° for 25 to 27 minutes or until lightly browned. Serve immediately. **Makes:** 8 servings.

Prep: 7 min., **Cook:** 30 min.

Sonja Jenkins
Tupelo, Mississippi

Sonja uses tiny sprigs of fresh sage, cilantro, or parsley to garnish the spoonbread in each stuffed pepper.

Fried Tomatoes With Gorgonzola Cheese

This recipe is best prepared with ripe, acidic summer tomatoes to balance the strong flavors of the cheese, basil oil, and vinegar.

1½ cups balsamic vinegar
2   ounces fresh basil leaves (about 1 large bunch)
¾   cup olive oil, divided
½   cup all-purpose flour
2   teaspoons salt
1   teaspoon garlic powder
1   teaspoon pepper
1   large egg, lightly beaten
¾   cup milk
4   small red tomatoes, each cut into 3 (¼-inch-thick) slices
¾   cup Italian-seasoned breadcrumbs
4   ounces Gorgonzola cheese, crumbled

Bring balsamic vinegar to a boil in a medium saucepan; cook until reduced to ½ cup (about 30 minutes).

Meanwhile, combine basil and ½ cup olive oil in a blender or food processor, and process until smooth, stopping to scrape down sides occasionally; set aside.

Combine flour and next 3 ingredients in a shallow bowl. Combine egg and milk. Dredge tomato slices in flour mixture in a shallow bowl; dip in egg mixture. Dredge tomato in breadcrumbs.

Heat remaining ¼ cup olive oil in a medium skillet over medium-high heat. Add tomato slices; cook 3 minutes on each side or until browned.

Transfer tomato slices to a baking sheet. Sprinkle Gorgonzola cheese evenly over slices. Bake at 400° for 5 minutes or until cheese is melted. Drizzle with basil oil and balsamic reduction; serve immediately. **Makes:** 4 servings.

Prep: 10 min., **Cook:** 49 min.

Tip: These flavorful tomatoes are wonderful served over mixed greens.

Margie Chiapel
St. Louis, Missouri

Tomato-Fig Vinaigrette Dressing

Tomato-Fig Vinaigrette Dressing

This dressing is good on salad greens, of course, but we also recommend pouring it over cream cheese to serve with crackers or use it as a marinade for chicken and pork.

¾ **cup drained dried tomatoes in oil, chopped**
½ **cup fig preserves**
½ **cup olive oil**
¼ **cup balsamic vinegar**
¼ **teaspoon salt**
Freshly ground pepper to taste

Whisk together all ingredients. Serve over salad greens. Store in refrigerator.
Makes: 1¾ cups.
Prep: 5 min.

Tip: Be sure to remove as much excess water as possible from the salad greens so the dressing will adhere to the greens better.

Kathy Collier
Fort Myers, Florida

If you don't have balsamic vinegar on hand, **Kathy** recommends red wine vinegar as a substitute.

Spiced Fig and Pineapple Preserves

If you like fig preserves, you'll love this version with allspice, cloves, cinnamon, and a sweet surprise . . . pineapple.

1 **(20-ounce) can crushed pineapple in syrup, undrained**
5 **cups stemmed and sliced fresh figs (about 2 pounds)**
7 **cups sugar**
½ **cup fresh lemon juice**
½ **teaspoon butter**
½ **teaspoon ground cinnamon**
¼ **teaspoon ground cloves**
¼ **teaspoon ground allspice**
1 **(3-ounce) package liquid pectin**

Drain pineapple, reserving ½ cup syrup. Add water to syrup to make ½ cup, if necessary.
Combine figs and next 6 ingredients in a large Dutch oven. Bring to a boil over medium-high heat; reduce heat, and simmer 3 minutes, stirring occasionally. Stir in pectin. Bring to a boil; cook 2 minutes, stirring constantly. Keep warm.
Pour hot fig mixture into 10 hot sterilized half-pint jars, filling ¼ inch from top.

Remove air bubbles; wipe jar rims. Cover at once with metal lids, and screw on bands.
Process in boiling-water bath 10 minutes.
Makes: 10 half-pints.
Prep: 40 min., **Cook:** 35 min.

Tip: Place washed jars in a 220° oven for 15 minutes to sterilize. This will allow more working space on the cooktop.

Amber T. Prince
Armuchee, Georgia

Black Bean, Ham, and Macaroni Salad

Quick, creamy, and a snap to prepare.

2 **cups uncooked elbow macaroni**
½ **cup mayonnaise**
2 **tablespoons red wine vinegar**
2 **tablespoons olive oil**
1 **teaspoon ground cumin**
1 **teaspoon dried oregano**
¾ **teaspoon salt**
½ **teaspoon pepper**
1 **(8-ounce) package diced cooked ham (1½ cups)**

1 **(15-ounce) can black beans, rinsed and drained**
¼ **cup chopped red onion**

Cook macaroni in boiling salted water according to package directions. Drain; rinse with cold water, and drain.

Stir together mayonnaise and next 6 ingredients in a medium bowl. Stir in macaroni, ham, black beans, and onion. Cover and chill at least 1 hour.
Makes: 7½ cups.
Prep: 10 min., **Cook:** 9 min., **Other:** 1 hr.

April Williams
Winter Park, Florida

By adding black beans and ground cumin, **April** updated a classic deli salad.

Ollie's Cheddar Potato Salad

Cheddar cheese gives this potato salad lots of color and flavor.

2½ pounds Yukon gold or yellow
   Finn potatoes, peeled and
   cubed
6   hard-cooked eggs, chopped
¾   cup chopped celery
½   cup chopped chives
¾   cup coarsely chopped dill pickle
1   tablespoon dill pickle juice
2   cups (8 ounces) shredded mild
   Cheddar cheese
1¾ cups (7 ounces) grated sharp
   white Cheddar cheese

¾   cup mayonnaise
2   tablespoons prepared mustard
1   teaspoon seasoned salt
1   teaspoon paprika
½   teaspoon salt

Combine potatoes and salted water to cover in a large saucepan; bring to a boil over medium heat, and cook 20 to 25 minutes or until tender. Drain and cool. Combine potatoes and remaining ingredients in a large bowl; toss gently. **Makes:** 8 to 10 servings.
Prep: 37 min., **Cook:** 25 min.

Tip: Potatoes can be cooled quickly in freezer if time is a factor.

Susan Oliver
Virginia Beach, Virginia

Susan uses kosher dill pickles in this salad because of their distinct flavor, but any dill pickle will work.

BLT Potato Salad

This recipe puts a spin on traditional potato salad with cream cheese, Ranch dressing, and Romano cheese. It received our highest rating.

3½ pounds Yukon gold potatoes,
   cubed
1   (8-ounce) package cream
   cheese, softened
½   cup sour cream
⅓   cup milk
1   cup mayonnaise
1   (1-ounce) package dry Ranch
   dressing mix
½   cup chopped fresh parsley
¼   cup finely chopped fresh basil
½   teaspoon onion salt
½   teaspoon ground white pepper
1   cup finely shredded Romano
   cheese, divided
2   (2.1-ounce) packages fully
   cooked bacon

1   pint grape tomatoes, halved
3   cups coarsely chopped romaine
   lettuce
1   tablespoon chopped fresh parsley

Cook potatoes in boiling water to cover 11 minutes or until tender. Drain well, and set aside to cool completely.
Meanwhile, whisk together cream cheese and next 3 ingredients until smooth. Add Ranch dressing mix and next 4 ingredients; stir well. Stir in ½ cup Romano cheese; set aside.
Cook bacon according to package directions; cool and coarsely chop.
Combine potatoes, cream cheese mixture, 1½ cups bacon, and tomatoes in a large bowl; stir gently to blend.

Place lettuce on a serving platter. Mound potato mixture on top of lettuce; sprinkle with remaining ½ cup Romano cheese, remaining ½ cup bacon, and 1 tablespoon parsley. **Makes:** 10 to 12 servings.
Prep: 48 min., **Cook:** 14 min.

Susan Rotter
Nolensville, Tennessee

Susan says this salad is best served at room temperature right after it's tossed. If the salad is made ahead and chilled, she recommends letting it stand at room temperature about 15 minutes before serving. See Susan's grand prizewinning recipe on page 23.

Creole Shrimp Lasagna With Béchamel Sauce

Using no-boil lasagna noodles really speeds up the preparation of this creative take on a classic. Shrimp and a white sauce replace the familiar ground beef and red sauce for a casserole fit for company. If you prefer to cook and peel your own shrimp, start with 1 pound raw in the shell.

4   tablespoons butter, divided
⅔   cup chopped green onions
½   cup chopped red bell pepper
½   pound cooked, peeled shrimp,
      coarsely chopped (about 1 cup)
1   cup ricotta cheese
1   cup cottage cheese
1   teaspoon salt, divided
1   (8-ounce) package cream
      cheese, softened
½   cup grated Parmesan cheese
2   large eggs, lightly beaten
1   tablespoon chopped fresh
      parsley
1   teaspoon Creole seasoning
1   teaspoon hot sauce
½   teaspoon pepper
3   tablespoons all-purpose flour
1½ cups half-and-half
6   no-boil lasagna noodles
1   cup (4 ounces) shredded Italian
      four-cheese blend
Paprika

Melt 1 tablespoon butter in a skillet over medium-high heat. Add green onions and red bell pepper; sauté 2 minutes. Stir in shrimp; set aside.

Combine ricotta cheese, cottage cheese, ½ teaspoon salt, and next 7 ingredients in a large bowl; set aside.

Melt remaining 3 tablespoons butter in a medium saucepan over medium heat; whisk in flour until smooth. Cook 1 minute, whisking constantly. Gradually whisk in half-and-half; cook over medium heat, whisking constantly, 3 to 4 minutes until thickened and bubbly. Stir in remaining ½ teaspoon salt.

Pour half of white sauce into a lightly greased 8-inch square baking dish. Layer 2 noodles, half of cheese mixture, and half of shrimp mixture.

Repeat layers with noodles, cheese mixture, and shrimp mixture, ending with remaining 2 noodles and remaining white sauce. Sprinkle with Italian cheese blend.

Bake, covered, at 350° for 30 minutes. Uncover and bake 10 more minutes or until lightly browned. Let stand 10 minutes. Sprinkle with paprika. **Makes:** 4 servings.
Prep: 35 min., **Cook:** 40 min., **Other:** 10 min.

Tip: You can substitute chopped cooked chicken for shrimp.

Myra Byanka
Dallas, Texas

Myra had the right idea by creating a lasagna that doesn't feed an army. She usually serves this creamy lasagna for two people, but it's so rich and satisfying, we made it four servings.

Collard Greens and Pasta

16 ounces uncooked dried angel
    hair pasta
2 tablespoons olive oil
1 pound ham steak, diced
2 cups thinly sliced onion
4 pounds fresh collard greens*
½ cup butter
½ teaspoon dried crushed red
    pepper
1¼ cups shredded Parmesan
    cheese
½ teaspoon salt
1 teaspoon coarsely ground black
    pepper

Cook pasta in boiling salted water according to package directions in a Dutch oven. Drain and return to pan; set aside.

Heat oil in a very large skillet over medium-high heat until hot; add ham, and cook 2 to 3 minutes or until just browned. Add onion, and cook 2 to 3 more minutes, stirring occasionally, until onions are just tender.

Check leaves of collards carefully; remove pulpy stems and discolored spots on leaves. Wash leaves thoroughly; drain and thinly slice. Add collard greens to skillet, and stir well. Cover, reduce heat to medium, and cook 5 to 6 minutes, stirring mixture occasionally.

Add butter and next 4 ingredients to skillet; stirring well.

Add collard green mixture to pasta in pan, tossing well. **Makes:** 6 servings.
Prep: 25 min., **Cook:** 25 min.

*Substitute 2 (16-ounce) bags trimmed fresh collard greens for the 4 pounds untrimmed collard greens. Collard greens will still need to be thinly sliced.

Kim Fabrizio
Seattle, Washington

Kim and our Test Kitchens' staff think alike when it comes to slicing collard greens. The easiest way to thinly slice them is to stack and roll the trimmed leaves into a tight bundle, then thinly slice the bundle of leaves crosswise with a sharp knife.

Cajun Rice and Sausage Stuffing

1 cup uncooked long-grain rice
2 cups chicken broth
½ cup butter
1 large onion, chopped
4 celery ribs, chopped
1 pound ground pork sausage
2 jalapeño peppers, seeded and
    finely chopped (about ⅓ cup)
3 tablespoons chopped fresh
    parsley
4 green onions, chopped
½ cup chopped red bell pepper
1 pound peeled crawfish tails
2 teaspoons Cajun seasoning
2 teaspoons poultry seasoning

Cook rice according to package directions, using 2 cups broth instead of water; set aside.

Meanwhile, melt butter in a large non-stick skillet over medium-high heat. Add onion, celery, and sausage; cook

Janis serves this robust stuffing two ways—as a side dish and as a stuffing for turkey. We tried it as a side dish and thought it paired well with roasted turkey, chicken, quail, and pork.

until sausage crumbles and is no longer pink and vegetables are tender. Add cooked rice, jalapeños, and remaining 6 ingredients; stir to blend. Cook 3 more minutes. Spoon rice mixture into a lightly greased 13- x 9-inch baking dish. Bake, uncovered, at 350° for 30 minutes. **Makes:** 8 to 10 servings.
Prep: 15 min., **Cook:** 39 min.

Janis Roberts
Spring, Texas

Collard Greens and Pasta

Bloody Mary's Cajun and Seafood Creole

Chorizo is a highly seasoned, spicy pork sausage used in Mexican and Spanish dishes. Mexican chorizo is made with fresh pork. Smoked pork is used to make Spanish chorizo and the sausage is firmer and sliceable like kielbasa.

1½ pounds unpeeled, medium-size fresh shrimp
1 pound fresh lump crabmeat
4 (8-ounce) containers fresh oysters, undrained
1 (10-ounce) can whole baby clams, undrained
Juice of 1 large lemon (about 2½ tablespoons)
2 teaspoons minced garlic
3 tablespoons olive oil
1 medium-size green bell pepper, chopped
1 small onion, chopped
4 celery ribs, chopped
8 ounces Mexican chorizo sausage
1 (8-ounce) bottle clam juice
1 cup Bloody Mary mix
1 cup spicy-hot vegetable juice
1 (16-ounce) package frozen sliced okra
1 cup frozen green peas
⅓ cup tomato paste
¼ cup vodka
1½ teaspoons Old Bay seasoning
1 teaspoon Worcestershire sauce
Hot cooked rice

Peel shrimp, and devein, if desired.
Drain crabmeat, removing any bits of shell. Drain oysters and clams, reserving ½ cup oyster liquid and ⅔ cup clam liquid. Combine shrimp, crabmeat, oysters, clams, and lemon juice in a large bowl, tossing well to coat.
Cook garlic in hot oil in a large Dutch oven over medium heat 1 minute. Stir in bell pepper, onion, and celery. Cook, stirring often, 10 minutes or until tender.
While vegetables cook, discard casings from sausage, if necessary. Add sausage to Dutch oven; cook over medium-high heat until browned, stirring until it crumbles. Add reserved oyster and clam juices, bottled clam juice, and next 8 ingredients. Bring to a boil; cover, reduce heat, and simmer over medium-low heat 45 minutes.
Stir in shrimp mixture; cook 3 to 5 minutes or just until shrimp turn pink and edges of oysters begin to curl. Serve over hot cooked rice. **Makes:** 8 servings.
Prep: 28 min., **Cook:** 62 min.

Terry Floyd
Tuscumbia, Alabama

Bayou Shrimp and Corn Chowder

1 pound unpeeled, medium-size fresh shrimp
1 cup dry white wine
5 bacon slices
3 celery ribs, finely chopped
1 medium onion, finely chopped
2 tablespoons all-purpose flour
2 cups chicken broth
3 tablespoons chopped fresh parsley
1 (14¾-ounce) can cream-style corn
3 large baking potatoes, cooked and diced
1 cup half-and-half
1 tablespoon Old Bay seasoning
2 tablespoons red wine vinegar
1½ teaspoons dried dillweed
½ teaspoon salt
½ teaspoon hot sauce
¼ teaspoon pepper

Peel shrimp and devein, if desired; rinse and drain shells, and place in a medium saucepan. Add white wine. Bring to a boil; reduce heat, and simmer, uncovered, 7 minutes. Strain broth mixture through a sieve over a bowl; discard solids. Set broth aside.

If you keep frozen uncooked shrimp on hand, feel free to use it in this chowder. That's what **Lisabeth** *does and we concur with her desire for convenience. However, this pot of bayou comfort is so tasty, we decided to splurge on fresh shrimp.*

Cook bacon in a Dutch oven over medium heat until crisp; remove bacon, reserving drippings in Dutch oven. Crumble bacon; set aside.
Cook celery and onion in bacon drippings, stirring constantly, 5 minutes or until tender. Stir in flour, and cook 3 minutes, stirring constantly. Add chicken broth, parsley, reserved shrimp broth, and corn. Bring to a boil; reduce heat to a simmer.
Add shrimp, potatoes, and next 7 ingredients. Cook over medium heat, stirring constantly until thoroughly heated and shrimp turn pink, about 3 to 5 minutes. Sprinkle with crumbled bacon before serving. **Makes:** 10 cups.
Prep: 28 min., **Cook:** 25 min.

Lisabeth LaFontaine
Beverly, Massachusetts

Crab Cakes With Corn Chowder

If you don't have wine on hand for the Corn Chowder, substitute an equal amount of chicken broth.

Corn Chowder
2 garlic cloves, minced
½ cup finely chopped celery
¼ cup finely chopped green bell pepper
¼ cup finely chopped red bell pepper
¼ cup butter or margarine, melted
1¼ cups chicken broth
2 tablespoons finely chopped fresh parsley
½ cup finely chopped green onions
¼ teaspoon salt
¼ teaspoon ground red pepper
1 (8-ounce) package herb-seasoned stuffing mix *
1 pound fresh lump crabmeat, drained
2 large eggs, lightly beaten
½ cup vegetable oil

Prepare Corn Chowder.
Cook garlic and next 3 ingredients in butter in a large Dutch oven over medium-high heat, stirring constantly, until vegetables are tender. Stir in broth and next 4 ingredients. Cook over medium-high heat until thoroughly heated.
Remove from heat; add stuffing mix, and toss gently to blend. Cover and let stand 30 minutes or until cool to touch.
Stir together crabmeat and eggs in a medium bowl; add to stuffing mixture, stirring gently. Shape mixture into 8 (3½-inch) patties.
Heat oil in a large skillet over medium-high heat until hot. Fry crab cakes 3 to 4 minutes on each side until golden. Divide Corn Chowder evenly among 8 shallow bowls; top each with 1 crab cake. Serve immediately. **Makes:** 8 crab cakes.
Prep: 20 min., **Cook:** 15 min., **Other:** 30 min.

Corn Chowder:
¾ cup chopped onion
¾ cup chopped celery
¼ cup butter or margarine, melted
3 medium baking potatoes, diced (about 4½ cups)
2 (15¼-ounce) cans whole kernel white corn, drained
1 (10½-ounce) can condensed chicken broth, diluted
½ cup chopped carrot
½ cup chopped green bell pepper
½ cup chopped red bell pepper
1 teaspoon salt
¼ teaspoon ground red pepper
2 tablespoons all-purpose flour
1 cup heavy whipping cream
½ cup dry white wine
3 tablespoons finely chopped fresh parsley
1 tablespoon Worcestershire sauce

Cook onion and celery in butter in a large Dutch oven, stirring constantly, until tender. Stir in potato and next 7 ingredients. Cover and cook over medium heat 15 minutes or until potato is very tender.
Place flour in a small bowl; gradually whisk in whipping cream. Add cream mixture to vegetable mixture, stirring constantly. Cook over medium heat, stirring constantly, until mixture begins to thicken. Stir in wine, parsley, and Worcestershire sauce. Simmer, covered, over medium heat 20 minutes, stirring occasionally. **Makes:** 11 cups.
Prep: 25 min., **Cook:** 44 min.

*For testing purposes only, we used Pepperidge Farm Herb-Seasoned Stuffing.

Karen L. Hildreth
Sarasota, Florida

Karen makes petite 1-inch crab cakes; they were so delicious we wanted more! We increased the crabmeat to get larger, more substantial cakes.

Turnip Green Soup

3 (15½-ounce) cans navy beans, undrained
2 (14-ounce) cans chicken broth
1 (16-ounce) package frozen chopped turnip greens
1 pound cooked ham, chopped*
3 cups peeled, chopped red potato (about 1½ pounds)
1½ cups chopped onion
1 cup chopped celery
1½ tablespoons sugar
1 teaspoon garlic salt
1 teaspoon pepper

Combine all ingredients in a large Dutch oven; bring to a boil. Reduce heat, and simmer, uncovered, 1 hour. **Makes:** 15 cups.
Prep: 14 min., **Cook:** 1 hr.

*Buy already-chopped ham in bags in the meat or lunchmeat department to save time.

Sandra Preuss
Monticello, Mississippi

Sometimes the simplest recipes are the best as **Sandra** proves with this soup that received our highest rating at taste testing. She always serves it with lots of hot buttered cornbread.

Chili With Jalapeño-Cheddar Dumplings

One thing is certain—this chili is loaded with flavor. So much so that it can stand alone without the dumplings. If you forgo the dumplings, serve the chili with cornbread or saltines.

1 pound ground beef
3 tablespoons olive oil
1 large onion, chopped
1 tablespoon minced garlic
3 tablespoons finely chopped jalapeño (about 1 large)
1 (16-ounce) can red beans, undrained
1 (16-ounce) can chili beans, undrained
2 (10-ounce) cans diced tomatoes and green chiles, undrained
1 (10-ounce) can diced tomatoes and green chiles in sauce, undrained
1 (6-ounce) can tomato paste
2 cups beef broth
1 (12-ounce) bottle beer
2 tablespoons Worcestershire sauce
1 tablespoon ground cumin
2 tablespoons chili powder
1 teaspoon ground black pepper
¼ teaspoon white pepper
Jalapeño-Cheddar Dumpling Batter
Garnishes: shredded Cheddar cheese, shredded Monterey Jack cheese, sour cream, chopped green onions

Brown ground beef in an 8-quart Dutch oven, stirring until it crumbles and is no longer pink. Drain and pat dry with paper towels. Heat oil over medium-high heat in Dutch oven; add onion, garlic, and jalapeño. Cook 6 minutes. Add beef, red beans, and next 11 ingredients. Bring to a boil; reduce heat, and simmer, uncovered, 1½ hours, stirring occasionally.
When simmering is almost completed, prepare Jalapeño-Cheddar Dumpling Batter.
Spoon batter over chili in biscuit-size dollops. (Do not stir into chili.) Cover and simmer 18 to 20 minutes or until dumplings are done. Spoon dumplings into bowls, and cover with chili. Garnish, if desired. **Makes:** 16 servings.
Prep: 15 min., **Cook:** 2 hrs.

Terri routinely freezes the chili and dumplings, but says they should be frozen (and thawed) separately.

Jalapeño-Cheddar Dumpling Batter:

2¼ cups all-purpose baking mix*
3 tablespoons finely chopped dried tomatoes in oil
1 teaspoon finely chopped jalapeño pepper
1 tablespoon finely chopped onion
1 tablespoon finely chopped cilantro
2 tablespoons sour cream
½ (12-ounce) can beer
¼ cup (1 ounce) finely shredded sharp Cheddar cheese
¼ cup (1 ounce) finely shredded Monterey Jack cheese

Combine all ingredients in a large bowl, stirring just until moistened. **Makes:** enough for 16 servings.
Prep: 5 min.

*For testing purposes only, we used Bisquick Original All-Purpose Baking Mix.

Terri Evans
Atlanta, Georgia

Turnip Green Soup

Corn Chowder

Heavy whipping cream, whole milk, and pureed fresh corn guarantee a rich and satisfying chowder.

- 4 **cups fresh corn kernels (about 8 ears), divided**
- 4 **bacon slices, chopped**
- 2 **large Vidalia onions, halved lengthwise and thinly sliced**
- 2 **celery ribs, thinly sliced**
- 2 **carrots, chopped**
- 4 **medium potatoes, peeled and cut into 1-inch chunks**
- 1 **(32-ounce) container chicken broth**
- 1 **cup heavy whipping cream**
- 1 **cup milk**
- 1 **teaspoon salt**
- ½ **teaspoon pepper**
- ¼ **teaspoon ground red pepper**
- 2 **tablespoons chopped fresh parsley**
- 1 **tablespoon chopped fresh chives**

Process 2 cups corn kernels in a food processor or blender until pureed; set pureed corn aside.

Cook bacon in a large Dutch oven until crisp. Remove bacon, and drain on paper towels, reserving 2 tablespoons drippings in pan. Add onion to reserved drippings; cook 10 minutes or until tender. Add celery and carrot; cook 10 minutes or until tender. Add 2 cups corn kernels, pureed corn, potatoes, and chicken broth. Bring to a boil; reduce heat to medium, and simmer 15 minutes or until potatoes are tender. Stir in cream and next 5 ingredients; cook 3 minutes or until thoroughly heated. Ladle into bowls; sprinkle with reserved bacon and chives. **Makes:** 13 cups.
Prep: 36 min., **Cook:** 44 min.

Kim Russell
North Wales, Pennsylvania

Tortilla Soup

Don't let the cook time fool you—this soup is super easy to make. Just a little chopping and you're ready to go. The time's in the simmering. This version is milder than many tortilla soups, so if you prefer a little more heat, simply add another jalapeño or use hot salsa instead of mild.

- 2 **tablespoons olive oil**
- 1 **large onion, chopped**
- 2 **garlic cloves, chopped**
- 1 **cup chopped celery**
- 1 **cup chopped carrot**
- 1 **jalapeño pepper, seeded and chopped**
- 1 **(32-ounce) container chicken broth**
- 2 **cups coarsely chopped roasted chicken (about 2 breast halves) ✱**
- 1 **(14.5-ounce) can diced tomatoes, undrained**
- ½ **cup salsa**
- 1 **tablespoon lime juice**
- 2 **teaspoons ground cumin**
- ½ **teaspoon salt**
- ¼ **teaspoon white pepper**
- **Crushed tortilla chips**
- **Chopped avocado**
- **Chopped fresh cilantro**
- **Shredded Monterey Jack cheese**

Heat oil in a Dutch oven over medium heat. Add onion and garlic; cook 5 minutes or until beginning to soften. Add celery, carrot, and jalapeño; cook 5 minutes or until almost tender. Add broth and next 7 ingredients. Bring to a boil; cover, reduce heat, and simmer 3 hours. Ladle into bowls; top with tortilla chips, avocado, cilantro, and cheese. **Makes:** 6 cups.
Prep: 28 min., **Cook:** 3 hrs., 10 min.

✱We used breast meat from a deli-roasted chicken and coarsely chopped it to yield 2 cups.

Marianne Chalange
Orlando, Florida

Marianne adds the cilantro to the soup before it simmers and serves the soup over crushed tortilla chips. We sprinkled the cilantro over the top of each serving for a fresher flavor and more color, and served the crushed chips over the soup for extra crunch.

Chipotle-Bacon Cornbread

The key to a crisp crust on this "Southern favorite with a kick" is pouring the batter into a hot cast-iron skillet.

3   tablespoons butter
⅔   cup yellow cornmeal
⅔   cup all-purpose flour
1   teaspoon baking powder
½   teaspoon baking soda
½   teaspoon salt
1   tablespoon sugar
1   large egg
1   cup buttermilk
3   chipotle peppers in adobo sauce, drained and chopped
5   slices fully cooked bacon, chopped

Place butter in an 8-inch cast-iron skillet. Place skillet in a preheated 425° oven for 5 minutes or until butter melts (do not let butter brown).

Meanwhile, combine cornmeal and next 5 ingredients in a large bowl; make a well in center of mixture. Stir together egg and next 3 ingredients; add to dry ingredients, stirring just until moistened. Pour batter into hot skillet. Bake at 425° for 20 minutes or until golden. Remove from skillet immediately. Cut into wedges, and serve hot. **Makes:** 6 servings.
Prep: 6 min., **Cook:** 25 min.

Tip: Be sure to use a well-seasoned cast-iron skillet. This insures that the bread will come out easily when it's hot.
Anna Ginsberg
Austin, Texas

Anna uses 1½ tablespoons sugar to balance the fiery chipotle chiles, but we reduced it a little with tasty results.

Black Bean and Sausage Cornbread

1   (16-ounce) package hot ground pork sausage
1   cup chopped green bell pepper
1   cup chopped red bell pepper
1   cup chopped onion
2   large eggs, lightly beaten
1⅓ cups milk
2   (6.5-ounce) packages yellow cornbread mix
1   cup (4 ounces) shredded Cheddar cheese
1   (15-ounce) can black beans, rinsed and drained

Cook sausage in a large skillet, stirring until it crumbles and is no longer pink; drain. Add bell peppers and onions to skillet; cook 8 minutes, stirring often. Remove from heat.

Combine eggs, milk, and cornbread mix in a large bowl; add cheese, beans, and sausage mixture, stirring just until dry ingredients are moistened.

Spoon batter into a lightly greased 13- x 9-inch baking dish. Bake at 425° for 25 to 27 minutes or until golden.
Makes: 8 servings.
Prep: 15 min., **Cook:** 37 min.

Carol Oakes
San Antonio, Texas

When **Carol** makes this hearty cornbread, she's sure to put lots of butter and sour cream on the table to top each piping hot square.

Squash Puppies With Dill Dipping Sauce

Squash Puppies With Dill Dipping Sauce

Paired with a lemony dill sauce for dipping, these zucchini and onion hush puppies earned our highest rating at taste testing. Don't limit this delicious sauce to these hush puppies; try it with fish and chicken, too.

2   **medium zucchini, shredded**
1   **small onion, chopped**
Vegetable oil
½   **cup yellow cornmeal**
¼   **cup cornstarch**
¼   **cup all-purpose baking mix ＊**
½   **teaspoon salt**
½   **teaspoon lemon pepper**
1   **large egg, lightly beaten**

Drain squash and onion well, pressing between several layers of paper towels. Let stand 15 minutes.
Pour oil to a depth of 2 inches into a large Dutch oven; heat to 375°.
Meanwhile, combine squash mixture, cornmeal, and next 4 ingredients in a large bowl; stir in egg.

Drop mixture by tablespoonfuls into hot oil; fry in batches 2 minutes or until golden, turning once. Drain on paper towels. Serve immediately with Dill Dipping Sauce. **Makes:** 4 to 6 servings.
Prep: 11 min., **Cook:** 17 min., **Other:** 15 min.

＊For testing purposes only, we used Bisquick Original All-Purpose Baking Mix.

Mary advises for best results not to crowd the pan when frying the puppies.

Dill Dipping Sauce:
½   **cup sour cream**
½   **cup mayonnaise**
2   **tablespoons minced fresh dill**
2   **teaspoons grated lemon rind**
2   **tablespoons fresh lemon juice**

Combine all ingredients in a small bowl. Cover and chill until ready to serve.
Makes: 1 cup.
Prep: 10 min.

Tip: Gently spoon batter into hot oil to prevent dangerous oil splashes and burns.

Mary Tichenor
Spruce Pine, North Carolina

Sweetest Sweet Potato Biscuits

Extra sugar makes these spiced biscuits soft and tender.

2   medium-size sweet potatoes
⅔   cup milk
3   cups all-purpose flour
¾   cup sugar
4   teaspoons baking powder
½   teaspoon salt
1   teaspoon ground cinnamon
¼   teaspoon ground nutmeg
¼   teaspoon ground ginger
½   cup butter-flavored shortening

Place potatoes on a baking sheet lined with aluminum foil. Bake at 450° for 1 hour or until tender; cool completely. Peel and mash enough sweet potato to measure 2 cups. Reserve remaining sweet potato for other uses. Combine sweet potato and milk in a small bowl.

Combine flour and next 6 ingredients in a large bowl. Cut shortening into flour mixture with a pastry blender until crumbly; add sweet potato mixture, stirring until dry ingredients are moistened.

Turn dough out onto a lightly floured surface; knead 3 or 4 times. Pat or roll dough to ½-inch thickness; cut with a 2½-inch round cutter, and place on a lightly greased baking sheet.

Bake at 400° for 15 minutes or until lightly browned. **Makes:** 16 biscuits.
Prep: 9 min., **Cook:** 1 hr., 15 min.

Deanna Swits
Nashville, Tennessee

Deanna serves these golden biscuits with honey butter, which we agree is wonderful. We also like them with country ham.

Monte Cristo Pancakes

For your next brunch, try these savory pancakes that combine all the traditional ingredients of a Monte Cristo sandwich.

2   cups all-purpose baking mix *
1   cup milk
2   large eggs, lightly beaten
2   tablespoons lemon juice
1   tablespoon sugar
1   teaspoon baking powder
1   cup chopped cooked turkey breast
1   cup chopped cooked ham
1   cup (4 ounces) shredded Swiss cheese
2   cups sliced strawberries
2   tablespoons granulated sugar
1   cup seedless strawberry jam
2   tablespoons powdered sugar
Whipped cream (optional)

Stir together first 6 ingredients in a large bowl. Fold in turkey, ham, and cheese.

Pour about ½ cup batter for each pancake onto a hot, lightly greased griddle. Cook pancakes until tops are covered with bubbles and edges look cooked; turn and cook other side.

Meanwhile, gently toss strawberries with granulated sugar; set aside.

Microwave jam in a microwave-safe bowl at HIGH 30 seconds to melt; stir until smooth.

Sift powdered sugar over each pancake. Top each with ¼ cup strawberries and 2 tablespoons jam. Serve with whipped cream, if desired. **Makes:** 8 pancakes.
Prep: 14 min., **Cook:** 8 min.

*For testing purposes only, we used Bisquick Original All-Purpose Baking Mix.

Ashley Rawls
Frisco, Texas

Ashley uses canned whipped topping to create a decorative dollop on each pancake.

Peach Scones

These scones are best made with fresh summer peaches, but frozen peaches can be used year-round.

1   **cup diced fresh or frozen peaches, thawed**
1½ **tablespoons lemon juice**
2   **tablespoons sugar, divided**
2   **cups all-purpose baking mix ***
¼   **teaspoon ground cinnamon**
⅔   **cup milk**
1   **teaspoon sugar**

Toss peaches, lemon juice, and 1 table-spoon sugar in a medium bowl; set aside.
Combine baking mix, cinnamon, and 1 tablespoon sugar in a large bowl.

Slowly add milk; stirring just until dry ingredients are moistened. Fold in peach mixture.
Drop by spoonfuls onto a lightly greased baking sheet. Sprinkle evenly with 1 teaspoon sugar.
Bake at 350° for 25 to 28 minutes or until lightly browned. Remove to a wire rack to cool. **Makes:** 9 scones.
Prep: 10 min., **Cook:** 28 min.

*****For testing purposes only, we used Bisquick Original All-Purpose Baking Mix.

Tip: If using frozen peaches, make sure to pat dry with a paper towel after thawing.

S. Alicia Seecharan
Jackson Heights, New York

S. Alicia uses buttermilk to prepare this fruity breakfast bread, but we got better results using milk.

Orange Sally Lunn Bread

1   **(15-ounce) can mandarin oranges, undrained**
2   **cups all-purpose flour**
¾   **cup sugar, divided**
1   **tablespoon baking powder**
¼   **teaspoon salt**
2   **large eggs, lightly beaten**
¼   **cup milk**
½   **cup orange juice**
2   **tablespoons butter, melted**
Orange sherbet (optional)

Drain mandarin oranges, reserving oranges and ¼ cup juice. Set aside.
Combine flour, ½ cup sugar, baking powder, and salt in a bowl; make a well in center of mixture. Stir together reserved juice, eggs, and next 3 ingredients; add to dry ingredients, stirring

Elizabeth enjoys this bread with tea, or she recommends dressing it up with additional mandarin oranges and sherbet for a light dessert. We liked it toasted with butter for breakfast.

well. Spoon mixture into a lightly greased 8- x 4-inch loafpan; sprinkle with remaining ¼ cup sugar.
Bake at 350° for 45 minutes or until a wooden pick inserted in center comes out clean. Cool in pan on a wire rack 10 minutes; remove from pan, and cool on wire rack. Cut into slices, and serve with reserved oranges and, if desired, orange sherbet. **Makes:** 1 loaf.
Prep: 8 min., **Cook:** 45 min.

Elizabeth Clites
Locust Grove, Virginia

Orange Rolls

These rolls will build character: patience, because they can't be made in an instant; and self-control, because they are so tender and decadent, it's hard to eat just one. We gave them our highest rating, and all agreed, "They're worth it."

1　(10-ounce) baking potato, peeled and cut into ¾-inch cubes
1　cup warm milk (100° to 110°)
1　(¼-ounce) envelope active dry yeast
1　cup butter, softened
½　cup sugar
1　large egg
2　teaspoons salt
5　cups all-purpose flour, divided
3　cups Orange Filling, divided

Cook potato in boiling water to cover 10 minutes or until tender; drain. Mash enough potato to measure 1 cup. Cool completely.

Stir together warm milk and yeast; cool completely.

Beat butter and sugar at medium speed with an electric mixer until creamy. Add 1 cup potato, egg, salt, and 3 cups flour; beat well. Add cooled milk mixture, beating well. Stir in 1½ cups flour to form a soft dough.

Dust work surface with 3 tablespoons remaining ½ cup flour. Turn dough out onto floured surface, and knead dough until smooth and elastic (8 minutes), gradually adding remaining 5 tablespoons flour as needed to prevent sticking. Place dough in a lightly greased bowl, turning to grease top. Cover and chill at least 8 hours.

Divide dough in half. Place half of dough on lightly floured work surface. Cover and refrigerate remaining half of dough. Roll first half of dough into a 13- x 9-inch rectangle. Spread 1 cup Orange Filling over dough to edges. Cut dough into 20 squares. Pinch together 2 opposite corners of each square; arrange rolls, pinched corners up, in a lightly greased 13- x 9-inch pan.

Cover; let rise at room temperature 3 to 4 hours or until rolls have spread together; pinch corners together again. (Corners will have spread apart by time for baking, but this is normal.) Repeat procedure with remaining half of dough and 1 more cup of filling, placing rolls in a second lightly greased 13- x 9-inch pan.

Bake, uncovered, at 375° for 25 minutes. (Roll tips should be very brown.) Remove rolls from oven; let stand 5 minutes. Spread each pan of rolls with ½ cup remaining Orange Filling. Serve warm. **Makes:** 40 rolls.
Prep: 1 hr., **Cook:** 35 min., **Other:** 12 hrs.

Tip: Be sure that milk mixture and mashed potato are cool so as not to melt the butter mixture during mixing.

Note: This roll dough contains a large amount of fat and should be kept cold for best results. Work quickly when rolling and shaping the dough. You can make and chill the roll dough up to 2 days before baking.

Orange Filling:

You'll have about a cup of filling left over to spread on toast, biscuits, or pound cake. Store it in the refrigerator up to 5 days.

1　cup butter, softened
½　cup shortening
¼　cup grated orange rind
¼　cup frozen orange juice concentrate, thawed
1　teaspoon orange extract
5½ cups sifted powdered sugar

Beat butter and shortening at medium speed with an electric mixer until creamy. Beat in orange rind, orange juice concentrate, and orange extract. Reduce speed to low, and gradually add powdered sugar, beating until fluffy.
Makes: 4⅓ cups.
Prep: 12 min.

Note: Orange Filling should be at room temperature for ease in spreading. It can be made the day before and refrigerated.

Ann Henderson
Selmer, Tennessee

Once **Ann** has prepared the roll dough and chilled it, she often keeps it in the refrigerator several days before she assembles and bakes the rolls. We tried this and it works great.

Sweet Potato Pie Cookies With Pecan Praline and Coconut Divinity Filling

These cookies are so rich—just one will suffice for dessert. Serve with steaming black coffee to balance the sweetness.

1   cup plus 2 tablespoons butter, softened
¾   cup firmly packed light brown sugar
1   cup granulated sugar
⅓   cup cooked mashed sweet potato
2   large eggs
2   teaspoons vanilla extract
2¼ cups all-purpose flour
1   teaspoon baking powder
½   teaspoon salt
1   cup almond toffee bits*
1   cup chopped pecans
1   cup white chocolate morsels
Pecan Praline
Coconut Divinity Filling

Beat butter in a large mixing bowl at medium speed with an electric mixer until creamy; gradually add sugars and next 3 ingredients.

Combine flour, baking powder, and salt; add to butter mixture, mixing well. Stir in toffee bits, pecans, and white chocolate morsels. Drop by rounded teaspoonfuls onto ungreased baking sheets. Bake at 350° for 12 minutes or until lightly browned. Cool on pan 2 minutes. Remove cookies to a wire rack to cool completely.

Prepare Pecan Praline. Spread about 1 teaspoon hot Pecan Praline onto the bottoms of 28 cooled cookies.

Prepare Coconut Divinity Filling. Spread about 1 teaspoon Coconut Divinity Filling over Pecan Praline; top with 28 more cookies. (You'll have about 9 cookies leftover.) **Makes:** 42 sandwich cookies.
Prep: 19 min., **Cook:** 12 min. per batch

Pecan Praline:

If desired, skip the cookies and make a small batch of chewy praline candy by dropping candy mixture onto nonstick aluminum foil.

1   cup firmly packed light brown sugar
2   tablespoons buttermilk powder
½   cup evaporated milk
¼   cup butter
2   teaspoons vanilla extract
⅔   cup finely chopped pecans

Combine brown sugar and buttermilk powder in a small saucepan. Stir in milk, and add butter. Bring to a boil over medium-low heat, stirring until butter melts. Using a pastry brush dipped in hot water, wash down any sugar crystals on sides of pan.

Cook, stirring constantly, until a candy thermometer registers 234° (soft ball stage). Remove from heat. Stir in vanilla and pecans. Immediately spoon onto cookies as directed. Spoon any leftover mixture onto nonstick aluminum foil to make praline candy. **Makes:** 2 cups.
Prep: 5 min., **Cook:** 10 min.

Tip: Because of the small amount of Pecan Praline mixture, you may have to tip the pan to keep the candy thermometer submerged. It's essential to do this for an accurate reading.

Coconut Divinity Filling:

1½ ounces cream cheese, softened
1   (7-ounce) jar marshmallow cream
1   teaspoon vanilla extract
1   cup white chocolate morsels, melted and cooled slightly
½   cup frozen grated coconut, thawed
½   cup finely chopped pecans

Beat cream cheese in a small mixing bowl at medium speed with an electric mixer until smooth. Stir in marshmallow cream and vanilla until blended. Stir in melted white chocolate, coconut, and pecans. Let mixture stand 15 minutes or until thickened, stirring occasionally. Fill cookies as directed. **Makes:** 1½ cups.
Prep: 7 min., **Other:** 15 min.

*For testing purposes only, we used Heath Almond Toffee Bits.

Tamy White
Hartwell, Georgia

Tamy brought several favorite Southern desserts together in one sandwich cookie with this creative recipe.

Southern Peanut Squares

You can substitute any nuts for peanuts. Sweet, buttery macadamia nuts are especially prized.

2   cups all-purpose baking mix *
¼   cup sugar
½   teaspoon salt
½   cup peanut butter
1   cup sugar
1   cup corn syrup
3   large eggs, lightly beaten
2   tablespoons peanut butter
1   teaspoon vanilla extract
1   (12-ounce) can cocktail
    peanuts, coarsely chopped

Combine first 3 ingredients in a large bowl. Cut in ½ cup peanut butter with a pastry blender until mixture is crumbly; press into a greased 13- x 9-inch pan. Bake at 350° for 18 minutes.

Combine 1 cup sugar and next 5 ingredients; pour over warm crust. Bake at 350° for 35 minutes or until mixture is set. Cool in pan on a wire rack. Cut into squares. **Makes:** 2 dozen.
Prep: 11 min., **Cook:** 53 min.

*For testing purposes only, we used Bisquick Original All-Purpose Baking Mix.

Gloria Kirchman
Eden Prairie, Minnesota

Gloria often serves this rich and nutty treat with sweetened whipped cream.

Graham Slams

These frozen treats taste like peanut butter pie sandwiched between graham crackers.

1   (8-ounce) package cream
    cheese, softened
½   cup creamy peanut butter
¼   cup milk
1   cup powdered sugar
1   (8-ounce) container frozen
    whipped topping, thawed
36 sheets honey or chocolate-
    flavored graham crackers
    (about 1 box plus 1 sleeve)

Beat first 4 ingredients at medium speed with an electric mixer until smooth. Fold in whipped topping.

Break crackers in half. Dollop 1 heaping tablespoon filling over 1 cracker half, top with remaining half. Repeat with remaining crackers and filling. Place sandwiches in a single layer on jellyroll pans; cover and freeze at least 2 hours.
Makes: 36 sandwich cookies.
Prep: 34 min., **Other:** 2 hrs.

Jane Neeley
Eldorado, Oklahoma

Jane wraps leftover sandwiches individually in nonstick aluminum foil and returns them to the freezer for a grab-and-go treat.

Holiday Ambrosia Cake

Although this recipe triggers thoughts of wintry Christmas holidays, its delicious citrus fillings and creamy coconut frosting may have you thinking of holiday fun in summer sun rather than in a winter wonderland.

½ **cup shortening**
¼ **cup unsalted butter, softened**
1½ **cups sugar**
3 **egg yolks**
1 **cup coconut milk**
1 **teaspoon vanilla extract**
½ **teaspoon almond extract**
1½ **cups cake flour**
¾ **cup all-purpose flour**
1 **tablespoon baking powder**
½ **teaspoon salt**
¼ **teaspoon ground nutmeg**
5 **egg whites**
1 **teaspoon cream of tartar**
Orange Filling
Pineapple Filling
Coconut Frosting
2 **cups sweetened flaked coconut**

Beat shortening and butter in a large mixing bowl at medium speed with an electric mixer until creamy; gradually add sugar, beating well. Add egg yolks, 1 at a time, beating until blended after each addition.

Combine coconut milk and extracts. Combine flours and next 3 ingredients; add to butter mixture alternately with coconut milk mixture, beginning and ending with flour mixture. Beat at low speed until blended after each addition.

Combine egg whites and cream of tartar in a large mixing bowl. Beat at high speed with an electric mixer until stiff peaks form; fold into batter. Pour batter into 2 greased and floured parchment paper-lined 9-inch round cakepans.

Bake at 350° for 25 to 27 minutes or until a wooden pick inserted in center comes out clean. Cool in pans on wire racks 10 minutes. Remove from pans; cool completely on wire racks.

Split layers horizontally; place bottom layer, cut side up, on a cake stand or plate. Spread with one-third each of Orange Filling and Pineapple Filling.

Replace top of cake layer, cut side down; spread with one-third each of fillings. Repeat procedure with remaining split cake layer (do not spread filling on top of cake). Spread Coconut Frosting evenly on top and sides of cake. Gently press coconut onto sides of cake. Chill at least 1 hour. Store in refrigerator.
Makes: 12 to 15 servings.
Prep: 30 min., **Cook:** 25 min., **Other:** 8 hrs.

Orange Filling:
2 **(10-ounce) jars orange marmalade**
½ **cup orange juice**
⅛ **teaspoon salt**
2 **tablespoons cornstarch**
2 **tablespoons orange juice**

Combine first 3 ingredients in a large saucepan; bring to a boil over medium-high heat, stirring constantly. Whisk together cornstarch and 2 tablespoons orange juice until smooth; stir into marmalade mixture. Cook 2 minutes or until thickened, stirring constantly. Cool completely. Cover and chill at least 8 hours. **Makes:** 2¼ cups.
Prep: 5 min., **Cook:** 5 min., **Other:** 8 hrs.

Pineapple Filling:
1 **(20-ounce) can crushed pineapple in syrup, undrained**
¼ **cup sugar**
⅛ **teaspoon salt**
2 **tablespoons cornstarch**
2 **tablespoons orange juice**

Combine first 3 ingredients in a large saucepan; bring to a boil over medium heat, stirring constantly. Whisk together cornstarch and orange juice until smooth; stir into pineapple mixture. Cook 1 minute or until thickened, stirring constantly. Cool completely. Cover and chill at least 8 hours. **Makes:** 2¼ cups.
Prep: 5 min., **Cook:** 5 min., **Other:** 8 hrs.

Coconut Frosting:
½ **cup shortening**
½ **cup unsalted butter, softened**
4 **cups sifted powdered sugar**
¼ **cup coconut milk**
1 **teaspoon vanilla extract**

Beat shortening and butter at medium speed with an electric mixer until creamy. Gradually add powdered sugar alternately with coconut milk, beating at low speed until light and fluffy. Stir in vanilla. **Makes:** 2½ cups.
Prep: 5 min.

Tip: Freeze unsplit cake layers overnight while the fillings chill. This will help in removing crumbs from the cake for assembly, and it will allow you to split the frozen cakes with ease.

Theresa Thetford
Midland, Texas

As a child, **Theresa's** mother always served Coconut Cake on Christmas morning. Her mother used star-shaped pans and baked, milked, peeled, and ground fresh coconuts for the cake. Theresa simplified her mother's recipe by using canned rather than fresh coconut, and we simplified the fruit fillings, creating a beautiful moist and tender cake.

Holiday Ambrosia Cake

"Tennessee Jam Cake" Beignets With Blackberry and Penuche Dipping Sauces

These little puffs have more of a cakelike texture than traditional French Quarter beignets.

2¼ cups all-purpose flour
1¾ teaspoons pumpkin pie spice
2 teaspoons baking powder
¼ teaspoon baking soda
¼ teaspoon salt
⅔ cup chopped pecans, toasted
½ cup currants
⅔ cup buttermilk
⅓ cup firmly packed dark brown sugar
1 large egg, lightly beaten
1 tablespoon butter, melted
1½ teaspoons vanilla extract
1½ cups butterscotch morsels
10 caramels
¾ cup evaporated milk
1¼ cups fresh blackberries
⅓ cup seedless blackberry jam
Vegetable oil
Powdered sugar

Combine first 7 ingredients in a large bowl. Whisk together buttermilk and next 4 ingredients in a small bowl until brown sugar dissolves. Add to dry ingredients, stirring to form a stiff dough. Turn dough out onto a lightly floured surface. Knead 10 to 12 times. Divide dough in half; wrap dough in wax paper. Chill 20 minutes.

Meanwhile, combine butterscotch morsels, caramels, and evaporated milk in a medium saucepan. Place over low heat, and cook, stirring often, until caramels melt and mixture is smooth. Set sauce aside.

Process blackberries and jam in blender until smooth. Set sauce aside.

Roll each portion of dough into a 9-inch square. Cut each portion of dough into 16 (2¼-inch) squares.

Pour oil to a depth of 1½ inches into a large deep skillet; heat to 375°. Fry 8 beignets at a time, 1 minute on each side or until golden. Drain on paper towels; sprinkle with powdered sugar. Serve immediately with dipping sauces. **Makes:** 32 beignets.
Prep: 27 min., **Cook:** 13 min., **Other:** 20 min.

Kevin West
Bloomington, Indiana

Kevin based this recipe on his wife's favorite cake recipe—Tennessee Jam Cake made with blackberry jam and penuche frosting.

Apple-Pecan Spice Cake With Buttermilk Sauce

This cake is incredibly moist, thanks to the creamy Buttermilk Sauce that absorbs into the warm cake.

3 cups all-purpose flour
1 teaspoon baking soda
½ teaspoon salt
2 teaspoons ground cinnamon
2 cups sugar
3 large eggs, lightly beaten
1¼ cups vegetable oil
2 teaspoons vanilla extract
¼ cup orange juice
2½ cups shredded Granny Smith apple (about 3 apples)
1½ cups chopped pecans
1 cup sweetened flaked coconut
Buttermilk Sauce

Combine first 4 ingredients in a medium bowl; set aside. Combine sugar and next 4 ingredients in a large bowl; add flour mixture, and combine well. Fold in apple, pecans, and coconut. Pour batter into a greased and floured 10-inch tube pan.

Bake at 325° for 1 hour and 15 minutes or until a long wooden pick inserted in center comes out clean. Cool in pan on a wire rack 10 to 15 minutes; remove from pan.

Poke holes in top of cake using long wooden pick; spoon hot Buttermilk Sauce over warm cake (cake will absorb most of the sauce). Cool completely before serving. **Makes:** 16 servings.
Prep: 25 min., **Cook:** 1 hr., 15 min.

Buttermilk Sauce:
1 cup sugar
½ cup butter
½ teaspoon baking soda
½ cup buttermilk

Combine all ingredients in a small saucepan. Cook over medium heat 5 minutes or until butter is melted and mixture is bubbly. **Makes:** 1½ cups.
Prep: 5 min., **Cook:** 5 min.

Kimberlie Henris
Le Roy, Illinois

The key to **Kimberlie's** ultra moist cake is spooning the hot Buttermilk Sauce over the cake while it's still warm.

Peanut-Glazed Brown Sugar Pound Cake

You'll find more than a handful of chopped peanuts sprinkled over the glaze on this wonderfully moist cake, and another load of peanuts inside the cake. It's a peanut lover's paradise.

1   cup butter, softened
⅓   cup shortening
2   cups firmly packed light brown sugar
¾   cup granulated sugar
5   large eggs
1   cup evaporated milk
1   teaspoon vanilla extract
½   teaspoon maple flavoring
2¾ cups all-purpose flour
1   teaspoon baking powder
½   teaspoon salt
1½ cups chopped peanuts, divided
Peanut Glaze

Beat butter and shortening in a large mixing bowl at medium speed with an electric mixer until creamy; gradually add sugars, and beat 2 minutes. Add eggs, 1 at a time, beating just until yellow disappears.
Combine milk and flavorings. Combine flour, baking powder, and salt; add to butter mixture alternately with milk mixture, beginning and ending with flour mixture. Beat at low speed just until blended. Stir in 1 cup peanuts.
Pour batter into a greased and floured 10-inch tube pan.
Bake at 325° for 1 hour and 15 minutes (cake will not test clean with a wooden pick). Cool in pan on a wire rack 15 minutes. Remove from pan, and cool completely on a wire rack. Drizzle with Peanut Glaze, and sprinkle with remaining ½ cup peanuts. **Makes:** 16 servings.
Prep: 17 min., **Cook:** 1 hr., 15 min.

While the cake is still warm, **Marie** drizzles the glaze and sprinkles the peanuts over it. We prefer to let the cake cool completely. The glaze clings to the cooled cake and the peanuts bask in the glaze.

Peanut Glaze:
1   cup powdered sugar
3   tablespoons evaporated milk
2   tablespoons butter, softened
½   teaspoon vanilla extract

Combine all ingredients in a medium bowl; beat at medium speed with an electric mixer until smooth. **Makes:** ½ cup.
Prep: 5 min.

Tip: Quickly chop peanuts in a food processor.

Note: Although most cakes are done when a wooden pick inserted near the center comes out clean, this cake is one of the exceptions. Remove it from the oven after 1 hour and 15 minutes for a wonderfully moist cake.

Marie Rizzio
Traverse City, Michigan

White Silk Lemon Mousse Cake With Ginger Praline Topping

White Silk Lemon Mousse Cake With Ginger Praline Topping

This creamy mousse cake is dressed up with a wonderful praline topping that hardens to resemble a praline when it hits the cool cake.

2 cups finely crushed crisp gingersnap cookies (about 40 cookies)
1 tablespoon dark brown sugar
5 tablespoons butter, melted
1 (.25-ounce) envelope unflavored gelatin
6 tablespoons lemon juice
2½ cups whipping cream, divided
1⅓ cups white chocolate morsels
3 (8-ounce) packages cream cheese, softened
1 cup sugar
1½ tablespoons grated lemon rind
Ginger Praline Topping

Brenda uses a food processor to quickly and finely crush the gingersnap cookies.

Stir together first 3 ingredients. Press mixture in bottom and 1 inch up sides of a greased 10-inch springform pan.
Sprinkle gelatin over lemon juice in a small bowl; set aside.
Heat ½ cup cream over low heat until hot, whisking rapidly (do not boil). Remove from heat, and whisk in white chocolate morsels until morsels melt. Add gelatin mixture, and stir well; cool slightly.
Beat cream cheese, 1 cup sugar, and lemon rind until creamy. Gradually add white chocolate mixture, beating until blended.
Beat remaining 2 cups cream just until stiff peaks form; fold into cream cheese mixture. Pour into prepared crust. Cover and chill 8 hours. Serve with warm Ginger Praline Topping. **Makes:** 16 servings.
Prep: 30 min., **Cook:** 14 min., **Other:** 8 hrs.

Ginger Praline Topping:
½ cup butter
¾ cup firmly packed dark brown sugar
¼ cup whipping cream
½ teaspoon ground ginger
1 cup pecan pieces

Melt butter in a medium saucepan over medium-high heat; add brown sugar, cream, and ginger. Bring to a boil; cook 3 minutes, stirring constantly. Stir in pecans; set aside to cool slightly. **Makes:** 1¼ cups.
Prep: 2 min., **Cook:** 3 min.

Note: Reheat leftover topping in microwave on HIGH at 30-second intervals until hot.

Brenda Huff
Fresno, California

Southwest Florida Mint-Key Lime Pie

Steeping fresh mint leaves in the Key lime filling refreshingly updates an old favorite. Omit the mint if you don't have the fresh herb because dried is not a good substitute.

½ (15-ounce) package refrigerated piecrusts
1 (14-ounce) can sweetened condensed milk
4 egg yolks
⅓ cup fresh Key lime juice
1 tablespoon cream cheese, softened
½ cup mint leaves
4 egg whites
½ teaspoon cream of tartar
6 tablespoons sugar

Fit 1 piecrust into a 9-inch pieplate according to package directions. Fold edges under, and crimp. Prick bottom and sides of piecrust with a fork. Bake at 450° for 8 minutes or until golden. Remove piecrust to a wire rack, and cool completely.

Whisk together condensed milk, egg yolks, lime juice, and cream cheese in top of a double boiler until smooth. Place mint leaves in a double layer of cheesecloth. Gather edges of cheesecloth together; tie securely. Add to milk mixture. Cook over hot (not boiling) water, whisking constantly, until temperature reaches 160°. Remove from heat. Cover and keep warm.

Beat egg whites and cream of tartar at high speed with an electric mixer until foamy. Gradually add sugar, 1 tablespoon at a time, beating until stiff peaks form.

Remove mint bundle from filling, scraping excess filling from bundle. Pour filling into prepared crust. Immediately spread meringue over hot filling, sealing to edge of crust. Bake at 325° for 25 minutes or until golden.

Makes: 8 servings.
Prep: 20 min., **Cook:** 35 min.

Tip: Begin beating egg white mixture when milk mixture is almost 160° so filling is as hot as possible before pouring into crust. To prevent "weeping," spread meringue over hot filling to begin cooking the meringue from the bottom.

Allison Carmichael
Birmingham, Alabama

According to **Allison**, this is a real Floridian recipe from an old Key native.

Heavenly Butterscotch Cream Pie

If you love creamy desserts, this one will steal your heart. Sweet whipped cream is spread over a soft-set homemade butterscotch filling.

8 pecan shortbread cookies, finely crushed
½ cup sweetened flaked coconut
2 tablespoons granulated sugar
2 tablespoons butter, melted
1 cup firmly packed dark brown sugar
½ cup all-purpose flour
¼ teaspoon salt
2 cups half-and-half
3 egg yolks, lightly beaten
3 tablespoons butter
1 teaspoon vanilla extract
1 cup whipping cream
¼ cup powdered sugar
½ teaspoon vanilla extract

Combine first 4 ingredients in a small bowl; press into a lightly greased 9-inch pieplate. Bake at 325° for 10 minutes; remove piecrust to a wire rack, and cool completely.

Whisk together brown sugar and next 4 ingredients in a medium saucepan. Cook over medium heat, stirring

After spreading the pie with whipped cream, **Linda** adds a drizzling of bottled butterscotch topping. We omitted the topping and let the homemade butterscotch filling steal the show.

constantly, 8 minutes or until thickened. Remove from heat; stir in butter and 1 teaspoon vanilla; cool slightly. Pour cooled filling into prepared crust; cover pie, and chill at least 8 hours.

Beat whipping cream, powdered sugar, and ½ teaspoon vanilla with an electric mixer until soft peaks form. Spread evenly over pie. **Makes:** 8 servings.
Prep: 22 min., **Cook:** 18 min., **Other:** 8 hrs.

Linda G. Baker
Montgomery, Alabama

Florida Chess Pie

Pineapple gives this chess pie a tropical twist.

½ (15-ounce) package refrigerated
   piecrusts
2 cups sugar
2 teaspoons all-purpose flour
2 teaspoons cornmeal
¼ teaspoon salt
4 large eggs, lightly beaten
6 tablespoons butter, melted
1 (8-ounce) can crushed
   pineapple in juice, well drained
½ cup sweetened flaked coconut

Fit 1 piecrust into a 9½-inch deep-dish pieplate according to package directions. Fold edges under, and crimp.

Whisk together sugar and next 3 ingredients. Whisk in eggs and melted butter until smooth. Stir in pineapple and coconut. Pour filling into prepared crust.

Bake at 325° for 1 hour or until set.

Makes: 8 servings.

Prep: 11 min., **Cook:** 1 hr.

Mary Cudd
West Columbia, Texas

After the pie has baked for 1 hour, **Mary** often removes the pie from the oven and covers it with nonstick aluminum foil. She then returns the pie to the oven for 30 to 45 minutes and says that the filling will crisp up, creating and an entirely new dessert.

Sweet Potato Pecan Pie With Coconut Custard

This rectangular sweet potato "pie" features a pecan shortbread crust topped with a creamy sweet potato filling and a rich coconut custard. To serve, cut into squares and serve chilled.

2 cups all-purpose flour
¾ cup chopped pecans
1½ cups sugar, divided
1 cup butter
½ cup butter, softened
2 large eggs, lightly beaten
3 medium-size sweet potatoes,
   cooked and mashed (about
   2½ cups)
½ cup evaporated milk
1 teaspoon vanilla extract
⅓ cup sugar
¼ cup cornstarch
¾ cup water
1 (14-ounce) can coconut milk
Garnishes: toasted coconut,
   toasted chopped pecans

Combine flour, pecans, and ½ cup sugar in a medium bowl; cut in 1 cup butter with a pastry blender until crumbly. Press dough into a lightly greased 13- x 9-inch baking dish. Bake at 350° for 20 to 22 minutes or until lightly browned.

Beat ½ cup butter and 1 cup sugar at medium speed with an electric mixer until blended. Stir in eggs and next 3 ingredients; blend well. Pour over baked crust. Bake at 350° for 35 minutes or until set.

Combine ⅓ cup sugar and cornstarch in a small saucepan. Add water and coconut milk; stir with a wire whisk. Bring mixture to a boil, and cook 1 minute or until thickened. Cool slightly; pour over baked sweet potato layer. Cover and chill 8 hours or overnight. Cut into squares. **Makes:** 15 servings.

Prep: 29 min., **Cook:** 57 min., **Other:** 8 hrs.

Tip: An easy way to cook 3 sweet potatoes is to pierce them several times with a fork; place 1 inch apart on paper towels in a microwave oven. Microwave on HIGH 8 to 10 minutes or until done.

Jennifer LaPeters
Winter Springs, Florida

Praline Sweet Potato Pie

Praline Sweet Potato Pie

½ (15-ounce) package
    refrigerated piecrusts
Praline Crumbles, divided
1¾ cups cooked mashed sweet
    potatoes (about 2 pounds)
1 (8-ounce) can crushed
    pineapple in juice, drained
3 egg yolks
1 cup sugar
6 tablespoons butter, softened
½ cup milk
½ cup half-and-half
1 tablespoon lemon extract
½ teaspoon ground nutmeg
½ teaspoon ground cinnamon
Frozen whipped topping, thawed

Fit 1 piecrust into a 9-inch pieplate according to package directions; fold edges under, and crimp. Sprinkle 1 cup Praline Crumbles into piecrust.

Process sweet potatoes and next 9 ingredients in a food processor until smooth, stopping to scrape down sides; pour into prepared crust.

Bake at 450° for 15 minutes. Reduce oven temperature to 350°; bake 35 minutes or until almost set (knife will not test clean), shielding edges after 15 minutes to prevent excessive browning, if necessary. Remove pie to a wire rack, and cool completely. Cover and chill at least 8 hours. Serve with whipped topping and remaining Praline Crumbles, if desired. **Makes:** 8 servings.
Prep: 31 min., **Cook:** 50 min., **Other:** 8 hrs.

Carol brought two Southern favorites together in one delectable dessert—bits of praline candy are buried in each mouthwatering bite of sweet potato pie.

Praline Crumbles:
¾ cup firmly packed light brown
    sugar
¾ cup granulated sugar
¾ cup half-and-half
3 tablespoons butter
1¼ cups pecan pieces
½ teaspoon vanilla extract

Combine first 4 ingredients in a large saucepan; cook over medium heat 5 minutes or until sugar dissolves, stirring constantly. Stir in pecans. Bring to a boil over medium heat; cook 9 to 10 minutes or until a candy thermometer registers 238° (soft ball stage), stirring constantly. Remove from heat.

Add vanilla; stir constantly 3 minutes. Working rapidly, drop by tablespoonfuls onto wax paper. Let stand until firm; chop. **Makes:** 3 cups.
Prep: 5 min., **Cook:** 24 min.

Tip: Although you may be tempted to use the clean-knife test to make sure this pie is done, it's an inaccurate test for this moist pie. The knife will never come out clean. Simply bake until the center looks like it's almost set. It will still jiggle just a little.

Carol Gillespie
Chambersburg, Pennsylvania

Piña Colada Li'l Fried Pies

A sweet concoction of pineapple is tucked inside pie pastry, then fried to a flaky golden brown. Dusted with powdered sugar, these simply melt in your mouth.

1 **(20-ounce) can crushed pineapple in juice, undrained**
⅓ **cup cream of coconut**
1 **tablespoon rum**
2 **(15-ounce) packages refrigerated piecrusts**
4 **cups vegetable oil**
¼ **cup powdered sugar**

Combine pineapple, cream of coconut, and rum in a small saucepan. Cook over medium-high heat, stirring often, 15 minutes or until mixture is thickened and liquid has evaporated. Cool mixture slightly.

Meanwhile, unfold piecrusts onto a cutting board. Cut 4 circles out of each crust, using a 4½-inch round cutter. Spoon about 1 tablespoon pineapple mixture onto half of each pastry circle. Moisten edges with water; fold pastry over pineapple mixture, pressing edges to seal. Crimp edges with a fork dipped in flour.

Heat oil in a deep 12-inch skillet to 375°. Fry pies, in batches, 1 to 2 minutes or until golden brown, turning once. Drain on paper towels. Sprinkle with powdered sugar. Serve warm. **Makes:** 16 pies.
Prep: 5 min., **Cook:** 16 min.

Loanne Chiu
Fort Worth, Texas

Southern Citrus Cheesecake Tart With Walnut Shortbread Crust

1¼ cups all-purpose flour
2 tablespoons granulated sugar
2 tablespoons light brown sugar
½ teaspoon salt
1¼ cups walnut halves
10 tablespoons cold unsalted butter, cut into pieces
1 (8-ounce) can pineapple tidbits in juice, drained
1 (10-ounce) jar lemon curd
½ cup orange marmalade
1 (8-ounce) package cream cheese, softened
¾ cup granulated sugar
2 large eggs
1 teaspoon vanilla extract

Process first 6 ingredients in a food processor or blender until mixture is crumbly. Press into bottom and up sides of a 9-inch deep-dish pieplate.
Bake at 350° for 15 minutes or until lightly browned.
Meanwhile, stir together pineapple, lemon curd, and marmalade; set aside.
Beat cream cheese and ¾ cup sugar at medium speed with an electric mixer until smooth. Add eggs, 1 at a time, beating until blended after each addition; stir in vanilla.
Carefully spread pineapple mixture over prepared crust. Pour cream cheese mixture over pineapple mixture.

Bake at 350° for 38 minutes or until center is almost set and top is lightly browned. Remove tart from oven, and let stand on a wire rack at least 2 hours before serving. Serve warm. **Makes:** 8 servings.
Prep: 20 min., **Cook:** 53 min., **Other:** 2 hrs.

Gaynell Lawson
Maryville, Tennessee

Gaynell uses black walnuts when she prepares her crust. Our Test Kitchens enjoyed it, but preferred regular walnuts in the crust.

Piña Colada Li'l
Fried Pies

Southern Peach Empanadas

Tender pastry, gooey fruit filling, and crunchy nuts create a trinity of textures in these easy turnovers. They're best eaten with a knife and fork rather than out of hand.

½   cup cold butter, cubed
2   cups all-purpose baking mix *
1   large egg, beaten
2   to 3 tablespoons water
¾   cup peach preserves
¼   teaspoon ground cinnamon
¼   cup chopped walnuts
¼   cup raisins
1   large egg, lightly beaten
1   tablespoon water

Cut butter into baking mix with a pastry blender until crumbly. Add 1 beaten egg, stirring with a fork until dry ingredients are moistened. Gradually stir in 2 to 3 tablespoons water until dough forms a ball. Roll out dough on a floured surface to ⅛-inch thickness. Cut 8 circles out of dough, using a 5-inch round cutter.

Combine peach preserves and next 3 ingredients in a medium bowl; stir well. Spoon 1 rounded tablespoon filling onto half of each dough circle. Moisten edges with water; fold circles in half, making sure edges are even. Press edges of filled pastry firmly together with fingers. Place pastries on baking sheets lined with parchment paper. Crimp edges of pastries with a fork dipped in flour. Whisk together remaining egg and 1 tablespoon water. Brush pastries with egg mixture.
Bake at 375° for 15 minutes or until golden. Remove to wire racks, and cool.
Makes: 8 turnovers.
Prep: 20 min., **Cook:** 15 min.

*For testing purposes only, we used Bisquick Original All-Purpose Baking Mix.

Tip: For ease in securing dough around filling, cradle folded side of each filled pastry in palm of one hand while pinching edges together with fingers.

Susan Griffin
Charlotte, North Carolina

Susan fills these little turnovers and keeps them in the refrigerator until she's ready to bake and serve them. She likes the make-ahead element because she says, "They're ready when you are."

Mint Julep Compote

Fresh mint and sweet fruit make this dessert simple and refreshing.

1½ cups orange juice
1   cup sugar
¼   cup fresh mint leaves, chopped
1   (1-inch) piece orange rind
2   tablespoons bourbon
2   cups chopped fresh pineapple *
1   banana, sliced
1   large peach, diced
8   maraschino cherries, sliced
2   tablespoons golden raisins
Lemon sorbet
Garnish: fresh mint sprigs

Combine first 5 ingredients in a medium saucepan over medium-high heat. Bring to a boil; reduce heat, and simmer 6 minutes or until thickened. Remove from heat; cool 2 minutes. Pour liquid through a wire-mesh strainer into a small bowl, discarding leaves and rind. Cover and chill 2 hours.
Divide fruit evenly among 4 bowls; spoon syrup over fruit, and top with lemon sorbet. Garnish, if desired.
Makes: 4 servings.
Prep: 4 min., **Cook:** 9 min., **Other:** 2 hrs.

*If fresh pineapple isn't available, substitute a 20-ounce can of pineapple chunks in syrup or juice instead. Just be sure to drain the liquid.

Roxanne Chan
Albany, California

You can use a 20-ounce can of pineapple chunks like **Roxanne** does, but we opted for fresh pineapple since it's readily available in most supermarkets.

Dessert Spoonbread With Lemon Berries

Topped with tangy strawberries, this dessert is a cross between spoonbread and rice pudding.

2   cups milk
2   tablespoons butter
2   large eggs, lightly beaten
⅓   cup white cornmeal
2   tablespoons sugar
1   tablespoon all-purpose flour
1   teaspoon salt
1   cup cold cooked rice
Lemon Berries
Garnish: whole strawberries

Lemon Berries:
1   quart strawberries
¾   cup sugar
2   tablespoons cornstarch
½   cup water
1   egg yolk, lightly beaten
1   teaspoon lemon rind
3   tablespoons fresh lemon juice
    (about **2 large lemons**)
1   tablespoon butter

Combine milk and butter in a medium saucepan over low heat; cook until butter is melted. In a small bowl, combine eggs and next 4 ingredients. Gradually stir egg mixture into milk mixture until combined. Add rice; cook 1 minute, stirring constantly, or until mixture thickens.

Pour mixture into a buttered 2-quart baking dish. Bake at 375° for 35 minutes or until browned and set. Remove to a wire rack, and cool completely. Serve with Lemon Berries. Garnish, if desired. **Makes:** 6 servings.
Prep: 5 min., **Cook:** 45 min.

Slice strawberries into a large bowl; set berries aside.

Combine sugar, cornstarch, and water in a small saucepan over medium heat; stir until smooth. Add egg yolk, lemon rind and lemon juice; cook, stirring constantly, until mixture is thickened. Remove from heat; stir in butter until melted. Cool completely. Fold lemon sauce into strawberries. Refrigerate until ready to serve. **Makes:** 4 cups.
Prep: 15 min., **Cook:** 6 min., **Other:** 1 hr.

Tip: This dessert is a great way to use leftover rice.

Connie Moore
Medway, Ohio

We applaud **Connie** for her creativity. She turned a traditional Southern side dish into a creamy dessert with the addition of a little sugar, some rice for texture, and a strawberry-lemon sauce.

Cinnamon-Vanilla Bread Pudding
With Praline Sauce

Cinnamon-Vanilla Bread Pudding With Praline Sauce

By the way this dressed-up bread pudding tastes, no one will ever guess it's so quick and easy.

2 cups milk
1 cup heavy whipping cream
3 tablespoons butter
1 cup white chocolate morsels
5 slices white bread, cut into ½-inch cubes
3 large eggs
½ cup sugar
½ teaspoon salt
2 teaspoons ground cinnamon
1 teaspoon vanilla extract
Praline Sauce

Combine first 4 ingredients in a medium saucepan; cook, stirring often, over medium heat until morsels are melted. Remove from heat; add bread cubes, and let stand 2 minutes.

Whisk together eggs and next 4 ingredients in a medium bowl. Add bread mixture. Pour into a lightly greased 11- x 7-inch baking dish.

Bake, uncovered, at 350° for 1 hour or until set and crust is golden. Let stand 5 minutes. Serve with warm Praline Sauce.

Makes: 8 servings.
Prep: 11 min., **Cook:** 1 hr.

Praline Sauce:
½ cup butter
2 cups chopped pecans
1 cup heavy whipping cream
1 cup sugar
1 tablespoon cornstarch
2 tablespoons pure maple syrup
1 cup white chocolate morsels
1 teaspoon vanilla extract

Melt butter in a medium saucepan over medium heat; add pecans and cook 5 minutes. Whisk together cream, sugar, cornstarch, and syrup in a small bowl. Add to pecan mixture. Stir in white chocolate morsels. Bring to a boil, and cook, stirring constantly, 1 minute or until mixture begins to thicken. Remove from heat; stir in vanilla. Serve over Cinnamon-Vanilla Bread Pudding.

Makes: about 4 cups.
Prep: 1 min., **Cook:** 9 min.

Tip: Serve leftover Praline Sauce over ice cream or pound cake.

Paula Cox
Texarkana, Texas

Southern Iced Tea Cake Parfaits

This moist, crumbly cake—delicately flavored with orange and ginger—is an instant crowd-pleaser.

Buttery Tea Topping
Whipped Cream Filling
1   **cup water**
⅓   **cup lemon-flavored iced tea liquid concentrate**
1   **(18.25-ounce) package spice cake mix**
⅓   **cup vegetable oil**
3   **large eggs**
2   **tablespoons grated orange rind**
1   **tablespoons grated fresh ginger**
Garnish: grated orange rind

Prepare Buttery Tea Topping and Whipped Cream Filling.

Combine 1 cup water and tea concentrate in a small bowl. Prepare cake according to package directions, using tea concentrate mixture, ⅓ cup oil, and 3 eggs. Add 2 tablespoons orange rind and ginger; beat 2 minutes at medium speed with an electric mixer. Pour batter into a lightly greased 13- x 9-inch pan.

Bake at 350° for 35 minutes or until a wooden pick inserted in center comes out clean. Place on a wire rack.

Pierce top of warm cake with a long wooden pick; pour Buttery Tea Topping over cake. Cool cake in pan on a wire rack for 30 minutes. Cut cake into 8 portions.

Crumble one-third of 1 cake portion into an 8-ounce parfait glass; top with 3 tablespoons Whipped Cream Filling. Repeat procedure twice to fill parfait glass (glass will be full). Repeat procedure with remaining cake portions and Whipped Cream Filling to make remaining parfaits. Cover and chill at least 1 hour before serving. Garnish, if desired. **Makes:** 8 servings.

Prep: 4 min., **Cook:** 35 min., **Other:** 2 hrs.

Buttery Tea Topping:
½   **cup sugar**
½   **cup lemon-flavored iced tea liquid concentrate**
⅓   **cup orange juice**
¼   **cup unsalted butter**

Combine all ingredients in a small saucepan over medium-high heat. Bring to a boil; cook 2 to 4 minutes or until mixture is syrupy. Remove from heat. **Makes:** 1½ cups.

Prep: 5 min., **Cook:** 4 min.

Whipped Cream Filling:
2   **cups heavy whipping cream**
3   **tablespoons sifted powdered sugar**
1   **tablespoon orange juice**

Combine all ingredients in a medium bowl. Beat with an electric mixer at medium speed 7 minutes or until soft peaks form. Cover and chill. **Makes:** 4¾ cups.

Prep: 7 min.

Tip: This is a good make-ahead dessert because the flavor of the cake improves overnight. Just be sure to cover each parfait well before refrigerating. If you don't have parfait glasses, serve the parfaits in large balloon-style red wine glasses.

Pamela M. Sanford
New Market, Tennessee

Pamela garnishes the top of each parfait with twisted strips of orange peel and fresh mint leaves. She places a thin slice of orange on the side of each parfait glass and inserts a long iced teaspoon into each dessert.

Simple and Scrumptious Entrées

Rules had to be rules at the Cook-Off competition.
But to give you the best in this book, we bent
the rules a bit. A few of these easy-to-make
main dishes take more than 30 minutes to prep
and 1 hour to cook. One taste and we bet
you won't mind the extra wait.

Melt-in-Your-Mouth Braised
and Barbecued Chicken

"I'm not creative in any other way, so cooking is my passion," says Carol Daggers. Letting loose in the kitchen takes the edge off a day at work in clinical research, monitoring scientific trials regulated by the U.S. Food and Drug Administration. Carol's work is logical, careful, controlled. In her kitchen, anything goes.

Carol's job often takes her on the road, so she does culinary research when she eats out. "I'm inspired by foods I discover at restaurants," she says. "When I get home to Delaware, I try to recreate those wonderful dishes in my kitchen."

Carol's prizewinning recipe uses ginger, soy sauce, and citrus fruit juices to add traditional Asian flavoring to the barbecue sauce in which chicken thighs are simmered. "I love the ribs they serve in Chinese restaurants," says Carol. "I developed this recipe to come up with a dish that has that type of flavor but is less fattening and easier to make."

Head judge Andria Hurst says the hands-off ease of braising makes this dish great for weeknight suppers. "Who knew chicken thighs could be this wonderful?"

$11,000
Category & Brand
Winner!

TROPICANA® Brand Winner
Melt-in-Your-Mouth Braised and Barbecued Chicken
Carol created a main dish that mimics Asian-style barbecue.

2 **tablespoons vegetable oil**
8 **bone-in chicken thighs, skinned (about 2 pounds)**
½ **cup orange juice**
½ **cup pineapple juice**
1 **tablespoon cornstarch**
⅓ **cup soy sauce**
⅓ **cup firmly packed light brown sugar**
2 **tablespoons minced fresh ginger**
3 **tablespoons cider vinegar**
3 **tablespoons ketchup**
½ **teaspoon dried crushed red pepper**
2 **garlic cloves, minced**
2 **regular-size bags boil-in-bag long-grain rice, uncooked**
¼ **cup chopped green onions**

Heat oil in a large skillet over medium-high heat. Add chicken, and sauté 6 minutes, turning once.
Combine fruit juices in a large bowl. Stir together cornstarch and 1 tablespoon juice mixture until smooth; set aside.
Stir soy sauce and next 6 ingredients into remaining juice mixture; pour over chicken. Bring mixture to boil; cover, reduce heat, and simmer 35 minutes, turning chicken after 20 minutes.

Prepare rice according to package directions. Keep warm.
Uncover chicken, and stir in cornstarch mixture. Cook, stirring constantly, 5 minutes or until sauce thickens.
Spoon rice onto a serving platter; top with chicken and sauce. Sprinkle with chopped green onions. **Makes:** 4 servings.
Prep: 15 min., **Cook:** 50 min.

Carol Daggers
Wilmington, Delaware

Carol likes thighs for this dish because they are more manageable in her one-skillet braising technique and produce better flavor than other chicken parts.

When Texan Lynne Milliron was 8 years old, she pried open the door of her toy oven because she couldn't wait for the cake to be ready. Luckily, her cooking is more sophisticated now.

It was her sister-in-law who actually had the inspiration one evening to combine shrimp and rice with an unorthodox sauce. "She mixed olives and other things in a blender, then poured it over sautéed shrimp—so simple and wonderful," Lynne recalls.

Later, a happy accident took the idea a step farther. "I wanted to try shrimp with pesto one night, but I didn't have any basil. So I used cilantro instead, because that's what was in the fridge."

Lynne's creative use of ingredients made her dish a finalist in the entrées category, making her first Cook-Off a great success. Lynne is determined to win again, so the Milliron family is enjoying her experiments. Her new recipes are likely to explore the Mexican-style cuisine that they love. Lynne says, "If I could have only one seasoning to cook with, I'd choose cumin, which is essential in Mexican cooking. I love that flavor."

$2,000
Finalist & Brand
Winner!

SUCCESS/MAHATMA® Brand Winner

Texas Pesto Shrimp Over Rice

If you like pesto, give this recipe a try. It's made with cilantro instead of the traditional basil.

1½ pounds unpeeled, large fresh shrimp
1 cup fresh cilantro leaves
3 green onions, cut into thirds
¼ cup freshly grated Parmesan cheese
½ small jalapeño pepper, unseeded
½ medium tomato
2 tablespoons pine nuts, toasted
3 tablespoons fresh lemon juice (about 1 lemon)
1 teaspoon minced garlic
½ teaspoon salt
½ teaspoon pepper
¼ cup olive oil, divided
Hot cooked rice

Peel shrimp; devein, if desired. Set aside.

Process cilantro, next 9 ingredients, and 3 tablespoons olive oil in a food processor until smooth.

Sauté shrimp in remaining 1 tablespoon hot oil in a large skillet over medium-high heat 3 to 4 minutes or just until shrimp turn pink. Pour cilantro mixture over shrimp, stirring well. Serve shrimp mixture over hot cooked rice. **Makes:** 4 servings.

Prep: 15 min., **Cook:** 15 min.

Lynne Milliron
Austin, Texas

For quick weeknight suppers, **Lynne** thaws frozen peeled and deveined shrimp for this dish. She toasts the pine nuts in the same skillet that she'll use to cook the shrimp so she doesn't have to dirty a second pan.

Texas Pesto Shrimp
Over Rice

Gloria Bradley's mother was not a good cook—though she made a great checkerboard cake—so it's no surprise that Gloria was a young bride who couldn't cook. "I tried to make a pie that first Thanksgiving in 1958, but the dough I made was so hard I couldn't roll it out—we ended up having Twinkies for dessert," she recalls.

Irma Rombauer's classic *The Joy of Cooking* became Gloria's ticket to culinary glory. The Illinois mother of five is now so accomplished in the kitchen that she's a veteran of numerous cook-offs and adept with highly flavored ingredients such as Jamaican jerk seasoning and Gorgonzola cheese.

An entrées finalist, Gloria chose to grill rib-eyes, which she often makes at home. "Everyone uses chile powder now, so I mixed ancho chile powder with olive oil to make a paste to rub on the steaks before they're grilled," she explains. A dollop of herbed cream cheese provides the finishing touch.

Gloria says her key to a winning recipe is thinking creatively about combining ingredients that taste good together.

$2,000 Finalist & Brand Winner!

WEBER® Brand Winner

Grilled Chile-Rubbed Rib Eyes With Herb Cheese and Asparagus Bundles

4   tablespoons cream cheese, softened
2   tablespoons minced shallots
1   teaspoon fresh lemon juice
2   teaspoons minced fresh chives
2   teaspoons minced fresh basil
1½ tablespoons ancho chile powder*
1   tablespoon paprika
1   teaspoon garlic salt
½   teaspoon ground red pepper
2   tablespoons olive oil
4   (12-ounce) rib-eye steaks (1 to 1½ inches thick)
1   tablespoon salt
4½ quarts water
20 fresh asparagus spears (about ½ pound)
4   prosciutto slices
Garnishes: fresh basil sprigs, lemon wedges

Stir together first 5 ingredients in a small bowl until blended. Shape into a 4-inch log; wrap in plastic wrap, and chill until firm.

Combine chile powder and next 3 ingredients in a small bowl. Stir in olive oil to form a paste. Rub mixture on both sides of steaks.

Combine salt and 4½ quarts water in a large Dutch oven. Bring water to a boil; add asparagus. Cook 2 minutes or until crisp-tender; drain. Plunge asparagus into ice water to stop the cooking process; drain.

Gather 5 asparagus spears into a bundle; wrap with 1 slice of prosciutto. Repeat procedure with remaining asparagus and prosciutto. Set aside.

Preheat grill according to manufacturer's instructions.

Place steaks on grill rack over direct high heat; grill, covered with grill lid, 10 minutes, turning once. Turn off burners that are directly below steaks. Reduce heat to medium; grill, covered with grill lid, 6 to 8 minutes or until done.

Remove steaks to serving plates; top each steak immediately with 1 tablespoon of herb cheese log. Serve asparagus bundles with steaks. Garnish, if desired. **Makes:** 4 servings.

Prep: 30 min., **Cook:** 23 min.

*For testing purposes only, we used McCormick Ancho Chile Powder.

Gloria Bradley
Naperville, Illinois

Gloria uses indirect heat to finish off the steaks on the grill. The result is tender, perfectly cooked steaks.

**Grilled Chile-Rubbed Rib Eyes With
Herb Cheese and Asparagus Bundles**

Judy's Brisket

Judy's Brisket

Slowly cooking this budget-cut of beef in a hearty amount of red wine results in a mouthwatering, tender roast with a French flair. Round out the meal with egg noodles or mashed potatoes.

1 **cup dry red wine**
1 **tablespoon chili sauce**
1 **teaspoon salt**
1 **(14½-ounce) can diced tomatoes, undrained**
2 **garlic cloves, minced**
½ **teaspoon freshly ground black pepper**
1 **(4-pound) beef brisket, trimmed**
8 **carrots, peeled and halved**
1 **large Vidalia onion, sliced**

Combine first 6 ingredients in a bowl; stir well.

Place brisket in a large greased roasting pan. Arrange carrot and sliced onion around brisket; pour wine mixture over brisket and vegetables.

Bake, covered, at 350° for 3 hours or until brisket is tender. Remove from oven; let stand 15 minutes.

Shred brisket into bite-size pieces with 2 forks, or cut diagonally across the grain into thin slices; place on a platter. Remove vegetables from pan with a slotted spoon, and arrange around meat. Spoon about 1 cup pan drippings over brisket and vegetables. Serve with remaining pan drippings. **Makes:** 6 to 8 servings.

Prep: 14 min., **Cook:** 3 hrs., **Other:** 15 min.

Judy Pincus
Boca Raton, Florida

Pat's Chi-Town Sirloin Steak

Don't be intimidated by the length of this ingredient list. Many of the items are seasonings from a bottle so the recipe goes together quickly. If you can't find the handy black and red pepper blend, you can substitute ½ teaspoon each of black pepper and ground red pepper.

¼ **cup spicy steak sauce**
¼ **cup olive oil**
1 **tablespoon minced fresh garlic**
1 **tablespoon prepared horseradish**
1 **teaspoon salt**
1 **teaspoon garlic powder**
1 **teaspoon onion powder**
1 **teaspoon Cajun seasoning**
1 **teaspoon ground black and red pepper blend** *
1 **teaspoon spicy steak seasoning** *
¼ **teaspoon hot sauce**
1 **(2-pound) boneless top sirloin steak, trimmed**
1 **green bell pepper, halved and seeded**
1 **red bell pepper, halved and seeded**
1 **yellow bell pepper, halved and seeded**
2 **tablespoons olive oil**

Combine first 11 ingredients in a shallow dish or large zip-top freezer bag; add steak. Cover or seal, and marinate in refrigerator 8 hours, turning occasionally.

Coat bell peppers with 2 tablespoons olive oil; set aside.

Remove steak from marinade, discarding marinade. Grill, covered with grill lid, over medium-high heat (350° to 400°) 6 to 8 minutes on each side or to desired degree of doneness. During last 5 minutes, add peppers, and grill, covered, 5 minutes or until pepper skins are bubbly and blackened.

Cut steak diagonally across the grain into thin slices. Peel peppers; cut into strips. Serve peppers with steak. **Makes:** 6 servings.

Prep: 18 min., **Cook:** 16 min., **Other:** 8 hrs.

*For testing purposes only, we used McCormick Hot Shot Black and Red Pepper Blend and McCormick Grill Mates Spicy Montreal Steak Seasoning.

Patrick Coppock
Fort Worth, Texas

Mediterranean Beef Rolls

To dress up this dish, simply slice each beef roll crosswise, fan the slices over a serving of seasoned orzo or soft polenta, then drizzle with the cheesy tomato sauce.

1   (1-pound) boneless sirloin steak
½   teaspoon salt
½   teaspoon ground black pepper
⅓   cup pesto sauce *
1   (12-ounce) jar roasted red bell peppers, drained and sliced
1   (14½-ounce) can petite diced tomatoes, undrained
¼   cup dried tomatoes in oil, drained and chopped
2   tablespoons chopped fresh basil
¼   teaspoon dried crushed red pepper
⅓   cup freshly grated Parmesan cheese
3   tablespoons olive oil

Place steak between 2 sheets of heavy-duty plastic wrap, and flatten to ¼-inch thickness, using a meat mallet or rolling pin. Sprinkle steak with salt and black pepper. Spread pesto over steak.

Pat peppers dry with paper towels; arrange over steak. Roll up steak, jelly-roll fashion, starting with a long edge; secure at 2-inch intervals with twine or wooden picks. Cut into 4 equal pieces.

Combine diced tomatoes and next 3 ingredients in a medium saucepan. Bring to a boil; reduce heat, and simmer 10 minutes, stirring occasionally. Remove from heat; stir in cheese.

Meanwhile, heat oil in a large nonstick skillet over medium-high heat 1 minute. Add beef rolls; cook 8 to 10 minutes or until done, turning to brown on all sides. Arrange beef rolls on individual serving plates, and top with tomato mixture. **Makes:** 4 servings.
Prep: 29 min., **Cook:** 11 min.

*For testing purposes only, we used Classico Creations Basil Pesto.

Diane Sparrow
Osage, Iowa

Luscious Blue Cheese Steak Sandwiches

Crusty French bread topped with a three-cheese spread, thin slices of flavorful steak, and arugula earned this sandwich our highest rating. Plan on making this open-faced sandwich a sit-down meal with a knife and fork.

4   ounces goat cheese
4   ounces blue cheese
½   (8-ounce) package cream cheese, softened
1   tablespoon freshly ground pepper
3   tablespoons olive oil
1   pound skirt steak
½   teaspoon salt
¼   teaspoon freshly ground pepper
3   tablespoons Dijon mustard
2   medium onions, cut into strips
1   (16-ounce) loaf French bread
3   tablespoons butter or margarine, softened
2   garlic cloves, minced
1   bunch arugula or watercress (about 1½ cups)

Beat first 4 ingredients at medium-high speed with an electric mixer in a medium mixing bowl until creamy; set aside.

Place a large cast-iron skillet over high heat until almost smoking; add oil.

Meanwhile, sprinkle both sides of steak with salt and pepper. Spread Dijon mustard over steak. Place steak in hot skillet. Cook 4 to 5 minutes on each side or until a meat thermometer inserted in thickest portion registers 150°. Remove from skillet; let stand on a cutting board 5 minutes. Cut into thin slices, cutting diagonally across the grain.

Add onions to skillet; cook, stirring constantly, 6 minutes or until crisp-tender; remove from skillet.

Cut bread in half crosswise; split each half lengthwise. Combine butter and garlic; spread mixture evenly over cut sides of bread.

Place bread halves, 2 at a time, cut side down, in skillet. Toast bread 1 to 2 minutes or until browned.

Spread toasted bread evenly with cheese mixture; top with arugula, steak slices, and onion strips. **Makes:** 4 servings.
Prep: 16 min., **Cook:** 23 min.

Shelley Madan
Winter Park, Florida

My Mom's Best Dinner

This is true comfort food. Tangy, salty dill pickles and Dijon mustard are enveloped in a hearty steak roll, then the steak is browned and smothered in gravy. We loved the beef rolls sliced and served over hot rice or egg noodles.

5   tablespoons Dijon mustard
6   cubed steaks (about 2 pounds)
½   teaspoon salt
½   teaspoon pepper
12   bacon slices, cooked and crumbled
1   cup chopped onion (1 medium onion)
1   cup chopped dill pickle
2   tablespoons vegetable oil
2   (1.2-ounce) envelope brown gravy mix
4   cups water

Spread mustard evenly over 1 side of each steak. Sprinkle evenly with salt and pepper. Combine bacon, onion, and dill pickle. Top each steak evenly with bacon mixture, spreading it almost to edges. Roll up, starting with a short side, and secure with wooden picks.

Brown meat on all sides in hot oil in a large skillet; remove meat, and keep warm. Whisk in gravy mix and water; bring to a boil. Return meat to pan; cover and reduce heat. Cook 20 minutes or until done. **Makes:** 6 servings.

Prep: 25 min., **Cook:** 28 min.

Linda Adkins
Charlotte, North Carolina

Linda uses thinly cut eye of round steak, but we got a more tender product using cubed steaks. Cubed steaks are pieces of top or bottom round that are run through a butcher's tenderizing machine, leaving a perforated appearance.

Orange Peel Beef and Rice With Ginger Green Beans

Delicious beef tenderloin earned this dish a high rating, but you can easily substitute less pricey sirloin steak. Partially freeze the beef for about 30 minutes for easier slicing.

¼   cup soy sauce, divided
1   tablespoon cornstarch
1   pound beef tenderloin fillets, thinly sliced
3   regular-size bags boil-in-bag long-grain rice, uncooked
3   tablespoons peanut oil, divided
1   tablespoon grated orange rind
1   tablespoon bottled minced garlic
3   green onions, chopped
⅓   cup orange marmalade
⅓   cup chili garlic sauce
2   teaspoons light brown sugar
½   teaspoon salt
     Ginger Green Beans

Combine 2 tablespoons soy sauce and cornstarch in a medium bowl; stir well. Add sliced beef; stir well. Let stand 10 minutes.

Meanwhile, cook rice according to package directions.

While rice cooks, heat 1 tablespoon oil in a large nonstick skillet over medium-high heat. Add half of beef; cook 4 minutes, stirring often. Remove beef from skillet; set aside. Repeat procedure with 1 tablespoon oil and remaining half of beef. Remove beef from skillet.

Heat remaining 1 tablespoon oil in skillet. Add orange rind, garlic, and green onions; cook 1 minute. Stir in remaining 2 tablespoons soy sauce, orange marmalade, chili garlic sauce, brown sugar, and salt. Return beef to skillet; cook 1 minute or until thoroughly heated.

Spoon rice onto a large serving platter; top with beef mixture. Arrange Ginger Green Beans around beef mixture and rice. **Makes:** 4 servings.

Prep: 15 min., **Cook:** 10 min.

Ginger Green Beans:
1   tablespoon peanut oil
1   tablespoon butter or margarine
1   pound small fresh green beans, trimmed, or 1 (16-ounce) package frozen whole green beans, partially thawed
3   tablespoons minced fresh ginger
1   tablespoon bottled minced garlic
¼   cup soy sauce
1   tablespoon light brown sugar

Heat oil and butter in a large nonstick skillet over medium-high heat. Add green beans and remaining ingredients. Cover; reduce heat to low, and cook 8 minutes or until crisp-tender, stirring occasionally. **Makes:** 4 servings.

Prep: 4 min., **Cook:** 8 min.

Leslie S. Couick
Rock Hill, South Carolina

Peppercorn Beef Fillets With
Orange Fennel Sauce

Peppercorn Beef Fillets With Orange Fennel Sauce

The sweet aroma of fennel accents the buttery Gorgonzola and crunchy toasted pecans in this peppery company entrée.

4   (8-ounce) beef tenderloin fillets
    (about 1½ inches thick)
3   tablespoons olive oil, divided
1   tablespoon coarsely ground
    pepper
2   tablespoons butter
1   fennel bulb, cut into thin strips*
¾   cup fresh orange juice
½   teaspoon salt
3   ounces Gorgonzola cheese,
    crumbled
⅓   cup chopped pecans, toasted

Brush steaks with 2 tablespoons oil; sprinkle with pepper, pressing pepper into steaks.

Grill, covered with grill lid, over medium-high heat (350° to 400°) 3 minutes on each side or to desired degree of doneness. Transfer steaks to a platter, and tent loosely with aluminum foil for juices to settle.

Meanwhile, melt butter in remaining 1 tablespoon oil in a large skillet over medium-high heat. Add fennel; sauté 2 minutes or until tender. Stir in orange juice and salt. Cook, stirring constantly, 3 minutes. Remove from heat.

Arrange steaks on individual serving plates. Spoon fennel mixture over steaks; sprinkle with cheese and pecans. **Makes:** 4 servings.
Prep: 14 min., **Cook:** 11 min.

*Substitute 1 large Vidalia onion, sliced, for the fennel, if desired.

Diane Sparrow
Osage, Iowa

Diane reserves a few feathery fennel tops to garnish this dish.

Aunt Peggy's Shish Kabobs

If using wooden skewers, be sure to soak in water 30 minutes before skewering to prevent them from burning.

1   cup vegetable oil
¾   cup low-sodium soy sauce
¼   cup Worcestershire sauce
2   garlic cloves, crushed
¼   cup fresh lemon juice
¼   cup prepared mustard
1   tablespoon cracked pepper
1½ pounds beef tenderloin steaks,
    cut into 1-inch pieces
1   large red onion, cut into
    12 pieces
1   green bell pepper, cut into
    1-inch pieces
½   pound whole mushrooms
½   pound cherry tomatoes
Hot cooked rice

Combine first 7 ingredients in a large zip-top freezer bag. Add steak and next 4 ingredients. Seal and toss. Marinate in refrigerator 2 hours.

Remove steak and vegetables from bag; discard marinade. Thread onto 8 (12-inch) skewers.

Grill kabobs, covered with grill lid, over medium-high heat (350° to 400°) 8 minutes on each side or to desired doneness. Serve with rice. **Makes:** 6 servings.
Prep: 26 min., **Cook:** 16 min., **Other:** 2 hrs.

Tip: For even cooking, thread meat onto separate skewers from vegetables. Also, to prevent overcooking tomatoes, add tomatoes halfway through cooking.

Mary Ann Archer
Pueblo West, Colorado

Pan de Maiz con Gusto Carne y Arroz

Roughly translated to "Cornbread with Tasty Meat and Rice," this spin-off of tamale pie has a double cornmeal crust and a rich, thick meaty filling.

1 pound lean ground beef
1 large onion, chopped
1 large green bell pepper, chopped
3 tablespoons minced garlic
½ teaspoon salt
¼ teaspoon pepper
2 (14½-ounce) cans diced tomatoes with green pepper, celery, and onion, drained
1 (15-ounce) can tomato sauce
4 jalapeño peppers, seeded and chopped
½ cup chopped fresh parsley
1 tablespoon lemon juice
1½ teaspoons ground cumin
1 (6.5-ounce) can sliced black olives, drained
1 cup hot cooked rice

3 cups self-rising buttermilk cornmeal mix
1 tablespoon sugar
2¼ cups buttermilk
⅓ cup olive oil
2 large eggs, lightly beaten

Combine first 4 ingredients in a large skillet over medium heat; sprinkle with salt and pepper. Cook 5 minutes, stirring until meat crumbles and is no longer pink; drain well. Return to skillet; stir in diced tomatoes and next 6 ingredients. Simmer, uncovered, 10 minutes or until slightly thickened. Stir in rice.

Combine cornmeal mix and next 4 ingredients in a large bowl, stirring well.

Pour half of cornmeal mixture into a greased 13- x 9-inch baking dish. Spoon meat mixture into center of dish, leaving a 1-inch border around edges. Spoon remaining cornmeal mixture evenly over meat mixture, spreading to edge.

Bake at 400° for 35 minutes or until browned. **Makes:** 12 servings.

Prep: 30 min., **Cook:** 50 min.

Note: The cornmeal batter on the bottom will edge up the sides of the dish when spooning in the filling. This helps the batter on the top layer spread easily and also seals in the filling during baking.

G. Steven Krogh
Norfolk, Virginia

Pine-Nut Beef and Hummus

Serve this entrée with pita wedges, or try stuffing it into a pita for a quick supper. Extra hummus makes a tasty dip for vegetables or pita wedges, or use it as a sandwich spread.

1 (15.5-ounce) can chickpeas, drained
¼ cup lemon juice
¼ cup tahini
2 tablespoons olive oil
3 large garlic cloves, halved
½ cup chopped onion
1 tablespoon minced garlic
1 tablespoon olive oil
1 pound ground beef
2 tablespoons lemon juice
1 teaspoon salt
¼ cup pine nuts, toasted
Pita rounds

Combine first 5 ingredients in a blender or food processor; process until smooth. Set aside.

Sauté onion and minced garlic in 1 tablespoon hot oil until tender; add ground beef, and cook, stirring until it crumbles and is no longer pink. Add lemon juice and salt; reduce heat, and simmer 2 minutes. Stir in pine nuts. Serve with hummus and pita bread.

Makes: 4 servings.

Prep: 13 min., **Cook:** 12 min.

Tip: Tahini, which is a ground sesame seed paste, is often found with the peanut butter in your grocery store; if it's not there, try the ethnic foods aisle.

Shari Ornstein
Burbank, California

Mexican Soup

Mexican Soup

The spicy flavor of this beef and bean soup is cooled a bit by the cheese and avocado sprinkled on top. If you prefer less spicy foods, reduce the chipotle pepper to 1 or 2 tablespoons.

1   poblano chile pepper*
6   large tomatoes (about 3
     pounds), cut into wedges
4   garlic cloves
1   pound ground beef
1   large onion, chopped (1½ cups)
2   (32-ounce) containers chicken
     broth
1   (16-ounce) package frozen
     whole kernel corn
1   (16-ounce) can pinto beans,
     drained
1   (15-ounce) can black beans,
     drained
3   chipotle peppers in adobo
     sauce, finely chopped (about
     ¼ cup)
2   cups coarsely crushed tortilla
     chips
1   cup (4 ounces) shredded
     Monterey Jack cheese
½   bunch fresh cilantro, chopped
     (about ⅓ cup)
1   avocado, diced

Broil poblano chile pepper on an aluminum foil-lined baking sheet 3 inches from heat about 3 minutes on each side or until pepper looks blistered. Place pepper in a zip-top freezer bag; seal and let stand 10 minutes to loosen skin. Peel pepper, and cut in half lengthwise; remove and discard seeds. Coarsely chop pepper; set aside.

Process tomato and garlic, in batches, in a blender until smooth.

Cook ground beef and onion in a large Dutch oven, stirring until beef crumbles and is no longer pink. Drain and return to pan. Add pureed tomato mixture, poblano chile pepper, chicken broth, and next 4 ingredients to beef mixture in pan. Bring to a boil; reduce heat, and simmer, stirring occasionally, 40 minutes. Ladle soup into bowls, and top with tortilla chips, cheese, cilantro, and avocado. **Makes:** 16 cups.
Prep: 12 min., **Cook:** 46 min.

*You can substitute 1 (4.5-ounce) can chopped green chiles for the poblano chile pepper, if desired.

Betty Criesco
Novato, California

Asian Meatballs Over Sesame Noodles

Try this Asian spin on spaghetti and meatballs. With a complementary blend of sweet grape jelly, chili garlic sauce, and fresh ginger, these meatballs pull off that ethnic Asian flavor with a classic American twist. Look for chili garlic sauce in the Asian section of large supermarkets or at Asian markets.

2　pounds ground round
1　garlic clove, minced
1　(8-ounce) can diced water chestnuts, drained and chopped
1　cup fine, dry breadcrumbs (store-bought)
½　cup diced green bell pepper
3　tablespoons soy sauce
2　teaspoons minced fresh ginger
½　teaspoon salt
½　teaspoon pepper
Vegetable cooking spray
Sesame Noodles
½　cup grape jelly
½　cup chili garlic sauce
3　tablespoons seasoned rice vinegar

Combine first 9 ingredients, and shape into 1½-inch balls. Place a rack coated with cooking spray in an aluminum foil-lined broiler pan. Arrange meatballs on rack, and lightly spray meatballs with cooking spray.
Bake at 400° for 15 minutes or until meatballs are no longer pink.

While meatballs bake, prepare Sesame Noodles.
Combine jelly, chili sauce, and vinegar in a small saucepan; cook over medium heat 3 minutes or until jelly melts and mixture is smooth, stirring constantly.
Combine meatballs and sauce, gently tossing to coat. Serve over Sesame Noodles. **Makes:** 8 servings.
Prep: 35 min., **Cook:** 18 min.

Sesame Noodles:
16　ounces uncooked spaghetti
½　cup chopped green onions
1　tablespoon butter or margarine
¼　cup creamy peanut butter
½　cup chicken broth
2　tablespoons sesame seeds, toasted
1　tablespoon dried crushed red pepper
1　tablespoon dark sesame oil

Cook pasta in boiling salted water according to package directions; drain and keep warm.

Meanwhile, sauté green onions in butter in a medium saucepan over medium-high heat until tender. Add peanut butter, and cook 1 minute or until melted, stirring constantly. Whisk in chicken broth and next 3 ingredients; cook, stirring constantly, 1 minute or until mixture is smooth.
Combine noodles and peanut butter sauce in a large bowl; gently toss to coat. **Makes:** 8 cups.
Prep: 3 min., **Cook:** 23 min.

Tip: Use a 1½-inch scoop to make perfectly round meatballs.

Leslie A. Mann
Charlotte, North Carolina

Leslie really has a flair for flavor in this dish. We replaced orange juice with seasoned rice vinegar to zest up the sauce even more and used fresh ginger instead of ground for maximum impact.

Five-Cheese Meatballs

Start with this meatball recipe to create all sorts of dishes, from appetizers and pasta dishes to sandwiches.

2 pounds ground sirloin
1 pound ground pork
   sausage
6 cups soft breadcrumbs
   (homemade)
2 large eggs
1 tablespoon salt
1 tablespoon pepper
1 (8-ounce) package shredded
   Italian four-cheese blend
¾ cup grated Romano cheese
½ cup tomato sauce
3 garlic cloves, minced

Crumble beef and sausage into a large bowl; gradually add breadcrumbs, mixing well with hands. Make a well in center of mixture. Add eggs, salt, and pepper; mix well. Add cheese blend, Romano, tomato sauce, and garlic; mix well.

Shape mixture into 1½-inch balls. Place on a 15- x 10-inch jellyroll pan lined with nonstick aluminum foil. Bake at 375° for 40 minutes or until done.
Makes: 70 meatballs.
Prep: 40 min., **Cook:** 40 min.

To freeze: Place meatballs on a jellyroll pan; freeze 1 hour. Place in zip-top freezer bags, and freeze up to 6 weeks.

To reheat: Place meatballs in a microwave-safe dish. Cover with heavy-duty plastic wrap. Microwave on HIGH until thoroughly heated. Frozen meatballs can also be added directly to pasta sauce. Cook over medium heat 20 to 30 minutes.

Mary Stacy
Fredericksburg, Virginia

Grilled Lebanese Lamb Chops With Minted Pine Nut Couscous

½ cup ketchup
½ cup olive oil
½ cup fresh lemon juice
1 tablespoon bottled roasted
   minced garlic
1 teaspoon salt
1 teaspoon ground cumin
1 teaspoon ground sumac
1 teaspoon dried thyme
1 teaspoon dried mint flakes
1 teaspoon ground coriander
1 teaspoon freshly ground black
   pepper
½ teaspoon ground cinnamon
½ teaspoon ground allspice
8 (1-inch-thick) lamb loin chops
Vegetable cooking spray
Minted Pine Nut Couscous
20 grape tomatoes, halved
Garnishes: lemon wedges, fresh
   mint sprigs

Combine first 13 ingredients in a large zip-top freezer bag; add lamb. Seal and marinate in refrigerator 8 hours, turning occasionally.

Remove lamb from marinade, discarding marinade. Spray chops evenly on both sides with cooking spray.
Grill, covered with grill lid, over medium-high heat (350° to 400°) 8 minutes on each side or to desired degree of doneness (145° for medium rare). Serve with Minted Pine Nut Couscous. Top with tomato halves. Garnish, if desired.
Makes: 8 servings.
Prep: 5 min., **Cook:** 16 min., **Other:** 8 hrs.

Whether spelled sumac or sumaq, this tart and sour spice is the secret ingredient to this Lebanese marinade. While it's hard to find in your local grocery store, it's readily available at most Mediterranean or Middle Eastern markets. If you can't find it, **Kelly** recommends doubling the amount of dried thyme.

Minted Pine Nut Couscous:
2 cups chicken broth
4 green onions, chopped
1 tablespoon bottled roasted
   minced garlic
1 tablespoon chopped fresh mint
1 tablespoon olive oil
1 (10-ounce) package plain
   couscous, uncooked
½ cup pine nuts, toasted

Bring first 5 ingredients to a boil in a medium saucepan over high heat. Add couscous and pine nuts; remove from heat. Let stand 5 minutes; fluff with a fork. **Makes:** 8 servings.
Prep: 5 min., **Cook:** 5 min., **Other:** 5 min.

Tip: Bone-in pork loin chops are a great substitute in this recipe. Simply grill them 8 minutes on each side or until a meat thermometer inserted into thickest portion, without touching bone, registers 160° (medium).

Kelly Evans
Atlanta, Georgia

Parmesan, Pistachio, and
Pepper-Crusted Veal Chops

Parmesan, Pistachio, and Pepper-Crusted Veal Chops

To reduce prep time, look for shelled pistachios in your supermarket around the holidays; freeze in zip-top freezer bags for use throughout the year.

½   cup finely chopped pistachios
½   cup grated Parmesan cheese
1½ teaspoons cracked black pepper*
1   teaspoon salt
1   teaspoon garlic powder
1   teaspoon paprika
½   teaspoon onion powder
½   teaspoon dried oregano
½   teaspoon dried thyme
½   teaspoon ground red pepper
½   teaspoon ground black pepper
4   (1-inch-thick) bone-in veal chops (about 1½ pounds)
½   cup all-purpose flour
2   large eggs, lightly beaten
2   tablespoons olive oil

Combine first 3 ingredients in a shallow dish; set aside.

Combine salt and next 7 ingredients. Sprinkle ¼ teaspoon salt mixture on each side of veal chops. Combine remaining salt mixture and flour in a shallow dish.

Dredge veal chops in flour mixture; dip in egg, then dredge in pistachio mixture.

Heat oil in a large ovenproof skillet over medium-high heat. Add veal chops, and cook 2 minutes on each side or until lightly browned. Bake at 350° for 8 to 10 minutes or to desired degree of doneness (veal should reach at least 145°). **Makes:** 4 servings.

Prep: 24 min., **Cook:** 14 min.

*We liked the taste and texture of cracked black pepper in the crust. If you use ground black pepper, decrease the amount to ¾ teaspoon.

Kelly Ellis
Huntsville, Alabama

Kelly finishes off these tender veal chops in the oven instead of on the cooktop to seal in their juices and to prevent the delicate pistachios from burning.

Viva Italian Burgers

Get out the knives and forks to enjoy these moist and mighty burgers.

¾   pound ground veal
¼   pound mild Italian sausage
1   (10-ounce) can diced tomatoes and green chiles, drained
½   cup Italian-seasoned breadcrumbs
1   teaspoon garlic powder
1   teaspoon dried crushed red pepper
¼   teaspoon salt
⅛   teaspoon ground black pepper
1   large portobello mushroom, cut into 4 slices
1   medium-size red onion, cut into 4 slices
1   yellow bell pepper, seeded and quartered
4   slices provolone cheese

1   (16-ounce) loaf unsliced Italian bread, cut into 8 (¾-inch) slices
½   cup pesto sauce
2   medium plum tomatoes, sliced
¼   cup chopped black olives
¼   cup crumbled feta cheese

Combine first 8 ingredients, mixing well. Form into 4 patties.

Place mushroom, onion, and bell pepper on a food grate coated with cooking spray. Grill, covered with grill lid, over medium-high heat (350° to 400°) 15 to 20 minutes, turning occasionally.

Meanwhile, place patties on food grate. Grill, covered, 7 to 8 minutes on each side or until no longer pink.

Top patties with grilled mushroom slices and provolone cheese. Cook until cheese is melted.

Remove vegetables and patties from grill. Grill bread slices 1 minute on each side or until toasted.

Spread each bread slice with 1 tablespoon pesto sauce. Place tomato slices, patties, and grilled vegetables on each of 4 bread slices; sprinkle with olives and feta cheese. Top with remaining bread slices. **Makes:** 4 sandwiches.

Prep: 14 min., **Cook:** 22 min.

Christina Valenta
Friendswood, Texas

Five-Spice Pork and Rice

Dredging strips of pork in cornstarch gives them a wonderfully crispy coating.

½ **cup light molasses**
¼ **cup soy sauce**
1 **tablespoon tomato paste**
1 **teaspoon granulated garlic**
½ **teaspoon Chinese five spice**
1 **pound boneless pork loin roast, cut into thin strips**
1 **cup cornstarch**
1 **cup canola or vegetable oil, divided**
½ **cup dry-roasted peanuts**
1 **cup chopped green onions (about 1 bunch)**
2 **cups hot cooked rice**
Garnish: green onion strips

Whisk together first 5 ingredients until smooth. Reserve ½ cup molasses mixture; set aside. Place remaining molasses mixture and pork in a shallow dish or large zip-top freezer bag. Cover or seal, and marinate in refrigerator 30 minutes, turning once.

Remove pork from marinade, discarding marinade. Place cornstarch in a shallow dish; dredge pork in cornstarch.

Heat ¼ cup oil in a large nonstick skillet or wok over medium-high heat. Cook one-fourth of pork 5 minutes or until crisp and no longer pink. Drain on paper towels. Repeat procedure 3 times with remaining oil and pork.

Discard all but 1 tablespoon oil in skillet; stir-fry peanuts and green onions 2 minutes. Return pork to skillet; add reserved ½ cup molasses mixture, stirring to coat. Serve over rice. Garnish, if desired. **Makes:** 2 to 3 servings.
Prep: 10 min., **Cook:** 22 min., **Other:** 30 min.

Rick Hasley
Lavergne, Tennessee

For an added boost of flavor, **Rick** cooks his rice in chicken broth instead of water.

Roasted Pork Loin With Creamy Mint Sauce

Leftover Creamy Mint Sauce can be served another night with grilled or roasted lamb.

5 **bacon slices**
2 **tablespoons dried mint flakes**
2 **tablespoons seasoning blend** *
1 **tablespoon freshly ground pepper**
1 **(4-pound) boneless pork loin roast**
Creamy Mint Sauce

Cook bacon in a large skillet 9 minutes or until crisp. Remove bacon, and drain on paper towels, reserving drippings in pan. Crumble bacon.

Combine mint flakes, seasoning blend, and pepper. Rub half of mixture over pork loin. Brown on all sides in reserved drippings in pan over medium heat. Place pork on a piece of aluminum foil, and sprinkle with remaining seasoning mixture; sprinkle with bacon. Fold foil to seal. Place pork in a roasting pan.

Bake at 400° for 50 minutes or until a meat thermometer inserted into thickest portion registers 155°. Cover and let stand 10 minutes or until thermometer registers 160° before slicing. Serve with Creamy Mint Sauce. **Makes:** 8 to 10 servings.
Prep: 8 min., **Cook:** 59 min., **Other:** 10 min.

Creamy Mint Sauce:
½ **cup mint jelly**
1 **(8-ounce) container sour cream**
1 **cup plain low-fat yogurt**
2 **teaspoons seasoning blend** *
2 **teaspoons dried mint flakes**
1 **jalapeño pepper, seeded and chopped**

Melt jelly in a saucepan over low heat. Remove from heat. Whisk in sour cream and remaining ingredients until blended. **Makes:** 2½ cups.
Prep: 3 min., **Cook:** 5 min.

＊For testing purposes only, we used Morton's Nature's Seasons Seasoning Blend.

Joyce O. Johnson
Athens, Texas

Joyce prepares this recipe using Morton's seasoning salt; however, we tested it with Morton's seasoning blend because we weren't able to find their seasoning salt in our area.

Jerk Pork Tenderloin

If you prefer this Jamaican favorite with more spicy heat, pump up the amounts of red and black pepper.

6   tablespoons brown sugar
1   tablespoon ground allspice
1   tablespoon dried thyme
2   teaspoons ground ginger
2   teaspoons garlic salt
2   teaspoons ground cinnamon
2   teaspoons ground red pepper
2   teaspoons ground black pepper
1   teaspoon onion powder
1   teaspoon ground cumin
1   teaspoon ground nutmeg
3   (1-pound) pork tenderloins
½   cup water
¼   cup vegetable oil
¼   cup cider vinegar

Combine first 11 ingredients in a large zip-top freezer bag. Add tenderloins; seal and shake to coat. Pour water, oil, and vinegar over pork in bag; seal bag, and marinate in refrigerator 8 hours, turning occasionally.

Traditionally made with habanero peppers, jerk-seasoned meats are fiery hot, but **Natalie's** milder version is ideal for family meals.

Grill tenderloins, covered with grill lid, over medium-high heat (350° to 400°) 25 minutes or until a meat thermometer inserted into thickest portion registers 155°, turning occasionally. Transfer tenderloins to a serving platter; cover and let stand 5 minutes or until thermometer registers 160° before slicing. **Makes:** 6 to 8 servings.

Prep: 6 min., **Cook:** 25 min., **Other:** 8 hrs., 5 min.

Natalie Brooks
Pelham, Alabama

Spicy Southern Pork Tenderloins

½   cup olive oil, divided
3   tablespoons Creole mustard
½   teaspoon garlic powder
¼   teaspoon salt
¼   teaspoon pepper
1   (2-pound) package pork
     tenderloins
3   bell peppers (1 each of red,
     green, and yellow), halved and
     seeded
1   large onion, cut into
     ½-inch-thick slices
1   (15-ounce) can black beans,
     drained
2   tablespoons chopped pickled
     jalapeño peppers

Combine ¼ cup olive oil and next 4 ingredients in a shallow dish or large zip-top freezer bag; add pork tenderloins. Cover or seal, and marinate in refrigerator 2 to 4 hours.

Remove pork from marinade; discard marinade. Grill pork, covered with grill lid, over medium-high heat (350° to 400°) 5 minutes. Brush peppers with remaining ¼ cup oil. Add peppers and onion to grill; cover and grill 15 minutes or until a meat thermometer inserted into thickest portion of tenderloin registers

155° and peppers are lightly blackened, turning as necessary. Cover pork; let stand 5 minutes or until thermometer registers 160° before slicing.

Slice grilled peppers into strips; coarsely chop onion. Stir together peppers, onion, beans, and jalapeño. Cut pork tenderloin into ¼-inch-thick slices; serve with grilled pepper mixture.

Makes: 6 to 8 servings.

Prep: 17 min., **Cook:** 20 min., **Other:** 2 hrs., 5 min.

Vicki Dickinson
Norman, Oklahoma

When **Vicki** prepares this entrée, she grills the pork and peppers in a foil pouch up to a day before she serves the meal. Then she refrigerates the pork and peppers and reheats them in the microwave (in a microwave-safe container) just before serving. We couldn't resist trading the foil pouch for some grill marks and smoky flavor. It smelled so good coming off the grill we sampled it right away instead of refrigerating it first.

Peanut and Herb-Encrusted Pork Tenderloin

The chunky peanut coating really makes this pork special. Be careful not to go too long in the food processor or the mixture will turn into a paste.

1½ cups dry-roasted, unsalted peanuts
2 garlic cloves
2 tablespoons unsalted butter, melted
½ teaspoon salt
½ teaspoon ground red pepper
¼ teaspoon ground black pepper
1 (1½- to 2-pound) herb-marinated boneless pork tenderloin

Combine first 6 ingredients in a food processor; pulse 6 to 8 times or until mixture is blended but still chunky.

Brown tenderloins on all sides in a large skillet over medium heat. Place tenderloin in a lightly greased roasting pan; press peanut mixture on top and sides of tenderloin.

Bake, uncovered, at 350° for 40 minutes or until a meat thermometer inserted in thickest portion registers 155°. Cover and let stand 5 minutes or until thermometer registers 160° before slicing. **Makes:** 4 servings.
Prep: 11 min., **Cook:** 40 min., **Other:** 5 min.

Note: Some of the crust for the tenderloin may crumble to the bottom of the roasting pan while it's cooking, but this imparts a hearty roasted flavor to the peanuts. Sprinkle the roasted nuts over the roast for a quick and easy garnish.

Anne Gerry
Atlanta, Georgia

Mississippi Maple Pork With Garlic Mashed Potatoes

We recommend using real maple syrup in this recipe instead of maple-flavored pancake syrup.

4 (1-inch-thick) boneless pork chops (about 1½ pounds)
¼ cup all-purpose flour
1 teaspoon kosher salt
½ teaspoon freshly ground pepper
6 tablespoons butter or margarine, divided
⅓ cup minced shallots
1½ cups chicken broth
¼ cup maple syrup
3 tablespoons balsamic vinegar
2 tablespoons Dijon mustard
½ teaspoon kosher salt
¼ teaspoon freshly ground pepper
Garlic Mashed Potatoes

Butterfly each chop by making a lengthwise cut down center of rounded edge, cutting to within ½ inch of other side. Open chops, and place between 2 sheets of heavy-duty plastic wrap; flatten to ¼-inch thickness, using a meat mallet or rolling pin.

Combine flour, 1 teaspoon salt, and ½ teaspoon pepper in a shallow dish; dredge chops in flour mixture.

Melt 2 tablespoons butter in a large nonstick skillet over medium-high heat.

Cook chops, in batches, 3 minutes on each side or until browned. Remove chops from skillet, reserving drippings in skillet; keep chops warm.

Melt 1 tablespoon butter in reserved drippings in skillet over medium-high heat. Add shallots; cook 2 minutes or until tender. Add broth; bring to a boil over high heat. Reduce heat to medium-high, and simmer 3 minutes or until reduced by half. Add maple syrup and next 4 ingredients; cook 6 minutes, stirring constantly, or until slightly thickened. Remove from heat; add remaining 3 tablespoons butter, stirring until smooth. Serve over chops and Garlic Mashed Potatoes. **Makes:** 4 servings.
Prep: 25 min., **Cook:** 31 min.

Garlic Mashed Potatoes:

4 medium russet potatoes (about 2¾ pounds), peeled and cubed
2 garlic cloves
⅓ cup warm milk
2 tablespoons butter or margarine
1 teaspoon kosher salt
¼ teaspoon freshly ground pepper

Cook potato and garlic in a Dutch oven in boiling salted water to cover 20 minutes or until tender; drain. Return potato to Dutch oven; add milk and remaining ingredients. Mash with a potato masher to desired consistency. **Makes:** 5 cups.
Prep: 7 min., **Cook:** 20 min.

Tip: There's no right way to mash potatoes. Some like them lumpy, while others like them smooth and creamy. If you like them on the smooth side, use an electric mixer instead of a potato masher.

Randolph Bush
Bridgeport, Connecticut

Randolph keeps the chops warm in a 150° oven while he stirs up the gravy in the same skillet he used for browning the chops. That way, the caramelized browned bits in the skillet add extra flavor to the gravy.

Caramelized Pork Chops and Onions
With Mashed Potatoes and Gravy

Caramelized Pork Chops and Onions With Mashed Potatoes and Gravy

This recipe is one of our favorites in this book. We liked the flavor of maple sausage in this country-style gravy, but feel free to substitute your favorite variety.

¼   **cup olive oil, divided**

2   **medium-size sweet onions (about 1¼ pounds), cut in half and thinly sliced**

7   **tablespoons butter or margarine, divided**

1   **teaspoon brown sugar**

4   **medium baking potatoes (about 1½ pounds), peeled and cubed**

⅓   **cup half-and-half**

1   **teaspoon salt, divided**

¾   **teaspoon ground black pepper, divided**

4   **(10-ounce) boneless pork loin chops (1 to 1¼ inches thick)**

6   **ounces maple-flavored ground pork sausage**

1   **cup chicken broth**

½   **cup half-and-half**

2   **tablespoons all-purpose flour**

Heat 2 tablespoons olive oil in a large skillet over medium heat. Add onions; cover and cook, stirring occasionally, 10 minutes or until soft. Add 1 tablespoon butter and brown sugar; cook, uncovered, stirring occasionally, 20 minutes or until onions are caramelized.

Meanwhile, cook potatoes in boiling salted water to cover 15 minutes or until tender; drain and return to pot. Add 4 tablespoons butter, ⅓ cup half-and-half, ½ teaspoon salt, and ¼ teaspoon pepper. Mash well with a potato masher; set aside, and keep warm.

While potatoes cook, sprinkle pork chops evenly with ¼ teaspoon salt and ¼ teaspoon pepper. Heat remaining 2 tablespoons oil in a large skillet over medium heat. Add pork chops, and cook 8 to 10 minutes on each side or until a meat thermometer inserted into thickest portion registers 155°. Remove chops; cover and let stand 5 minutes or until temperature registers 160°. Remove 2 tablespoons pan drippings from skillet; set aside. Discard remaining pan drippings.

Add sausage to skillet, and cook over medium-high heat, stirring until it crumbles and is no longer pink. Reduce heat to medium. Add 2 tablespoons reserved pan drippings, 2 tablespoons butter, and chicken broth; bring to a simmer.

Whisk together remaining ¼ teaspoon salt, remaining ¼ teaspoon pepper, ½ cup half-and-half, and flour until smooth. Add flour mixture to sausage mixture, whisking until blended. Simmer, stirring often, 4 to 5 minutes or until thickened.

Spoon mashed potatoes evenly onto individual serving plates. Top each serving with caramelized onions, a pork chop, and gravy. **Makes:** 4 servings.

Prep: 14 min., **Cook:** 42 min., **Other:** 5 min.

Note: You can prepare potatoes ahead and reheat before serving. To save a few minutes, use prepared refrigerated mashed potatoes and heat according to package directions.

Melissa Cusano
Granite Bay, California

Melissa arranges this dish with an artful eye. She places the potatoes in the center of the plate and tops them with some of the onions. She leans the pork chop to the side of the potatoes, placing the prettiest browned side up. Then she finishes it off with a generous amount of the gravy.

Chipotle Chops

Serve saffron rice or mashed potatoes with these spicy chops to temper the heat. Or create a South American meal with black beans and sautéed plantains. Look for ground chipotle chile pepper on the spice rack at large supermarkets. This ingredient adds a smoky essence that's vital to the flavor of the dish. If you want to tone down the heat, omit the black pepper.

3 tablespoons olive oil, divided
4 (8-ounce) bone-in center-cut pork chops
1 cup chopped onion
3 tablespoons minced garlic
1 (14.5-ounce) can diced tomatoes
2 tablespoons ground chipotle chile pepper*
3 tablespoons fresh lemon juice
1 teaspoon salt
1 teaspoon dried oregano
1 teaspoon ground black pepper

Heat 1 tablespoon oil in a large skillet over medium-high heat. Add pork chops; cook 3 minutes on each side or until browned. Transfer chops to a lightly greased 11- x 7-inch baking dish.
Sauté onion and garlic in remaining 2 tablespoons oil in skillet over medium-high heat 5 minutes or until onion is tender. Stir in tomatoes and next 5 ingredients. Pour tomato mixture over chops; cover with aluminum foil.
Bake, covered, at 350° for 1 hour and 50 minutes or until pork is tender.
Makes: 4 servings.
Prep: 6 min., **Cook:** 2 hrs.

*For testing purposes only, we used McCormick Chipotle Chile Pepper.

William Blacksmith
Albuquerque, New Mexico

William divides these ingredients into two 11- x 7-inch baking dishes for the long simmer in the oven, but we found that they fit fine and cook evenly when layered slightly in one dish.

Spicy Asian Grilled Chops

Grilling these chops accentuates the sweet and spicy flavor of the spice rub.

1 tablespoon Chinese five spice
2 tablespoons dark sesame oil
1 teaspoon kosher salt
1 teaspoon garlic powder
1 teaspoon dried crushed red pepper
½ teaspoon dark brown sugar
½ teaspoon ground red pepper
4 (1-inch-thick) boneless pork loin chops (about 2½ pounds)

Combine first 7 ingredients in a small bowl; stir to form a paste. Rub paste on both sides of chops.
Grill chops, covered with grill lid, over medium-high heat (350° to 400°) 10 minutes on each side or until a meat thermometer inserted into thickest portion registers 155°. Transfer to a serving plate; cover and let stand 5 minutes or until temperature registers 160° before slicing. **Makes:** 4 servings.
Prep: 10 min., **Cook:** 20 min., **Other:** 5 min.

Monique Jackson-Fitzgerald
Hayes, Virginia

We prefer the thick chops **Monique** calls for in this recipe, but when you're pinched for time, use thinner chops and decrease the cook time.

Roasted Red Pepper Lasagna

This lasagna boasts a meaty sauce and lots of cheese—ingredients guaranteed to satisfy hearty appetites.

16   lasagna noodles, uncooked
1   large sweet onion, cut into ¼-inch slices (about 2 cups)
2   pounds ground hot pork sausage
1   pound ground chuck
1   large carrot, finely chopped (⅔ cup)
3   garlic cloves, minced
1   (26-ounce) jar tomato-basil pasta sauce
1   (14.5-ounce) can diced tomatoes
1   (12-ounce) jar roasted red bell peppers, drained and coarsely chopped
½   teaspoon salt
¼   teaspoon pepper
2   large eggs, lightly beaten
2   (15-ounce) containers ricotta cheese
⅔   cup minced fresh parsley
2   (8-ounce) packages shredded Italian 6-cheese blend cheese, divided

Cook lasagna noodles in boiling salted water according to package directions. Drain and keep warm.

Cut onion slices in half crosswise. Cook onion, sausage, and next 3 ingredients in a large deep skillet or Dutch oven 10 minutes, stirring until meats crumble and are no longer pink; drain. Return meat mixture to pan. Stir in pasta sauce and next 4 ingredients. Bring to a boil; cover, reduce heat, and simmer 5 minutes.

Meanwhile, stir together eggs, ricotta cheese, and parsley in a medium bowl.

Spread 3 cups meat sauce in a lightly greased 15- x 10-inch lasagna dish.

Arrange 4 lasagna noodles evenly over sauce.

Spread half of ricotta mixture over noodles. Arrange 4 noodles over ricotta, and top with 4 cups meat sauce; sprinkle with 1 cup cheese.

Arrange 4 noodles over cheese, and top with remaining half of ricotta mixture and remaining 4 noodles. Sprinkle 1 cup cheese over noodles, and top with remaining meat mixture (Dish will be very full.)

Bake, covered, at 375° for 45 minutes or until bubbly. Uncover, sprinkle with remaining 2 cups cheese, and bake 5 more minutes or until cheese melts. Let stand 15 minutes before serving.

Makes: 12 servings.

Prep: 44 min., **Cook:** 1 hr., 5 min., **Other:** 15 min.

Nancy Weiss
Middletown, Maryland

Plantation Minced Pork in Lettuce Cups

Peaches provide a unique sweetness that perfectly balances the spicy pork sausage.

1   (15-ounce) can diced peaches in light syrup, undrained
1   (16-ounce) package hot pork sausage
1   tablespoon minced fresh ginger
1   tablespoon minced garlic
1   teaspoon grated lime rind
1   tablespoon fresh lime juice
1   tablespoon creamy peanut butter
2   tablespoons chopped fresh mint
2   tablespoons chopped fresh cilantro
½   cup dry-roasted peanuts, chopped
1   large head iceberg lettuce

Drain peaches, reserving ¾ cup peaches and 3 tablespoons syrup. Reserve remaining peaches and syrup for another use.

Cook sausage in a large nonstick skillet, stirring until it crumbles and is no longer pink. Remove from heat; stir in reserved ¾ cup peaches, reserved 3 tablespoons peach syrup, ginger, and next 7 ingredients.

Separate lettuce leaves, counting out 16 leaves. Reserve remaining lettuce for other uses. Spoon ¼ cup sausage mixture onto each lettuce leaf; roll up. Serve immediately. **Makes:** 3 to 4 servings.

Prep: 27 min., **Cook:** 8 min.

Gail Singer
Calabasas, California

Gail serves this family style with everyone filling and rolling their own lettuce leaves. She says it's fun for the whole family.

Monte Cristo Casserole

Monte Cristo Casserole

To present this casserole in true Monte Cristo style, serve it with a dusting of powdered sugar and a dab of jam.

8   white bread slices, trimmed and cut into cubes
1   (12-ounce) package Canadian bacon, chopped
8   ounces oven-roasted turkey breast, chopped
2   cups (8 ounces) shredded Swiss cheese
6   large eggs
2   cups milk
3   tablespoons mayonnaise
1½ tablespoons spicy brown mustard
1   teaspoon salt

Place bread cubes in a lightly greased 13- x 9-inch baking dish. Top with Canadian bacon and turkey; sprinkle with cheese.

Beat eggs and next 4 ingredients in a large bowl at medium speed with an electric mixer until blended; pour evenly over bread mixture.

Bake, uncovered, at 350° for 43 to 45 minutes or until set and lightly browned. Serve immediately. **Makes:** 8 servings.
Prep: 19 min., **Cook:** 45 min.

Note: To quickly trim bread slices, stack 4 slices, and cut off crusts on each side, using a serrated knife.

Anita Ledoux
Salem, Alabama

Anita had a clever idea when she turned a classic American sandwich into a casserole. Pair it with steamed asparagus, and serve it for brunch, lunch, or dinner.

Gorgonzola Fettuccine With Pears, Prosciutto, and Pistachios

Most of the prep in this recipe is easily done while your pasta cooks. We used Bosc pears for testing, but any variety of pears will work well in this recipe. You may prefer to leave the peel on the pears for added color—and it saves a little time, too.

1   pound uncooked fettuccine
¾   cup butter, melted
8   ounces crumbled Gorgonzola cheese
¼   pound thinly sliced prosciutto, coarsely chopped
½   cup coarsely chopped pistachios
2   pears, peeled, cored, and thinly sliced

Cook fettuccine in boiling salted water according to package directions; drain. Add butter and cheese; toss until cheese begins to melt. Add prosciutto and remaining ingredients, and toss until blended. Serve immediately. **Makes:** 6 to 8 servings.
Prep: 17 min., **Cook:** 10 min.

Annelle Williams
Martinsville, Virginia

Annelle has a large shallow pasta bowl that she tosses the mixture in right at the table. Toss it in the pot you cooked the pasta in if you don't have a bowl large enough.

Cuban Grills

These Cuban sandwiches are made with crispy cornbread cakes instead of traditional Cuban bread.

1 (6-ounce) package yellow or
  buttermilk cornbread mix *
1 large egg, lightly beaten
⅔ cup milk
2 tablespoons vegetable oil,
  divided
3 teaspoons honey mustard
3 teaspoons hot mustard
6 thin slices deli ham (about
  ¼ pound)
6 thin slices deli spicy pork roast
  (about ¼ pound)
6 thin slices baby Swiss cheese
  (about ¼ pound)
6 bacon slices, cooked
15 dill pickle slices

Combine first 3 ingredients in a small bowl. Heat 1 teaspoon oil in a large nonstick skillet over medium heat. Pour ¼ cup cornbread batter into hot skillet; cook 1 to 2 minutes on each side or until lightly browned. Repeat procedure with remaining oil and batter to make 5 more corncakes. Transfer corncakes to a wire rack.

Spread honey mustard on 1 side of 3 corncakes; spread hot mustard on 1 side of remaining 3 corncakes. Layer 2 slices ham, 2 slices pork, and 2 slices cheese over 3 corncakes; top each with 2 slices bacon and 5 pickle slices. Top with remaining corncakes, mustard side down.

Grill sandwiches, 1 at a time, in skillet over medium-low heat 2 minutes on each side, pressing sandwiches down with a small heavy skillet. **Makes:** 3 sandwiches.
Prep: 13 min., **Cook:** 36 min.

*For testing purposes only, we used Martha White cornmeal mix.

Tip: Look for precooked bacon in your grocer's refrigerator case, and heat according to package directions.

Valerie Holt
Cartersville, Georgia

Valerie uses a package of cornbread mix to speed up the preparation time.

Easy Glazed Ham

1 (7½-pound) fully cooked ham
  half
1½ cups sweetened applesauce
1 cup sugar
½ cup molasses
1 teaspoon ground allspice

Place ham in a large Dutch oven.
Stir together applesauce and next 3 ingredients; pour over ham. Bake, covered, at 350° for 1½ to 2 hours or until a meat thermometer registers 140°, basting every 30 minutes. Let stand 15 minutes before carving.
Makes: 8 servings.
Prep: 5 min., **Cook:** 2 hrs., **Other:** 15 min.

Lisa Campbell
Pleasantville, Pennsylvania

With this recipe, **Lisa** proves you don't have to spend all morning in the kitchen to make an entrée for eight people. In only 5 minutes the hands-on work is done; then you're free to do other things while the ham bakes.

Cuban Grills

Ancho Grilled Chicken With Cilantro-Yogurt Sauce

If hot and spicy food causes your tongue to tremble, think twice before running for the fire hose. Water simply transports the chile oils to different spots on your tongue, but creamy dairy mixtures, such as this tasty cilantro sauce, contain casein, a milk protein, that breaks down the hot chile oils and tames the heat. We enjoyed this dish with a cool, refreshing tomato-avocado salad.

5   ancho chile peppers
4   cups boiling water
3   garlic cloves
½   cup chopped red onion
½   cup fresh cilantro leaves
2   tablespoons tomato paste
1   tablespoon ground cumin
1   teaspoon kosher salt
1   teaspoon dried oregano
½   teaspoon freshly ground
     pepper
2   tablespoons olive oil
3½ pounds bone-in chicken pieces
Cilantro-Yogurt Sauce

Combine chile peppers and water in a bowl; let stand 30 minutes. Remove chile peppers from liquid, reserving 1½ cups liquid.

Process chile peppers, garlic, and next 7 ingredients in a food processor until blended. Add oil and reserved liquid; process until smooth, stopping to scrape down sides.

Place chicken and marinade in a zip-top freezer bag; seal bag, and marinate in refrigerator 30 minutes, turning occasionally. Remove chicken from marinade, discarding marinade.

Coat food grate with cooking spray; place on grill over medium-high heat (350° to 400°). Place chicken on grate, and grill, covered with grill lid, 10 minutes on each side or until done. Serve with Cilantro-Yogurt Sauce.
Makes: 4 servings.
Prep: 18 min., **Cook:** 20 min., **Other:** 1 hr.

Cilantro-Yogurt Sauce:
2   cups low-fat plain yogurt
½   cup chopped fresh cilantro
2   tablespoons fresh lime juice
¾   teaspoon kosher salt
½   teaspoon freshly ground pepper

Combine all ingredients in a small bowl. Cover and chill. **Makes:** 2¼ cups.
Prep: 5 min.

Tip: Prepare yogurt sauce while rehydrating ancho chile peppers. No need to chop rehydrated peppers. Just toss them into a food processor with the other marinade ingredients.

Jonathan Goldman
San Antonio, Texas

Ancho Grilled Chicken With Cilantro-Yogurt Sauce

Raspberry Tea Chicken Stir-Fry

Raspberry-flavored liquid iced tea concentrate puts a new spin on this easy chicken stir-fry, but you can substitute 2 tablespoons pineapple juice, if you'd rather.

1 pound skinned and boned chicken breasts, sliced into strips
½ cup soy sauce
2 tablespoons raspberry-flavored iced tea liquid concentrate*
3 garlic cloves, minced
1 tablespoon butter
1 small onion, sliced
1 large green bell pepper, cut into 1-inch pieces
1 (12-ounce) package fresh broccoli florets (about 4 cups)
1 (8-ounce) can pineapple chunks in juice, drained
½ cup dry-roasted peanuts
2 tablespoons cornstarch
2 tablespoons cold water
Hot cooked rice

Combine first 4 ingredients in a large zip-top freezer bag. Seal and marinate in refrigerator at least 15 minutes.

Heat butter in a wok or skillet coated with cooking spray over medium heat. Add onion; sauté 3 minutes or until tender. Add chicken and marinade; stir-fry 5 minutes. Add bell pepper and broccoli; stir-fry 2 minutes. Add pineapple and peanuts; stir-fry 1 minute.

Combine cornstarch and water, stirring until smooth. Stir cornstarch mixture into skillet; bring to a boil. Boil 1 minute. Serve over hot cooked rice. Serve with additional soy sauce, if desired. **Makes:** 4 to 6 servings.
Prep: 20 min., **Cook:** 14 min., **Other:** 15 min.

*For testing purposes only, we used Nestea Iced Tea Liquid Concentrate.

Barb Nash
Fairview, Pennsylvania

Rosemary-Sun Dried Tomato Stuffed Chicken

The amount of stuffing you'll be able to fit in each chicken breast will depend on the size of the pocket and shape of the chicken breast.

6 large skinned and boned chicken breasts
1 cup orange juice
1 cup dried tomatoes
½ cup pine nuts, toasted
½ cup fine, dry breadcrumbs (store-bought)
½ cup shredded Parmesan cheese
1 egg white, lightly beaten
1½ teaspoons butter, melted
1 teaspoon chopped fresh rosemary
½ teaspoon salt
½ teaspoon pepper
2 teaspoons olive oil
2 (5-ounce) packages long-grain and wild rice mix

Place chicken breasts in a large zip-top freezer bag. Pour orange juice over chicken; seal and marinate in refrigerator 1 hour, turning occasionally.

Place tomatoes in a 2-cup glass measuring cup. Add boiling water to cover. Let stand 30 minutes. Drain and chop, reserving 2 tablespoons liquid.

Combine tomatoes, pine nuts, and next 7 ingredients. Add reserved liquid, stirring until blended.

Remove chicken from marinade, reserving marinade. Cut a 3½-inch-long horizontal slit through thickest portion of each chicken breast, cutting to, but not through, other side, forming a pocket. Shape about ¼ cup tomato mixture into an oval; stuff firmly into pocket. Repeat procedure with remaining chicken and tomato mixture.

Heat olive oil in a large nonstick skillet over medium-high heat. Add chicken; cook 2 minutes on each side or until browned. Transfer chicken to a lightly greased 13- x 9-inch baking dish. Pour reserved marinade over chicken.

Bake, covered, at 350° for 20 minutes. Uncover and bake 10 more minutes or until done.

While chicken bakes, prepare rice according to package directions.

To serve, spoon marinade mixture over chicken. Serve chicken over rice. **Makes:** 4 servings.
Prep: 24 min., **Cook:** 38 min., **Other:** 1 hr.

Erica Murphy
Palm Harbor, Florida

Erica stuffs this yummy tomato filling into four extra-large chicken breasts, which can sometimes be hard to find. We used six large breasts, instead.

Spicy Ranch Chicken Burritos

Use a fork and a knife to tackle these burritos—they're stuffed!

4   (6-ounce) skinned and boned chicken breasts
3   tablespoons olive oil
¼   teaspoon salt
¼   teaspoon ground black pepper
2   (15-ounce) cans black beans, drained
1   (4.5-ounce) can chopped green chiles, drained
1   cup Ranch-style dressing
¼   cup hot taco sauce*
2   teaspoons lime juice
¼   teaspoon ground red pepper
8   (10-inch) flour tortillas
1   (10-ounce) can diced tomatoes and green chiles, drained
1   small onion, chopped
½   cup chopped fresh cilantro (about 1 bunch)
1   (8-ounce) package shredded iceberg lettuce (about 4 cups)
1   cup (4 ounces) shredded Cheddar cheese

Cut chicken into 2- x ¼-inch strips.
Heat oil in a large skillet over medium heat. Add chicken; cook 5 to 6 minutes on each side or until done. Sprinkle with salt and pepper. Set chicken aside, and keep warm.

Combine black beans and chiles in a medium saucepan; cook over medium heat until thoroughly heated.

Stir together Ranch-style dressing and next 3 ingredients.

Heat tortillas according to package directions. Spoon chicken, bean mixture, tomatoes and green chiles, onion, cilantro, lettuce, and cheese evenly down center of each tortilla. Drizzle with 2 tablespoons spicy Ranch sauce; roll up. Serve with remaining spicy Ranch sauce, if desired. **Makes:** 8 servings.

Prep: 27 min., **Cook:** 12 min.

*For testing purposes only, we used Taco Bell Hot Sauce. It's the same taco-type sauce you find in the packets at the restaurant. It has a very distinctive flavor, and other products typically labeled hot sauce should not be substituted.

Jenny Flake
Gilbert, Arizona

Caribbean Chicken Fans With Tropical Fruit Salsa

Tamarind paste is a tangy East Indian and Middle Eastern flavoring often used in chutneys and curry dishes. Tamarind paste can be found in East Indian and Asian markets. We sampled the chicken with and without the tamarind paste and enjoyed it both ways. Feel free to omit it if you can't find it.

4   skinned and boned chicken breasts
2   garlic cloves, minced
1   teaspoon minced fresh thyme
¾   teaspoon ground allspice
½   teaspoon salt
½   teaspoon tamarind paste (optional)
2   tablespoons olive oil
1   (15-ounce) can pineapple tidbits in juice, drained
¼   cup diced red bell pepper
2   green onions, thinly sliced
1   small jalapeño pepper, seeded and minced
2   tablespoons minced fresh basil
2   tablespoons fresh lime juice
Garnish: fresh basil sprigs

Place chicken between 2 sheets of heavy-duty plastic wrap, and flatten to ½-inch thickness, using a meat mallet or rolling pin. Combine garlic, thyme, allspice, salt, tamarind paste, if desired, and olive oil, stirring to form a paste. Rub paste over both sides of chicken breasts; cover and refrigerate while preparing salsa.

Combine pineapple and next 5 ingredients in a small bowl; set aside.

Cook chicken in a large nonstick skillet coated with cooking spray over medium heat 6 to 7 minutes on each side or until done. Cut chicken into slices, and fan out on a serving plate. Spoon salsa at center of fan. Garnish, if desired.

Makes: 4 servings.

Prep: 17 min., **Cook:** 14 min.

Note: Use a mortar and pestle or the tines of a fork to mash the garlic and spices into a paste.

Jeanette Atwood
Oklahoma City, Oklahoma

Jeanette uses canned tropical fruit salad in her salsa, but we liked the simplicity of pineapple tidbits.

Grilled Peanut-Tea Chicken With Pineapple Salsa

You'll want to remember the salsa part of this recipe to serve with grilled salmon.

½ cup olive oil

½ cup creamy peanut butter

3 garlic cloves, minced

6 tablespoons lemon-flavored iced tea liquid concentrate, divided *

¼ cup chili sauce

¼ teaspoon ground red pepper

6 skinned and boned chicken breasts

1 (20-ounce) can pineapple tidbits in juice, drained

½ cup peeled, seeded, and chopped cucumber

½ cup finely chopped red bell pepper

3 tablespoons finely chopped red onion

3 tablespoons chopped fresh cilantro

Garnishes: chopped dry-roasted peanuts, fresh mint sprigs

Heat olive oil in a small saucepan just until hot.

Stir together peanut butter and garlic in a shallow dish large enough to marinate chicken; pour hot oil over peanut butter mixture, and stir well. Whisk in 4 tablespoons tea concentrate, chili sauce, and ground red pepper into peanut butter mixture. Add chicken to peanut butter mixture, turning to coat all sides. Cover and marinate in refrigerator 20 minutes.

Meanwhile, combine remaining 2 tablespoons tea concentrate, pineapple, and next 4 ingredients in a bowl; toss gently. Cover and chill.

Remove chicken from marinade, discarding marinade. Grill chicken, covered with grill lid, over medium heat (300° to 350°) 7 minutes on each side or until done.

Slice chicken into ½-inch slices; serve with salsa. Garnish, if desired. **Makes:** 6 servings.

Prep: 22 min., **Cook:** 14 min., **Other:** 20 min.

*For testing purposes only, we used Nestea Iced Tea Liquid Concentrate.

Gloria Bradley
Naperville, Illinois

We enjoyed **Gloria's** creative use of tea concentrate to flavor this Asian-inspired dish. See her winning recipe on page 98 in this chapter.

Grilled Chicken Breasts With Candied Sweet Potatoes, Apples, Raisins, and Chipotle Chiles

Grilled Chicken Breasts With Candied Sweet Potatoes, Apples, Raisins, and Chipotle Chiles

If you want to prepare a chicken dish that's simple but special enough for the holidays, this recipe is a great one to try.

½   **cup butter**
2   **pounds sweet potatoes, peeled and cut into 1-inch chunks**
2   **Granny Smith apples, sliced**
1   **cup firmly packed light brown sugar**
¾   **cup light corn syrup**
3   **chipotle peppers in adobo sauce, minced**
½   **cup raisins**
¼   **teaspoon ground cinnamon**
4   **skinned and boned chicken breasts**
1   **tablespoon peanut oil**
1   **teaspoon seasoning blend***

Melt butter in a 12-inch nonstick skillet over medium-high heat. Sauté sweet potatoes, in batches, in butter 8 minutes or until they begin to brown. Add apple; sauté 5 more minutes or until potatoes and apples are tender. Stir in brown sugar and corn syrup; cook 3 minutes or until mixture is bubbly. Stir in peppers, raisins, and cinnamon; cook 5 more minutes. Remove mixture from heat; keep warm.

Meanwhile, brush chicken breasts with oil; sprinkle evenly with seasoning blend. Grill, covered with grill lid, over medium-high heat (350° to 400°) 5 to 6 minutes on each side or until done. Remove from heat. Add chicken to sweet potato mixture, turning to coat chicken. **Makes:** 4 servings.
Prep: 13 min., **Cook:** 38 min.

Note: Preheat grill before starting this recipe so that it's ready when you need it.

*For testing purposes only, we used Morton's Nature's Seasons Seasoning Blend.

Mary Clifft
Cave Creek, Arizona

If you're trying to watch your sodium intake, use Morton's seasoned salt substitute, like **Mary** does, instead of seasoning blend. We preferred the recipe with the little bit of salt that the seasoning blend contributes.

Greenville Avenue Mesquite Chicken Sandwich

This spicy sauce is well worth the number of ingredients. Use any leftover sauce as a dip for chips or fries.

4　(5-ounce) skinned and boned chicken breasts
1　cup water
⅓　cup light teriyaki sauce
2　tablespoons lime juice
3　garlic cloves, minced
1　teaspoon mesquite liquid smoke
¼　teaspoon salt
¼　teaspoon ground ginger
1　tablespoon tequila or light teriyaki sauce
4　teaspoons mesquite chicken seasoning*
1　(4-ounce) can whole green chiles, drained and cut in half lengthwise
4　ounces Monterey Jack cheese with peppers or Monterey Jack, thinly sliced
4　kaiser rolls, split
Greenville Avenue Sauce

If desired, place chicken between 2 sheets of heavy-duty plastic wrap, and pound chicken to even out thickness.

Combine water and next 7 ingredients in a shallow dish or zip-top freezer bag; add chicken. Cover or seal, and marinate in refrigerator 20 minutes. Remove chicken from marinade, discarding marinade.

Grill, covered with grill lid, over medium-high heat (350° to 400°) 4 minutes on each side or until done. Sprinkle chicken breasts with chicken seasoning, and top each breast with ½ green chile and cheese; cover with grill lid, and cook until cheese is melted.

Place kaiser rolls, cut side down, on grill during last 2 minutes chicken grills; grill just until warmed.

To serve, spread each roll half with 1 teaspoon Greenville Avenue Sauce; top bottom half with chicken breast and remaining roll half. Serve with additional sauce, if desired. **Makes:** 4 servings.

Prep: 18 min., **Cook:** 17 min., **Other:** 20 min.

Tip: To keep your grill tidy, Bonnie recommends putting a piece of aluminum foil on your grill, then place cooked chicken breasts on foil before topping with chiles and cheese. This will keep cheese from dripping into grill.

*For testing purposes only, we used McCormick Mesquite Chicken Seasoning.

Greenville Avenue Sauce:

½　cup light mayonnaise
¼　cup nonfat sour cream
1　tablespoon milk
1　tablespoon minced dried tomatoes in oil
2　teaspoons minced pickled jalapeño peppers
2　teaspoons minced onion
1½ teaspoons white vinegar
¼　teaspoon dried parsley flakes
¼　teaspoon salt
¼　teaspoon garlic powder
¼　teaspoon seasoned pepper
¼　teaspoon hot sauce
⅛　teaspoon dried dillweed
⅛　teaspoon paprika
⅛　teaspoon ground cumin
⅛　teaspoon ground red pepper
⅛　teaspoon chili powder

Combine all ingredients in a small bowl; cover and chill. **Makes:** ¾ cup.
Prep: 10 min.

Note: This sauce can be prepared ahead and stored, covered, in the refrigerator until ready to serve.

Bonnie Nichols
Southlake, Texas

Bonnie created this recipe trying to duplicate a favorite dish she and her husband enjoy at a restaurant on Greenville Avenue in Dallas. Her husband wholeheartedly confirms that Bonnie succeeded. Don't let the long ingredient list discourage you—it's mostly small amounts of seasonings that add up to big flavor in the sauce. Her use of several light products keeps the sandwich on the healthy side.

Italian Dijon Chicken With Tomato Cream Pasta

Breadcrumb-crusted chicken adds crisp contrast to a bed of pasta with cream sauce.

2   cups soft breadcrumbs (homemade)
½   cup grated Parmesan cheese
½   cup chopped fresh parsley
1½ teaspoons salt
2   tablespoons dried Italian seasoning
¼   cup butter, melted
2   garlic cloves, minced
1   tablespoon Worcestershire sauce
2   tablespoons Dijon mustard
6   (6-ounce) skinned and boned chicken breasts
2   cups heavy whipping cream
3   (8-ounce) cans tomato sauce
1   (14.5-ounce) can diced tomatoes, drained
5   fully cooked bacon slices, chopped
⅓   cup chopped fresh basil
½   teaspoon pepper
12 ounces penne pasta, cooked

Combine first 6 ingredients in a shallow bowl; set aside.

Combine garlic, Worcestershire sauce, and mustard in a small bowl. Brush mustard mixture onto chicken breasts; press breadcrumb mixture on tops of chicken breasts. Place chicken on a baking sheet lined with nonstick aluminum foil. Bake at 375° for 25 to 27 minutes or until done.

Meanwhile, over medium-high heat, bring heavy cream to a boil in a large saucepan. Reduce heat, and simmer, uncovered, 15 minutes or until reduced by half. Add tomato sauce and next 4 ingredients; simmer 5 more minutes. Drizzle a little sauce over chicken. Toss pasta with remaining sauce. Serve chicken over pasta. **Makes:** 6 servings.
Prep: 8 min., **Cook:** 30 min.

Tip: Make your own soft breadcrumbs in a food processor using leftover bread.

Kerri Davis
Lexington, Kentucky

Chutney Chicken Bake

This stuffed chicken features a creamy center and a crispy coating topped with a wonderfully fruity sauce.

1   (8-ounce) package cream cheese, softened
2   teaspoons grated lemon rind
2   teaspoons grated orange rind
6   skinned and boned chicken breasts (about 3 pounds)
2   cups crushed cornflakes cereal
½   cup yellow cornmeal
1   teaspoon chopped fresh rosemary
½   teaspoon salt
½   teaspoon garlic powder
½   teaspoon pepper
¼   cup olive oil
2   (9-ounce) jars mango chutney

Combine first 3 ingredients in a small bowl; stir well.

Cut a 3½-inch horizontal slit through the thickest portion of each chicken breast, cutting to, but not through, other side, forming a pocket. Stuff cream cheese mixture evenly into each pocket.

Combine crushed cornflakes and next 5 ingredients in a shallow dish. Pour oil into a separate shallow dish. Dip each chicken breast in oil, then dredge in cornflakes mixture; transfer to a lightly greased 13- x 9-inch pan. Bake, uncovered, at 350° for 1 hour or until chicken is done.

Meanwhile, heat chutney in a small saucepan over medium heat until hot and bubbly. Serve over chicken breasts.
Makes: 6 servings.
Prep: 36 min., **Cook:** 1 hr.

Tip: To crush cornflakes easily, place cereal in a zip-top plastic bag, and seal. Crush cereal, using the ball of your hand, a rolling pin, or a heavy can.

Lisa Davis
Hallsville, Texas

Soba Noodles With Tarragon Grilled Chicken and Peppers

Soba are dark brownish-gray Japanese noodles made with buckwheat and wheat flour. You can substitute whole wheat spaghetti noodles for the soba noodles, if desired.

- 1¼ cups soy sauce, divided
- 4 teaspoons grated fresh ginger
- 1 cup extra-virgin olive oil, divided
- ⅔ cup finely chopped fresh tarragon, divided
- 1 teaspoon paprika, divided
- 2 teaspoons cracked pepper, divided
- 2 pounds skinned and boned chicken breasts
- 1 (12-ounce) jar roasted red bell peppers, drained
- 1 (12-ounce) package dried soba noodles
- 1 teaspoon salt
- 1½ teaspoons minced garlic
- 1 bunch green onions, chopped
- 1 (4-ounce) package goat cheese, crumbled
- Garnish: fresh tarragon sprigs

Stir together 1 cup soy sauce, ginger, ½ cup oil, ⅓ cup tarragon, ½ teaspoon paprika, and 1 teaspoon pepper in a large bowl.

Place chicken and bell peppers in a shallow dish; pour marinade over chicken and peppers. Cover and marinate in refrigerator 30 minutes.

Meanwhile, cook noodles in boiling salted water according to package directions, using 1 teaspoon salt. Drain and keep warm.

Remove chicken and peppers from marinade, discarding marinade.

Coat food grate with cooking spray; place on grill. Place chicken on grate.

Grill, covered with grill lid, over medium heat (300° to 350°) 6 minutes on each side or until done. Remove chicken to a serving platter. Place peppers on grill; cook 1 minute on each side or until thoroughly heated. Dice chicken, and slice peppers into strips.

Stir together remaining ¼ cup soy sauce, ½ cup oil, ⅓ cup tarragon, ½ teaspoon paprika, 1 teaspoon pepper, and garlic in a small bowl; pour over noodles. Stir in green onions, chicken, and peppers. Sprinkle with goat cheese; toss well. Garnish, if desired. **Makes:** 8 to 10 servings.

Prep: 22 min., **Cook:** 17 min., **Other:** 30 min.

Angela Doss
Edmond, Oklahoma

Crunchy Baked Chicken

Ranch-flavored croutons give everyday chicken a flavorful crunch.

- 1 cup Ranch-flavored croutons, crushed
- ¼ cup (1 ounce) shredded mozzarella cheese
- ¼ cup (1 ounce) shredded Parmesan cheese
- 1 teaspoon salt
- ½ teaspoon ground pepper
- 4 (6-ounce) skinned and boned chicken breasts
- ¼ cup milk
- ¼ cup butter or margarine, melted
- 1 teaspoon garlic powder
- 2 tablespoons lemon juice

Combine first 5 ingredients in a zip-top plastic bag. Dip chicken in milk. Add chicken to crouton mixture; seal and shake until coated.

Remove chicken from bag, discarding crouton mixture. Place chicken in a lightly greased 13- x 9-inch baking dish. Combine melted butter, garlic powder, and lemon juice. Drizzle over chicken.

Bake, uncovered, at 350° for 35 to 40 minutes or until chicken is done. **Makes:** 4 servings.

Prep: 12 min., **Cook:** 40 min..

Carey Collier
Dripping Springs, Texas

Soba Noodles With Tarragon
Grilled Chicken and Peppers

Asian Chicken, Cilantro, and Mandarin Salad

Ginger and citrus complement toasted sesame flavors to dress this entrée salad accented by crisp cabbage and pungent cilantro.

3 teaspoons dark sesame oil, divided
1 teaspoon kosher salt
1 teaspoon ground white pepper
1 pound chicken tenderloins
3 tablespoons rice wine vinegar
2 tablespoons canola oil or vegetable oil
2 tablespoons honey
2 tablespoons soy sauce
2 teaspoons sesame seeds, toasted
1 tablespoon grated fresh ginger
1 tablespoon orange juice
Vegetable cooking spray
2 (6-ounce) bags baby spinach
¼ small green cabbage, finely shredded (2 cups)
½ cup chopped fresh cilantro
¼ cup pine nuts, toasted
4 green onions, sliced (½ cup)
1 (11-ounce) can mandarin oranges, drained

Combine 2 teaspoons sesame oil, salt, and pepper in a medium bowl. Add chicken, and toss well. Cover and marinate in refrigerator 10 minutes.

Meanwhile, whisk remaining 1 teaspoon sesame oil, vinegar, and next 6 ingredients in a 1-cup glass measuring cup. Cover and set aside.

Remove chicken from marinade; discard marinade.

Coat chicken with cooking spray, and sauté in a large nonstick skillet over medium-high heat 3 minutes or until done. Remove chicken from skillet; set aside to cool.

Combine spinach and next 4 ingredients in a large bowl. Slice chicken diagonally into 1-inch pieces; toss with spinach mixture. Pour desired amount of dressing over spinach mixture; add oranges, and toss gently. **Makes:** 4 servings.
Prep: 21 min., **Cook:** 3 min.

Tip: Use a Microplane to grate peeled fresh ginger with ease.

Olga Czekalski
Olney, Maryland

Olga has a little dressing left over that she chills and uses as an Asian-inspired salad dressing for greens later in the week.

Enchiladas Verde

2 tablespoons olive oil
1 cup chopped onion (about 1 medium)
1 cup chopped green bell pepper (about 1 medium)
¾ cup diced poblano chile pepper (about 1 medium)
2 garlic cloves, chopped
4 cups shredded roasted chicken
1 (16-ounce) jar salsa verde, divided
½ cup chopped fresh cilantro
1 teaspoon ground cumin
20 (6-inch) corn tortillas*
1 cup milk
½ (8-ounce) package cream cheese, softened
⅛ teaspoon ground red pepper
½ teaspoon salt
¼ teaspoon ground black pepper
1 cup (4 ounces) shredded Monterey Jack cheese with peppers

Heat oil in a large skillet over medium-high heat. Add onion and next 3 ingredients; cook 3 minutes or until tender. Add shredded chicken, 1 cup salsa verde, cilantro, and cumin; toss well to blend.

Wrap tortillas loosely in heavy-duty plastic wrap; heat in microwave according to package directions. Spoon about ¼ cup chicken mixture down center of each tortilla; roll up. Place seam side down in a lightly greased 13- x 9-inch baking dish.

Combine remaining salsa verde, milk, and next 4 ingredients in a small saucepan. Cook over medium heat 5 minutes or until smooth, whisking occasionally. Pour sauce evenly over tortillas; sprinkle with Monterey Jack cheese. Bake, uncovered, at 350° for 15 to 20 minutes or until cheese melts.
Makes: 10 servings.
Prep: 40 min., **Cook:** 28 min.

*We used traditional corn tortillas in this recipe, but if your family prefers the flour variety, substitute 10 (8-inch) flour tortillas, and use ½ cup filling in each.

Tip: Salsa verde is a green salsa usually made from tomatillos, cilantro, and peppers; look for it in the ethnic foods section of supermarkets.

Thom McCarthey
San Francisco, California

We spiced up **Thom's** recipe by adding salsa verde to the cream sauce and filling, and a sprinkle of pepper Jack cheese to the top before baking. We also decreased the prep time a bit by using a deli-roasted chicken instead of cooking our own. If you're watching the fat in your diet, you can use nonfat milk and cream cheese like Thom did, but we preferred the full fat products in this particular recipe.

Indonesian-Style Chicken With Confetti Rice

This chicken dish will really tease your taste buds. The sweet taste of grilled pineapple mixed with the oh-so-good taste of the peanutty marinade gives this dish a cause for celebration.

1 (20-ounce) can pineapple chunks in juice, undrained
1 pound chicken breast tenders, cut into 1-inch cubes
⅓ cup all-purpose flour
⅓ cup honey-roasted chunky peanut butter
2½ teaspoons Chinese hot mustard
¾ teaspoon dried crushed red pepper
¼ teaspoon kosher salt
Confetti Rice

Drain pineapple chunks, reserving 6 tablespoons juice.

Dredge chicken in flour; place in a large zip-top freezer bag.

Combine 3 tablespoons reserved pineapple juice, peanut butter, and next 3 ingredients. Add peanut butter paste to freezer bag; seal and squeeze bag until chicken is coated. Let stand 10 minutes.

Remove chicken from marinade, discarding marinade.

Thread chicken and pineapple alternately onto 8 (12-inch) skewers.

Coat a food grate with cooking spray; place on grill over medium-high heat (350° to 400°). Place kabobs on grate, and grill, covered with grill lid, 3 minutes on each side or until done. Serve with Confetti Rice. **Makes:** 4 servings.

Prep: 15 min., **Cook:** 6 min., **Other:** 10 min.

Vickie choreographed this recipe to make use of all the down time, making the total time to prepare both recipes under 40 minutes. While the chicken marinates 10 minutes, she gets the rice going; while the rice simmers, she grills the kabobs.

Confetti Rice:

3 tablespoons butter or margarine
⅓ cup chopped onion
¾ cup uncooked long-grain rice
1½ cups water
3 tablespoons reserved pineapple juice
1 tablespoon chopped fresh parsley
1 teaspoon kosher salt
1 teaspoon dried crushed red pepper

Melt butter in a medium saucepan; add onion, and sauté over medium-high heat 2 minutes or until tender. Stir in rice, and sauté 1 minute. Stir in water and remaining 4 ingredients; cover, reduce heat, and simmer 20 minutes or until tender. **Makes:** 4 servings.

Prep: 5 min., **Cook:** 24 min.

Note: If using wooden skewers, soak them in water for 30 minutes to prevent them from burning.

Vickie Medlin
Dallas, Texas

Lemony Chicken Couscous

This dish tastes great served hot or cold, making leftovers handy for brown-bag lunches. Try it in pita pockets.

1 (10-ounce) package couscous
4 cups chopped cooked chicken, heated if desired
¾ cup olive oil
3 tablespoons lemon juice
1 (15.8-ounce) can great Northern beans, rinsed and drained
3 medium carrots, sliced
2 celery ribs, chopped
6 green onions, chopped
1½ teaspoons salt
½ teaspoon pepper

Cook couscous according to package directions. Spoon couscous into a large serving bowl, and fluff with a fork. Stir in chicken and remaining ingredients. Serve immediately, or cover and chill. **Makes:** 4 to 6 servings.

Prep: 12 min., **Cook:** 5 min.

Kimberley Theobald
Owings Mills, Maryland

Kimberley cooks 4 boned chicken breasts to yield 4 cups chopped cooked chicken. This is a great dish for using leftover chopped cooked chicken or turkey.

Confetti Chicken Cakes With White Wine Cream Sauce

Look for ground chicken in the meat department of your grocery store. If you can't find it, ask the butcher to grind chicken breasts for you, or grind them yourself in the food processor.

½ cup ground pecans
½ cup all-purpose flour
2 tablespoons butter or margarine
¼ cup finely chopped green bell pepper
¼ cup finely chopped red bell pepper
¼ cup finely chopped yellow bell pepper
¼ cup finely chopped red onion
¼ cup fine, dry breadcrumbs (store-bought)
¼ cup mayonnaise
1 tablespoon dried parsley flakes
2 teaspoons salt
½ teaspoon garlic powder
½ teaspoon ground red pepper
⅛ teaspoon ground nutmeg
2 pounds ground chicken
½ cup vegetable oil
White Wine Cream Sauce

Combine ground pecans and flour in a shallow dish; set aside.

Melt butter over medium-high heat in a large skillet. Add green bell pepper and next 3 ingredients; sauté 3 minutes or until tender.

Combine vegetables, breadcrumbs, and next 6 ingredients in a large bowl. Crumble in ground chicken; mix gently to combine. Shape mixture into 8 (1-inch-thick) patties, and dredge in pecan mixture.

Heat oil in a large skillet over medium-high heat; cook chicken cakes, in batches, 3 to 4 minutes on each side or until golden brown and chicken is done. Drain on paper towels. Serve with White Wine Cream Sauce.
Makes: 4 servings.
Prep: 19 min., **Cook:** 12 min.

White Wine Cream Sauce:

½ (8-ounce) package cream cheese, cubed
4 ounces pasteurized prepared cheese product, cubed
½ cup dry white wine
½ cup chicken broth
½ cup whipping cream
¼ cup all-purpose flour
⅛ teaspoon salt
⅛ teaspoon ground nutmeg
⅛ teaspoon ground red pepper
⅛ teaspoon ground black pepper

Combine all ingredients in a small saucepan; cook over medium heat, whisking constantly, 5 minutes or until thickened and cheese melts. **Makes:** 2½ cups.
Prep: 7 min., **Cook:** 5 min.

Tip: Find ground pecans in the baking or snack section of your grocery store, or grind your own in the food processor.

Gail P. Mathis
Rayne, Louisiana

Sometimes **Gail** turns these golden chicken cakes into a sandwich by serving them on burger buns.

Hawaiian Turkey Tournedos With Cranberry Chutney

Served with a wonderful cinnamon-berry chutney, this tangy-sweet turkey recipe is to die for.

1   cup soy sauce
¾   cup sugar
½   cup red wine vinegar
1   teaspoon sherry or soy sauce
1   teaspoon garlic powder
2   (1½-pound) turkey tenderloins
2   (20-ounce) cans pineapple slices in juice, drained
Cranberry Chutney

Combine first 5 ingredients in a large zip-top freezer bag; add tenderloins. Seal bag, and marinate in refrigerator 8 hours, turning occasionally.

Remove tenderloins from marinade, discarding marinade.

Coat a food grate with cooking spray; place on grill over medium-high heat (350° to 400°). Place tenderloins on grate, and grill, covered with grill lid, 11 minutes on each side or until a meat thermometer inserted into thickest portion registers 165°. Remove from heat; cover and let stand 5 minutes or until temperature registers 170° before slicing.

Add pineapple slices to grill; grill 3 minutes on each side. Serve turkey with Cranberry Chutney and grilled pineapple. **Makes:** 4 servings.
Prep: 8 min., **Cook:** 29 min., **Other:** 8 hrs.

Cranberry Chutney:

1   (16-ounce) can whole-berry cranberry sauce
⅓   cup raspberry preserves
1½   tablespoons sugar
1   tablespoon orange juice
¼   teaspoon ground cinnamon
⅓   cup chopped pecans, toasted

Combine first 5 ingredients in a large saucepan; cook over medium heat 6 minutes or until smooth, stirring constantly. Remove from heat; stir in pecans. Cool completely. **Makes:** 2¼ cups.
Prep: 5 min., **Cook:** 6 min.

Jamie Tarence
Birmingham, Alabama

Jamie slices the turkey into tournedos before grilling, but we sliced them after grilling for easier handling on the grill and extra moist meat.

Turkey Rollatini With Fruit and Nut Stuffing

Your family will love these aromatic turkey rolls with fruit, toasted nuts, and fresh breadcrumbs inside and a tasty mushroom wine sauce drizzled over the top.

1½ teaspoons salt, divided
1   cup cooked long-grain rice *
⅓   cup raisins
¼   cup chopped dried apricots
¼   cup chopped pecans, toasted
¼   cup soft breadcrumbs (homemade)
¼   cup butter or margarine, softened
1   egg white, lightly beaten
6   (4-ounce) turkey breast cutlets
2   tablespoons all-purpose flour
2   tablespoons olive oil, divided
1   (8-ounce) package sliced fresh mushrooms
¼   cup minced shallots
½   teaspoon dried thyme
1   cup dry white wine
1   tablespoon butter or margarine
Garnish: fresh thyme sprigs

Combine ½ teaspoon salt and next 7 ingredients in a large bowl; set aside.

Place turkey between 2 sheets of heavy-duty plastic wrap; flatten to ¼-inch thickness, using a mallet or rolling pin.

Spread rice mixture evenly over turkey, leaving a ¼-inch border.

Roll up turkey, jellyroll fashion, starting with short sides; secure with string.

Sprinkle turkey rolls evenly with ½ teaspoon salt; dredge in flour.

Heat 1 tablespoon oil in a large nonstick skillet over medium heat. Add mushrooms, shallots, and dried thyme; cook 6 minutes or until tender. Remove from skillet; set aside.

Heat remaining 1 tablespoon oil in skillet over medium-high heat. Add turkey rolls; cook 8 to 10 minutes or until browned, turning as needed. Add wine and mushroom mixture. Bring to a boil; cover, reduce heat, and simmer 20 minutes or until turkey is done. Transfer turkey rolls to a cutting surface; keep warm.

Increase heat, and bring mushroom mixture to a boil; cook 3 minutes or until slightly thickened. Stir in 1 tablespoon butter and remaining ½ teaspoon salt. Slice turkey rolls, and place on a serving platter; spoon mushroom sauce evenly over turkey. Garnish, if desired.
Makes: 6 servings.
Prep: 26 min., **Cook:** 39 min.

*Start with ⅓ cup uncooked long-grain rice to yield 1 cup cooked rice.

Gilda Lester
Wilmington, North Carolina

Mexican Stuffed Peppers With Chipotle-Sour Cream Sauce

This meat mixture also makes a tasty filling for flour tortillas.

1   pound ground turkey
1   pound Mexican chorizo
    sausage, crumbled
½   cup chopped sweet onion
½   cup roasted red bell peppers,
    drained and chopped
1   jalapeño pepper, seeded and
    diced
1   Anaheim pepper, seeded and
    diced
4   garlic cloves, minced
½   cup frozen whole kernel corn,
    thawed
¼   cup crushed tortilla chips
1   teaspoon lime juice
1   tablespoon chopped fresh
    cilantro
¼   teaspoon salt
½   teaspoon pepper
1   teaspoon ground cumin
½   teaspoon chili powder
2   cups (8 ounces) shredded
    Monterey Jack cheese with
    peppers, divided
4   red bell peppers, halved
    lengthwise and seeded
1   (14.5-ounce) can diced
    tomatoes, drained

1   (10-ounce) can mild enchilada
    sauce
    Chipotle-Sour Cream Sauce

Cook first 7 ingredients in a large skillet over medium-high heat, stirring until meat crumbles and is no longer pink; drain and return to skillet.
Add corn and next 7 ingredients to meat mixture; stir gently. Stir in 1 cup cheese. Spoon meat mixture evenly into pepper halves. Arrange in a lightly greased 13- x 9-inch baking dish.
Stir together tomatoes and enchilada sauce in a small bowl; pour over peppers.
Bake, uncovered, at 350° for 40 to 45 minutes. Top evenly with remaining 1 cup cheese; bake 5 more minutes or until cheese melts. Serve with Chipotle-Sour Cream Sauce. **Makes:** 8 servings.
Prep: 44 min., **Cook:** 50 min.

Debbie uses mild chorizo and enchilada sauce in these perky peppers, but you can crank up the heat by using hot versions, if you'd like.

Chipotle-Sour Cream Sauce:

There's plenty of time to stir up this sauce while the peppers bake, but for a quick and easy substitution, stir ½ cup bottled chipotle salsa or your favorite salsa into sour cream.

1   (16-ounce) container sour
    cream
½   cup roasted corn with black
    bean salsa
2   chipotle peppers in adobo sauce
1   tablespoon adobo sauce from
    can
1   tablespoon chopped fresh
    cilantro
1   teaspoon lime juice
½   teaspoon salt
½   teaspoon ground cumin
¼   teaspoon pepper
2   garlic cloves, halved

Process all ingredients in a blender or food processor until blended. Cover and chill. **Makes:** 2¾ cups.
Prep: 10 min.

Debbie Figueroa
Bellingham, Washington

Savory Cilantro-Lime Fish Tacos

Cilantro, lime, and fish give these tacos a light, refreshing change from traditional beef tacos.

1   tablespoon fresh lemon juice
2   teaspoons fresh lime juice
2   teaspoons fajita seasoning
¼   teaspoon salt
¼   teaspoon pepper
4   (6-ounce) grouper fillets
    (about 2 pounds)
1   tablespoon butter or margarine,
    cut into thin slices
1   tablespoon chopped fresh
    cilantro
10 (8-inch) flour tortillas
    Cilantro-Lime Sauce
    Shredded Monterey Jack cheese
    Chopped tomatoes
    Guacamole
    Salsa

Combine first 5 ingredients in a small bowl; brush over fish to coat. Place fish fillets in a large skillet coated with cooking spray over medium heat; top each fillet with butter and cilantro. Sauté 4 minutes on each side or until fish flakes with fork. Break fish into pieces with fork.

Heat tortillas according to package directions. Divide fish evenly among tortillas; drizzle with Cilantro-Lime Sauce. Top with cheese, chopped tomatoes, guacamole, and salsa; fold in half. **Makes:** 5 servings.

Prep: 7 min., **Cook:** 8 min.

Cilantro-Lime Sauce:

½   cup fresh cilantro leaves
½   cup lime juice
½   cup sour cream
¼   cup olive oil
1   tablespoon sugar
½   teaspoon salt
½   teaspoon pepper

Place all ingredients in a food processor or blender; process until smooth, stopping to scrape down sides.

Prep: 7 min.

Tip: Mahi mahi and snapper are good substitutes for grouper in this recipe.

Amy Templeton
Mount Pleasant, South Carolina

Grilled Halibut With Mediterranean Salsa

The distinctive flavors of fennel, grapefruit, and kalamata olives pair nicely with mild-flavored halibut.

½   cup ruby red grapefruit juice
3   tablespoons olive oil
2   tablespoons dry white wine
1   shallot, minced
2   garlic cloves, minced
½   teaspoon salt
¼   teaspoon pepper
4   (8-ounce) halibut fillets*
1   pink or red grapefruit, peeled
    and sectioned
1   fennel bulb, vertically sliced
1   cup chopped fresh arugula
½   cup chopped red onion
⅓   cup pitted, chopped kalamata
    olives
1   garlic clove, minced
2   tablespoons olive oil
1   teaspoon sugar
½   teaspoon salt
¼   teaspoon pepper

Combine first 7 ingredients in a large zip-top freezer bag; add fish. Seal and marinate in refrigerator while preparing salsa, turning occasionally.

Coarsely chop grapefruit sections. Combine grapefruit sections and next 9 ingredients; toss gently. Remove fish from marinade; discard marinade.

Coat food grate with cooking spray; place on grill over medium-high heat (350° to 400°). Place fish on grate, and grill, covered with grill lid, 6 to 8 minutes on each side or until fish flakes with a fork. Serve with salsa.

Makes: 4 servings.

Prep: 30 min., **Cook:** 16 min.

*If halibut isn't available, use any firm white fish such as grouper or orange roughy.

Amy Sutherland
Portland, Maine

Amy serves this Mediterranean-inspired medley over couscous. She also adds coriander seeds to the salsa, but we omitted them to highlight the other distinctive flavors in the dish.

Bourbon-Marinated Grilled Salmon

¼ cup fresh lemon juice (about 6 small lemons)
¼ cup soy sauce
¼ cup bourbon
3 garlic cloves, pressed
3 tablespoons dark brown sugar
2 tablespoons extra-virgin olive oil
4 teaspoons seafood seasoning*
4 teaspoons chopped fresh chives
2 teaspoons finely chopped onion
½ teaspoon salt
½ teaspoon cracked pepper
4 (8-ounce) salmon fillets (1 inch thick)
Garnish: fresh chives

Combine first 11 ingredients in a large zip-top freezer bag. Add salmon, and seal bag. Marinate in refrigerator at least 3 hours.

Remove salmon from marinade, discarding marinade. Grill, covered with grill lid, over medium-high heat (350° to 400°) 12 minutes or until fish flakes with a fork, turning once. Garnish, if desired. **Makes:** 4 servings.

Prep: 13 min., **Cook:** 12 min., **Other:** 3 hrs.

Note: Grill the salmon with the flesh side down first for the prettiest grill marks. If using a different thickness of salmon, adjust grilling time accordingly.

*For testing purposes only, we used McCormick Seafood Seasoning.

Jeani Smith
Lewisville, North Carolina

For even more flavor, **Jeani** marinates the fish overnight.

Sensational Stuffed Salmon

This simple but impressive stuffed salmon will wow any dinner guest.

4 fully cooked bacon slices, chopped
1½ cups chopped baby portobello mushrooms
½ cup chive-and-onion cream cheese
½ (16-ounce) loaf French bread, crust removed
2 tablespoons unsalted butter, melted
¼ cup minced fresh Italian parsley
4 (6-ounce) skinless salmon fillets (about 1 inch thick)
½ teaspoon salt
¼ teaspoon freshly ground pepper
Garnish: lemon wedges

Cook bacon in a medium skillet over medium-high heat 1 minute; remove and drain on paper towels. Sauté mushrooms in hot drippings, stirring occasionally, 5 minutes or until lightly browned. Place mushrooms in a small bowl; cool 10 minutes. Add bacon and cream cheese to mushrooms; stir until blended.

Meanwhile, tear bread into pieces, and pulse in a food processor or blender to make coarse crumbs. Stir in melted butter and parsley; set aside.

Cut a slit about 2 inches long down the top of each salmon fillet without cutting through the bottom. Divide cream cheese mixture evenly among fillets, pressing into slits. Sprinkle with salt and pepper. Press breadcrumbs onto top of fillets. Place on an aluminum foil-lined baking sheet. Bake at 450° for 12 to 15 minutes or until fish flakes with a fork. Place on a serving platter, and garnish, if desired. **Makes:** 4 servings.

Prep: 11 min., **Cook:** 21 min.

Jamie Miller
Maple Grove, Minnesota

Jamie cooks the ready-to-serve bacon for 1 minute to crisp it a little before stirring it into the filling and to get a little bit of drippings for sautéing the mushrooms.

Cherry-Chipotle Salmon Steaks

Chipotle peppers and cherry preserves mingle to make a spicy-sweet sauce to serve over the salmon and wild rice duo.

1　(5-ounce) package long-grain and wild rice
⅓　cup dried cherries
1　tablespoon vegetable oil
¼　cup chopped shallots
1　tablespoon minced garlic
1　teaspoon minced fresh ginger
½　cup dry red wine
⅓　cup cherry preserves
3　chipotle peppers in adobo sauce, minced (about 2 tablespoons)
4　(6-ounce) salmon fillets
½　teaspoon salt
½　teaspoon freshly ground black pepper
1　tablespoon vegetable oil

Cook rice according to package directions, adding dried cherries.

Meanwhile, heat 1 tablespoon oil over medium-high heat in a small saucepan. Add shallots, garlic, and ginger; cook 2 minutes or until tender. Add wine, preserves, and minced peppers. Bring to a boil over medium-high heat, and cook 2 minutes; set aside, and keep warm.

Sprinkle fillets with salt and pepper. Heat 1 tablespoon oil in a large nonstick skillet over medium-high heat; add salmon, and cook 4 to 5 minutes on each side or until fish flakes with a fork. Serve over wild rice with cherry chipotle sauce. **Makes:** 4 servings.

Prep: 12 min., **Cook:** 22 min.

Margee Berry
White Salmon, Washington

Margee uses the dried cherries in the sauce, but we added them to the rice for more texture. Margee grills the salmon, which adds great flavor, but we found it easier to cook indoors with the rice and sauce that need preparing. The salmon was just as good sizzled over medium-high heat, which browns it nicely.

Butter Pecan Salmon en Croûte

This sweet, buttery-tasting fish melts in your mouth.

¼　cup butter or margarine, softened
½　cup chopped pecans, toasted
2　tablespoons chopped green onions
2　garlic cloves, minced
2　tablespoons light brown sugar
1　tablespoon hazelnut liqueur
12　sheets frozen phyllo pastry, thawed in the refrigerator
¼　cup butter or margarine, melted
4　(6-ounce) skinless salmon fillets

Combine first 6 ingredients in a small bowl; set aside.

Unfold phyllo on a lightly floured surface. Stack 3 sheets, brushing lightly with melted butter between sheets. (Keep remaining sheets covered with a damp towel.)

Place 1 salmon fillet topped with one-fourth of pecan mixture on a short side of phyllo stack; gently roll up, folding in long sides. Repeat procedure with remaining phyllo sheets, melted butter, salmon, and pecan mixture. Place on a lightly greased baking sheet.

Bake at 425° for 20 minutes or until crispy and light brown. **Makes:** 4 servings.

Prep: 18 min., **Cook:** 20 min.

Kristine Leo Belile
Geneva, New York

Kristine uses twice as much brown sugar and adds vanilla extract to these pastry-wrapped salmon fillets. We added green onions and garlic for a savory touch.

Grilled Salmon With Capers

Grilled Salmon With Capers

½ cup balsamic vinegar
¼ cup turbinado sugar or
   2 tablespoons brown sugar
1 teaspoon sesame oil
½ teaspoon minced fresh ginger
2 green onions, chopped
6 (6-ounce) salmon fillets
1 cup mayonnaise
2 tablespoons Dijon mustard
2 tablespoons drained capers
1 tablespoon lemon juice
1 tablespoon chopped fresh
   dill
½ teaspoon sugar
Garnish: fresh dill

Combine vinegar, sugar, oil, ginger, and green onions in a zip-top freezer bag; add salmon. Seal and marinate in refrigerator 4 hours, turning occasionally.

Meanwhile, stir together mayonnaise and next 5 ingredients; cover and chill until serving time.

Remove salmon from marinade, discarding marinade. Coat food grate with cooking spray; place on grill over medium-high heat (350° to 400°).

Place salmon on grate, and grill, covered with grill lid, 5 to 6 minutes on each side or until fish flakes with a fork. Serve salmon with mayonnaise mixture. Garnish, if desired. **Makes:** 6 servings.

Prep: 10 min., **Cook:** 12 min., **Other:** 4 hrs.

Judy Travis
Demopolis, Alabama

Judy grills the salmon over indirect heat, but we had good results grilling it over direct coals, which is a little quicker.

Pineapple-Glazed Sea Bass With Tropical Rice Pilaf

If sea bass isn't available in your area, simply substitute another firm white fish such as grouper or halibut.

Tropical Rice Pilaf
2 tablespoons sugar
2 tablespoons pineapple tidbits *
1 tablespoon pineapple juice
1¼ teaspoons minced fresh ginger
1 garlic clove, minced
2 tablespoons rice vinegar
1 tablespoon chopped fresh basil
¼ teaspoon ground red pepper
4 (6-ounce) sea bass fillets
½ teaspoon salt
½ teaspoon ground black pepper
1 teaspoon canola oil

Prepare Tropical Rice Pilaf.

Meanwhile, combine sugar and next 4 ingredients in a small saucepan. Bring to a boil over high heat; reduce heat, and simmer 3 minutes, stirring occasionally. Remove from heat; stir in vinegar, basil, and red pepper.

Sprinkle both sides of fish fillets with salt and black pepper.

Heat oil in a large ovenproof nonstick skillet over medium-high heat. Add fish; cook 2 minutes. Turn fish over. Spoon pineapple glaze evenly over fish.

Broil 4 minutes or until fish flakes with a fork. Serve over Tropical Rice Pilaf.

Makes: 4 servings.

Prep: 8 min., **Cook:** 11 min.

Tropical Rice Pilaf:

2 cups water
1 cup uncooked long-grain rice
2 teaspoons salt
1 cup pineapple tidbits *
½ cup chopped carrot
½ cup lightly salted cashews
1 to 2 habanero peppers, seeded
   and minced *
1 garlic clove, minced
1 teaspoon lime rind
2 tablespoons fresh lime juice
1 tablespoon canola oil
1 tablespoon chopped fresh
   cilantro
1 tablespoon fresh lemon juice
1 teaspoon grated fresh
   ginger

Bring water to a boil in a medium saucepan; stir in rice and salt. Cover, reduce heat, and simmer 20 minutes or until rice is tender. Stir in pineapple and next 10 ingredients. Remove from heat; cover and keep warm. **Makes:** 5 cups.

Prep: 22 min., **Cook:** 22 min.

Tip: If you don't own an ovenproof skillet, wrap the handle of your skillet with heavy-duty aluminum foil.

*Reserve pineapple juice from a 20-ounce can of pineapple tidbits for this recipe. Habanero peppers are extremely hot, so use only 1 chile if you prefer a tad less heat. Or you can substitute milder jalapeño pepper for the habanero.

Maya Packard
Charlotte, North Carolina

Grilled Swordfish With Olive Tapenade

This tapenade pairs well with just about any fish. It's also delicious served with pita chips.

- **4** **(6-ounce) swordfish fillets (about 1 inch thick)**
- **2** **tablespoons olive oil**
- **¼** **teaspoon salt**
- **¼** **teaspoon pepper**
- **1** **(4½-ounce) can sliced ripe olives**
- **2** **tablespoons capers**
- **¼** **cup dried tomatoes in oil, coarsely chopped**
- **3** **anchovy fillets, minced**
- **3** **tablespoons fresh lemon juice**
- **2** **garlic cloves, minced**
- **1** **tablespoon minced fresh thyme**
- **1** **tablespoon minced fresh oregano**
- **¼** **cup olive oil**

Brush fish with 2 tablespoons olive oil, and sprinkle salt and pepper evenly on both sides of fish.

Grill fish, covered with grill lid, over medium-high heat (350° to 400°) 6 to 8 minutes on each side or until fish flakes with a fork.

Stir together olives and next 8 ingredients. Serve over grilled swordfish. **Makes:** 4 servings.

Prep: 5 min., **Cook:** 16 min.

Tip: Tapenade can be prepared a day in advance and chilled.

Louis deLaunay
Grapevine, Texas

Louis has a flair for pairing big flavors—olives, capers, dried tomatoes, anchovies, garlic, and herbs—as seen in this dish hailing from France's Provence region.

Grilled Swordfish With Olive Tapenade

Grilled Sicilian Swordfish

This chunky tomato sauce adds a sweet and tangy twist to any grilled fish.

3   tablespoons olive oil
2   tablespoons grated lemon rind
⅓   cup fresh lemon juice
2   tablespoons minced fresh rosemary, divided
1½ teaspoons salt, divided
1   teaspoon pepper, divided
4   swordfish steaks (about 1 inch thick)
1   medium onion, halved and thinly sliced
2   celery ribs, thinly sliced
2   teaspoons fennel seeds
1   bay leaf
1   cup orange juice
1   (14.5-ounce) can stewed tomatoes with sweet onions, undrained
½   cup raisins
1½ teaspoons balsamic vinegar
¼   cup minced fresh Italian parsley
Lemon wedges

Combine first 3 ingredients, 1 tablespoon rosemary, 1 teaspoon salt, and ½ teaspoon pepper in a large zip-top freezer bag. Add swordfish; seal and marinate in refrigerator 15 minutes.

Coat a medium nonstick skillet with cooking spray. Cook onion and celery over medium-high heat 5 minutes or until vegetables are tender. Add fennel seeds, bay leaf, and remaining 1 tablespoon rosemary; cook 1 more minute. Add orange juice, increase heat, and boil 8 minutes. Add tomatoes and raisins; reduce heat, and simmer 10 minutes. Stir in balsamic vinegar and remaining salt and pepper; discard bay leaf. Cover sauce, and keep warm.

Remove swordfish from marinade; discard marinade. Grill fish, covered with grill lid, over high heat (400° to 500°) 3 to 4 minutes on each side or until fish flakes with a fork.

Divide sauce evenly among 4 serving plates; top with swordfish steaks. Sprinkle with parsley, and serve with lemon wedges. **Makes:** 4 servings.
Prep: 18 min., **Cook:** 31 min., **Other:** 15 min.

Tip: Substitute any firm fish for swordfish.

Jamie Miller
Maple Grove, Minnesota

Pistachio-Crusted Trout With Pineapple-Lime Sauce

Lime marmalade imparts a unique flavor to the sauce, but if you can't find it, substitute orange or lemon marmalade.

1   cup lime marmalade *
¼   cup chicken broth
1   (8-ounce) can crushed pineapple in juice, drained
2   dashes hot sauce
6   tablespoons butter or margarine, divided
½   cup pistachios
¼   cup yellow cornmeal
¼   cup fine, dry breadcrumbs (store-bought)
2   tablespoons chopped fresh parsley
¼   teaspoon salt
⅛   teaspoon pepper
4   (8-ounce) filleted whole trout
¼   cup mayonnaise
Garnish: lime wedges

Combine first 4 ingredients and 2 tablespoons butter in a 1-quart saucepan; cook, uncovered, over medium-low heat until marmalade and butter melt, stirring occasionally. Remove from heat; cover and keep warm.

Meanwhile, process pistachios in a food processor until finely ground, but still dry (do not overprocess into a paste). Combine ground pistachios, cornmeal, and next 4 ingredients in a shallow dish.

Brush trout with mayonnaise; dredge in pistachio mixture. Melt 2 tablespoons butter in a large nonstick skillet over medium-high heat. Cook 2 trout, skin side up, in butter 2 to 3 minutes or until browned; turn trout, and cook 3 more minutes or until fish flakes with a fork. Repeat procedure with remaining 2 tablespoons butter and remaining 2 trout. Serve trout with sauce. Garnish, if desired. **Makes:** 4 servings.
Prep: 6 min., **Cook:** 12 min.

*For testing purposes only, we used Rose's Lime Marmalade.

Melinda Womack
Highlands, North Carolina

Melinda uses trout fillets weighing about 8 ounces each for this recipe, but we had a hard time finding trout that large locally. We used 8-ounce whole trout fillets, or butterflied trout. If you use larger single fillets, you may need to cook them a little longer.

Peanut-Encrusted Tilapia With Orange Curry Sauce on Coconut-Basil Rice

This dish gives you a taste of the tropics with a combination of coconut, fish, and citrus flavors. It's quicker to make than it looks. Simply start the rice and prepare the fish and sauce as the rice cooks.

Coconut-Basil Rice
Orange Curry Sauce
1½ cups dry-roasted peanuts
1½ cups classic seasoned croutons
2   large eggs
¼   cup milk
4   (6-ounce) tilapia fillets
2   tablespoons olive oil
1   (11-ounce) can mandarin
     oranges, drained

Prepare Coconut-Basil Rice.
Prepare Orange Curry Sauce.
While the rice cooks, process peanuts and croutons in a food processor or blender until finely chopped. Whisk together eggs and milk. Dip fish in egg mixture; dredge in peanut mixture.
Heat oil in a large nonstick skillet over medium heat. Add fish; cook 4 minutes on each side or until fish flakes with a fork. Serve over Coconut-Basil Rice. Pour Orange Curry Sauce over fish. Top each serving with mandarin oranges.
Makes: 4 servings.
Prep: 7 min., **Cook:** 8 min.

Pamela recommends refrigerating the peanut-coated fish while the oil heats in the skillet, or up to 20 minutes, so the coating will stick to the fish and not fall off when fried.

Coconut-Basil Rice:
1   cup water
1   cup coconut milk
1   cup uncooked long-grain rice
6   green onions, thinly sliced
6   tablespoons chopped fresh basil
2   tablespoons olive oil
1   teaspoon ground ginger
3   garlic cloves, minced
2   serrano chile peppers, seeded
     and minced

Combine water and coconut milk in a medium saucepan; bring to a boil. Stir in rice and remaining 6 ingredients. Cover, reduce heat, and simmer 20 minutes or until rice is tender. **Makes:** 3 cups.
Prep: 7 min., **Cook:** 22 min.

Orange Curry Sauce:
¼   cup butter or margarine
¼   cup all-purpose flour
1   cup orange juice
1   cup milk
1   tablespoon curry powder

Melt butter in a small heavy saucepan over medium-low heat. Gradually add flour, whisking until smooth; cook 1 minute, whisking constantly. Gradually add orange juice; cook over medium heat, whisking constantly, until thickened and bubbly. Gradually add milk and curry powder; cook 5 minutes or until thickened, whisking constantly.
Makes: 2 cups.
Prep: 2 min., **Cook:** 12 min.

Note: When working with hot peppers, wear plastic gloves to protect your hands from irritating oils.

Pamela Van Fleet
Alpharetta, Georgia

Caribbean Peach Salsa on Grilled Tuna Steaks

Canned peaches work well in this recipe year-round, but sweet, juicy fresh peaches are wonderful in the summer.

3 tablespoons olive oil, divided
¾ teaspoon salt, divided
½ teaspoon freshly ground pepper, divided
2 (15¼-ounce) cans sliced peaches in heavy syrup, drained and diced (about 2 cups diced)
¾ cup drained canned black beans, rinsed
⅔ cup diced red onion
2 tablespoons minced, seeded serrano chile peppers (about 2 small)
1 garlic clove, minced
1½ tablespoons chopped fresh cilantro
1 teaspoon ground cumin
1 teaspoon chili powder
1 teaspoon grated lime rind
1½ tablespoons fresh lime juice
¼ cup fresh lemon juice
6 (6-ounce) tuna steaks (1 inch thick)

Stir together 1 tablespoon olive oil, ¼ teaspoon salt, ¼ teaspoon pepper, and next 10 ingredients in a medium bowl. Cover and set aside.

Combine remaining 2 tablespoons olive oil, remaining ½ teaspoon salt, remaining ¼ teaspoon pepper, and lemon juice; brush over tuna steaks. Grill, covered with grill lid, over medium-high heat (350° to 400°) 8 to 10 minutes or to desired degree of doneness, turning once. Serve tuna with peach mixture. **Makes:** 6 servings.
Prep: 25 min., **Cook:** 10 min.

Sally Hastings
Stuart, Florida

White Bean Tuna Salad

Linda serves this zesty tuna salad as a gyro, encased in a pita that she heats on the grill. We enjoyed it as a main-dish salad over lettuce with toasted pita chips on the side.

1 (12-ounce) can white tuna in water, drained and flaked
1 (15.8-ounce) can great Northern beans, rinsed and drained
2 (2-ounce) jars diced pimiento, drained
3 tablespoons chopped red onion
2 teaspoons chopped fresh dill
1 teaspoon dried oregano
½ teaspoon salt
½ teaspoon pepper
2 tablespoons creamy Caesar dressing
2 tablespoons mayonnaise
1 teaspoon fresh lemon juice
¾ cup crumbled feta cheese
Lettuce leaves
Toasted pita chips

Combine first 8 ingredients in a medium bowl. Add Caesar dressing, mayonnaise, and lemon juice, stirring until blended. Sprinkle with feta cheese. Serve on lettuce leaves with toasted pita chips. **Makes:** 6 servings.
Prep: 12 min.

Linda Spranger
Farmington Hills, Michigan

Spicy Crab Enchiladas

If you like your food on the milder side, use mild picante sauce and the lesser amount of the dried crushed red pepper. Otherwise, this is one hot enchilada!

1 small onion, chopped (about 1 cup)
4 ounces sliced fresh mushrooms
3 tablespoons minced garlic
3 tablespoons butter or margarine
½ cup chopped fresh parsley, divided
1 teaspoon salt
1 teaspoon ground black pepper
1 to 2 teaspoons dried crushed red pepper
½ cup dry white wine
½ cup drained canned diced tomatoes and green chiles
1 tablespoon Worcestershire sauce
2 (3-ounce) packages cream cheese, softened
1 pound jumbo lump crabmeat, drained

5 (8-inch) flour tortillas
1½ cups (6 ounces) shredded Monterey Jack cheese
1 cup heavy whipping cream
2 tablespoons chopped green onions
2 tablespoons chopped red bell pepper
1 (16-ounce) jar medium picante sauce
Garnish: lemon wedges

Cook onion, mushrooms, and garlic in butter in a large nonstick skillet over medium-high heat 5 minutes or until tender, stirring often. Stir in ¼ cup parsley and next 3 ingredients.

Stir in wine, tomatoes, and Worcestershire sauce. Bring to a simmer over medium-high heat; reduce heat, and simmer 5 minutes. Remove from heat, and stir in cream cheese; gently fold in crabmeat.

Spoon crab mixture evenly down center of each tortilla; bring edges to center, overlapping. Place tortillas, seam side down, in a lightly greased 13- x 9-inch baking dish. Sprinkle Monterey Jack cheese evenly over enchiladas; pour cream over cheese.

Sprinkle remaining ¼ cup parsley, green onions, and red bell pepper over cheese. Bake, uncovered, at 350° for 25 minutes or until cheese is lightly browned and bubbly. Serve with picante sauce. Garnish, if desired. **Makes:** 5 servings.
Prep: 38 min., **Cook:** 35 min.

Jayne Lawson
Tampa, Florida

Presentation is one of **Jayne's** strong suits. She plates each enchilada with a serving of yellow rice, and then garnishes with fresh parsley sprigs and a lemon half cut in the shape of a flower.

Herby Crab Cakes

Seasoned stuffing mix, bacon, and Dijon mustard create a powerhouse of flavor in these crisp cakes.

1½ cups herb-seasoned stuffing
    mix, crushed and divided
1   pound lump crabmeat, drained
1   large egg, lightly beaten
2   tablespoons finely chopped
    carrot
2   tablespoons finely chopped
    celery
2   tablespoons finely chopped
    onion
1   tablespoon fresh lemon juice
2   tablespoons mayonnaise

2   bacon slices, cooked and
    crumbled
½   teaspoon salt
½   teaspoon hot pepper sauce
½   teaspoon Dijon mustard
3   tablespoons extra-virgin olive oil
Garnish: lemon wedges

Combine ¼ cup crushed stuffing mix and next 11 ingredients; stir well. Shape crabmeat mixture into 5 (½-inch-thick) patties. Dredge patties in remaining stuffing mix crumbs; cook patties in hot olive oil 3 minutes on each side or until golden. Garnish, if desired. **Makes:** 5 servings.

Prep: 31 min., **Cook:** 6 min.

Vivian Zingarelli
Virginia Beach, Virginia

Vivian makes these yummy crab cakes using canned crab, but we found the seasonings so sensational we couldn't resist splurging for fresh crabmeat.

Bourbon-Bacon Scallops With Tropical Salsa

Be sure not to overcook the bacon so the slices will wrap around the scallops easily.

2   green onions, chopped
3   tablespoons bourbon
3   tablespoons maple syrup
1½ tablespoons soy sauce
1½ tablespoons Dijon mustard
½   teaspoon pepper
24 sea scallops (about 1½
    pounds)
4   (12-inch) wooden skewers
½   cup diced fresh pineapple
½   cup diced mango
½   cup peeled and diced cucumber
½   cup diced red bell pepper
3   tablespoons chopped fresh
    cilantro
4   teaspoons fresh lime juice
¼   teaspoon salt
⅛   teaspoon pepper
1   jalapeño pepper, seeded and
    minced
12 bacon slices, cut in half

Stir together first 6 ingredients in a bowl; reserve ⅓ cup marinade, and set aside. Add scallops to remaining marinade. Cover and marinate in refrigerator 1 hour, stirring occasionally.

Meanwhile, soak wooden skewers in water at least 30 minutes. Combine pineapple and next 8 ingredients in a medium bowl; toss gently. Cover salsa and chill.

Partially cook bacon in a large skillet 8 minutes or until just beginning to brown; set aside.

Remove scallops from marinade, discarding marinade. Wrap each scallop with a half slice of bacon. Thread onto skewers, securing bacon edges.

Coat food grate with cooking spray; place on grill over medium-high heat (350° to 400°). Place scallops on grate, and grill, covered with grill lid, 5 minutes on each side or until done, basting with ⅓ cup reserved marinade.

Serve scallops immediately with salsa.
Makes: 4 servings.
Prep: 29 min., **Cook:** 18 min., **Other:** 1 hr.

Shane Goodoff
Sherman Oaks, California

We grilled these bourbon-and-bacon kissed scallops, but you can broil them about 8 minutes like **Shane** does.

Southern Scallops With Sweet Tea Chili Sauce

These golden scallops are bathed in a sweet-and-sour sauce with just a hint of tea.

Sweet Tea Chili Sauce

¼ cup extra-virgin olive oil, divided

2 tablespoons fresh lemon juice

2 tablespoons fresh lime juice

1 teaspoon salt

1 teaspoon freshly ground pepper

18 large sea scallops (about 1½ pounds)

2 tablespoons sour cream

3 tablespoons chopped fresh chives

Prepare Sweet Tea Chili Sauce. Cool completely.

Combine 2 tablespoons oil and next 4 ingredients in a large zip-top freezer bag; add scallops. Seal bag; marinate in refrigerator 15 minutes. Drain, discarding marinade; pat scallops dry.

Heat 1 tablespoon oil in a large nonstick skillet over high heat. Sear half of scallops, 2 minutes on each side or until browned. Remove scallops to individual serving plates. Repeat procedure with remaining 1 tablespoon oil and remaining scallops.

Drizzle 3 tablespoons Sweet Tea Chili Sauce over each serving. Dollop each serving with 2 teaspoons sour cream; sprinkle with chives. **Makes:** 3 servings.

Prep: 9 min., **Cook:** 8 min., **Other:** 15 min.

Sweet Tea Chili Sauce:

You'll have a little of this spicy, sweet sauce leftover; use it with pot stickers or won tons.

½ cup sugar

½ cup rice vinegar

¼ cup ketchup

¾ teaspoon dried crushed red pepper

½ teaspoon salt

½ teaspoon iced tea liquid concentrate *

2 tablespoons plum sauce

1 tablespoon minced fresh ginger

2 teaspoons minced garlic

1 teaspoon cornstarch

Combine all ingredients in a medium microwave-safe bowl; whisk until blended. Microwave at HIGH 5 minutes, whisking after each minute. **Makes:** 1¼ cups.

Prep: 8 min., **Cook:** 5 min.

* For testing purposes only, we used Nestea Iced Tea Liquid Concentrate.

Dann Rains
Lyman, South Carolina

Dann crowns these sea jewels with crème fraîche, but we used sour cream instead, since it's more available and it was such a small amount.

Southern Scallops With
Sweet Tea Chili Sauce

Shrimp With Peanut Coconut Sauce

We used already-peeled and deveined shrimp in this recipe. If you have the time, substitute 1⅓ pounds unpeeled shrimp and peel them yourself.

1   tablespoon cornstarch
3   tablespoons fish sauce, divided *
1   pound peeled and deveined, large fresh shrimp
2½ tablespoons chunky peanut butter
½   cup coconut milk
2   tablespoons peanut oil
2   garlic cloves, minced
1   teaspoon red curry paste *
1   red bell pepper, cut into thin strips
1   (8-ounce) can bamboo shoots, drained
1   tablespoon lime juice
¼   cup chopped fresh cilantro
Hot cooked jasmine rice *

Combine cornstarch and 1 tablespoon fish sauce in a medium bowl. Add shrimp, and toss well to coat; set aside.
Combine remaining 2 tablespoons fish sauce, peanut butter, and coconut milk in a small bowl; set aside.
Heat oil in a wok or large nonstick skillet over medium-high heat. Add garlic, and sauté 1 minute or until beginning to brown; stir in red curry paste. Add bell pepper and bamboo shoots; sauté 2 to 3 minutes or until tender. Add shrimp, and cook 3 minutes or until shrimp turn pink. Stir in peanut butter mixture, lime juice, and cilantro. Cook 1 minute or just until heated. Serve over jasmine rice.
Makes: 4 servings.
Prep: 9 min., **Cook:** 8 min.

*Look for fish sauce and red curry paste in the ethnic foods section of your grocery store. Jasmine rice is an aromatic white rice from Thailand. It has a nutlike flavor and buttery aroma. You can substitute basmati rice or regular long-grain rice.

Daljeet Singh
Coral Springs, Florida

Jamaican Jerk Shrimp

This recipe doesn't have the ground spices and habanero heat traditionally found in Jamaican jerk dishes, so it's ideal for those who prefer less fire and spice. And it goes together in about 17 minutes—perfect for weeknight family meals.

2   tablespoons butter or margarine
¼   cup extra-virgin olive oil
3   garlic cloves, minced
1   pound peeled and deveined, large fresh shrimp
1   teaspoon dried parsley flakes
1   teaspoon dried thyme
2   tablespoons concentrated jerk marinade *
¼   cup water
2   tablespoons fresh lemon juice
1   loaf Cuban or French bread (optional)

Melt butter with olive oil in a large saucepan over medium-high heat. Add garlic; sauté 1 minute. Add shrimp, parsley, and thyme; cook, stirring often, 3 to 5 minutes or until shrimp turn pink.
Reduce heat to medium-low; add marinade, water, and lemon juice. Cook 1 minute or until thoroughly heated. Serve with bread, if desired.
Makes: 2 or 3 servings.
Prep: 10 min., **Cook:** 7 min.

*For testing purposes only, we used Island Pit Jerk Marinade.

Note: We bought 1 pound peeled and deveined shrimp with the tails on for a pretty presentation. If you peel and devein shrimp yourself, start with 1⅓ pounds raw shrimp in the shell.

Lacie Griffin
Tampa, Florida

Lacie serves this with lemon wedges to squeeze over the shrimp and with Cuban bread to sop up the flavorful juices.

Perdido Key Shrimp

This indulgent pasta has a surprisingly light garlic and herb sauce. It comes together quickly because much of the prep and cook times overlap. Put the pasta on to cook as soon as you start the dish. Buying peeled shrimp saves time, but if you'd like to peel your own, buy 2⅔ pounds in the shell.

12 ounces uncooked dried linguine
1 tablespoon salt
1 red bell pepper
2 tablespoons butter or margarine
5 tablespoons olive oil, divided
4 shallots, sliced
4 garlic cloves, chopped
1 teaspoon chopped fresh rosemary
1 tablespoon lemon juice
½ teaspoon freshly ground black pepper
1 teaspoon Worcestershire sauce
2 pounds peeled and deveined, large fresh shrimp
½ cup white wine
1 tablespoon chopped fresh marjoram
½ teaspoon salt
1 (8-ounce) package sliced fresh mushrooms
1 cup shredded Parmesan cheese, divided
2 tablespoons chopped fresh parsley

Cook linguine according to package directions, adding 1 tablespoon salt to water; drain and keep warm.

Broil bell pepper on an aluminum foil-lined baking sheet 5 inches from heat about 5 minutes on each side or until pepper looks blistered. Place pepper in a zip-top freezer bag; seal and let stand 10 minutes to loosen skins. Peel pepper; remove and discard seeds. Slice pepper into thin strips; set aside.

Heat butter and 3 tablespoons olive oil in a medium skillet over medium-high heat; add shallots and garlic, and sauté until tender. Add roasted bell pepper strips, rosemary, and next 3 ingredients; cook 6 minutes. Add shrimp and next 4 ingredients; cook 3 minutes or until shrimp turn pink.

Toss pasta with remaining 2 tablespoons olive oil and ½ cup Parmesan cheese. Top with shrimp mixture, remaining Parmesan cheese, and parsley. Toss well just before serving. **Makes:** 6 servings.
Prep: 18 min., **Cook:** 21 min., **Other:** 10 min.

Tip: Substitute ⅔ cup roasted red bell peppers in a jar for speedy preparation.

Barbara Erhart
Pensacola, Florida

Barbara is our kind of cook—she recommends pouring a glass of wine as you start this dish to sample its appropriateness in the dish. She follows our recommendation of never cooking with a wine you wouldn't drink.

Bacon-Wrapped Shrimp Salad

This elegant salad is simpler than you'd expect; it uses precooked shrimp and bacon to speed up the cooking process. If you'd rather cook and peel the shrimp yourself, start with 3 pounds raw in the shell.

24 cooked, peeled jumbo shrimp (about 1½ pounds)
24 fully cooked bacon slices
½ cup olive oil
¼ cup chopped fresh parsley
1 tablespoon fresh lemon juice
½ teaspoon chopped garlic
¼ teaspoon salt
⅛ teaspoon pepper
1 (5-ounce) package gourmet mixed salad greens

Wrap each shrimp with a bacon slice; secure with a wooden pick. Place shrimp on an aluminum foil-lined 15- x 10-inch jellyroll pan. Bake at 425° for 3 to 4 minutes or until shrimp are thoroughly heated.

Combine olive oil and next 5 ingredients in a blender; pulse until pureed.

To serve, divide salad greens evenly among serving plates; top each salad with shrimp, and drizzle with dressing.
Makes: 4 servings.
Prep: 26 min., **Cook:** 4 min.

Note: You can easily prepare the shrimp up to the cooking point; store it in the refrigerator until cook time.

Gina De Roma
Pasadena, California

Gina submitted this recipe with a pimiento cheese risotto, but the salad was so delicious, quick, and easy, we thought it merited standing on its own.

Bayou Shrimp, Okra, and Corn Cakes With Stone-Ground Mustard and Honey Vinaigrette

Bayou Shrimp, Okra, and Corn Cakes With Stone-Ground Mustard and Honey Vinaigrette

This is a twist on your typical corn cake recipe because whole kernel corn is used instead of cornmeal. These little cakes also have just a touch of shrimp in them to make them unique.

½ cup stone-ground mustard
½ cup white balsamic vinegar
½ cup orange blossom honey
1 tablespoon peanut or canola oil
1 cup finely chopped Vidalia onion
1 pound cooked, peeled shrimp, chopped
1½ cups frozen cut okra, thawed
1 cup frozen whole kernel corn, thawed
4 large eggs
1 tablespoon Old Bay seasoning
1 tablespoon lemon juice
1 teaspoon salt
1 teaspoon onion powder
3 cups all-purpose baking mix *
1½ cups peanut or canola oil
3 (5-ounce) packages gourmet mixed salad greens

Whisk together first 5 ingredients in a small bowl; cover and chill.
Combine shrimp and next 7 ingredients in a large bowl; stir well. Stir in baking mix; let stand 10 minutes.

Heat 1½ cups oil in a 10-inch cast-iron skillet over medium-high heat. Pour about ⅓ cup batter for each cake into hot oil. Cook in batches 4 minutes on each side or until golden; keep warm.
Divide salad greens evenly among serving plates. Place 2 cakes on greens; drizzle with dressing. **Makes:** 8 servings.
Prep: 10 min., **Cook:** 8 min. per batch, **Other:** 10 min.

*For testing purposes only, we used Bisquick Original All-Purpose Baking Mix.

Frank Setera
Naples, Florida

Frank uses precooked and peeled shrimp and packaged salad greens to keep things simple. If you'd rather start with fresh shrimp in the shell, buy 2 pounds. Size doesn't matter since you'll chop it anyway.

Ginger-Grilled Shrimp With Pineapple-Orange Sauce on Saffron Rice

1 (10-ounce) package saffron yellow long-grain rice
1 tablespoon light brown sugar
1 teaspoon salt
½ teaspoon ground ginger
½ teaspoon ground cinnamon
¼ teaspoon onion powder
¼ teaspoon pepper
1 pound peeled and deveined, large fresh shrimp, tails removed (about 36 shrimp) *
2 tablespoons butter or margarine, melted
Lemon wedges
Pineapple-Orange Sauce

Cook rice according to package directions; set aside.

Combine sugar and next 5 ingredients. Sprinkle shrimp with seasoning mixture; thread shrimp onto 6 (12-inch) skewers. Place skewers on a food grate coated with cooking spray. Grill, covered with grill lid, over medium-high heat (350° to 400°) 8 to 10 minutes or until shrimp turn pink, turning once and brushing with melted butter. Remove shrimp from skewers onto a bed of rice. Serve with lemon wedges and warm Pineapple-Orange Sauce. **Makes:** 4 to 6 servings.
Prep: 15 min., **Cook:** 35 min.

Pineapple-Orange Sauce:

This sauce is also great with crispy chicken fingers, grilled tuna steaks, or coconut shrimp.

¼ cup sugar
1½ teaspoons cornstarch
½ cup water
1 tablespoon grated fresh ginger (optional)
1 (18-ounce) jar orange marmalade
1 (8-ounce) can crushed pineapple, drained
¼ cup sweetened flaked coconut
¼ cup sliced almonds

Combine sugar and cornstarch in a medium saucepan. Slowly stir in water. Cook over medium heat 5 minutes or until mixture starts to thicken. Reduce heat to low; stir in ginger, if desired, orange marmalade, and pineapple. Cook 1 more minute. Stir in coconut and almonds. **Makes:** 3⅓ cups.
Prep: 5 min., **Cook:** 6 min.

*If you'd rather peel and devein the shrimp yourself, start with 1⅓ pounds raw shrimp in shell to yield 1 pound peeled and deveined shrimp.

Note: If you're using wooden skewers, soak them in water at least 30 minutes before threading shrimp and grilling.

Paula Cox
Texarkana, Texas

Jumbo Shrimp in Tequila-Lime Sauce

Because of its high alcohol content, just a touch of tequila is needed in this south-of-the-border flavored dish.

8 ounces uncooked dried fettuccine
1 pound unpeeled, jumbo fresh shrimp
3 tablespoons olive oil
1 onion, chopped
2 celery ribs, chopped
1 teaspoon minced garlic
1 medium tomato, chopped
½ cup drained and chopped bottled roasted red bell pepper
¼ cup chopped fresh basil
½ teaspoon grated lime rind
½ teaspoon grated lemon rind
¼ cup fresh lime juice
2 tablespoons fresh lemon juice
2 tablespoons tequila
1 tablespoon minced seeded pickled jalapeño pepper
1 tablespoon dried tomato pesto
1 teaspoon salt
½ teaspoon freshly ground black pepper
½ teaspoon dried thyme
½ teaspoon dried parsley flakes
Garnishes: fresh basil, lime slices

Cook pasta in boiling salted water according to package directions. Drain; set aside, and keep warm.

Meanwhile, peel shrimp, and devein, if desired. Set aside.

Heat oil in a large nonstick skillet over medium heat. Add onion, celery, and garlic; sauté 5 minutes. Add shrimp, tomato, and next 13 ingredients to skillet; cook 8 minutes or until shrimp turn pink, stirring occasionally. Serve shrimp mixture over pasta. Garnish, if desired. **Makes:** 4 servings.
Prep: 11 min., **Cook:** 13 min.

Tip: Peeling and deveining shrimp is one smooth move if you use a tool called a shrimp peeler and deveiner. The handy tool is sold in seafood and household gadget departments in grocery stores or kitchen supply shops.

Jerry Alessi
Rochester, New York

Spicy Shrimp and Vegetables With Creamy Cheese Polenta

The creamy polenta cooks while you prepare the shrimp and vegetables.

Creamy Cheese Polenta

2 pounds unpeeled, large fresh shrimp
¼ cup unsalted butter
1 large sweet onion, chopped (about 2 cups)
1 medium-size red bell pepper, chopped (about 1 cup)
1 medium-size yellow bell pepper, chopped (about 1 cup)
1 (8-ounce) package sliced fresh mushrooms
1 tablespoon hot sauce
1 (10-ounce) package fresh spinach, coarsely chopped
6 bacon slices, cooked and crumbled

Prepare Creamy Cheese Polenta.

While polenta cooks, peel shrimp, and devein, if desired.

Melt butter in a large nonstick skillet over medium-high heat. Add onion and next 4 ingredients; sauté 5 minutes or until tender. Add shrimp; cook 4 to 5 minutes or until shrimp turn pink. Add spinach; cook 5 minutes or until wilted.

Spoon polenta onto 6 serving dishes; spoon shrimp mixture over polenta using a slotted spoon. Sprinkle with bacon. **Makes:** 6 servings.

Prep: 15 min., **Cook:** 15 min.

Creamy Cheese Polenta:

1 cup yellow cornmeal
1 (10-ounce) package frozen shoepeg corn
1 cup milk
1 (14-ounce) can low-sodium fat-free chicken broth
1 tablespoon hot sauce
¼ cup unsalted butter
1 teaspoon salt
1 teaspoon cracked black pepper
1 cup (4 ounces) shredded sharp Cheddar cheese

Combine cornmeal, corn, and milk in a small bowl; set aside.

Bring broth and next 4 ingredients to a boil in a 3-quart saucepan over medium heat. Gradually whisk in cornmeal mixture. Reduce heat to low, and simmer, stirring often, 20 minutes. Remove from heat; stir in cheese. **Makes:** 5½ cups.

Prep: 5 min., **Cook:** 26 min.

Pamela M. Sanford
New Market, Tennessee

Pamela always warms her serving dishes so the polenta stays piping hot, then she garnishes each serving with fresh spinach leaves and red bell pepper strips.

Creamy Alfredo Artichoke-Spinach Lasagna

When you're pushed for time, try using 4 cups of store-bought Alfredo sauce for the homemade sauce in this recipe.

¼ cup butter or margarine
2 garlic cloves, minced
3 cups half-and-half
1 (8-ounce) package cream cheese, cubed
½ cup grated Parmesan cheese
¼ teaspoon ground nutmeg
¼ teaspoon pepper
1 (10-ounce) package frozen chopped spinach, thawed
2 cups (8 ounces) shredded mozzarella cheese, divided
1 (12-ounce) jar quartered marinated artichokes, drained and chopped
1 (1.4-ounce) package dried vegetable soup mix
2 green onions, sliced
1 (15-ounce) container ricotta cheese
1 (8-ounce) container sour cream
½ (8-ounce) package cream cheese, softened
¼ cup grated Parmesan cheese
1 (9-ounce) package no-boil lasagna noodles (16 noodles)

Melt butter in a medium saucepan over medium heat; add garlic, and cook 1 minute. Add half-and-half and next 4 ingredients; cook over medium heat 12 minutes or until slightly thickened. Remove from heat. Set sauce aside, and keep warm.

Drain spinach well, pressing between paper towels. Combine spinach, 1 cup mozzarella cheese, and next 7 ingredients in a large bowl, stirring until blended.

Spread ¾ cup sauce in a lightly greased 13- x 9-inch baking dish. Top sauce in dish with 4 lasagna noodles.

Spread one-third of spinach mixture over noodles. Continue layering noodles and spinach mixture in same manner (without Alfredo sauce), ending with noodles. Pour remaining Alfredo sauce over noodles; top with remaining 1 cup mozzarella cheese.

Bake, covered, at 350° for 30 minutes. Uncover and bake 15 more minutes. Let stand 10 minutes before serving.

Makes: 8 servings.

Prep: 15 min., **Cook:** 58 min., **Other:** 10 min.

Michele Landers
Royal Palm Beach, Florida

We enjoyed **Michele's** rich Alfredo sauce so much that we doubled it for this recipe. It's a creamy vegetable lasagna made easy by using no-boil lasagna noodles.

Tortellini With Lemon Wine Sauce

Add a little something extra to each serving with a sprinkling of freshly grated Parmesan cheese.

1   (9-ounce) package refrigerated spinach and cheese-filled tortellini, uncooked
¼   cup butter or margarine
1   teaspoon olive oil
2   garlic cloves, minced
1   medium tomato, chopped
1   tablespoon lemon juice
¼   cup dry white wine
1   cup chicken broth
1   cup chopped fresh spinach
1   (8-ounce) can mushroom pieces and stems, or 1 cup sliced fresh mushrooms
1   (6-ounce) jar marinated artichoke hearts, drained and chopped
1   teaspoon dried oregano
¼   teaspoon pepper
1   tablespoon capers

Cook pasta in boiling salted water according to package directions; drain well.

Meanwhile, heat butter and oil in a medium saucepan over medium heat until butter is melted. Add garlic; sauté 1 minute. Add tomato; cook 2 minutes. Add lemon juice, wine, and broth; bring to a boil. Stir in spinach and next 5 ingredients. Return to a boil; reduce heat, and simmer 10 minutes. Add pasta, tossing to combine. Serve immediately. **Makes:** 3 to 4 servings.
Prep: 7 min., **Cook:** 17 min.

Tip: You save a lot of time by using refrigerated pasta instead of dried pasta.

Marianne Chalange
Orlando, Florida

Marianne says the simmer time is key to the reduction to concentrate the flavors in this pasta dish.

Four-Cheese Portobello

Portobello mushrooms are sold loose and prepackaged. The prepackaged mushrooms are usually a bit smaller and fit better in the skillet.

1   (28-ounce) can whole tomatoes, drained
2   garlic cloves, minced
1   tablespoon sugar
2   tablespoons red wine vinegar
1   tablespoon olive oil
½   teaspoon salt
½   teaspoon dried basil
½   teaspoon dried oregano
½   teaspoon dried parsley flakes
½   teaspoon pepper
4   large portobello mushroom caps (about 5 inches in diameter)
¼   cup Italian-seasoned breadcrumbs
4   thick slices mozzarella cheese (about 2 ounces each)
4   slices provolone cheese (about 1 ounce each)

1   (7-ounce) package baby spinach
1   tablespoon grated Romano cheese
1   tablespoon grated Parmesan cheese

Pulse first 10 ingredients in a food processor until pureed; set aside.

Place mushrooms, gills side down, in a large nonstick skillet coated with cooking spray. Cook, uncovered, over medium heat 3 minutes or until mushrooms begin to soften; turn mushrooms, gills side up.

Sprinkle breadcrumbs evenly over mushrooms. Top each mushroom with 1 slice each mozzarella and provolone cheese. Pour tomato mixture evenly over mushrooms; top with spinach. Sprinkle with Romano and Parmesan cheeses. Cook, uncovered, over medium heat 25 minutes or until cheese melts and spinach wilts. **Makes:** 4 servings.
Prep: 15 min., **Cook:** 28 min.

G. Anthony DelFranco
Bristol, Pennsylvania

G. Anthony's explicit directions told us that he has this recipe procedure down to a science, which was helpful when testing. He cautions that because you don't stir the contents while cooking, it's important to use a nonstick skillet.

Guatemalan Leek and Onion Pie

2   large baking potatoes,
    peeled and chopped (about
    4½ cups)
1   (15-ounce) package refrigerated
    piecrusts
3   large eggs, lightly beaten
1   cup (4 ounces) shredded
    mozzarella cheese
1   (2-ounce) jar diced pimientos,
    drained
¼   cup heavy whipping cream
1   (16-ounce) package bacon
4   medium leeks, sliced (about
    4 cups)
1   large onion, chopped (about
    1¾ cups)
½   teaspoon salt
¼   teaspoon pepper

Cook potatoes in boiling salted water to cover in a large Dutch oven 15 minutes or until potatoes are tender; drain well. **Meanwhile,** fit 1 piecrust into a 9-inch pieplate according to package directions. **Combine** eggs and next 3 ingredients in a small bowl; set aside.

Cook bacon in a large skillet over medium heat until crisp; remove bacon, reserving 2 tablespoons drippings in skillet. Crumble bacon. Sauté leeks and onion in reserved drippings 5 minutes or until tender. Add salt, pepper, cooked potatoes, and bacon; sauté 2 minutes. Remove from heat; stir in egg mixture. Spoon into prepared crust.

Roll remaining piecrust to press out fold lines; place over filling. Fold edges under, and crimp; cut slits in top for steam to escape. Bake at 350° for 45 to 55 minutes or until golden. **Makes:** 4 to 6 servings.

Prep: 19 min., **Cook:** 1 hr., 10 min.

Liz Tillit
Fitchburg, Massachusetts

Liz makes this dish with a homemade piecrust, but we simplified the procedure by using a ready-made refrigerated piecrust. She also uses pre-cooked bacon, but we cooked our own so we'd have some drippings leftover for sautéing the leeks and onion.

Guatemalan Leek
and Onion Pie

Portobello Sauté With Rice and Spinach

Use your favorite white wine to add depth to the flavor of this simple dish.

1	cup uncooked brown rice
½	cup dried tomatoes, sliced
1	cup white wine
2	tablespoons olive oil
1	medium onion, chopped
2	garlic cloves, minced
1	(6-ounce) package portobello mushroom caps, cut into 1-inch cubes
2	teaspoons dried oregano
1	teaspoon salt
½	teaspoon dried basil
½	teaspoon pepper
⅛	teaspoon mesquite liquid smoke
2	cups fresh baby spinach
2	tablespoons freshly grated Parmesan cheese

Cook rice according to package directions; keep warm.

Place tomatoes and wine in a small bowl; let stand 15 minutes. Drain, reserving liquid.

Heat oil in a large skillet over medium heat. Add onion and garlic; sauté until tender. Add mushrooms and next 5 ingredients; reduce heat, and simmer, stirring occasionally, 15 minutes. Stir in spinach, and cook 3 minutes or just until spinach wilts. Serve over rice; sprinkle with cheese before serving.
Makes: 2 servings.
Prep: 6 min., **Cook:** 45 min., **Other:** 15 min.

Tip: For easy slicing, cut dried tomatoes with kitchen shears.

Vanessa Chaney
Marietta, Georgia

Vanessa serves this mushroom medley over raw spinach leaves and rice, but we wilted the spinach along with the mushrooms to add color and texture to the mushrooms.

Easy Chile Rellenos With Spicy Tomato Sauce

All-purpose baking mix makes a quick and easy substitute for the traditional batter in these zesty stuffed peppers. You can also stir up the chunky Mexican sauce while the rellenos bake. For a pretty presentation, serve chile rellenos on a pool of sauce. Serve any leftover Spicy Tomato Sauce with tortilla chips.

3	(4-ounce) cans whole green chiles, drained
2	cups (8 ounces) shredded sharp Cheddar cheese, divided
½	(8-ounce) package cream cheese, softened
1	teaspoon garlic powder
¼	cup butter or margarine, divided
1	cup all-purpose baking mix *
½	cup yellow cornmeal
1	teaspoon garlic salt
1	teaspoon ground cumin
3	large eggs, lightly beaten

Chopped fresh cilantro
Spicy Tomato Sauce

Carefully cut 8 chiles lengthwise down 1 side. Reserve any remaining chiles for another use. Set aside 2 tablespoons Cheddar cheese. Stir together remaining Cheddar cheese, cream cheese, and garlic powder in a bowl. Shape cheese mixture into an 8-inch log; cut into 8 pieces. Stuff each chile pepper with a piece of cheese mixture, and gently reshape chiles.

Place 2 tablespoons butter in an 11- x 7-inch baking dish; place in a 425° oven for 3 to 5 minutes or until butter melts.

Meanwhile, combine baking mix and next 3 ingredients in a shallow dish. Dip each chile in egg, and dredge in cornmeal mixture. Arrange stuffed peppers in melted butter in dish. Place remaining 2 tablespoons butter in a microwave-safe bowl. Microwave at HIGH 1 minute or until butter melts; drizzle butter over chiles. Sprinkle chiles with reserved Cheddar cheese.

Bake, uncovered, at 425° for 20 minutes or until golden. Sprinkle with cilantro. Serve with Spicy Tomato Sauce.
Makes: 4 servings.
Prep: 22 min., **Cook:** 20 min.

For a complete meal, **Peggy** serves these chile rellenos with flour tortillas, Mexican-style corn, and green salad with Ranch-style dressing.

Spicy Tomato Sauce:

½	cup chopped onion
1	tablespoon minced garlic
1	tablespoon olive oil
1	(14.5-ounce) can diced tomatoes with zesty mild green chiles, undrained
1	(15-ounce) can tomato sauce
1	teaspoon light brown sugar
1	teaspoon ground cumin
1	teaspoon garlic salt
¼	teaspoon dried oregano
1	bay leaf

Sauté onion and garlic in hot oil in a saucepan over medium-high heat until onion is tender. Stir in tomatoes and remaining ingredients. Bring to a boil; cover, reduce heat, and simmer 10 minutes, stirring occasionally. Discard bay leaf. **Makes:** 3¼ cups.
Prep: 7 min., **Cook:** 15 min.

*For testing, we used Bisquick Original All-Purpose Baking Mix.

Peggy Woodhouse
Richardson, Texas

Sun-Dried Tomato Ratatouille
Over Polenta

Sun-Dried Tomato Ratatouille Over Polenta

This savory mixture of eggplant, peppers, tomatoes, and fresh herbs is a vegetarian's dream come true.

4 small Japanese eggplants, peeled and cut into 1½-inch pieces (about 1 pound)
1 teaspoon salt
1 (8-ounce) jar dried tomatoes in oil, undrained (about 1 cup)
1 medium-size red onion, cut into eighths
1 medium-size red bell pepper, sliced
4 garlic cloves, pressed (about 1 tablespoon)
1 (14½-ounce) can stewed tomatoes, undrained
1½ cups water
1 medium zucchini, cut into ½-inch slices
1 tablespoon chopped fresh parsley
1 tablespoon chopped fresh oregano
1 tablespoon chopped fresh basil
1 tablespoon balsamic vinegar
2 teaspoons chopped fresh rosemary
1 teaspoon sugar
1 teaspoon dried marjoram
¼ teaspoon freshly ground black pepper
3½ cups water
1 teaspoon salt
1 cup yellow cornmeal
½ cup grated Parmesan cheese
Garnish: shredded Parmesan cheese

Place eggplant in a large bowl of water to cover; add 1 teaspoon salt. Let stand 20 minutes; drain well.

Drain dried tomatoes, reserving 3 tablespoons tomato oil. Coarsely chop tomatoes; set aside.

Heat 2 tablespoons reserved oil in a large nonstick skillet over medium heat. Add red onion and bell pepper; sauté until tender, about 5 minutes. Add garlic; cook 2 minutes. Stir in eggplant, stewed tomatoes, and 1½ cups water. Bring to boil; cover, reduce heat, and simmer 10 minutes. Add zucchini, ¾ cup chopped dried tomatoes, parsley, and next 7 ingredients; cover and simmer, stirring occasionally, 30 minutes or until tender.

Meanwhile, bring 3½ cups water and 1 teaspoon salt to a boil in a medium saucepan. Gradually add cornmeal, stirring constantly with a wire whisk. Simmer 2 minutes or until thick. Remove from heat; stir in remaining 1 tablespoon reserved oil, remaining chopped dried tomatoes, and ½ cup Parmesan cheese. Cool slightly.

Spoon polenta evenly into bowls; top with ratatouille. Garnish, if desired.

Makes: 4 servings.

Prep: 22 min., **Cook:** 49 min., **Other:** 20 min.

Note: Add an additional ½ cup water to ratatouille during cooking, if necessary.

Kathleen Ligon
Austin, Texas

Mediterranean Grilled Pizza

Mediterranean Grilled Pizza

1   (1-pound) loaf frozen bread
    dough, thawed and cut in half
½   cup canned tomato sauce with
    roasted garlic
2   garlic cloves, chopped
¼   teaspoon dried Italian
    seasoning
8   teaspoons olive oil, divided
20 pitted kalamata olives,
    quartered
¼   cup dried tomatoes in oil,
    drained and cut into thin strips
2   tablespoons pine nuts, toasted
2   tablespoons drained capers
2   shallots, vertically sliced
¼   cup crumbled feta cheese
1   cup (4 ounces) shredded
    mozzarella cheese

Roll out each half of bread dough into a 9-inch round pizza crust on a lightly floured surface. Stir together tomato sauce, garlic, and Italian seasoning.

Brush 1 side of each pizza crust with 2 teaspoons olive oil. Place crust, oiled side down, on a food grate.

Grill, covered with grill lid, over medium-high heat (350° to 400°) 2 to 3 minutes or until crisp. Lightly brush top of each pizza crust with 2 teaspoons oil; turn crusts over. Quickly brush half of tomato sauce mixture over each pizza. Sprinkle olives and next 6 ingredients, in order given, over sauce. Grill, covered, 2 to 3 minutes or until cheese melts. **Makes:** 2 servings.
Prep: 18 min., **Cook:** 6 min.

Tip: If you use a gas grill, you may need to adjust the heat even lower if crust is browning too quickly.

Renee Pokorny
Ventura, California

Renee offers frozen bread dough as a substitute for home-made pizza dough, and we liked her suggestion. The dough was easy to work with on the grill, and we loved the smoky flavor.

One-Dish Wonders

Mealtime possibilities are endless
with these simple weeknight family meals.
Take your pick from skillet dinners, pasta dishes,
casseroles, and much more—dinner's
on the table in a flash.

uth Kendrick's childhood shares a common thread with those of several other cook-off winners: a mother who encouraged her to cook and who put up with the mess. "I would tell Mother that I needed milk for my mud pies because that made them better . . . she gave it to me."

Ruth carries on the tradition of baking, candy-making, and cooking the kind of all-American fare her mother made for hungry hands on an Idaho farm. But she also goes beyond the basics to experiment with more exotic foods, herbs, and spices.

Successful experiments have taken Ruth to four other national cook-offs, but she intended to skip this one. Between boating and camping with her family and piloting a private plane, Ruth says, "I have less time than I used to." But a friend who shares her cooking contest hobby convinced Ruth to send in the recipe at the last minute.

$11,000 Category & Brand Winner!

BISQUICK® Brand Winner
Spicy Tex-Mex Chicken Cobbler
Ruth hoped the name "cobbler" might catch the judges' attention.

1	**medium onion, sliced**
2	**tablespoons vegetable oil**
1	**(15-ounce) can black beans, rinsed and drained**
1	**(10-ounce) can Mexican festival diced tomatoes with lime juice and cilantro**
1	**(10-ounce) can enchilada sauce**
2	**cups cubed cooked chicken**
1	**teaspoon salt**
½	**teaspoon ground cumin**
½	**teaspoon chili powder**
½	**teaspoon dried oregano**
½	**teaspoon ground pepper**
1½	**cups all-purpose baking mix** ✱
1	**large egg**
⅔	**cup milk**
1	**cup (4 ounces) shredded extra-sharp Cheddar cheese, divided**
½	**cup chopped fresh cilantro, divided**
2	**avocados, sliced**
1	**tablespoon lime juice**

Sour cream

Sauté onion in hot oil in a 10-inch cast-iron skillet over medium-high heat 3 to 4 minutes or until tender. Stir in beans and next 8 ingredients. Bring to a boil; reduce heat, and simmer, uncovered, 15 minutes.

Combine baking mix, egg, and milk in a medium bowl, stirring until smooth. Fold in ½ cup cheese and ¼ cup cilantro; pour over simmering chicken mixture.

Bake at 400° for 20 minutes or until a wooden pick inserted in topping comes out clean. Sprinkle with remaining ½ cup cheese and remaining ¼ cup cilantro. Sprinkle avocado slices with lime juice, and arrange over cobbler. Serve with sour cream. **Makes:** 4 to 6 servings.
Prep: 10 min., **Cook:** 45 min.

✱ For testing purposes only, we used Bisquick Original All-Purpose Baking Mix.

Ruth Kendrick
Ogden, Utah

Ruth's cobbler is a one-dish meal that can come to the table in the skillet. Judge Andria Hurst says the savory dish has the texture of cobbler—moist with gravy inside and a crispy crust outside.

Spicy Tex-Mex Chicken Cobbler

Tomato-Leek-Bacon Tart

"I'm like a mad scientist in the kitchen," admits Nancy Fazakerley. "My specialty is using whatever happens to be in the cupboard to come up with a gourmet dish. My husband likens it to the traditional Swedish folktale of nail soup."

This tart—her first-ever cook-off entry—is evidence of Nancy's talent for dressing up a plain dish. Starting with a neighbor's basic recipe, she omitted two ingredients, and added five others, including her husband's beloved bacon as well as homegrown tomatoes and basil. She experimented with the recipe until the flavor "had the 'wow' it deserves." Tinkering with recipes must come naturally to someone who once dared to boil spaghetti in beer rather than point her boat into shore to get fresh water.

"I like food to have *punch*," says Nancy. "Beer and coconut milk are both interesting, powerful flavors that I like to experiment with. Garlic is indispensable; its aroma invites you to the table. The more I cook, the more fun I have, and the more interesting and delicious the food."

$2,000 Finalist & Brand Winner!

OSCAR MAYER® *Ready to Serve BACON Brand Winner*

Tomato-Leek-Bacon Tart

½ (15-ounce) package refrigerated piecrusts
1 (8-ounce) package shredded Italian three-cheese blend, divided
3 medium leeks, thinly sliced (about 1 cup)
2 tablespoons olive oil
8 plum tomatoes, sliced
1 cup loosely packed fresh basil leaves, coarsely chopped
3 garlic cloves, coarsely chopped
½ (2.1-ounce) package ready to serve bacon, chopped
½ cup mayonnaise
¼ cup freshly grated Parmesan cheese
1 tablespoon fresh lemon juice
½ teaspoon pepper
Garnishes: fresh basil leaves, plum tomato slices

Coat a 9-inch tart pan with cooking spray. Fit piecrust into pan according to package directions.

Bake at 450° for 10 minutes or until golden. Remove crust from oven; sprinkle with 1 cup cheese blend.

Sauté leeks in hot oil in a skillet over medium-high heat until tender; sprinkle over crust. Arrange tomato over leeks; sprinkle with basil and garlic.

Stir together remaining 1 cup cheese blend, chopped bacon, and next 4 ingredients in a bowl. Spoon cheese mixture over tart, spreading to edges.

Bake at 375° for 25 minutes or until golden. Garnish, if desired. **Makes:** 4 servings.

Prep: 30 min., **Cook:** 40 min.

Nancy Fazakerley
Mechanicsburg, Pennsylvania

Don't forget the garnish. **Nancy** is an artist who strives for presentation as well as flavor. "The sight of a beautiful dish is just as rewarding as the happy faces after the first sampling."

How does an Italian girl from New Jersey get to make chicken 'n' dumplings in a *Southern Living* cook-off? "Maybe I was Southern in another life," laughs Karen Peters, who counts sweet potato pie, grits, and chili among her specialties. But much of her cooking is Southern with a definite Italian accent.

Cooking is in Karen's blood. As a child shaping meatballs for Sunday dinner, she worked beside three generations of Italian cooks who taught her a classic repertoire that includes a host of fish dishes as well as homemade pasta, pasta sauces, and pizza.

"My Italian mother, grandmother, and great-grandmother never treated cooking as a chore," says Karen. "They saw it as a labor of love . . . they never were happier than when the whole family was at the table, enjoying the meals they'd prepared."

That joy of cooking helped Karen give prizewinning flavor to a humdrum recipe. Once married to "a non-Italian guy" who yearned for old-fashioned chicken and dumplings, Karen tried his grandmother's recipe. "I don't know if it was supposed to taste like that, but it was way too bland for Italian taste buds," she says.

Karen's spiced-up version was a huge success that outlasted the marriage, she laughs. "My daughter's birthday party was the night before I left for Nashville," says Karen. "I was cooking for 12 preteens, with two big Dutch ovens going simultaneously. My daughter's friends always ask to be invited for dinner when they know I'm making this dish."

That holds with Karen's family traditions. "We associate food with good times, sweet memories, and most of all, love."

$1,000 Finalist Winner!

Quick-and-Spicy Chicken 'n' Dumplings

8   **skinned and boned chicken thighs**
4   **cups all-purpose baking mix, divided** *
1   **teaspoon paprika**
1   **teaspoon ground red pepper**
½   **teaspoon garlic powder**
½   **teaspoon onion powder**
½   **teaspoon poultry seasoning**
¼   **teaspoon freshly ground black pepper**
Dash of salt
2   **tablespoons vegetable oil, divided**
3   **(14.5-ounce) cans chicken broth, divided**
¼   **(1.41-ounce) box coriander and annatto seasoning (2 packets)**
⅔   **cup milk**

Rinse chicken with cold water; pat dry. Combine 2 cups baking mix, paprika, and next 6 ingredients in a large zip-top freezer bag. Add chicken thighs, 1 at a time; seal bag, and shake to coat.

Heat 1 tablespoon oil in a 6-quart Dutch oven over medium heat. Add half of chicken, and cook 5 minutes on each side or until golden brown; remove chicken. Repeat procedure with remaining oil and chicken.

Add ½ cup chicken broth to drippings in pan, stirring to loosen browned bits from bottom.

Return chicken to pan; stir in remaining broth and 2 seasoning packets. Bring to a boil; cover, reduce heat, and simmer 25 minutes.

Combine milk and remaining 2 cups baking mix in a medium bowl, stirring just until moistened. Drop dough by tablespoonfuls onto simmering chicken mixture; cook, uncovered, 10 minutes. Cover and cook 10 more minutes. Serve immediately. **Makes:** 4 servings.
Prep: 25 min., **Cook:** 1 hr., 5 min.

*For testing purposes only, we used Bisquick Original All-Purpose Baking Mix.

Karen Peters
Hawthorne, New Jersey

Karen's secret ingredient is the coriander and annatto seasoning that she discovered in the Hispanic foods section of her local supermarket. She says the seasoning gives the dish savory flavoring as well as wonderful color and aroma.

Quick-and-Spicy Chicken
'n' Dumplings

HUNT'S® Brand Winner

Baked Chicken-and-Cheese Enchiladas

1 (8-ounce) package cream cheese
2 cups chopped cooked chicken
1 (4-ounce) can diced green chiles, undrained
¼ cup chopped onion
½ teaspoon salt
½ teaspoon pepper
3 cups (12 ounces) shredded Monterey Jack cheese, divided
10 (6-inch) corn tortillas
1 (14.5-ounce) can petite diced tomatoes with mild green chilies, undrained
1 (15-ounce) can tomato sauce
½ cup whipping cream
Toppings: sour cream, shredded lettuce

Stir together first 6 ingredients and 1 cup cheese in a large bowl until well-blended.

Wrap tortillas in heavy-duty plastic wrap; heat in microwave according to package directions. Spoon about ⅓ cup chicken mixture down center of each warm tortilla; roll up. Place in a lightly greased 13- x 9-inch baking dish.

Cook diced tomatoes, tomato sauce, and cream in a 2-quart saucepan over medium-high heat, stirring often, 10 minutes or until thoroughly heated. Pour tomato mixture over tortillas, spreading to ends of tortillas; sprinkle with remaining 2 cups cheese.

Bake, uncovered, at 350° for 20 minutes or until cheese melts and tomato mixture is bubbly. Serve with desired toppings. **Makes:** 5 servings.
Prep: 20 min., **Cook:** 30 min.

Stephanie created a deliciously creamy dish by adding cream cheese to the enchilada filling and whipping cream to the sauce.

Stephanie Wood
Woodstock, Georgia

VELVEETA® CHEESY POTATOES Brand Winner

Sunday Night Spicy Cheesy Sausage-Spud Bake

1 (16-ounce) package ground pork sausage
1 large shallot, finely chopped
1 garlic clove, minced
1 (10-ounce) can diced tomatoes and green chilies, undrained
1 (10.23-ounce) package cheesy au gratin potatoes
¼ cup chopped fresh parsley, divided
3 cups milk
8 large eggs
2 tablespoons all-purpose baking mix *
½ teaspoon salt

Cook sausage in a skillet over medium-high heat, stirring until it crumbles and is no longer pink. Using a slotted spoon, transfer sausage to a 13- x 9-inch baking dish coated with cooking spray; reserve drippings in skillet.

Sauté shallot and garlic in sausage drippings over medium heat 2 minutes or until tender. Spoon shallot mixture evenly over sausage. Pour diced tomatoes and green chilies over sausage mixture. Set aside cheese mix packet from au gratin potatoes. Spread potatoes over tomatoes.

Whisk together reserved cheese mix, 2 tablespoons parsley, milk, and next 3 ingredients in a large bowl; pour over sausage mixture, covering potatoes completely.

Bake, uncovered, at 375° for 36 minutes or until a knife inserted in center comes out clean and top begins to brown. Remove from oven; let stand 5 minutes. Sprinkle with remaining 2 tablespoons parsley. Serve immediately.
Makes: 8 servings.
Prep: 25 min., **Cook:** 48 min., **Other:** 5 min.

*For testing purposes only, we used Bisquick Original All-Purpose Baking Mix.

Ellen Cavallaro
Berkeley Heights, New Jersey

**Baked Chicken-and-Cheese
Enchiladas**

Pot Roast to Make the Neighborhood Jealous

It's easy to put this yummy four-ingredient roast together. Just throw soup mix, a roast, and tomato and orange juices in the slow cooker before work, and you'll have a meal ready to serve your family when you get home.

3 **(1-ounce) envelopes dry onion soup mix**
1 **(6-pound) beef brisket, halved crosswise**
3 **cups low-acid orange juice**
3 **cups tomato juice**

Sprinkle 1 envelope soup mix in a 5-quart electric slow cooker. Place half of brisket over soup mix; sprinkle with 1 envelope soup mix. Place remaining half of brisket over soup mix; sprinkle with remaining envelope soup mix.

Pour juices over brisket.

Cook, covered, on HIGH 1 hour. Reduce heat to LOW; cook 8 hours or until tender. **Makes:** 12 servings.

Prep: 5 min., **Cook:** 9 hrs.

Tip: Thicken the juices remaining in the Dutch oven with flour or cornstarch, and serve the gravy over mashed potatoes.

Evelyn Fine
Daytona Beach, Florida

Grandma's Pot Roast

This roast will make your family think of Sunday lunch at Grandma's.

3 **tablespoons olive oil**
3 **teaspoons salt, divided**
2 **teaspoons pepper, divided**
1 **(4-pound) chuck roast**
3 **medium onions, quartered**
4 **celery ribs, coarsely chopped**
2 **beef bouillon cubes**
½ **cup dry red wine**
½ **cup hickory-flavored barbecue sauce**
6 **carrots, cut into 2-inch pieces**
1 **medium-size green bell pepper, diced**
6 **baking potatoes, cubed**
3 **tablespoons water**
3 **tablespoons cornstarch**

Heat olive oil in a large Dutch oven. Combine 2 teaspoons salt and 1 teaspoon pepper. Sprinkle on both sides of roast. Cook roast over medium heat in Dutch oven until browned on both sides. Add onions and celery. Combine bouillon cubes, wine, and barbecue sauce; pour over meat. Cover, reduce heat, and simmer 1½ hours.

Add carrots, bell pepper, and potatoes, and cook 1½ more hours or until tender.

Transfer meat to a serving platter. Spoon vegetables around meat using a slotted spoon, reserving liquid in Dutch oven.

Whisk together water and cornstarch; add to reserved liquid. Whisk in remaining 1 teaspoon salt and remaining 1 teaspoon pepper; cook over medium heat, stirring constantly, until thickened. Serve with roast. **Makes:** 6 to 8 servings.

Prep: 22 min., **Cook:** 3 hrs., 8 min.

Shirley Peake
Fort Myers, Florida

Shirley uses an eye of round roast in this recipe, but we found that a chuck roast cooks up very tender in this barbecue-flavored pot roast.

Braised Beef Ribs With New Potatoes, Vidalia Onion, and Fennel

Serve these succulent ribs to that meat-and-potatoes man in your family, and you'll definitely score points.

4	pounds beef short ribs, trimmed
2	tablespoons all-purpose flour, divided
1	tablespoon salt
1	teaspoon freshly ground black pepper
½	cup vegetable oil, divided
4	cups chicken broth
12	small red potatoes, halved
1	large Vidalia onion, cut into 6 wedges
2	large fennel bulbs, quartered and cored
1	(14-ounce) can beef broth
¼	cup creamy peanut butter
1	tablespoon paprika

Sprinkle ribs with 1 tablespoon flour, salt, and pepper. Brown half of ribs in half of oil in a large ovenproof Dutch oven over medium high heat 8 to 9 minutes, turning occasionally. Repeat procedure with remaining ribs and oil. Remove ribs from pan, reserving 2 tablespoons drippings in pan.

Add chicken broth to pan, stirring to loosen browned bits from bottom of pan. Return ribs to pan. Add potatoes, onion, and fennel. Bring to a boil; immediately cover with lid, and remove from heat.

Bake at 325° for 3 hours or until ribs are tender. Transfer ribs and vegetables to a serving platter, reserving 2 tablespoons broth mixture; keep warm.

Whisk together beef broth and peanut butter. Combine reserved drippings, remaining 1 tablespoon flour, and paprika in pan; cook over medium heat 1 minute. Whisk in beef broth mixture, stirring until smooth; cook over medium-high heat 6 minutes or until slightly thickened. Serve with ribs and vegetables. **Makes:** 4 to 6 servings.

Prep: 21 min., **Cook:** 3 hrs., 30 min.

Teri Fermo
Tulsa, Oklahoma

French-Style Short Ribs

If you can't find, or just don't want to use, baby yellow beets, you can substitute new potatoes, baby golden potatoes, or fingerling potatoes. Don't be tempted to substitute red beets for the golden, however, because they'll tint the dish red.

2	tablespoons olive oil, divided
4	pounds beef short ribs, trimmed
4	(14-ounce) cans beef broth
½	teaspoon dried crushed rosemary
½	teaspoon dried thyme
¼	teaspoon pepper
3	(½-ounce) packages dried morel mushrooms
15	whole baby yellow beets, peeled
2	teaspoons grated lemon rind
4	medium leeks, sliced
1	tablespoon all-purpose flour
⅓	cup sour cream

Heat 1 tablespoon oil in a large nonstick skillet. Add half of ribs; brown on all sides, turning occasionally. Remove from skillet, and place in a large Dutch oven; repeat procedure with remaining 1 tablespoon oil and remaining ribs.

Combine broth and next 3 ingredients; pour over ribs. Bring to a boil; cover, reduce heat, and simmer 1 hour.

Meanwhile, soak mushrooms according to package directions. Drain mushrooms, and cut in half; set aside.

Add beets and lemon rind to pan; simmer, covered, 30 minutes. Add mushrooms and leeks; simmer, covered, 30 minutes or until meat and beets are tender.

Remove meat and vegetables to individual serving dishes with a slotted spoon, reserving 1¼ cups liquid; drain remaining liquid. Whisk together reserved liquid and flour; pour into Dutch oven over medium heat; cook 5 minutes or until slightly thickened, stirring constantly. Remove from heat, and whisk in sour cream. Spoon sauce evenly over meat and vegetables. **Makes:** 8 servings.

Prep: 28 min., **Cook:** 2 hrs., 16 min.

John Foster, Jr.
Orland Park, Illinois

Baked Fajita Supreme

2 (10-ounce) cans milder-flavored diced tomatoes and green chilies, undrained*
2 beef bouillon cubes
1 large onion, chopped
½ (20-ounce) package frozen grilled seasoned steak strips, cut into 1-inch pieces (about 3 cups)*
2 (16-ounce) cans pinto beans, rinsed and drained
1 cup frozen whole kernel corn
2 cups crumbled cornbread
1 (8-ounce) package shredded colby Jack cheese (2 cups)
½ cup chopped fresh cilantro
1 (8-ounce) container sour cream
Garnish: fresh cilantro sprigs

Combine first 3 ingredients in a 4-quart saucepan. Bring to a boil; cover, reduce heat, and simmer 10 minutes. Stir in steak strips, beans, and corn. Mash beans slightly with a potato masher; stir well. Bring to a boil; cover, reduce heat, and simmer 5 minutes.

Pour bean mixture into a lightly greased 13- x 9-inch baking dish. Toss together cornbread crumbs and cheese; sprinkle over bean mixture.

Bake, uncovered, at 350° for 25 minutes or until bubbly. Sprinkle with ½ cup cilantro. Serve immediately with sour cream. Garnish, if desired. **Makes:** 8 servings.

Prep: 18 min., **Cook:** 42 min.

*For testing purposes only, we used RoTel Milder Diced Tomatoes and Green Chilies and Tyson Grilled Seasoned Beef Steak Strips.

Tip: About 4 regular-size corn muffins yield 2 cups crumbs. Purchase the muffins from the bakery or freezer section of the store, or make your own favorite recipe.

Mary Holt
Kerrville, Texas

Mexican Dish

If you like burritos, you'll like this quick-and-easy skillet supper.

1 pound ground chuck
¾ cup chopped onion
1 (1.25-ounce) package taco seasoning
1 (14½-ounce) can stewed tomatoes, undrained
1 (16-ounce) can refried beans
2 (3-ounce) packages cream cheese, cubed
6 (8-inch) flour tortillas, cut into 1-inch squares
Shredded lettuce
Shredded Cheddar cheese
Chopped tomato
Cubed avocado
Sour cream

Cook ground chuck and onion in a large skillet, stirring until beef crumbles and is no longer pink; drain. Stir in taco seasoning until blended; stir in tomatoes, refried beans, and cream cheese. Bring to a boil; cover, reduce heat, and simmer 10 minutes or until cream cheese melts, stirring often.

Stir in tortilla pieces. Heat just until tortillas soften. Spoon immediately onto serving plates. Top with lettuce and remaining ingredients. **Makes:** 4 to 5 servings.

Prep: 6 min., **Cook:** 18 min.

Alisha Binns
Cedar Rapids, Iowa

Alisha stirs pieces of flour tortilla into the meat mixture, and cooks them just until they soften. The tortillas become somewhat like dumplings in this south-of-the-border meal.

Spicy Skillet Supper

Spicy Skillet Supper

Known as picadillo in Central America and the Caribbean, this spicy-sweet hash is a favorite served over rice or as a filling for tortillas.

1   cup uncooked brown rice
1   tablespoon olive oil
1   pound ground chuck
1   green bell pepper, chopped
1   small onion, chopped
2   garlic cloves, minced
⅓   cup sliced pimiento-stuffed green olives
⅓   cup golden raisins
1   tablespoon brown sugar
1   tablespoon chili powder
½   teaspoon salt
½   teaspoon ground cumin
½   teaspoon ground coriander
½   teaspoon ground cinnamon
¼   teaspoon freshly ground pepper
2   tablespoons water

2   tablespoons cider vinegar
1   cup chunky salsa
1   cup (4 ounces) shredded Monterey Jack cheese
¼   cup chopped fresh cilantro

Cook rice according to package directions; keep warm.

Meanwhile, heat oil in a large skillet. Add ground chuck and next 3 ingredients; cook over medium-high heat, stirring until beef crumbles and is no longer pink and bell pepper is tender. Drain well. Add olives and next 10 ingredients; stir until blended. Cook mixture, stirring occasionally, 5 minutes or until thoroughly heated.

Divide rice evenly among 4 plates. Spoon meat mixture over rice; top each serving evenly with salsa, cheese, and cilantro. **Makes:** 4 servings.
Prep: 10 min., **Cook:** 45 min.

Tip: For added flavor and crunch, sprinkle with toasted, slivered almonds before serving.

Lee Burdett
Altamonte Springs, Florida

Classic Pasta Fagioli

This hearty, meaty soup will warm you up on a cold winter's day.

1½ cups uncooked bow tie pasta
1½ tablespoons olive oil
1½ pounds lean ground beef
5 fully cooked bacon slices, chopped
½ small onion, chopped (about ½ cup)
1 teaspoon salt
¼ cup chopped fresh basil
¼ cup chopped fresh parsley
3 tablespoons chopped fresh oregano
1 teaspoon pepper
¾ teaspoon ground red pepper
2 teaspoons minced garlic
1 (46-ounce) can vegetable juice
1 (28-ounce) can petite diced tomatoes, undrained
1 (26-ounce) can Italian-style tomato sauce

1 (16-ounce) can light red kidney beans, drained
1 (16-ounce) can dark red kidney beans, drained
1 (15.8-ounce) can great Northern beans, drained
4 celery ribs, diagonally sliced (1½ cups)
2 cups shredded carrots
Grated Parmesan cheese

For an extra-special meal, **Georgia** adds precooked frozen meatballs with the celery and carrots.

Cook pasta in boiling salted water according to package directions; drain. **Meanwhile,** heat oil in a large Dutch oven over medium heat. Add beef, bacon, and onion; cook, stirring occasionally, until meat crumbles and is no longer pink and onion is tender, about 7 minutes; drain. Stir in salt and next 6 ingredients. Add vegetable juice and next 7 ingredients; simmer, uncovered, 45 minutes. Add pasta, and cook 5 minutes or until thoroughly heated. Serve with Parmesan cheese. **Makes:** 12 cups.
Prep: 4 min., **Cook:** 57 min.

Tip: To save time, begin cooking the meat when you start to cook the pasta.

Georgia White
Dandridge, Tennessee

Minaste

1 pound lean ground beef
1 medium onion, chopped
3 garlic cloves, minced
3 cups peeled and cubed potato (about 3 medium baking potatoes)
1 (6-ounce) can tomato paste
1½ teaspoons salt
½ teaspoon black pepper
4 cups water
3 cups chopped fresh kale, stems removed
⅛ teaspoon dried crushed red pepper
⅛ teaspoon dried Italian seasoning

Cook ground beef, onion, and garlic in a Dutch oven over medium-high heat, stirring until beef crumbles and is no longer pink; drain and return mixture to Dutch oven.
Add potato and next 4 ingredients. Bring to a boil; reduce heat, and simmer, uncovered, 30 minutes.
Add kale, red pepper, and Italian seasoning. Simmer 25 minutes or until potato and kale are tender. **Makes:** 7 cups.
Prep: 7 min., **Cook:** 1 hr., 2 min.

Tip: For easier preparation, buy bagged kale that's already cleaned and chopped.

Tara Tuckwiller
Charleston, West Virginia

A staple in Northern Italy, *minaste* is a hearty soup made with chicken broth, cannellini beans, Italian sausage, and a dark, leafy green, such as kale, escarole, or spinach. **Tara's** version uses ground beef instead of beans. She also starts with water, which becomes part of a flavorful broth as the soup cooks.

Honey-Gingered Pork Chops With Peanuts and Cilantro

Fresh ginger gives this dish a definite Asian accent.

1 ounce dried cèpe or porcini mushrooms
1 (14-ounce) can beef broth
2 tablespoons soy sauce
1 tablespoon butter or margarine
1 tablespoon peanut oil
4 (6-ounce) pork chops (about 1 inch thick)
1 medium leek, sliced
2 tablespoons grated fresh ginger
2 tablespoons honey
½ cup chopped fresh cilantro
2 carrots, sliced
Hot cooked somen noodles
1½ cups coarsely chopped peanuts, divided
Garnish: fresh cilantro sprigs

Combine mushrooms, broth, and soy sauce in a small bowl; cover and let stand 20 minutes.

Heat butter and oil in a large skillet over medium-high heat; add pork chops, and cook 3 minutes on each side. Add leek; cook 4 minutes or until tender. Add mushroom mixture, ginger, and next 3 ingredients. Cover, reduce heat, and simmer 15 minutes, turning pork chops once.

Increase heat to high; uncover and cook until liquid is reduced by half. Remove from heat; stir in 1 cup peanuts. Remove pork chops from skillet; cut into thin slices.

Place somen noodles in each of 4 shallow bowls. Arrange pork slices over noodles. Spoon vegetables and sauce over pork slices; top each serving evenly with remaining peanuts. Garnish, if desired.
Makes: 4 servings.
Prep: 18 min., **Cook:** 31 min., **Other:** 20 min.

Joan W. Churchill
Dover, New Hampshire

If you're a fan of fresh cilantro, you might want to try 1 cup chopped as **Joan** does. We preferred half that amount of the potent herb. Joan serves the combo with steamed rice or soy noodles. We liked somen noodles.

Honey-Gingered Pork Chops With Peanuts and Cilantro

Bacon Cheeseburger Salad

It's hard to beat Thousand Island dressing on this "think-outside-the-bun" burger salad, but blue cheese and Ranch-style dressing are also good choices.

1   **pound ground sirloin**
⅓   **cup ketchup**
2   **teaspoons steak seasoning** ★
4   **fully cooked bacon slices**
1   **small head romaine lettuce, shredded**
½   **small red onion, chopped**
4   **plum tomatoes, chopped**
1   **cup (4 ounces) shredded sharp Cheddar cheese**
Thousand Island dressing
Dill pickle slices

Cook ground sirloin in a large skillet, stirring until it crumbles and is no longer pink; drain. Return to skillet. Stir in ketchup and seasoning; set aside, and keep warm.

Heat bacon according to package directions; crumble and set aside.

Layer lettuce, onion, and tomato on a large platter; top with beef mixture. Sprinkle with cheese and bacon. Serve with dressing and pickle slices. **Makes:** 4 to 6 servings.

Prep: 10 min., **Cook:** 15 min.

★ For testing purposes only, we used McCormick Grill Mates Montreal Steak Seasoning.

Tip: You can substitute extra-lean ground beef, turkey bacon, reduced-fat cheese, and reduced-fat salad dressing.

Sara Davis
Bedford, Texas

Asian Peanut-Pork Lettuce Wraps

1   **(1-pound) pork tenderloin**
2   **tablespoons prepared peanut sauce** ★
Salt to taste
Pepper to taste
1¼   **cups chopped dry-roasted peanuts, divided**
12   **Bibb lettuce leaves (about 2 heads)**
1   **(20-ounce) can pineapple tidbits in juice, drained**
1   **cup shredded carrot**
½   **cup sliced green onions**
½   **cup chopped fresh cilantro**
Asian Peanut Sauce

Butterfly tenderloin by making a lengthwise cut down center of 1 flat side, cutting to within ½ inch of other side. Unfold tenderloin, forming a rectangle; brush with peanut sauce, and sprinkle with salt and pepper.

Press 1 cup chopped peanuts over tenderloin to coat; place on a lightly greased rack in a roasting pan. Bake, uncovered, at 400° for 20 to 22 minutes or until a meat thermometer inserted into thickest portion registers 155°. Remove from oven; let stand, covered, 5 minutes until temperature rises to 160°. Cut into ¼-inch slices.

To serve, place pork slices in center of lettuce leaves. Top evenly with pineapple, carrot, green onions, cilantro, and remaining ¼ cup chopped peanuts. Roll up and secure with wooden picks. Serve with Asian Peanut Sauce. **Makes:** 4 servings.

Prep: 12 min., **Cook:** 22 min., **Other:** 5 min.

Asian Peanut Sauce:

¾   **cup prepared peanut sauce** ★
¾   **cup lite coconut milk**

Combine peanut sauce and coconut milk in a small bowl; stir well. **Makes:** 1½ cups.

Prep: 3 min.

★ For testing purposes only, we used House of Tsang Bangkok Padang Peanut Sauce.

Lou Rapp
Mason, Ohio

Santa Fe Sausage With Toasted Seed Biscuits

Cheese-topped sunflower seed biscuits cook right on top of the sausage mixture in this hearty one-dish supper.

1   pound mild ground pork sausage
1   (10-ounce) can diced tomatoes and green chiles, undrained
1   (11-ounce) can yellow corn with red and green bell peppers, undrained
1   (16-ounce) can chili beans, undrained
1   canned chipotle pepper in adobo sauce, minced
2¼ cups all-purpose baking mix *
1   teaspoon chili powder
⅓   cup roasted sunflower seed kernels
1   cup milk
1   cup (4 ounces) shredded Cheddar cheese

Cook sausage in an ovenproof Dutch oven over medium-high heat, stirring until it crumbles and is no longer pink; drain well, and return to pan. Stir in tomatoes and next 3 ingredients. Bring to a boil, reduce heat, and simmer, uncovered, 5 minutes, stirring occasionally.

Mary Ann is lucky enough to find Mexican chili powder and chili beans with chipotle peppers in her area. We found that regular chili powder makes a fine substitution, and we added a canned chipotle pepper to plain chili beans.

Meanwhile, stir together baking mix, chili powder, and sunflower seeds; stir in milk just until combined. Drop biscuit mixture by heaping tablespoonfuls onto hot sausage mixture.

Bake, uncovered, at 425° for 20 minutes or until biscuits are golden brown. Remove from oven; sprinkle cheese over biscuits. Cover with lid, and let stand 3 minutes or until cheese melts. **Makes:** 4 to 6 servings.
Prep: 7 min., **Cook:** 32 min., **Other:** 3 min.

＊For testing purposes only, we used Bisquick Original All-Purpose Baking Mix.

Mary Ann Lee
Hicksville, New York

Down-on-the-Bayou Dressing

Not only is this dish hearty enough to serve your family on a weeknight, but it's also an excellent side dish for a holiday crowd.

2   pounds ground pork sausage
1   cup butter or margarine
2   medium onions, chopped (about 3 cups)
2   green bell peppers, seeded and chopped (about 2 cups)
4   celery ribs, chopped (about 1½ cups)
8   green onions, chopped (about 1 cup)
1   teaspoon salt
2   cups uncooked long-grain rice
2   (10¾-ounce) cans cream of mushroom soup, undiluted
2   (10¾-ounce) cans cream of chicken soup, undiluted
1   cup sliced fresh mushrooms (optional)
½   cup chopped fresh parsley
½   cup frozen corn (optional)
¼   cup soy sauce
8   garlic cloves, chopped (about 3 tablespoons)

Cook sausage in a Dutch oven over medium heat, stirring until it crumbles and is no longer pink; drain. Remove from Dutch oven. Melt butter in Dutch oven; cook onion and next 4 ingredients in butter over medium-high heat, stirring constantly, 3 to 4 minutes. Add sausage, and cook 5 minutes, stirring often.

Add rice and remaining ingredients, stirring well. Spoon into a lightly greased 13- x 9-inch baking dish. Cover and bake at 350° for 1 hour and 5 minutes or until rice is tender. **Makes:** 15 servings.
Prep: 30 min., **Cook:** 1 hr., 22 min.

Beth Allen
Prairieville, Louisiana

We like the flexibility **Beth** offers in this rice dressing. She includes a couple of optional ingredients and the choice to feed a crowd or easily cut the recipe in half.

Slow-Cooker Sauerkraut and Sausage

Whether it's authentic or not, nothing celebrates German heritage like a dish of sauerkraut and sausage.

1 (16-ounce) package kielbasa sausage, cut into 3-inch pieces
3 large baking potatoes, peeled and cut into 1-inch pieces (about 6 cups)
2 large Fuji or Gala apples, peeled and cut into 1-inch pieces
4 fully cooked bacon slices, crumbled
3 tablespoons light brown sugar
2 tablespoons all-purpose flour
1 teaspoon caraway seeds
1 (27-ounce) can shredded sauerkraut, undrained
½ cup water

Combine first 7 ingredients in a 5-quart electric slow cooker; stir in sauerkraut and water.
Cook, covered, on HIGH 1 hour. Reduce heat to LOW, and cook for 7½ to 8 hours or until potatoes are tender.
Makes: 5 servings.
Prep: 15 min., **Cook:** 9 hrs.

Tip: Have the urge to sneak a peak at your dinner? Don't! Every time you remove the lid it adds 30 more minutes to the cook time.

Lori Schroeder
Canton, Michigan

Lori says reduced-fat smoked sausage works well in this recipe when you're trying to cut the amount of fat in your diet.

Brazilian Festive Feijoada

This spicy black bean and pork stew was prepared by colonial slaves in Brazil, using scraps of pork. Today, it's a must-have dish when visiting the South American country.

1 pound ground hot pork sausage
1 pound smoked sausage, cut into ¼-inch slices
5 garlic cloves, minced
1 small serrano chile pepper, chopped
1 cup chopped onion
3 cups chicken broth
3 (15-ounce) cans black beans, rinsed and drained
1 (14.5-ounce) can diced tomatoes with green peppers and onions, undrained
¼ cup chopped fresh cilantro
1⅓ cups uncooked jasmine rice
2 cups chicken broth
⅔ cup orange-pineapple juice
1½ tablespoons butter or margarine
¾ teaspoon salt

1 (1-pound) package bacon slices, cut into 1-inch pieces
5 garlic cloves, minced
1 pound chopped fresh collard greens

Place a lightly greased Dutch oven over medium-high heat. Add sausages, 5 garlic cloves, serrano pepper, and onion; cook 8 to 9 minutes, stirring until sausage crumbles and is no longer pink. Drain.

Norma serves sliced pineapple over her *feijoada*, but we liked it just as well without.

Add chicken broth and next 3 ingredients. Bring to a boil; reduce heat, and simmer 50 minutes or until slightly thickened, stirring occasionally. Transfer to a large bowl; keep warm.
Meanwhile, combine rice and next 4 ingredients in a medium saucepan. Bring to a boil; cover, reduce heat, and simmer 20 minutes or until tender. Let stand 10 minutes.
Wipe Dutch oven clean. Cook bacon over medium-high heat 9 minutes or until crisp. Add 5 garlic cloves and greens to pan; cook over medium heat 10 minutes or until tender, stirring often. Serve sausage mixture with rice and collard greens. **Makes:** 10 servings.
Prep: 15 min., **Cook:** 1 hr., 25 min.

Norma Fried
Denver, Colorado

**Slow-Cooker Sauerkraut
and Sausage**

Creamy Gnocchi With Basil and Prosciutto

Look for gnocchi on the pasta aisle of your local grocery store. It's sold vacuum-packed in a 1-pound box.

2 (16-ounce) boxes vacuum-packed gnocchi with potato
¼ cup butter or margarine
2 garlic cloves, minced
1 (8-ounce) package cream cheese, cubed
1 cup diced prosciutto
1 cup chicken broth
¼ cup chopped fresh basil
½ cup finely shredded Parmesan cheese
Garnish: fresh basil leaves

Cook gnocchi according to package directions, omitting salt. Drain well; set aside.

Meanwhile, melt butter in a large nonstick skillet over medium heat. Add garlic; cook 1 minute, stirring constantly. Add cream cheese and prosciutto, stirring until blended. Slowly stir in broth; cook 4 minutes or until slightly thickened. Stir in chopped basil and Parmesan cheese. **Pour** cheese sauce over gnocchi; stir gently to blend. Garnish, if desired. Serve immediately. **Makes:** 4 servings.
Prep: 7 min., **Cook:** 12 min.

Kelly Baxter
Olympia, Washington

Kelly brings together a handful of simple ingredients to create an ultra-creamy sauce that's packed with flavor. Gnocchi never had it so good.

Mex-etti Supper

8 ounces uncooked spaghetti, broken in half
½ cup chopped onion
3 garlic cloves, minced
2 teaspoons vegetable oil
1 (26-ounce) jar tomato, garlic, and onion pasta sauce
1 (16-ounce) can kidney beans, drained
1 (15¼-ounce) can whole kernel corn with red and green peppers, drained
1 (15-ounce) can black beans, drained
2 tablespoons chopped fresh cilantro
1½ cups (6 ounces) shredded Cheddar cheese
Salsa
Sour cream

Cook pasta in boiling salted water according to package directions; drain. **Cook** onion and garlic in hot oil in a Dutch oven 3 to 4 minutes; add pasta, pasta sauce, and next 4 ingredients, stirring well. Spoon mixture into a lightly greased 13- x 9-inch baking dish; sprinkle with cheese. Bake, uncovered, at 350° for 25 minutes or until thoroughly heated and bubbly. Serve with salsa and sour cream.
Makes: 4 servings.
Prep: 19 min., **Cook:** 25 min.

Melody Rudolph
Santee, California

Melody uses Parmesan cheese and baked beans to make this dish. We preferred kidney beans for a less sweet flavor, and we thought Cheddar cheese worked well with the other Mexican flavors.

Brined Lemon Chicken Waikiki

Brining the chicken (soaking it in a salt-water solution) tremendously improves the flavor and tenderizes the chicken.

4 cups water
¾ cup kosher salt
¾ cup sugar
4 skinned and boned chicken breasts (about 1½ pounds)
6 tablespoons pineapple preserves
1 tablespoon grated lemon rind
2 tablespoons fresh lemon juice
1 tablespoon grated fresh ginger
1 tablespoon dark sesame oil
2 tablespoons soy sauce
½ teaspoon dried crushed red pepper
1 to 2 teaspoons freshly ground black pepper
1 tablespoon vegetable oil
12 ounces mixed salad greens
2 tablespoons sesame seeds, lightly toasted
Garnishes: fresh pineapple, lemon slices

Combine water, salt, and sugar in a large bowl, stirring until salt and sugar dissolve. Add chicken; cover and refrigerate 1 hour.

Whisk together pineapple preserves and next 6 ingredients; set aside.

Remove chicken from brine; discard brine. Pat chicken with paper towels, and sprinkle with black pepper.

If you don't have kosher salt, **Janice** recommends using half the amount of regular salt in this flavorful chicken-topped green salad.

Heat oil in a 12-inch heavy skillet or chicken fryer over medium heat, and add chicken. Cook 16 to 18 minutes or until done, turning once. Remove chicken from skillet; set aside, and keep warm.

Add pineapple preserves mixture to skillet. Bring to a boil, stirring often. Reduce heat; add chicken, turning until chicken is well glazed. Remove chicken from skillet, reserving glaze. Cut chicken crosswise into thin slices; place over crisp greens on individual salad plates. Drizzle with remaining glaze, and sprinkle with sesame seeds. Garnish, if desired. **Makes:** 4 servings.
Prep: 12 min., **Cook:** 26 min., **Other:** 1 hr.

Tip: Because of the high sodium content in the brine, no additional salt is needed.

Janice Elder
Charlotte, North Carolina

Rosemary Chicken

Try this juicy, flavorful bird instead of turkey for your next holiday meal. With or without the vegetables, it's perfect for small gatherings, or if you don't want a lot of leftovers.

1   (7- to 7½-pound) roasting
    chicken
3   tablespoons chopped fresh
    rosemary
1   tablespoon salt
1   tablespoon fresh lemon juice
1   teaspoon freshly ground pepper
¼   cup raisins
2   tablespoons olive oil
½   pound fresh pearl onions, peeled
1   (16-ounce) package baby
    carrots
12 small round red potatoes,
    halved (about 1½ pounds)
Garnish: fresh rosemary

Remove and reserve giblets and neck from chicken for other uses. Rinse chicken with cold water; pat dry.

Stir together rosemary and next 3 ingredients to form a paste. Starting at neck cavity, loosen skin from breast and drumsticks by inserting fingers and gently pushing between skin and meat. (Do not totally detach skin.) Rub half of rosemary mixture under skin; rub remaining half in cavity. Sprinkle raisins in cavity.

Place chicken, breast side up, in a lightly greased large roasting pan. Tie ends of legs together with string; tuck wing tips under. Brush chicken with oil. Arrange onions, carrots, and potatoes around chicken.

Bake, uncovered, at 350° for 2 hours and 15 minutes until a meat thermometer inserted in thigh registers 180°, stirring vegetables halfway through. Cover loosely with foil, and let stand 10 minutes before slicing. Garnish, if desired.

Makes: 6 servings.

Prep: 20 min., **Cook:** 2 hrs., 15 min., **Other:** 10 min.

Tip: For ease in peeling pearl onions, cook them in boiling water 3 minutes. Drain, rinse with cold water, and peel.

Janine Newberry
Punta Gorda, Florida

To help the veggies cook evenly, we surrounded the chicken with them rather than stuffing half of them inside as **Janine** does.

Rosemary Chicken

Chicken Breasts With Guacamole

Chicken Breasts With Guacamole

Contrast is the operative word to describe this dish—hot-off-the-grill chicken, topped with cool, creamy guacamole, juicy tomato, and crunchy bacon.

4   **ripe avocados, mashed**
6   **tablespoons fresh lemon or lime juice**
½   **cup chopped red onion**
¼   **cup chopped fresh cilantro**
2   **garlic cloves, minced**
2   **jalapeño peppers, seeded and minced**
¼   **teaspoon salt**
¼   **teaspoon pepper**
8   **skinned and boned chicken breasts**
2   **tablespoons olive oil**
Shredded lettuce
2   **medium-size tomatoes, chopped**
4   **bacon slices, cooked and crumbled**
Garnish: fresh cilantro sprig

Stir together first 8 ingredients in a medium bowl. Press plastic wrap directly onto surface of guacamole to make an airtight seal; chill.

Place chicken between 2 sheets of heavy-duty plastic wrap; flatten to ¼-inch thickness, using a mallet or rolling pin. Rub chicken with olive oil. Grill chicken, covered with grill lid, over medium-high heat (350° to 400°) 2 minutes on each side or until done.

Place chicken breasts on lettuce-lined plates. Spoon desired amount of guacamole over each chicken breast; top with tomato, and sprinkle with bacon. Garnish, if desired. **Makes:** 8 servings.

Prep: 30 min., **Cook:** 4 min.

Tip: Be sure to seal the guacamole well; keeping out air prevents darkening. Serve extra guacamole with tortilla chips.

Carol Frederick
Oro Valley, Arizona

Carol tops this dish with shreds of prosciutto, but we used bacon instead to stay with the Southwestern theme.

Russian Chicken

You'll love this simple version of sweet-and-sour chicken. Put the rice on to cook during the latter part of the time the chicken cooks.

1 (8-ounce) bottle Russian dressing
1 (1.0-ounce) envelope dry onion soup mix
1 (10-ounce) jar apricot preserves
6 skinned and boned chicken breasts
Hot cooked rice

Combine first 3 ingredients in a small bowl; set aside.

Place chicken breasts in a lightly greased 13- x 9-inch baking dish. Pour dressing mixture evenly over chicken; cover with nonstick aluminum foil. Bake at 350° for 1½ hours. Serve with hot cooked rice.

Makes: 6 servings.

Prep: 4 min., **Cook:** 1½ hrs.

Tip: As an alternative to apricot preserves, use pineapple preserves or orange marmalade.

Janice Strout
Ada, Oklahoma

Janice ensures this meal is no-fuss all the way to the end by serving the chicken and sauce over boil-in-bag rice.

Salsie Chicken

Keep these ingredients on hand for this easy weeknight pleaser. Add a salad, and you're good to go.

4 skinned and boned chicken breasts
¼ teaspoon salt
2 teaspoons olive oil
1¾ cups hot cooked rice
1 (14.5-ounce) can diced tomatoes in sauce, undrained
1 (16-ounce) jar chunky salsa with cilantro
1 (8-ounce) package shredded Monterey Jack cheese with habanero peppers

Place chicken between 2 sheets of heavy-duty plastic wrap; flatten to ¼-inch thickness, using a meat mallet or rolling pin. Sprinkle chicken with salt. Place olive oil in a large nonstick skillet over medium-high heat until hot. Add chicken; cook 3 minutes on each side or until browned.

Spoon rice into a lightly greased 11- x 7-inch baking dish. Top with chicken. Combine tomatoes and salsa, stirring well. Spoon tomato mixture over chicken. Bake, covered, at 350° for 25 minutes or until chicken is done. Uncover and top with cheese. Bake 5 more minutes or until cheese melts.

Makes: 4 servings.

Prep: 15 min., **Cook:** 36 min.

Rex Smyser
Burbank, Washington

Rex's family says, "the more cheese, the better" when it comes to this picante chicken and rice casserole.

Asian Chicken Salad With Peanuts

For a more authentic Asian flavor, try a sesame dressing or other Asian-inspired dressing in place of poppy seed dressing.

¼ teaspoon salt
⅛ teaspoon **pepper**
4 skinned and boned chicken breasts
2 romaine lettuce hearts, chopped (about 9 cups)
1 (15-ounce) can mandarin oranges, drained
1 (8-ounce) can sliced water chestnuts, drained
1 red bell pepper, cut into strips
1 bunch green onions, sliced
1 cup shredded red cabbage
1 cup dry-roasted peanuts
1 cup poppy seed dressing
1 cup chow mein noodles

Sprinkle salt and pepper evenly over chicken. Grill chicken, covered with grill lid, over medium-high heat (350° to 400°) 6 to 8 minutes on each side or until done. Cut chicken into strips. **Combine** chicken strips, lettuce, and next 6 ingredients in a large bowl. Drizzle with poppy seed dressing, and gently toss to coat. Sprinkle with chow mein noodles. **Makes:** 6 to 8 servings.
Prep: 8 min., **Cook:** 16 min.

Tip: If time doesn't allow for grilling the chicken, look for grilled chicken strips in the meat department of your supermarket. Three (6-ounce) packages grilled chicken strips can be substituted for 4 chicken breasts.

Melissa Sherman
Alachua, Florida

We preferred large strips of chicken in this colorful main-dish salad, but **Melissa** suggests the chicken can be shredded or cubed, as well.

Lo Mein Salad With Grilled Asian Chicken

Dark sesame oil adds intense flavor to this recipe.

½ cup soy sauce
½ cup sherry
2 garlic cloves, pressed
1 (2-inch) piece fresh ginger, peeled and sliced
1 tablespoon sugar
½ teaspoon dried crushed red pepper
4 skinned and boned chicken breasts
8 ounces uncooked dried linguine
3 cups broccoli florets
1 carrot, shredded (about ¾ cup)
4 green onions, sliced
2 tablespoons dark sesame oil
3 tablespoons soy sauce
2 tablespoons rice wine vinegar
2 tablespoons chopped dry-roasted peanuts

Combine first 6 ingredients in a large zip-top freezer bag. Add chicken; seal and marinate in refrigerator 1 hour, turning occasionally.
Meanwhile, bring 2 quarts water to a boil in a large Dutch oven. Add pasta; cook 4 minutes. Add broccoli; cook 3 minutes. Add carrot; cook 1 minute or until pasta is al dente. Drain pasta and vegetables; rinse with cold water. Drain well. Place in a medium bowl; set aside. Combine green onions and next 3 ingredients in a small bowl; pour over pasta mixture, tossing well to coat. Set aside.
Remove chicken from marinade; discard marinade. Grill chicken, covered with grill lid, over high heat (400° to 500°) 5 minutes on each side or until done. Remove from heat; cut into strips.

Divide pasta mixture evenly among 4 plates; top each with sliced chicken. Sprinkle with peanuts before serving. **Makes:** 4 servings.
Prep: 10 min., **Cook:** 18 min., **Other:** 1 hr.

Tip: This salad works well with any long, thin pasta, so feel free to try it with spaghetti or fettuccine.

Lynch Orr
Nashville, Tennessee

If you don't have rice wine vinegar, use red wine vinegar like **Lynch** does. We used rice wine vinegar to carry out the Asian accent.

Asian Chicken Salad With Peanuts

Hot 'n' Spicy Rice 'n' Beans With Grilled Chicken and Sausage

¼ cup olive oil
1 tablespoon garlic powder
1 tablespoon Cajun seasoning
½ teaspoon mesquite liquid smoke
3 (6-ounce) skinned and boned chicken breasts
Hot 'n' Spicy Rice
1 (16-ounce) package kielbasa sausage
1 (14.5-ounce) can diced tomatoes with green pepper and onions, drained
1 (15-ounce) can black beans, drained
1 (16-ounce) can chili beans, drained

Combine first 4 ingredients in a large zip-top freezer bag. Add chicken; seal and marinate in refrigerator 30 minutes, turning once.
Prepare Hot 'n' Spicy Rice.
Remove chicken from bag; discard marinade. Grill chicken and sausage, covered with grill lid, over high heat (400° to 500°) 15 minutes or until sausage is hot and chicken is no longer pink, turning once.
Remove chicken from grill; let stand 5 minutes. Chop chicken into 1-inch pieces, and slice sausage.
Stir tomatoes, black beans, and chili beans into cooked rice mixture. Add chicken and sausage; cover and simmer, stirring occasionally, 12 minutes.
Makes: 6 to 8 servings.
Prep: 30 min., **Cook:** 27 min., **Other:** 35 min.

Hot 'n' Spicy Rice:
1 tablespoon olive oil
1 tablespoon minced garlic
1 cup uncooked long-grain rice
2 cups chicken broth
2 teaspoons dried thyme
1 teaspoon onion powder
1 teaspoon Cajun seasoning
1 teaspoon hot sauce
½ teaspoon celery salt
½ teaspoon ground cumin
¼ teaspoon salt
¼ teaspoon pepper

Heat oil in a 4½-quart Dutch oven over medium heat; add garlic, and sauté 1 minute. Add remaining ingredients; stir well. Bring to a boil; reduce heat, and simmer, covered, 20 minutes. **Makes:** 3 cups.
Prep: 5 min., **Cook:** 20 min.

Tip: You can easily adjust the "heat" of the rice by adding more hot sauce.

Suzy Weaver
Costa Mesa, California

Suzy serves this one-dish meal in bowls, and garnishes each serving with chopped green onions and diced red bell pepper. We found that it tastes just as good, if not better, the day after it's made.

Italian Chicken Florentine Napoleons

You'll recognize this dish because it has many of the components of lasagna, but it's assembled in stacks full of Italian flavor.

1 medium eggplant (about 1 pound)
Vegetable cooking spray
½ teaspoon salt, divided
½ teaspoon black pepper, divided
¼ teaspoon ground red pepper
2 teaspoons dried oregano, divided
1 pound skinned and boned chicken breasts, cut into ¼-inch strips
1 tablespoon olive oil
1 (10-ounce) package frozen leaf spinach
1 (26-ounce) jar chunky pasta sauce with tomato, garlic, and onion
1 (15-ounce) container ricotta cheese
1 large egg, beaten
½ cup freshly shredded Romano cheese, divided
8 ounces uncooked spaghetti
1 (2.2-ounce) package fully cooked bacon, cut crosswise into ½-inch pieces

Peel eggplant, if desired. Cut eggplant into 8 (¼-inch) slices, reserving any remaining eggplant for another use. Place slices on a lightly greased 15- x 10-inch jellyroll pan. Coat slices with cooking spray. Sprinkle with ¼ teaspoon salt, ¼ teaspoon black pepper, red pepper, and, 1 teaspoon oregano. Bake, uncovered, at 450° for 12 minutes.

Meanwhile, cook chicken strips in hot olive oil over medium-high heat 4 minutes or until done. Set aside. Puncture (microwave-safe) package of spinach with a knife; place package in a bowl. Microwave spinach in package at HIGH 4 minutes. Drain and squeeze excess moisture from spinach; set aside.

Set aside 1¾ cups pasta sauce. Spread remaining pasta sauce in a lightly greased 13- x 9-inch baking dish. Arrange eggplant slices in a single layer over sauce.

Combine ricotta cheese, egg, ¼ cup Romano cheese, remaining ¼ teaspoon salt, remaining ¼ teaspoon black pepper, and remaining 1 teaspoon oregano in a medium bowl; stir well. Spoon cheese mixture evenly on top of eggplant slices. (Do not spread cheese mixture.) Top ricotta cheese mixture with chicken strips and spinach, making 8 individual stacks. Spoon reserved 1¾ cups pasta sauce evenly on top of stacks. Sprinkle with remaining ¼ cup Romano cheese.

Bake, uncovered, at 450° for 15 minutes.

While eggplant mixture bakes, cook pasta in boiling salted water according to package directions; drain and keep warm. Microwave bacon at HIGH for 1 minute.

Remove casserole from oven; let stand, uncovered, 10 minutes. Sprinkle with bacon. Serve immediately over pasta.

Makes: 4 to 6 servings.
Prep: 47 min., **Cook:** 27 min., **Other:** 10 min.

Tip: Purchase an eggplant that's about 4 inches in diameter so 8 slices will fit in one layer in baking dish. Slices shrink slightly during the initial baking step.

Sharon Strain
Memphis, Tennessee

Angel hair pasta was **Sharon's** choice to serve as the base for these eggplant stacks, but we used sturdier spaghetti noodles to stand up to the hearty stacks.

Glazed Pecan Chicken With Tortellini

Pecans add texture to this simple pasta and chicken dish.

3   cups chicken broth, divided
3   tablespoons olive oil, divided
1   teaspoon salt
1   teaspoon dried thyme
½   teaspoon garlic powder with parsley
1½ pounds skinned and boned chicken breasts, sliced into 1-inch strips
2   tablespoons butter
½   cup sliced red onion (about ½ medium onion)
1   large red bell pepper, sliced
2   garlic cloves, minced
¾   cup coarsely chopped pecans
3   tablespoons white wine vinegar
1   (8.9-ounce) package dried three-cheese tortellini *
1   (14-ounce) can quartered artichoke hearts, drained
⅔   cup shredded Parmesan cheese

Combine ½ cup chicken broth, 1 tablespoon olive oil, and next 3 ingredients in a large zip-top freezer bag. Add chicken; seal and marinate in refrigerator 2 hours. Remove chicken; discard marinade.
Melt butter and remaining 2 tablespoons oil in a 12-inch skillet over medium-high heat. Add chicken; cook just until browned. Add onion and next 3 ingredients; sauté 6 minutes or until onion is tender and chicken is almost done. Add vinegar and remaining 2½ cups chicken broth; bring to a boil. Stir in tortellini and artichokes; simmer, uncovered, 12 minutes or until tortellini is tender. Sprinkle with Parmesan cheese before serving.
Makes: 6 servings.
Prep: 6 min., **Cook:** 20 min., **Other:** 2 hrs.

*For testing purposes only, we used Barilla tortellini. This tortellini can be found in the dried pasta section of your grocery store.

Barbie Lee
Tavernier, Florida

Barbie says you can marinate the chicken anywhere from 15 minutes to 24 hours, but we found it has more flavor from at least a 2-hour stint in the savory marinade, if you have the time.

Polynesian Teriyaki Chicken Salad

The cool fruity blend of mandarin oranges and pineapple mixed with the teriyaki dressing is the perfect meal for a hot summer night.

¼   cup water
4   teriyaki-marinated skinned and boned chicken breasts *
1   (10-ounce) package mixed salad greens
1   small red bell pepper, thinly sliced
2   carrots, grated
1   (11-ounce) can mandarin oranges, drained
1   (15-ounce) can pineapple chunks in juice, drained
2   tablespoons water
1   (0.7-ounce) envelope Italian dressing mix
¼   cup balsamic vinegar
3   tablespoons teriyaki sauce
¼   cup olive oil
2   cups wide chow mein noodles

Heat ¼ cup water in a large nonstick skillet over medium heat; add chicken, and cook 12 to 14 minutes or until chicken is browned and liquid is slightly thickened. Remove chicken from skillet; slice into strips.
Meanwhile, wash salad mix with cold water; drain well. Place in a large bowl; add bell pepper and next 3 ingredients, tossing well. Cover and chill 10 minutes. In a small bowl, combine 2 tablespoons water, dressing mix, vinegar, and teriyaki sauce, whisking until blended. Add oil; whisk briskly. Set aside.
Divide salad mixture among 4 plates; top with chicken strips. Serve with dressing and chow mein noodles.
Makes: 4 servings.
Prep: 4 min., **Cook:** 14 min., **Other:** 10 min.

*For testing purposes only, we used Tyson's Teriyaki-Marinated Chicken Breasts.

Dulce Castillo
Charlotte, North Carolina

Dulce typically serves the hot chicken over the salad greens. We discovered the salad is also delicious when the chicken is made ahead, chilled, and served cold, making this a great make-ahead dinner option.

Chicken Florentine With Mushrooms and Artichokes

6 ounces dried angel hair pasta
2 garlic cloves, minced and divided
6 tablespoons olive oil, divided
4 skinned and boned chicken breasts, cut into 1-inch pieces
½ (10-ounce) package fresh spinach
6 tablespoons butter or margarine
3 green onions, chopped
1 (8-ounce) package sliced fresh mushrooms
¼ cup all-purpose flour
2 tablespoons chopped fresh parsley
1 teaspoon salt
½ teaspoon freshly ground pepper
1 cup milk
½ cup dry white wine *
½ cup (2 ounces) shredded Swiss cheese

1 (6-ounce) jar marinated quartered artichoke hearts, drained
3 tablespoons fresh lemon juice

Cook pasta in boiling salted water according to package directions; drain.
Sauté 1 garlic clove in 3 tablespoons olive oil in a large skillet over medium-high heat 2 minutes. Add to pasta, and toss; set aside.
Heat remaining 3 tablespoons olive oil in same skillet over medium-high heat. Add remaining garlic clove; sauté 2 minutes. Add chicken; cook 6 minutes or until browned.
Place pasta into a lightly greased 13- x 9-inch baking dish. Layer spinach over pasta; top evenly with chicken.
Melt butter in same skillet over medium heat. Add green onions and mushrooms; cook 3 minutes or until

mushrooms are tender. Stir in flour and next 3 ingredients. Reduce heat to medium-low. Gradually whisk in milk and wine; cook 1 minute. Add cheese, stirring just until melted. Remove from heat; stir in artichokes and lemon juice. Pour sauce mixture evenly over chicken.
Bake at 350° for 30 minutes. Serve immediately. **Makes:** 4 servings.
Prep: 21 min., **Cook:** 57 min.

*Substitute chicken broth for dry white wine, if desired.

James D. Odom
Leroy, Alabama

James recommends serving French bread with olive oil for dipping and a Pinot Grigio with this sensational dish.

Easy Green Chile Chicken

The no-hassle cleanup that comes with using a foil oven bag makes this easy dish even easier.

1 large-size foil oven bag
Vegetable cooking spray
1 tablespoon fajita seasoning
2 pounds chicken breast tenders
1 (14.5-ounce) can diced tomatoes, undrained
1 tablespoon chopped fresh cilantro
2 (4-ounce) cans whole green chiles, drained and cut in half
1 cup (4 ounces) shredded Monterey Jack cheese
Tortilla chips

Coat inside of oven bag with cooking spray; place bag on a baking sheet, and set aside.

Sprinkle fajita seasoning over chicken tenders. Place chicken in oven bag; top evenly with tomatoes, cilantro, and chiles. Fold edges of the bag over to seal. Bake at 350° for 35 to 40 minutes or until chicken is done. Remove from oven; open bag with a sharp knife, and peel back foil. Immediately sprinkle with cheese. Serve with tortilla chips.

Makes: 6 servings.
Prep: 3 min., **Cook:** 40 min.

Tip: Cooking chicken in a foil oven bag keeps it moist.

Cynthia Clarke
Mira Loma, California

Cynthia sprinkles tortilla chips over the chicken mixture before it bakes, which steams and softens the chips. We enjoyed the crunch of the chips simply served alongside the chicken.

Peanut Chicken Pot Pie

2 tablespoons butter or margarine
½ cup chopped celery
½ cup chopped onion (1 small onion)
3 cups chopped cooked chicken
2 (10¾-ounce) can cream of chicken soup, undiluted
1 (10¾-ounce) can cream of celery soup, undiluted
1 (16-ounce) package frozen mixed vegetables, thawed
1 cup chicken broth
1 cup unsalted peanuts
½ teaspoon salt
½ teaspoon poultry seasoning
½ teaspoon pepper
1½ (15-ounce) packages refrigerated piecrusts (3 piecrusts)

Melt butter in a medium skillet over medium heat; add celery and onion, and sauté until tender.

Combine cooked vegetables, chicken, and next 8 ingredients in a large bowl.

Fit 2 piecrusts into an ungreased 13- x 9-inch baking dish; trim off excess pastry along edges. Pour chicken mixture into crust. Roll remaining piecrust to press out fold lines; cut into ¾-inch strips, and arrange in a lattice design over filling, pressing edges of lattice strips and bottom crust to dish to seal.

Bake at 425° for 40 minutes or until golden. Let stand 5 minutes before serving. **Makes:** 8 servings.
Prep: 26 min., **Cook:** 43 min., **Other:** 5 min.

Tip: Either 1 (20-ounce) package frozen diced cooked chicken or a deli rotisserie chicken will yield about 3 cups cooked chicken for this dish.

Julie McCormack
Killeen, Texas

Julie tells us this pot pie is always a hit at covered-dish suppers.

Chicken Nachos

Whether you have hungry boys who need a little snack while watching the game, or you just want a quick, no-fuss dinner, these cheesy chicken nachos are the perfect treat.

2   tablespoons olive oil
1   medium onion, chopped
2   garlic cloves, minced
3   cups chopped cooked chicken
1   (10-ounce) can diced tomatoes
    and green chiles, undrained
1   teaspoon salt
1½ teaspoons chili powder
½   teaspoon garlic pepper*
¾   (11-ounce) package
    scoop-shaped tortilla chips*
1   (8-ounce) package shredded
    colby and Monterey Jack
    cheese
Sour cream
Sliced pickled jalapeño peppers

Heat oil in a large nonstick skillet over medium-high heat. Add onion and garlic; cook 3 minutes or until onion is tender.

Add chicken and next 4 ingredients; cook 6 minutes or until liquid is absorbed.
Arrange tortilla chips in a 13- x 9-inch baking dish. Spoon chicken mixture over top of chips. Sprinkle with cheese.
Bake at 350° for 10 minutes or until cheese melts. Serve with sour cream and jalapeño peppers. **Makes:** 4 to 6 servings.
Prep: 11 min., **Cook:** 19 min.

*For testing purposes only, we used Lawry's Garlic Pepper and Tostitos Scoops.

Tip: You can purchase precooked skinned and boned chicken breasts in the meat department of your local supermarket.

Barry Moore
Lexington, South Carolina

Texas Ranch Casserole

Here's a new spin on the original King Ranch Chicken recipe.

4   cups chopped cooked chicken
1   (10¾-ounce) can cream of
    mushroom soup, undiluted
1   (10¾-ounce) can cream of
    chicken soup, undiluted
1   (15¼-ounce) can whole kernel
    corn, drained
1   (10-ounce) can diced tomatoes
    and green chiles, undrained
1   teaspoon chili powder
¼   teaspoon garlic powder
¼   teaspoon pepper
12 (6-inch) corn tortillas, cut into
    strips

2   cups (8 ounces) shredded
    Monterey Jack cheese
1   large tomato, chopped
½   cup sour cream
¼   cup chopped fresh cilantro

Combine first 8 ingredients in a large bowl; stir well.
Place half of tortilla strips in a lightly greased 13- x 9-inch baking dish; top with half the chicken mixture, and sprinkle with 1 cup cheese. Repeat layers.

Bake, uncovered, at 350° for 35 minutes. Serve with chopped tomato, sour cream, and cilantro. **Makes:** 6 to 8 servings.
Prep: 8 min., **Cook:** 35 min.

Patricia Griffin
Austin, Texas

Poppy Seed Chicken Divine

Poppy Seed Chicken Divine

This recipe marries two classic recipes into one dish your family is sure to love.

1   (4-ounce) package fast-cooking long-grain and wild rice mix *
1   (10-ounce) package frozen chopped broccoli
3   cups chopped cooked chicken
1½ cups (6 ounces) shredded sharp Cheddar cheese
1   (10¾-ounce) can cream of chicken soup, undiluted
1   (8-ounce) container sour cream
½   cup butter, melted
35 round buttery crackers, crushed *
1   tablespoon poppy seeds

Cook rice according to package directions. **Cook** broccoli according to package directions; drain.

Combine chicken, rice, broccoli, cheese, soup, and sour cream. Spoon into a lightly greased 8-inch square baking dish.

Alison cooks 3 chicken breasts to yield the 3 cups chopped cooked chicken called for in this recipe.

Combine butter, crushed crackers, and poppy seeds; sprinkle over chicken mixture. Bake, uncovered, at 350° for 30 minutes. **Makes:** 4 servings.
Prep: 32 min., **Cook:** 30 min.

*For testing purposes only, we used Success Long Grain and Wild Rice and Ritz crackers.

Tip: This casserole can easily be made ahead. Top with cracker mixture right before baking.

Alison Day
Charlotte, North Carolina

Chicken Enchiladas

8   (8-inch) flour tortillas
1   (10¾-ounce) can cream of mushroom soup, undiluted
1   (8-ounce) container sour cream
1   (4½-ounce) can chopped green chiles, undrained
1   medium onion, chopped (about 1 cup)
1   tablespoon olive oil
2   (6-ounce) packages Southwestern-flavored chicken breast strips, coarsely chopped
1   (8-ounce) package shredded Mexican four-cheese blend, divided

Wrap tortillas in aluminum foil. Bake at 350° for 10 minutes or until warm.

Meanwhile, stir together soup, sour cream, and green chiles in a medium bowl until blended; set aside.

Sauté onion in hot olive oil over medium-high heat 5 minutes or until tender. Stir in chicken and half of soup mixture. Cook 1 minute or until thoroughly heated.

Spoon about ½ cup chicken mixture down center of each tortilla; sprinkle with 2 tablespoons cheese, and roll up. Place enchiladas, seam sides down, in a lightly greased 13- x 9-inch baking dish. Spread remaining soup mixture over enchiladas. Cover and bake at 350° for 30 minutes; uncover and sprinkle with remaining cheese. Bake 10 more minutes or until cheese melts. Serve immediately. **Makes:** 4 servings.
Prep: 13 min., **Cook:** 46 min.

Barbara Bishop
Magee, Mississippi

Barbara layers all the ingredients in a baking dish to create a casserole. The flavors were great, but we preferred to make individual enchiladas. We also added sour cream to the filling for creaminess.

Italian Chicken Casserole

1   (15-ounce) container ricotta
    cheese
1½ cups grated Asiago cheese
¼   cup shredded Parmesan cheese
2   large eggs, lightly beaten
1   tablespoon dried parsley flakes
1   teaspoon salt
1   teaspoon black pepper
1   teaspoon dried minced onion
1   teaspoon bottled minced
    roasted garlic
⅛   teaspoon ground red pepper
1   (26-ounce) jar roasted garlic
    and onion pasta sauce
1   (24-ounce) package frozen
    cheese-filled ravioli, thawed

2   (6-ounce) packages Italian-
    flavored chicken breast strips,
    coarsely chopped
1   (10-ounce) package frozen
    chopped spinach, thawed and
    drained
1   cup (4 ounces) shredded
    mozzarella cheese
1   cup (4 ounces) shredded Italian
    three-cheese blend

Stir together first 10 ingredients in a medium bowl; set aside.

Spread ½ cup pasta sauce in a lightly greased 13- x 9-inch baking dish. Arrange ravioli over sauce; pour remaining sauce over ravioli. Layer with chopped chicken, spinach, and mozzarella cheese. Spread ricotta cheese mixture over mozzarella layer. Top with Italian cheese blend. Cover and bake at 350° for 30 minutes; uncover and bake 30 more minutes or until lightly browned. **Makes:** 8 servings.
Prep: 25 min., **Cook:** 1 hr.

Rita A. Lutz
Amelia, Ohio

Rita adds a little more than a pound of shredded hash browns to this one-dish meal, but we omitted them since ravioli was also in the recipe.

Savory Chicken Skillet

Mashed potatoes or rice pair well with this saucy dish.

6   chicken thighs, skinned (about
    1½ pounds)
½   teaspoon salt
½   teaspoon black pepper
1   tablespoon olive oil
6   garlic cloves, minced
1   (14½-ounce) can stewed
    tomatoes, undrained
1   cup frozen pearl onions
5   ounces andouille sausage, diced
    (1 cup)

1   cup dry red wine
2   tablespoons balsamic vinegar
1   (2½-ounce) jar pitted Spanish
    olives, drained and chopped
¼   teaspoon dried crushed red
    pepper
¼   cup chopped fresh parsley

Sprinkle chicken with salt and pepper. Brown chicken in hot olive oil in a large skillet over medium-high heat. Remove chicken from skillet; sauté garlic in drippings 3 seconds. Quickly stir in tomatoes and next 6 ingredients. Add chicken to tomato mixture, turning to coat. Bring to a boil; cover, reduce heat, and simmer 50 minutes or until chicken is tender. Sprinkle with parsley.
Makes: 3 to 6 servings.
Prep: 11 min., **Cook:** 1 hr.

Gilda Lester
Wilmington, North Carolina

Gilda browns the chicken in a skillet and then transfers it to a casserole dish and bakes it in the oven. We hate to dirty more dishes than necessary, so we tested the recipe a second time, cooking it in the skillet. It was equally yummy.

Oven-Fried Chicken With Potatoes and Raisin Sauce

You have to try this to believe it. We think you'll love this fried chicken glazed in a yummy raisin sauce.

Raisin Sauce
- 1 (1.0-ounce) envelope dry onion soup mix
- 1 cup all-purpose flour
- 2 teaspoons dried basil
- 2 teaspoons dried oregano
- 2 teaspoons dried parsley flakes
- 1 teaspoon garlic powder
- 1½ teaspoons salt, divided
- 1½ teaspoons pepper, divided
- 1 large egg
- ¼ cup milk
- 3½ pounds chicken pieces
- 5 medium baking potatoes, cut into 2-inch pieces
- ¾ cup sliced celery

Prepare Raisin Sauce.

Combine onion soup mix, next 5 ingredients, and 1 teaspoon each of salt and pepper in a large zip-top freezer bag.

Combine egg and milk in a shallow dish; dip chicken in egg mixture. Add chicken to flour mixture; seal and shake to coat.

Combine potatoes and celery in a lightly greased 12- x 8-inch baking dish. Sprinkle with ½ teaspoon each of salt and pepper. Arrange chicken over vegetable mixture. Pour Raisin Sauce over chicken.

Bake, uncovered, at 425° for 50 minutes or until potatoes are tender, basting with Raisin Sauce after 25 minutes.

Makes: 4 servings.

Prep: 20 min., **Cook:** 50 min.

The unusual combination of ingredients in this recipe shows **Barbara's** flare for flavors. All the components of the dish work perfectly together.

Raisin Sauce:
- ¾ cup sugar
- 2 tablespoons cornstarch
- 2 cups water
- 2 tablespoons lemon juice
- 2 tablespoons butter
- 1 tablespoon chopped fresh rosemary
- 1 cup raisins

Combine sugar and cornstarch in a medium saucepan; gradually stir in water and next 3 ingredients until smooth. Bring to a boil over medium-high heat; cook 3 minutes or until slightly thickened, stirring constantly. Stir in raisins. **Makes:** 3 cups.

Prep: 5 min., **Cook:** 3 min.

Barbara Bleigh
Colonial Heights, Virginia

Southwestern Fish

The intense spicy flavors are balanced by the mild sweetness of the fish.

2   (5-ounce) bags saffron rice
1   (19-ounce) can black beans, rinsed and drained
1   (10-ounce) can diced tomatoes and green chiles, undrained
1   tablespoon chili powder
1   teaspoon ground coriander
1   teaspoon ground cumin
½   teaspoon salt
½   teaspoon ground cumin
½   teaspoon ground coriander
1   teaspoon chili powder
1   tablespoon olive oil
4   (6-ounce) mahimahi fillets
2   teaspoons fresh lemon juice
Salsa
Sour cream
Shredded Cheddar or Monterey Jack cheese

Cook rice according to package directions; keep warm.

Meanwhile, combine beans and next 4 ingredients in a medium saucepan. Simmer 10 minutes or until slightly thickened.

Meanwhile, combine salt and next 4 ingredients in a small bowl. Rub mixture evenly over fillets. Sprinkle with lemon juice. Grill fillets, covered with grill lid, over medium-high heat (350° to 400°) 4 minutes on each side or until fish flakes with a fork.

To serve, divide rice evenly among 4 plates. Spoon bean mixture over rice; top with 1 fish fillet. Serve with salsa, sour cream, and shredded cheese.

Makes: 4 servings.
Prep: 6 min., **Cook:** 20 min.

Tip: Try this recipe with different kinds of fish, such as catfish or grouper.

Catherine Chandler
Charlotte, North Carolina

Catherine serves Cheddar cheese with this Southwestern sensation, but we liked the taste of Monterey Jack, too.

Southwestern Fish

South-of-the-Border Cordon Bleu

You'll be pleasantly surprised with the generous helping of ham and turkey rolled up in tortillas and smothered with a spicy cheese sauce.

2   (10¾-ounce) cans Cheddar
    cheese soup, undiluted
1   (12-ounce) can evaporated milk
1   (10-ounce) can extra-hot diced
    tomatoes and green chiles,
    drained
1½ pounds thinly sliced deli turkey
1½ pounds thinly sliced deli ham
6   (10-inch) flour tortillas
6   prepackaged sharp Cheddar
    cheese slices
6   prepackaged mozzarella cheese
    slices
½   cup chopped green onions
Sour cream

Whisk together soup, milk, and tomatoes in a large bowl until smooth. Pour 1 cup soup mixture in a lightly greased 13- x 9-inch baking dish.

Layer ¼ pound each of turkey and ham over each tortilla. Place 1 slice each of Cheddar and mozzarella cheese over ham layer. Roll up tightly, and place seam side down over soup mixture. Pour remaining soup mixture over tortilla wraps to cover.

Bake, uncovered, at 350° for 50 minutes or until thoroughly heated and bubbly. Let stand 10 minutes before serving. Sprinkle with green onions, and serve with sour cream. **Makes:** 6 servings.

Prep: 20 min., **Cook:** 50 min., **Other:** 10 min.

Tip: Tone down this dish by using mild diced tomatoes and green chilies.

Patricia Turner
Hudson, Florida

Breakfast Strata

Here's a real eye-opener: a breakfast dish with an Italian twist.

1   pound ground pork sausage
3   cups (12 ounces) shredded
    mozzarella cheese, divided
½   cup crumbled goat cheese
½   cup shredded Parmesan cheese
3   large eggs, lightly beaten
½   cup ricotta cheese
¼   cup whipping cream
1   medium tomato, cut into
    6 slices
2   tablespoons pesto sauce

Crumble sausage into bite-size pieces. Cook in a medium skillet over medium heat until browned; drain well.

Combine sausage, 2 cups mozzarella cheese, and next 5 ingredients in a large bowl; spread into a lightly greased 11- x 7-inch baking dish. Place tomato slices evenly on top of mixture; top with pesto sauce.

Bake, uncovered, at 350° for 25 minutes; remove from oven. Sprinkle remaining 1 cup mozzarella cheese over strata; return to oven. Bake 5 more minutes. **Makes:** 4 to 6 servings.
Prep: 9 min., **Cook:** 38 min.

Tip: This dish is hearty enough to serve for supper.

Jane Knight
Decatur, Alabama

Jane prepares this strata in a 13- x 9-inch baking dish. We opted for thicker squares, so we baked it in a smaller dish.

Crustless Bacon and Mushroom Quiche

10 large eggs
½ cup all-purpose flour
1 (16-ounce) container cottage cheese
½ cup butter or margarine, melted
1 teaspoon baking powder
¼ teaspoon salt
4 cups (16 ounces) shredded sharp Cheddar cheese, divided
15 bacon slices, cooked and crumbled
1 (8-ounce) package sliced fresh mushrooms

Beat eggs at medium speed with an electric mixer until foamy. Add flour and next 4 ingredients, beating well. Stir in 2 cups cheese, bacon, and mushrooms. Pour into a lightly greased 13- x 9-inch baking dish.

Karie uses precooked bacon to speed up the preparation for this no-crust quiche.

Bake, uncovered, at 350° for 40 minutes or until set. Sprinkle with remaining 2 cups cheese, and bake, uncovered, 5 more minutes or until cheese melts. **Makes:** 12 servings.
Prep: 15 min., **Cook:** 45 min.

Karie Fristoe
Newport Beach, California

Puffin' Stuffin' Croissants

A quick and easy alternative to fast food breakfast sandwiches . . . and tastier, too!

8 (½-ounce) slices Canadian bacon, halved
⅓ cup chopped red bell pepper
10 large eggs
½ teaspoon garlic powder
½ teaspoon ground red pepper
¼ teaspoon salt
8 large croissants
4 teaspoons spicy brown mustard
1 (8-ounce) can crushed pineapple in juice, drained
½ cup (2 ounces) shredded sharp Cheddar cheese

Cook bacon in a large nonstick skillet over medium heat until hot, turning once. Remove from pan; set aside. Cook bell pepper in pan drippings 1 minute or until tender. Stir together eggs and next 3 ingredients; add to bell pepper in skillet, and cook, without stirring, until eggs begin to set on bottom. Draw a spatula across bottom of skillet to form large curds. Continue cooking until eggs are slightly thickened but still moist (do not stir constantly).

Slice croissants in half horizontally. Spread mustard evenly over bottom halves of croissants; place 2 pieces bacon on each croissant bottom. Spoon egg mixture evenly over bacon; top evenly with pineapple. Sprinkle with cheese.

Place on a baking sheet lined with nonstick aluminum foil. Broil 3 inches from heat 2 minutes or until cheese is melted. Replace tops of croissants. **Makes:** 8 servings.
Prep: 10 min., **Cook:** 7 min.

Treena Tomlinson
Chesapeake, Virginia

Treena typically serves these croissants for lunch or supper and adds lettuce leaves to the stack. We omitted the lettuce since the sandwich seemed so fitting for breakfast or brunch, as well.

South-of-the-Border Quiche

We tried this soufflé-like quiche with and without the sazón con azafrán. The seasoning imparts a very mild saffron flavor and adds yellow color to the dish, but the quiche is just as good without it.

4 uncooked mild breakfast
sausage patties
1 (8-ounce) package cream
cheese, softened
3 tablespoons all-purpose baking
mix *
1 packet sazón con azafrán
(about 1¼ teaspoon) *
¼ teaspoon salt
¼ teaspoon freshly ground pepper
1 cup (4 ounces) shredded
Mexican four-cheese blend
1 (10-ounce) can diced tomatoes
and green chiles, undrained
7 large eggs
Sour cream

Place sausage patties in an 8-inch square baking dish. Cover dish loosely with wax paper. Microwave at HIGH 3 minutes or until done, turning patties over after 1½ minutes. Drain patties on paper towels; coarsely chop patties. Coat dish with cooking spray; set aside.

Beat cream cheese and next 5 ingredients at medium speed with an electric mixer until blended. Gradually add tomatoes, beating until blended. Add chopped sausage and eggs; beat well. Pour into prepared dish.

Bake, uncovered, at 350° for 40 minutes or until set. Let stand 10 minutes. Serve with sour cream. **Makes:** 4 servings.

Prep: 12 min., **Cook:** 40 min., **Other:** 10 min.

*For testing purposes only, we used Bisquick Original All-Purpose Baking Mix and Goya Sazón Con Azafrán. Look for this unique seasoning containing saffron in the Hispanic section of your supermarket.

Robert Capitano
Grayson, Georgia

Robert enjoys leftovers of this Mexican quiche cold, which makes it very convenient for a quick meal anytime of day.

Brunch Casserole

This cheesy sausage-egg casserole is a simple and delicious way to wow overnight guests.

1 pound ground pork sausage
2 tablespoons all-purpose flour
9 large eggs, lightly beaten
1 cup milk
3 (5.75-ounce) cans whole green chiles, drained and sliced
4 cups (16 ounces) shredded Cheddar cheese
4 cups (16 ounces) shredded Monterey Jack cheese

Cook sausage in a large skillet over medium heat, stirring until it crumbles and is no longer pink; drain well.

Combine flour, eggs, and milk in a medium bowl; set aside.

Spoon sausage into a lightly greased 13- x 9-inch baking dish. Arrange chiles over sausage; sprinkle evenly with cheeses. Pour egg mixture over cheeses. Bake, uncovered, at 350° for 45 minutes or until set. Let stand 5 minutes before slicing. **Makes:** 8 to 10 servings.

Prep: 9 min., **Cook:** 48 min., **Other:** 5 min.

Tip: Use ground hot sausage, if desired.

Vickie Fry
Muskogee, Oklahoma

With this recipe, **Vickie** shows how to prepare a no-hassle brunch for a small crowd.

Mexican Breakfast Casserole

With a spicy kick of jalapeños, this traditional blend of eggs, sausage, bread, and cheese is guaranteed to be a crowd-pleaser.

1 pound ground pork sausage
1 small onion, chopped
2 medium jalapeño peppers, seeded and chopped
6 white bread slices, crust removed
3 cups (12 ounces) shredded sharp Cheddar cheese, divided
6 large eggs
2 cups milk
1 teaspoon pepper
½ teaspoon salt
1 cup salsa

Cook sausage, onion, and jalapeños in a large skillet over medium-high heat, stirring until sausage crumbles and is no longer pink; drain.

Place bread slices in a lightly greased 11- x 7-inch baking dish. Sprinkle bread slices with sausage mixture and 1 cup cheese.

Whisk together eggs, milk, pepper, and salt; pour mixture over sausage mixture and cheese. Sprinkle with remaining 2 cups cheese. Cover and chill 8 to 24 hours. Bake, uncovered, at 350° for 45 minutes or until set. Let stand 5 minutes. Serve with salsa. **Makes:** 6 servings.

Prep: 12 min., **Cook:** 45 min., **Other:** 8 hrs., 5 min.

Gini Goldsmith
Omaha, Nebraska

As soon as it comes out of the oven, **Gini** spoons salsa over the top of the casserole. We recommend serving the salsa on the side in case you're lucky enough to have leftovers.

Spicy Bean and Tomato Tart

Spicy Bean and Tomato Tart

This spicy combination of chiles, beans, and tomatoes is sure to satisfy your craving for Mexican food.

1   **cup all-purpose baking mix** *
½   **cup yellow cornmeal**
1   **(8-ounce) package shredded extra-sharp Cheddar cheese, divided**
1   **teaspoon dried crushed red pepper**
2   **tablespoons chopped green chiles**
½   **cup chicken broth**
1   **(10-ounce) can diced tomatoes and green chiles, drained**
1   **(15-ounce) can chili beans, rinsed and drained**
¼   **cup chopped fresh cilantro**

2   **plum tomatoes, chopped (optional)**
Sour cream

Combine baking mix, cornmeal, 1 cup cheese, red pepper, and chiles in a medium bowl; add chicken broth, and stir until blended. Press dough into a lightly greased 10-inch springform pan. Bake at 350° for 20 minutes or until crust is set and just browned.

Sprinkle diced tomatoes, beans, and cilantro over crust; top with remaining cheese. Return to oven; bake 8 minutes or until cheese is melted and bubbly.

Remove from oven; sprinkle with chopped tomato, if desired. Remove sides of pan; cut tart into wedges. Serve immediately with sour cream. **Makes:** 4 to 6 servings.
Prep: 10 min., **Cook:** 28 min.

*For testing purposes only, we used Bisquick Original All-Purpose Baking Mix.

Tip: Serve this tart right out of the oven, while the cornbreadlike crust is firm.

Pat Neaves
Kansas City, Missouri

Pasta Alfredo With Steak and Mushrooms

Here's a great variation on classic Alfredo. It's a robust blend of garlic, basil, dried tomatoes, creamy Alfredo pasta sauce, and tender beef. It'll be the hit of your next party.

16 ounces uncooked spaghetti
2   tablespoons olive oil, divided
1½ teaspoons salt, divided
1   pound beef tenderloin fillets,
    cut into 1-inch cubes *
3   tablespoons minced dried
    tomatoes in oil
3   garlic cloves, pressed
1   (8-ounce) package sliced fresh
    mushrooms
1   (16-ounce) jar dried
    tomato-Alfredo pasta sauce
1   cup whipping cream
1   teaspoon dried oregano
1   teaspoon dried basil
½   teaspoon dried crushed red
    pepper

Cook pasta in boiling salted water according to package directions; drain. **Meanwhile,** heat 1 tablespoon oil in a large nonstick skillet over medium-high heat. Sprinkle ½ teaspoon salt evenly over beef, and add to pan; cook 6 minutes or to desired degree of doneness. Remove from skillet, and keep warm.

Add remaining 1 tablespoon oil, dried tomatoes, garlic, and mushrooms to pan; cook over medium heat 5 minutes or until tender. Stir in remaining 1 teaspoon salt, Alfredo sauce, and next 4 ingredients; cook 7 minutes or until thickened, stirring constantly. Stir in beef. **Combine** pasta and Alfredo mixture in a large bowl, tossing gently to coat.

Makes: 8 servings.
Prep: 10 min., **Cook:** 20 min.

*Use New York strip or rib-eye instead of tenderloin, if desired.

Lori Rosbrugh
Wrightsville Beach, North Carolina

Lori tried this recipe with several kinds of mushrooms before determining that she preferred baby portobellos. She also sometimes uses penne or bow tie pasta in place of spaghetti.

Italian Orzo Jambalaya

Orzo, pepperoni, herbs, and cheese lend Italian flare to a Cajun classic.

8   ounces mild Italian sausage
3   tablespoons olive oil
1   medium onion, chopped
½   medium-size green bell pepper,
    chopped
1   tablespoon minced garlic
16 ounces uncooked orzo
1   cup chopped pepperoni
1   (14.5-ounce) can stewed
    tomatoes, undrained and
    chopped
1   tablespoon tomato bouillon
    granules *
2   tablespoons chopped fresh
    parsley
1   tablespoon dried Italian
    seasoning
½   teaspoon black pepper
3   cups water
2   cups (8 ounces) shredded
    Italian three-cheese blend

Remove and discard sausage casings. Heat oil in a Dutch oven over medium-high heat. Crumble sausage into Dutch oven; add onion, bell pepper, and garlic. Sauté 5 minutes or until vegetables are tender. Add orzo and pepperoni; cook 1 minute, stirring constantly. Add stewed tomatoes and next 5 ingredients; bring to a boil, and cook 5 minutes. Reduce heat to low; cook, uncovered, 5 to 6 minutes or until orzo is done and water has evaporated. Spoon into individual bowls; top each serving with shredded cheese. **Makes:** 4 to 6 servings.
Prep: 14 min., **Cook:** 19 min.

*For testing purposes only, we used Knorr Caldo de Tomate. Look for tomato bouillon granules in the ethnic foods section of your grocery store.

Leah Lyon
Ada, Oklahoma

Stuffed Shells With a Twist

For any picky eaters in your family, divide the cheese filling and add only their favorite ingredients; this will please everyone with little extra work on your part.

26 jumbo pasta shells (about 7 ounces)
1 (29-ounce) can tomato sauce
1 (6-ounce) can tomato paste
2 tablespoons sugar
2 tablespoons dried Italian seasoning
2 tablespoons red wine vinegar
1½ teaspoons minced garlic
½ teaspoon salt
½ teaspoon pepper
4 cups (16 ounces) shredded mozzarella cheese, divided
1 (16-ounce) container small curd cottage cheese
1 (15-ounce) container part-skim ricotta cheese
½ cup shredded Parmesan cheese
1 tablespoon dried parsley flakes
2 teaspoons garlic salt
1 teaspoon pepper
2 large eggs
½ pound hot Italian sausage
1 cup coarsely chopped fresh mushrooms

Cook pasta in boiling salted water according to package directions; drain.

Meanwhile, combine tomato sauce and next 7 ingredients in a large saucepan; simmer 5 minutes over medium-low heat, stirring occasionally.

Stir together 3 cups mozzarella cheese and next 7 ingredients in a medium bowl; set aside.

Remove and discard sausage casings. Cook sausage and mushrooms in a medium skillet over medium-high heat, stirring until sausage crumbles and is no longer pink; drain well. Add to cheese mixture.

Spoon half of tomato sauce mixture into a lightly greased 15- x 10-inch baking dish. Spoon about 2 heaping table-spoons sausage mixture into each pasta shell, and place shells in baking dish. Pour remaining tomato sauce mixture over shells; top with remaining 1 cup mozzarella cheese. Bake, covered, at 375° for 25 minutes; uncover and bake 10 more minutes or until cheese melts and begins to brown. **Makes:** 8 servings.
Prep: 34 min., **Cook:** 48 min.

Joe Walls
Mabelvale, Arkansas

Italian Smoked Sausage

Smoked sausage adds distinct flavor to this homemade tomato sauce seasoned with basil, olives, and crushed red pepper. Serve over pasta, and top with Parmesan cheese.

16 ounces uncooked rotini
1 pound smoked sausage, thinly sliced
1 medium onion, chopped (about 1½ cups)
1 tablespoon butter or margarine, melted
1 (28-ounce) can diced tomatoes, undrained
1 (15-ounce) can tomato sauce
1 (6-ounce) can pitted ripe olives, rinsed and drained
3 tablespoons chopped fresh basil
½ teaspoon salt
½ teaspoon dried crushed red pepper
½ teaspoon black pepper
¼ cup freshly grated Parmesan cheese

Cook pasta in boiling salted water according to package directions; drain.

Meanwhile, sauté sausage and onion in butter in a large nonstick skillet over medium-high heat 9 minutes or until browned; drain and return to skillet.

Ellen stirs the cooked pasta into the sauce during the last few minutes of cooking, but we liked spooning the robust sauce over the pasta instead.

Stir in tomatoes and next 6 ingredients; bring to a boil. Reduce heat to medium, and simmer 8 minutes or until slightly thickened. Serve over pasta. Sprinkle with Parmesan cheese. **Makes:** 6 servings.
Prep: 7 min., **Cook:** 21 min.

Tip: For true Italian flavor, use Italian sausage as a substitute. Remove casings, and cook sausage, stirring until it crumbles and is no longer pink; drain.

Ellen Lemme
Orlando, Florida

Four-Meat Hearty Pasta Bake

In a dish like this, what's not to love? You have the robust, Italian flavors of garlic, basil, tomato, and pepperoni all stirred up into one meal.

1   (16-ounce) package uncooked penne pasta
1   pound Italian sausage
1   pound ground beef
2   (8-ounce) packages sliced fresh mushrooms
3   (26-ounce) jars tomato and basil pasta sauce
3   (2.25-ounce) cans sliced ripe olives, drained
1   (14.5-ounce) can diced tomatoes with sweet onions, undrained
1   (14.5-ounce) can diced tomatoes with roasted garlic, undrained
1   (8-ounce) package sliced pepperoni
½   cup chopped fresh cilantro
1   teaspoon salt
6   cups (24 ounces) shredded mozzarella cheese, divided
1   (2.1-ounce) package fully cooked bacon, crumbled

Cook pasta in boiling salted water according to package directions. Drain and set aside.

Meanwhile, remove and discard sausage casings. Cook sausage, beef, and mushrooms in an 8-quart Dutch oven over medium-high heat until meat crumbles and is no longer pink; drain. Combine pasta and meat mixture in pan pasta cooked in. Stir in pasta sauce and next 6 ingredients.

Stir in 3 cups cheese. Spoon pasta mixture evenly into 2 lightly greased 13- x 9-inch baking dishes.

Cover and bake at 350° for 35 minutes or until thoroughly heated. Sprinkle evenly with bacon and remaining 3 cups cheese. Bake, uncovered, 5 more minutes. **Makes:** 16 servings.
Prep: 20 min., **Cook:** 46 min.

Tip: Not having a large guest list tonight? Simply cover and freeze one dish to have for dinner another night. Just thaw and bake, covered, at 350° for 1 hour or until thoroughly heated and cheese melts.

Denise Moore
Hoover, Alabama

Denise loves this recipe because it freezes well and makes two pans full—one to eat right away and the other to share with a new mom or to take to a potluck dinner.

Four-Meat Hearty Pasta Bake

Hey, Cook Man's 3-Cheese Spinach Lasagna

9   uncooked lasagna noodles
1   ounce pancetta, chopped (about 5 thin slices)
1   medium onion, chopped
2   garlic cloves, minced
2   tablespoons dried Italian seasoning
2   (14.5-ounce) cans diced tomatoes, undrained
¼   teaspoon salt
¼   teaspoon ground black pepper
6   tablespoons butter or margarine
¼   cup all-purpose flour
3   cups milk
1⅓   cups freshly grated Parmesan cheese, divided
1⅓   cups freshly grated Gruyère cheese, divided
1⅓   cups freshly grated Romano cheese, divided
1   (10-ounce) package frozen chopped spinach, thawed and drained

Cook lasagna noodles in boiling salted water according to package directions; drain and set aside.

Meanwhile, heat a large nonstick skillet over medium-high heat; add pancetta, and cook 2 minutes or until crisp. Remove pancetta; set aside, reserving drippings in skillet. Sauté onion in drippings 3 minutes or until soft; add garlic, and sauté 1 minute. Add reserved pancetta and Italian seasoning; sauté 30 seconds. Stir in tomatoes, salt, and pepper; bring to a boil, reduce heat and simmer, uncovered, 15 minutes.

Meanwhile, melt butter in a large saucepan over medium heat; whisk in flour until smooth. Cook 1 minute, whisking constantly. Gradually whisk in milk; cook over medium heat, whisking constantly, until mixture is slightly thickened and bubbly. Add 1 cup each of Parmesan, Gruyère, and Romano cheeses, stirring until melted.

Spoon ½ cup tomato mixture into a lightly greased 13- x 9-inch baking dish. Top with 3 lasagna noodles, one-third remaining tomato mixture, one-third spinach, and one-third cheese mixture. Repeat layers twice, ending with cheese mixture. Sprinkle with remaining ⅓ cup each of Parmesan, Gruyère, and Romano cheeses. Cover and bake at 375° for 1 hour. Uncover and bake 10 more minutes or until cheese is lightly browned. Remove from oven; let stand 10 minutes before serving. **Makes:** 8 servings.

Prep: 25 min., **Cook:** 1 hr., 35 min., **Other:** 10 min.

Robert Haroth
Millersville, Maryland

Crazy "Lasagna"

This layered casserole eliminates cooking lasagna noodles by using cheese-filled ravioli. Onion soup mix and sausage boost the flavor in the meat sauce.

1 pound ground pork sausage
1 pound ground chuck
1 (26-ounce) jar pasta sauce
1 cup water
1 medium onion, chopped
3 garlic cloves, pressed
2 green onions, chopped
1 tablespoon Worcestershire sauce
1 teaspoon dried crushed red pepper
1 teaspoon dried Italian seasoning
1 (1-ounce) package dry onion soup mix
1 teaspoon black pepper
½ teaspoon salt
1 (8½-ounce) can sweet peas, drained
1 (4-ounce) can sliced mushrooms, drained

1 (24-ounce) package frozen cheese ravioli, thawed and divided
4 cups (16 ounces) shredded sharp Cheddar cheese, divided
4 cups (16 ounces) shredded mozzarella cheese, divided
1 (12-ounce) container cottage cheese, divided
½ cup grated Parmesan cheese

Cook sausage and beef in a Dutch oven, stirring until meat crumbles and is no longer pink; drain. Return meats to skillet; stir in pasta sauce and next 10 ingredients. Bring to a boil; cover, reduce heat, and simmer 10 minutes. Remove from heat; stir in peas and mushrooms.

Spoon 1 cup meat mixture into a lightly greased 15- x 10-inch baking dish. Layer half of ravioli over sauce. Top with half of remaining sauce and half each of Cheddar and mozzarella cheeses. Spoon half of cottage cheese over Cheddar and mozzarella cheeses. Top with remaining ravioli, remaining meat sauce, and remaining cottage cheese. Cover and bake at 375° for 50 minutes.

Uncover and sprinkle with remaining Cheddar cheese, remaining mozzarella cheese, and Parmesan cheese. Bake, uncovered, 5 more minutes or until cheeses melt. Let stand 15 minutes before serving. **Makes:** 12 to 15 servings.
Prep: 25 min., **Cook:** 1 hr., 8 min., **Other:** 15 min.

Margaret Parnell
Crossett, Arkansas

Sausage-Lasagna Roll-Ups

12 uncooked lasagna noodles
1 pound ground pork sausage
2 cups (8 ounces) shredded mozzarella cheese, divided
4 large eggs, lightly beaten
1 (8-ounce) package cream cheese, softened
¾ cup ricotta cheese
¼ cup chopped fresh chives, divided
½ teaspoon freshly ground pepper
¼ teaspoon salt
1 (29-ounce) can tomato sauce

Cook lasagna noodles in boiling salted water according to package directions. Drain and set aside.

Meanwhile, cook sausage in a large skillet until it crumbles and is no longer pink. Drain.

Stir together sausage, 1 cup mozzarella cheese, eggs, cream cheese, ricotta cheese, 3 tablespoons chives, pepper, and salt in a large bowl.

Spoon half of tomato sauce into a lightly greased 13- x 9-inch baking dish.

Spread about 3 tablespoons sausage mixture evenly on 1 side of each lasagna noodle. Roll up, starting at short ends. Place seam sides down in prepared dish. Pour remaining half of tomato sauce evenly over rolls. Sprinkle with remaining 1 cup mozzarella cheese.

Bake, covered, at 350° for 25 minutes. Uncover and bake 15 more minutes or until golden and bubbly. Let stand 5 minutes before serving. Sprinkle roll-ups evenly with remaining 1 tablespoon chopped chives.

Makes: 6 servings.
Prep: 41 min., **Cook:** 40 min., **Other:** 5 min.

Tip: To prevent cheese from sticking to aluminum foil, spray foil with cooking spray or use nonstick foil.

Robin Jones
Cary, North Carolina

Robin serves these lasagna roll-ups for breakfast since they're loaded with eggs, sausage, and cheese. We loved the novelty of that, but they're great for lunch or supper, too.

Chicken Scampi

½ cup olive oil
¼ cup unsalted butter
1 large onion, chopped
4 garlic cloves, minced
2 bay leaves
16 ounces uncooked spaghetti
4 skinned and boned chicken breasts, cut into 1-inch pieces
1 large egg, lightly beaten
½ teaspoon lemon juice
1 cup Italian-seasoned breadcrumbs
¾ cup all-purpose flour
1 cup white Zinfandel wine
¼ cup fresh lemon juice
1 teaspoon dried oregano
1 teaspoon dried basil
1 teaspoon dried parsley flakes
1 teaspoon salt
½ teaspoon pepper
¼ cup grated Parmesan cheese
6 tablespoons vegetable oil, divided

Heat olive oil and butter in a 1½-quart saucepan over medium heat until hot; add onion and garlic. Cook, stirring constantly, 5 minutes. Add bay leaves; cover, reduce heat, and simmer 25 minutes or until onions are soft. Remove and reserve bay leaves. Let onion mixture cool 15 minutes.

Cook pasta in boiling salted water according to package directions; drain and keep warm.

Meanwhile, stir together chicken, egg, and ½ teaspoon lemon juice, tossing to coat. Stir together breadcrumbs and flour in a shallow dish. Dredge chicken pieces in breadcrumb mixture; set aside.

Process cooled onion mixture in a blender until smooth; pour into a 1½-quart saucepan. Add reserved bay leaves, wine, and next 6 ingredients. Bring to a boil; cover, reduce heat, and simmer 20 minutes. Stir in Parmesan cheese. Remove and discard bay leaves.

While onion mixture simmers, heat 3 tablespoons vegetable oil in a large skillet until hot. Cook half of chicken until browned, turning once. Remove chicken to a bowl; set aside, and keep warm. Repeat procedure with remaining oil and chicken. Toss chicken with 2 tablespoons onion mixture. Pour remaining onion mixture over hot cooked pasta, tossing well. Place pasta on a large serving platter. Spoon chicken over pasta. **Makes:** 4 servings.
Prep: 53 min., **Cook:** 1 hr., 5 min., **Other:** 15 min.

Cathy Pandelo
Bradenton, Florida

Spicy Chicken Spaghetti

For a less fiery sauce, omit the jalapeño seeds. Put a pot of water for the pasta on to boil after the sauce has simmered 25 minutes, and the pasta and sauce will be ready to serve about the same time.

3 tablespoons olive oil
1½ pounds skinned and boned chicken breasts, cut into ½-inch cubes
1 medium onion, chopped
2 garlic cloves, minced
1 large jalapeño pepper, sliced into ⅛-inch slices
1 (29-ounce) can tomato sauce
1 (15-ounce) can tomato sauce
1 (6-ounce) can tomato paste
1 (4-ounce) can sliced mushrooms, drained

2 teaspoons dried oregano
2 teaspoons dried basil
1 teaspoon black pepper
½ teaspoon sugar
½ teaspoon dried crushed red pepper
¼ teaspoon salt
¼ teaspoon dried thyme
¼ teaspoon celery seeds
⅓ cup grated Parmesan cheese
8 ounces spaghetti, cooked

Heat olive oil in a large Dutch oven until hot. Add chicken; cook until browned, stirring after 2 minutes. Stir in onion, garlic, and jalapeño pepper; cook, stirring constantly, until onion is tender. Stir in tomato sauces and next 10 ingredients. Bring to a boil; cover, reduce heat, and simmer 45 minutes, stirring occasionally. Stir in Parmesan cheese. Serve over hot cooked spaghetti. **Makes:** 6 servings.
Prep: 35 min., **Cook:** 58 min.

Anne Ross
Woodruff, South Carolina

Seafood Rigatoni

With oodles of creamy cheese sauce and a crusty crumb topping, this casserole is sure to make anybody love seafood.

1 (16-ounce) package uncooked rigatoni
1 pound unpeeled, medium-size fresh shrimp
2 tablespoons butter or margarine
8 green onions, chopped
2 garlic cloves, minced
1 (10¾-ounce) can cream of shrimp soup, undiluted
1 (8-ounce) package cream cheese, cubed
1 cup ricotta cheese
½ cup half-and-half
½ cup dry white wine
2 tablespoons chopped fresh basil
½ teaspoon salt
½ teaspoon white pepper
2 cups (8 ounces) shredded Swiss cheese, divided
8 ounces bay scallops
4 ounces fresh lump crabmeat, drained
½ cup fine, dry breadcrumbs
½ cup freshly grated Parmesan cheese

Cook pasta in boiling salted water according to package directions.

Meanwhile, peel shrimp, and devein, if desired; set shrimp aside.

Melt butter in a large Dutch oven over medium heat. Add green onions and garlic; cook 2 minutes or until tender. Stir in soup and next 7 ingredients; cook 3 minutes or until smooth, stirring constantly. Stir in 1½ cups Swiss cheese, stirring until cheese melts. Remove from heat.

Place shrimp, scallops, and crabmeat in a large colander. Drain pasta over seafood so hot water blanches seafood. Gently stir pasta and seafood into sauce.

Spoon seafood mixture into a lightly greased 13- x 9-inch baking dish. Combine remaining ½ cup Swiss cheese, breadcrumbs, and Parmesan cheese; sprinkle over seafood mixture.

Bake, uncovered, at 350° for 20 minutes or until lightly browned. **Makes:** 6 servings.

Prep: 18 min., **Cook:** 32 min.

Tip: Peel the shrimp while you bring the pasta water to a boil so everything's ready at the right time. Draining the hot pasta over the seafood in a colander blanches the seafood just enough so that it's perfectly cooked after the short time in the oven.

Diane Sparrow
Osage, Louisiana

Diane uses fresh basil and lemon slices to garnish this delectable meal of fresh seafood and cheesy pasta.

Crawfish Tetrazzini

8	ounces uncooked thin spaghetti
1	cup chopped onion
1	cup chopped green bell pepper
1	cup chopped fresh mushrooms
4	garlic cloves, minced
½	cup butter, melted
1	(10¾-ounce) can cream of mushroom soup, undiluted
½	cup dry white wine
1	(8-ounce) package cream cheese, cubed and softened
2	(16-ounce) packages frozen, cooked crawfish tailmeat, thawed and undrained
1	teaspoon hot sauce
1	teaspoon salt
½	teaspoon pepper
1	tablespoon finely chopped fresh parsley
1	cup shredded Parmesan cheese

Cook pasta in boiling salted water according to package directions. Drain; set aside, and keep warm.

Meanwhile, sauté onion, bell pepper, mushrooms, and garlic in butter in a Dutch oven over medium-high heat 6 minutes or until vegetables are tender. Add soup and wine, stirring well. Gradually add cream cheese, stirring until melted. Add crawfish tails, including liquid, hot sauce, salt, and pepper; stir until smooth. Stir in parsley.

Combine pasta and crawfish mixture, tossing well.

Spoon mixture into a lightly greased 13- x 9-inch baking dish. Sprinkle with Parmesan cheese. Bake, uncovered, at 350° for 20 minutes or until bubbly. Serve immediately. **Makes:** 6 to 8 servings.

Prep: 13 min., **Cook:** 28 min.

Note: Be sure to purchase already peeled and cooked crawfish tails. You can usually find them at the seafood counter or with the frozen foods in the grocery store.

Lucy Leger
Lafayette, Louisiana

From Louisiana, **Lucy** knows her crawfish. She also has a trick or two to speed up her cooking. Canned mushroom soup and cream cheese make a creamy sauce for this dish, and a splash of wine cuts the canned taste. Stirring in the thawed crawfish tails with all their juices adds lots of flavor.

Crawfish Tetrazzini

Quick-and-Easy Black Beans and Rice With Kielbasa

With a short prep time and a little bit of spice, this easy rice and beans dish will accommodate your busy schedule and satisfy your family's taste buds.

1   **(16-ounce) package kielbasa sausage, thinly sliced**
½   **cup chopped onion**
1   **tablespoon butter or margarine, melted**
1   **(15-ounce) can black bean soup**
1   **(15-ounce) can black beans, rinsed and drained**
½   **teaspoon garlic hot sauce ***
¼   **teaspoon salt**
⅛   **teaspoon ground red pepper**
4   **cups hot cooked rice**
Sour cream

Sauté sausage and onion in butter in a large nonstick skillet over medium-high heat 9 minutes or until browned; drain and return to skillet.

Stir in soup and next 4 ingredients; reduce heat, and simmer 3 minutes or until thoroughly heated. Serve over rice. Dollop with sour cream. **Makes:** 4 servings.

Prep: 5 min., **Cook:** 12 min.

*For testing purposes only, we used Tabasco Garlic Pepper Sauce.

Tip: For a little more heat, add more hot sauce.

Michelle Palmer
Orlando, Florida

Michelle cooks boil-in-bag rice to keep this dish simple. Two (3.5-ounce) bags will yield 4 cups cooked rice. Put the rice on to cook when you start the dish.

Pasta Jambalaya

Rotini pasta replaces the traditional rice in this jambalaya. Pump up the flavor by using a spicy smoked sausage.

1   **pound unpeeled, large fresh shrimp**
1½ **pounds smoked sausage, cut into ¼-inch slices**
1   **large onion, finely chopped**
½   **green bell pepper, finely chopped**
2   **celery ribs, finely chopped**
3   **large garlic cloves, minced**
1½ **teaspoons dried crushed red pepper**
5   **cups chicken broth, divided**
1   **pound uncooked rotini pasta**
¼   **teaspoon black pepper**

Peel shrimp, and devein, if desired; set shrimp aside.

Cook sausage and next 5 ingredients in a large Dutch oven over medium-high heat 7 to 8 minutes or until sausage is browned and vegetables are tender. Add 1 cup broth; bring to a boil, stirring to loosen brown bits from bottom of Dutch oven. Stir in pasta and remaining 4 cups chicken broth, and bring to a boil; cover, reduce heat, and simmer 15 minutes. Stir in shrimp; cook 3 to 5 more minutes or until shrimp turn pink. Stir in black pepper. Remove from heat; let stand 10 minutes before serving. **Makes:** 8 servings.

Prep: 22 min., **Cook:** 38 min., **Other:** 10 min.

Kelly Donathan
Fort Myers, Florida

Sometimes **Kelly** uses crawfish tails or chicken instead of shrimp to vary this dish.

Seafood Jambalaya New Orleans Style

This jambalaya is a mild version of the Creole classic. If you prefer a little more spice, add a dash of hot sauce to each serving.

2	pounds diced ham	½	teaspoon salt
2	pounds smoked sausage, sliced	½	teaspoon freshly ground black pepper
2	pounds unpeeled, medium-size fresh shrimp	½	teaspoon dried crushed red pepper
1	tablespoon vegetable oil	2	bay leaves
1	large onion, chopped	2	cups uncooked long-grain rice
1	cup chopped celery		
3	garlic cloves, chopped		
4	cups water		
1	(14.5-ounce) can diced tomatoes, undrained		
1	teaspoon dried thyme		
1	teaspoon dried rosemary, crushed		

Brown ham in a large nonstick skillet; transfer to a large Dutch oven. Brown sausage, in batches, in same skillet; transfer to Dutch oven. While meats brown, peel shrimp, and devein, if desired; set aside.

Heat oil in same skillet. Add onion, celery, and garlic; cook 6 minutes or until tender. Add onion mixture, water, and next 7 ingredients to Dutch oven; bring to a boil. Add rice; cover, reduce heat, and simmer 15 minutes. Add shrimp; cover, and simmer 5 more minutes or until shrimp turn pink and rice is tender. Discard bay leaves.
Makes: 15 cups.
Prep: 24 min., **Cook:** 36 min.

Terry Lenahan
Conway, Arkansas

Company Shrimp Casserole

Similar to Spanish paella—a saffron rice dish with assorted vegetables, meats, and shellfish—this recipe is easy to prepare with the help of a few convenience products.

1	(10-ounce) package yellow rice
¼	cup butter or margarine
6	ounces kielbasa sausage, cut into ¼-inch slices
½	cup chopped green bell pepper
½	cup chopped onion
½	cup chopped fresh mushrooms
2	(10¾-ounce) cans golden mushroom soup, undiluted
1	(8-ounce) container sour cream
1	(14.5-ounce) can diced tomatoes, undrained
12	ounces cooked and peeled medium-size fresh shrimp

Cook rice according to package directions; set aside.
Meanwhile, melt butter in a skillet over medium-high heat; add sausage and next 3 ingredients. Cook, stirring constantly, or until vegetables are tender.

Angie uses cooked and peeled shrimp to speed up this recipe. If you'd rather cook and peel your own, start with 1½ pounds raw in the shell.

Combine rice, soup, sour cream, sausage mixture, and tomatoes. Spoon mixture into a lightly greased 13- x 9-inch baking dish. Bake, uncovered, at 350° for 25 minutes. Stir in shrimp, and bake 5 more minutes. **Makes:** 6 to 8 servings.
Prep: 16 min., **Cook:** 35 min.

Tip: Substitute chopped cooked chicken for the shrimp.

Angie Hutchinson
Richmond, Virginia

Simply Shrimp Fried Rice

You can make this recipe faster than it takes to order "takeout."

1   **pound unpeeled, medium-size fresh shrimp**
1   **bunch green onions, chopped**
½   **cup chopped cooked ham**
3   **tablespoons olive oil, divided**
2   **cups cooked long-grain rice, chilled**
1   **large egg, lightly beaten**
¼   **cup water**
¼   **cup lite soy sauce**
1   **teaspoon garlic powder**
⅛   **teaspoon pepper**

Peel shrimp and devein, if desired. Coarsely chop shrimp.

Sauté green onions, ham, and shrimp in 1 tablespoon oil in a large skillet over medium-high heat 4 minutes or until shrimp turn pink. Remove from skillet.

Sharon recommends using chilled rice in this dish because hot rice may become sticky. It's a great way to use leftover cooked rice.

Heat remaining 2 tablespoons oil in skillet over medium-high heat. Add rice; stir-fry 6 minutes or until lightly browned. Push rice mixture to sides of skillet, forming a well in center. Pour egg into well, and cook, stirring occasionally, until set.

Return shrimp mixture to pan; add ¼ cup water and remaining ingredients, stirring well. **Makes:** 4 servings.
Prep: 15 min., **Cook:** 12 min.

Sharon Dempsey
Savannah, Georgia

Bubbly Cheddar, Chicken, and Rice Bake

Enjoy the comforts of home cooking with this creamy chicken casserole.

4   **cups cooked rice**
4   **cups diced cooked chicken**
1   **(8-ounce) package shredded sharp Cheddar cheese**
¼   **cup chopped green onions**
¼   **cup chopped pecans, toasted**
½   **teaspoon salt**
¼   **teaspoon pepper**
1½   **cups heavy whipping cream**
1   **cup chicken broth**
1½   **cups Japanese breadcrumbs***
3   **tablespoons butter, melted**

Stir together first 9 ingredients in a large bowl. Spoon into a lightly greased 13- x 9-inch baking dish.

Combine breadcrumbs and butter; sprinkle over chicken mixture.

Bake, uncovered, at 375° for 30 minutes or until bubbly and lightly browned.
Makes: 8 servings.
Prep: 24 min., **Cook:** 30 min.

*For testing purposes only, we used panko, which are Japanese breadcrumbs. You can find them in large supermarkets and in Asian food markets.

Tip: To yield 4 cups diced cooked chicken, sprinkle 4 chicken breasts with ¼ teaspoon each of salt and pepper, and bake at 350° for 25 minutes or until done. Let cool slightly, then dice.

Nikki Claassen
Austin, Texas

Nikki prepares the quick-cooking boil-in-bag rice for this dish. To yield 4 cups, cook 2 (3.5-ounce) bags.

Simply Shrimp Fried Rice

Polenta Lasagna With Spinach

You'll never miss the noodles in this meatless lasagna that layers polenta slices with spinach and Romano, ricotta, and provolone cheeses.

3½ cups water
1   cup yellow cornmeal
1   teaspoon salt
¼   cup freshly grated Romano cheese
3   tablespoons olive oil
½   cup chopped onion
2   garlic cloves, minced
2   (6-ounce) packages fresh baby spinach
¼   cup raisins
½   teaspoon salt
⅛   teaspoon ground nutmeg
½   cup ricotta cheese
3   tablespoons whipping cream
1   cup (4 ounces) shredded provolone cheese, divided
½   cup freshly grated Romano cheese

Combine first 3 ingredients in a large saucepan. Bring to a boil over high heat; cook 5 minutes or until thickened, stirring constantly. Stir in ¼ cup Romano cheese. Spread cornmeal mixture in a lightly greased 8-inch square baking dish; cool. Cover and chill 8 hours.

Cut polenta square in half, and cut crosswise into ½-inch-thick slices.

Heat oil in a large saucepan over medium-high heat. Add onion and garlic; cook 2 minutes or until tender. Add spinach and next 3 ingredients; cook 2 minutes or just until spinach wilts, stirring constantly. Remove from heat; stir in ricotta cheese and whipping cream.

Arrange half of polenta slices in a lightly greased 11- x 7-inch baking dish, and spoon half of spinach mixture on top. Sprinkle with half of provolone cheese. Repeat layers, ending with provolone cheese. Sprinkle with ½ cup Romano cheese.

Cover and bake at 350° for 45 minutes or until thoroughly heated and cheese melts. **Makes:** 6 servings.
Prep: 15 min., **Cook:** 55 min., **Other:** 8 hrs.

Tip: To prevent cheese from sticking to aluminum foil, spray foil with cooking spray or use nonstick foil.

Gilda Lester
Wilmington, North Carolina

Gilda rinses and trims a pound of fresh spinach for this dish. We preferred shortcutting the process by using bags of prewashed baby spinach that's ready to cook.

Cream of Crawfish, Asparagus, and Andouille Soup

This rich, creamy soup is sure to make anyone a crawfish fan.

½ cup butter
1 small Vidalia onion, diced (about 1 cup)
1 bunch green onions, chopped
8 ounces andouille sausage, chopped
1 pound fresh asparagus, cut into 1-inch pieces
1 pound peeled crawfish tails
2 cups chicken broth
1½ cups heavy whipping cream
1 (10-ounce) can diced tomatoes and green chiles, undrained
1 (8-ounce) package cream cheese, cubed
4 ounces pasteurized prepared cheese product, cubed *
¼ teaspoon pepper
1 tablespoon lemon juice

Melt butter over medium heat in a Dutch oven. Add onion and green onions, and sauté until tender. Add sausage and asparagus; cook 1 minute. Stir in crawfish and next 6 ingredients; bring to a simmer, and cook 10 minutes, stirring occasionally, until thoroughly heated (do not boil). Stir in lemon juice immediately before serving. **Makes:** 12 cups.
Prep: 5 min., **Cook:** 25 min.

*For testing purposes only, we used Velveeta cheese.

Tip: We used thicker asparagus spears in this soup because we liked having larger pieces of vegetables. Thin spears will also work well, but you may want to reduce the cook time.

Misty Mathews
Boyce, Louisiana

Living in the crawfish capital of the world, **Misty** knows just how to prepare the freshwater crustaceans in creative ways. This soup combines the succulent, sweet tail meat with Vidalia onion, asparagus, spicy sausage, and lots of cheese.

Chili

From Cincinnati to Texas, everyone has a personal definition of chili. Here's one version with a south-of-the-border twist.

2 pounds ground chuck
1 large green bell pepper, chopped
2 (14.5-ounce) cans Mexican-style stewed tomatoes, undrained
1 (16-ounce) can hot chili beans, undrained
1 (16-ounce) can refried beans with green chiles
1 (15.8-ounce) can black-eyed peas, rinsed and drained
1 (15-ounce) can black beans, rinsed and drained

1 (10¾-ounce) can tomato soup, undiluted
¼ cup chili powder
¾ teaspoon salt
¾ teaspoon pepper
Sour cream
Corn chips
Chopped onion
Cilantro

Cook beef and bell pepper in a large Dutch oven over medium-high heat 7 minutes or until beef crumbles and is no longer pink. Drain. Stir in tomatoes and next 8 ingredients; cook over medium heat until hot. Top each serving with sour cream and next 3 ingredients.
Makes: 14 cups.
Prep: 6 min., **Cook:** 14 min.

Mary Vaudreuil
Bloomington, Minnesota

Mary may have the quickest chili recipe we've ever seen. Spicy canned ingredients maximize the flavor.

Carne Adovada Southwestern Stew

Carne Adovada Southwestern Stew

Don't be tempted to substitute regular chili powder, which is a mixture of dried chiles, garlic, oregano, cumin, and coriander, for New Mexico chile powder. New Mexico chile power is made from pure dried New Mexico chiles, and no additional herbs are added.

¼ cup orange juice

2 tablespoons fresh lemon juice

¼ cup ground New Mexico chile powder *

1 tablespoon garlic powder

1 tablespoon dried Mexican or regular oregano

2 tablespoons cornstarch

2 tablespoons sugar

½ teaspoon salt

¼ teaspoon pepper

2 pounds boneless pork loin roast, cut into 1-inch cubes

1 pound Yukon gold potatoes, cubed

1 large red onion, coarsely chopped

1 (15.5-ounce) can white hominy, drained

2 (15-ounce) cans black beans, drained

1 (10-ounce) can diced tomatoes and green chiles, undrained

1 (14.5-ounce) can diced tomatoes, undrained

Toppings: sour cream, fresh cilantro sprig, tortilla chips

Combine first 9 ingredients in a large zip-top freezer bag. Place pork in bag. Seal and marinate in refrigerator at least 8 hours.

Place pork and marinade in a 5-quart electric slow cooker; stir in potatoes and next 5 ingredients.

Cook, covered, on HIGH 1 hour. Reduce heat to LOW; cook 7 hours or until pork is tender. Serve with desired toppings. **Makes:** 12 servings.

Prep: 20 min., **Cook:** 8 hrs., **Other:** 8 hrs.

*Look for New Mexico chile powder in gourmet and Latin markets.

Herman Liu
Edgewood, New Mexico

Herman lives in the heart of the Southwest where it's easy to find specialty seasonings. He uses them skillfully in this spicy stew.

Creole Chicken Bisque

Creole foods are generally cream based and are typically not as spicy as Cajun foods. This pleasantly spiced milk and sour cream-based bisque is true to its roots.

2   bacon slices, cut crosswise into ½-inch pieces
2   pounds skinned and boned chicken breasts, cut into ½-inch pieces
¾   teaspoon salt, divided
1   teaspoon freshly ground black pepper, divided
½   cup all-purpose flour
1   tablespoon olive oil
1   (14-ounce) can chicken broth
1   (14½-ounce) can diced tomatoes, undrained
1   (14½-ounce) can diced tomatoes with zesty mild green chiles, undrained
1   medium onion, chopped
1   large green bell pepper, chopped
1⅔   cups fresh corn kernels (about 5 small ears)

⅔   cup milk
¼   cup chopped fresh basil
½   teaspoon Cajun seasoning
½   teaspoon dried oregano
¼   teaspoon dried thyme
¼   teaspoon ground red pepper
⅓   cup sour cream

Cook bacon over medium-low heat in a 4-quart saucepan 7 minutes, stirring occasionally, or until crisp.

While bacon cooks, sprinkle chicken with ¼ teaspoon salt and ¼ teaspoon black pepper. Place chicken in a large zip-top plastic bag; add flour. Seal bag, and shake until chicken is coated. Remove bacon from pan; drain on paper towels, reserving drippings in skillet. Add olive oil to drippings. Cook chicken in drippings 9 minutes or until done, turning occasionally.

Stir in remaining ½ teaspoon salt, remaining ¾ teaspoon black pepper, chicken broth, and next 11 ingredients. Bring to a boil; cover, reduce heat, and simmer, stirring occasionally, 40 minutes. Remove soup from heat; stir in sour cream. **Makes:** about 11 cups.
Prep: 38 min., **Cook:** 1 hr.

Melinda Nickle
Fayetteville, Arkansas

Melinda recommends to cut the corn as for cream-style corn to help thicken the bisque. To do this, cut the tips of the kernels first, and then scrape the remaining pulp and milk from the cob using a paring knife.

Groundnut Chicken Stew

Because the peanut plant bends over and buries its pods in the earth after flowering, peanuts are also called groundnuts. The distinctive flavor in this stew comes from peanut butter.

4   skinned and boned chicken breasts, cut into ½-inch pieces (about 1½ pounds)
2   tablespoons peanut oil
1   small onion, chopped
1   garlic clove, minced
1   (16-ounce) can dark red kidney beans, rinsed and drained
1   (14.5-ounce) can diced tomatoes, undrained
1   cup water
¼   cup creamy peanut butter
2   tablespoons tomato paste
1   teaspoon salt
½   teaspoon ground red pepper
2   extra-large bags boil-in-bag rice
¼   cup chopped fresh parsley

Sauté chicken in hot oil in a large Dutch oven over medium-high heat 6 minutes or until done. Add onion and garlic; sauté 5 minutes or until onion is tender.

Add kidney beans and next 6 ingredients. Bring to a boil; cover, reduce heat, and simmer, stirring occasionally, 30 minutes.

Meanwhile, prepare rice according to package directions. Serve stew over rice; sprinkle with parsley. **Makes:** 4 to 6 servings.
Prep: 14 min., **Cook:** 46 min.

Gloria Bradley
Naperville, Illinois

Here's another great entry from **Gloria** who was a Finalist and Brand Winner in the Simple and Scrumptious Entrées category.

Fresh and Easy Minestrone

Need to feed a crowd? Warm them up with this minestrone recipe. There are so many flavored canned tomatoes on the market, experiment with different ones for added interest.

¼   cup olive oil
1⅓ cups chopped onion
1⅓ cups chopped celery
1   cup sliced carrot
1   garlic clove, minced
3   cups coarsely chopped cabbage
1½ cups frozen cut green beans
1   cup frozen whole kernel corn
1   cup frozen sweet peas
1   (46-ounce) bottle spicy-hot vegetable juice
1   (16-ounce) can navy beans, drained
1   (14.5-ounce) can diced tomatoes, undrained
6   cups water
1   tablespoon chopped fresh parsley
1½ teaspoons salt
1   teaspoon dried oregano
½   teaspoon pepper
1   teaspoon hot sauce
Pinch of dried crushed red pepper
2   cups uncooked large elbow macaroni

Heat oil in a large Dutch oven. Add onion and next 3 ingredients; cook 3 minutes over medium-high heat until tender. Add cabbage and next 13 ingredients; bring to a boil. Cover, reduce heat, and simmer 45 minutes. Stir in macaroni; cook 11 more minutes or until macaroni is tender.
Makes: 5 quarts.
Prep: 15 min., **Cook:** 1 hr.

Tip: For a boost in flavor, use diced tomatoes with oregano, basil, and garlic.

Sharon Strain
Memphis, Tennessee

Sharon uses ziti in this recipe, but we used macaroni to stay traditional to minestrone.

Butternut Squash Soup

Top off this hearty soup with a sprinkle of bacon and dollop of sour cream for added flavor.

1 **large butternut squash**
2 **tablespoons butter or margarine**
¼ **cup chopped onion**
4 **fresh thyme sprigs**
2 **cups chicken broth**
1½ **cups milk**
½ **teaspoon salt**
¼ **teaspoon pepper**

Cut squash in half lengthwise; remove seeds and membranes. Place on a lightly greased baking sheet, cut sides up. Bake at 400° for 45 minutes or until tender; cool. Scoop out pulp; set aside.

Melt butter in a Dutch oven over medium-high heat. Add onion and thyme; sauté 5 minutes or until onion is tender. Add reserved squash pulp and chicken broth. Bring mixture to a boil. Discard thyme sprigs.

Process mixture, in batches, in a blender or food processor until smooth.

Return mixture to pan. Stir in milk and remaining ingredients. Simmer over low heat 10 minutes. Serve immediately.

Makes: 6 cups.

Prep: 15 min., **Cook:** 60 min.

Tip: This soup can be prepared up to the processing step and frozen up to 1 month. Add milk, salt, and pepper after thawing.

Tracy Arthur
Petersburgh, New York

Tracy uses all milk in this smooth and creamy soup, but for our second test, we used less milk and added chicken broth for more flavor.

3 Bonus Side-Dish Entries

Spiced Glazed Parsnips

With a hint of orange juice and cider vinegar and a bit of brown sugar, the glaze dresses up parsnips or carrots deliciously.

1 **pound parsnips, cut into ¼-inch-thick slices**
3 **tablespoons butter or margarine**
¼ **cup firmly packed light brown sugar**
¼ **cup cider vinegar**
3 **tablespoons orange juice**
½ **teaspoon salt**

Place parsnips in a steamer basket over boiling water. Cover and steam 10 minutes or until crisp-tender.

Meanwhile, combine butter and next 3 ingredients in a medium saucepan. Bring to a boil; cook 5 minutes or until thickened, stirring constantly. Add parsnips and salt to pan. Spoon sauce over parsnips to glaze. **Makes:** 4 servings.

Prep: 8 min., **Cook:** 10 min.

Amy Tuten-Darrah
Cincinnati, Ohio

Baked Squash

You may not be able to find banana squash whole because it's so large (2 to 3 feet long). Look for banana squash in cut pieces in the produce section. The squash should have firm, bright orange-colored flesh. Butternut squash is a good substitute.

¼ **cup butter or margarine, melted**
½ **teaspoon salt**
2 **tablespoons light brown sugar**
2 **tablespoons orange juice**
1½ **pounds banana squash, peeled and cut into 1-inch cubes (about 4 cups)**

Combine first 4 ingredients in an 11- x 7-inch baking dish, stirring to blend well. Add squash, and toss to coat with butter mixture. Bake, uncovered, at 400° for 30 minutes; stir. Bake 15 more minutes or until tender. **Makes:** 4 servings.

Prep: 16 min., **Cook:** 45 min.

Carol Frederick
Oro Valley, Arizona

Roasted Asparagus With Orange and Hazelnuts

2 **pounds asparagus**
2 **teaspoons olive oil**
2 **tablespoons unsalted butter**
2 **teaspoons grated orange rind**
2 **tablespoons fresh orange juice**
¼ **teaspoon salt**
¼ **teaspoon pepper**
¼ **cup chopped hazelnuts, toasted**

Snap off tough ends of asparagus. Place asparagus on a 15- x 10-inch jellyroll pan; drizzle oil over asparagus, and toss.

Bake at 500° for 8 minutes, stirring after 5 minutes. Remove from oven; add butter, rind, juice, salt, and pepper to pan. Return to oven and bake 2 more minutes or until butter melts. Toss with nuts before serving. Serve warm. **Makes:** 8 servings.

Prep: 12 min., **Cook:** 10 min.

Carol Frederick
Oro Valley, Arizona

Kids Love It!

Let your kids lend a hand with some
of these recipes, or prepare dinner
while they play. You'll find enough variety
to please any age and dishes that will
make your kids say, "Yummy!"

High school teacher Stacy Lamons knows what kids like to eat in class (when they're not supposed to be eating at all)—finger food. With that certainty in mind, she cooked up this finger-licking recipe in her head while monitoring an exam.

But she almost didn't submit it. She had entered several recipes the previous year, but when none were chosen, Stacy decided she didn't have what *Southern Living* was looking for. At the last minute, she decided to enter this one recipe. "It happened to be one that the magazine *was* looking for," she says.

Stacy has travelled widely, learning languages and appreciating foods of different cultures. She learned to make Czech and German delicacies of her own heritage from her great-aunt, Elsa, and her mother. "My mom was good about letting me try things as long as I cleaned up my mess," Stacy says. "She taught me that a good chef always cleans up after herself."

$10,000 Category Winner!

Tex-Mex Egg Rolls With Creamy Cilantro Dipping Sauce

For a beautiful presentation, cut top from 1 large red bell pepper, reserving top; remove and discard seeds and membrane, leaving pepper intact. Arrange bell pepper on a serving plate, and fill with sauce.

1   (5-ounce) package Spanish rice mix
1   teaspoon salt
1   pound ground hot pork sausage
1   (15-ounce) can black beans, rinsed and drained
6   green onions, finely chopped
1   (1.25-ounce) envelope taco seasoning mix
2   cups (8 ounces) shredded Monterey Jack cheese
1   (14.5-ounce) can petite diced tomatoes with mild green chiles, undrained
28 egg roll wrappers
1   large egg, lightly beaten
4   cups peanut oil
Creamy Cilantro Dipping Sauce
Garnish: fresh cilantro sprigs

Cook rice according to package directions, using 1 teaspoon salt. Cool completely.
Cook sausage in a skillet over medium heat, stirring until it crumbles and is no longer pink; drain well. Cool.
Stir together rice, sausage, black beans, and next 4 ingredients in a large bowl. Spoon about ⅓ cup rice mixture in center of each egg roll wrapper. Fold top corner of wrapper over filling, tucking tip of corner under filling; fold left and right corners over filling. Lightly brush remaining corner with egg; tightly roll filled end toward the remaining corner, and gently press to seal.
Pour oil in a heavy Dutch oven; heat to 375°. Fry egg rolls, in batches, 2 to 3 minutes or until golden. Drain on a wire rack over paper towels. Serve with Creamy Cilantro Dipping Sauce. Garnish, if desired. **Makes:** 28 egg rolls.
Prep: 40 min., **Cook:** 3 min. per batch

Creamy Cilantro Dipping Sauce:

1   (8-ounce) package cream cheese, softened
1   cup sour cream
3   garlic cloves, minced
2   (10-ounce) cans Mexican festival diced tomatoes with lime juice and cilantro, undrained
2   cups loosely packed fresh cilantro leaves (about 1 bunch)
Garnish: finely chopped fresh cilantro

Process first 5 ingredients in a food processor until smooth. Garnish, if desired. **Makes:** 3 cups.
Prep: 10 min.

Stacy Lamons
Houston, Texas

For bite-size hors d'oeuvres, **Stacy** suggests substituting small won ton wrappers for the egg roll wrappers.

Tex-Mex Egg Rolls With Creamy
Cilantro Dipping Sauce

Caramel-Pecan French Toast

If you're cruising down a California highway behind a car with a tag that reads "LV2Bake," then toot your horn and wave hello to Kathy Specht.

A dyed-in-the-wool cook-off afficionado, Kathy has cooked everywhere from state fairs to the Pillsbury Bake-Off. She jokes that she's too busy in the kitchen to marry. She started young with a supportive mother whose only rules were to mind the budget and leave the kitchen as you found it. Waste not, want not, so whatever Kathy made was either dinner or fed to the birds. The Specht family ate many a strange experiment, and the vacant lot next door had the best-fed pigeons in town.

As a former child chef, Kathy knows what kids like to eat, and French toast is a perennial favorite—"My dad would make either waffles or French toast every Sunday before church." Her contest recipe combines the delights of stuffed French toast and a gooey cinnamon bun. "Eggs, raisins, and nuts make a good, wholesome breakfast before kids go off to school, and a few strips of bacon round it out," she says.

Desserts are her specialty, but Kathy enjoys all cooking, and has an extensive cookbook collection to prove it. "I look back at all the recipes I've saved over the years—some of them are great, but sometimes I wonder what I was thinking," she says.

Kathy urges those starting out in the kitchen to remember that practice makes perfect. In time, you may even catch the bug to enter contests. "Be confident about sending your recipes in," she says. "You must believe in yourself before anyone else will."

$1,000 Finalist Winner!

Caramel-Pecan French Toast

1   **cup firmly packed light brown sugar**
½   **cup butter**
2   **tablespoons light corn syrup**
12   **slices honey white bread**
¾   **cup raisins**
1   **cup chopped pecans, toasted and divided**
6   **large eggs**
½   **cup milk**
2   **teaspoons grated lemon rind**
1   **teaspoon vanilla extract**
½   **teaspoon ground cinnamon**
1½   **cups whipping cream, divided**
¼   **cup powdered sugar**
Maple syrup
Cooked bacon slices (optional)

Combine first 3 ingredients in a small saucepan; cook, stirring constantly, over medium heat 3 to 5 minutes or until sugar dissolves.

Pour brown sugar mixture into an ungreased 13- x 9-inch baking dish. Arrange 6 bread slices in brown sugar mixture, cutting slices as necessary to fit in dish. Sprinkle raisins and ¾ cup pecans over bread. Top with remaining bread slices.

Whisk together eggs, next 4 ingredients, and 1 cup cream. Pour egg mixture over bread slices in baking dish.

Bake, uncovered, at 350° for 40 minutes or until a wooden pick inserted in center comes out clean.

Beat remaining ½ cup whipping cream until foamy; gradually add powdered sugar, beating until stiff peaks form.

Divide French toast among 8 individual serving plates. Top each serving with whipped cream; drizzle with maple syrup, and sprinkle with remaining ¼ cup pecans. Serve with bacon, if desired. **Makes:** 8 servings.
Prep: 30 min., **Cook:** 45 min.

Kathy Specht
Cambria, California

Kathy sometimes varies the fruit filling when she makes this dish. Make your own version with your favorite fruit, such as apples, blueberries, cranberries, pineapple, or coconut.

Tex-Mex Chicken
Crunchies

Twenty years of experimenting with recipes and entering cooking contests certainly prepared Frances Benthin for our Cook-Off. She's a seasoned winner, having netted cash, a motorcycle, and trips to exotic locales. But it's her role as a wife and mother of five sons that put her cooking skills to the test.

"When you have five boys and a husband, you spend some time in the kitchen," says Frances. "Some of my best memories are of when I had all the boys in the kitchen while I cooked, sharing thoughts and telling me about their day" she says. "I was always moving someone from in front of the refrigerator, stove, or sink so I could get dinner on the table. I worked full-time, but I cooked dinner every night." Frances still cooks the way her mother taught her, from scratch. "Prepared foods are a great help, but food from scratch can't be beat," she says.

Take this sage advice from a successful cook and now grandmother: At least once a day, gather your family around the table to eat a meal together, with no television or other distractions. "And let your family help with the cooking," she says. "All my boys learned to cook."

$1,000 Finalist Winner!

Tex-Mex Chicken Crunchies

½ cup all-purpose baking mix *
1 large egg
½ cup enchilada sauce
2 cups crushed spicy tortilla chips
¼ cup minced fresh cilantro
6 skinned and boned chicken breasts, cut into 1½-inch pieces
1 cup vegetable oil
Ranch-style dressing
Barbecue sauce

Place baking mix in a shallow dish. Whisk together egg and enchilada sauce in a small bowl. Stir together crushed chips and cilantro in a separate shallow dish.
Dredge chicken pieces in baking mix; dip in egg mixture, and dredge in crumb mixture. Cover chicken, and chill 30 minutes.

Pour oil into a large skillet; heat to 375°. Fry chicken, in batches, 3 minutes on each side or until brown. Drain on wire racks over paper towels. Serve chicken with Ranch-style dressing or barbecue sauce. **Makes:** 8 to 10 servings.
Prep: 10 min., **Cook:** 6 min. per batch, **Other:** 30 min.

*For testing purposes only, we used Bisquick Original All-Purpose Baking Mix.

Frances Benthin
Scio, Oregon

Frances dips the chicken in baking mix first because it helps the subsequent ingredients stick to the meat and form an even, crispy crust.

Toffee Crunch Mix

Sweet, salty, crunchy—what more could kids want?

1	(15-ounce) box lightly sweetened whole grain oat cereal squares*
1	cup sliced almonds
2	cups chow mein noodles
2	cups pretzel sticks
2	cups raisins
2	cups firmly packed light brown sugar
1	cup butter
½	cup light corn syrup
1	teaspoon baking soda

Combine first 5 ingredients in a large bowl; toss well.

Combine brown sugar, butter, and corn syrup in a medium saucepan. Bring to a boil, stirring constantly, over medium-high heat. Stir in baking soda; remove from heat.

Pour glaze mixture over cereal mixture; mix thoroughly.

Spoon mixture into a lightly greased roasting pan. Bake at 350° for 30 minutes, stirring every 10 minutes. Cool completely. **Makes:** 18 cups.
Prep: 14 min., **Cook:** 30 min.

*For testing purposes only, we used Quaker Oat Life Cereal.

Tip: This mixture will keep up to 1 week if stored in an airtight container.

Anita Shutt
Spirit Lake, Iowa

Granny's Granola

Enjoy this wholesome treat by itself, with milk, or as a topping for yogurt.

4	cups uncooked regular oats
1½	cups firmly packed brown sugar
1	teaspoon ground cinnamon
⅓	cup butter or margarine, divided
1	cup golden raisins
1	cup dry-roasted peanuts
½	cup semisweet chocolate morsels

Combine first 3 ingredients in a large bowl; set aside.

Melt 3 tablespoons butter in a large skillet over medium heat. Add half of oat mixture; cook 6 minutes, stirring often, or until sugar is melted and mixture is golden brown. Remove from pan. Spread out on baking sheets lined with nonstick aluminum foil; cool to room temperature. Repeat process with remaining butter and oat mixture. Stir in raisins, peanuts, and chocolate morsels. Store in an airtight container or zip-top plastic bags. **Makes:** 8¾ cups.
Prep: 2 min., **Cook:** 13 min.

Tip: For easy portioning, measure and store this granola in small zip-top plastic bags.

Kathy Nichols-Lee
Baton Rouge, Louisiana

Peanut Ball

This recipe makes one large (6-inch) ball, but the mixture can easily be divided in half to form two smaller balls.

2	cups chunky peanut butter
1	cup semisweet chocolate mini-morsels
½	cup powdered sugar
1	cup chopped dry-roasted peanuts
	Chocolate and caramel syrups

Stir together peanut butter, chocolate morsels, and powdered sugar in a medium bowl; chill at least 1 hour.

Place chopped nuts in a shallow dish. Place peanut butter mixture on nuts; roll mixture into a ball, gently pressing nuts into ball.

Place Peanut Ball on a serving plate; drizzle chocolate and caramel syrups over ball. Serve with bananas, apple wedges, or graham crackers. **Makes:** 1 (6-inch) peanut ball.
Prep: 11 min., **Other:** 1 hr.

Joel Robertson
Bluff City, Tennessee

Berry Delicious Salsa and Cinnamon Chips

When we tested this recipe, the staff went back for seconds and thirds. Chances are your family and friends will do the same, but just in case you have leftovers, try the salsa over angel food cake, waffles, pancakes, or ice cream.

4 medium apples, cored and chopped
2 cups strawberries, chopped
2 kiwifruit, peeled and chopped
1 (20-ounce) can crushed pineapple in juice, drained
½ cup firmly packed light brown sugar
¼ cup apple jelly

3 tablespoons lemon juice (about 1 lemon)
2 tablespoons orange juice
Cinnamon Chips

Combine first 8 ingredients in a large bowl; cover and chill 1 hour. Serve with Cinnamon Chips. **Makes:** 10 cups.
Prep: 35 min., **Other:** 1 hr.

Cinnamon Chips:
6 (8-inch) flour tortillas
Vegetable cooking spray
¼ cup sugar
1½ teaspoons ground cinnamon

Cut each tortilla into 8 wedges; spray wedges evenly with cooking spray.
Combine sugar and cinnamon in a small bowl; sprinkle evenly over tortilla wedges. Place wedges on a baking sheet. Bake at 375° for 10 to 12 minutes or until crisp. Serve with fruit salsa. **Makes:** 4 dozen.
Prep: 7 min., **Cook:** 12 min.

Lori Patterson
Clanton, Alabama

Lori uses water to moisten the tortilla wedges before adding the cinnamon-sugar. We got crisp, perfectly golden chips using cooking spray instead of water.

Berry Delicious Salsa and Cinnamon Chips

Peanut Butter and Banana Milk Shakes

This shake is a surefire favorite of Elvis fans young and old.

2   medium bananas, sliced and frozen
2   tablespoons creamy peanut butter
1   cup milk
1   teaspoon vanilla extract
3   cups vanilla ice cream
Garnishes: chocolate candy sprinkles, chopped peanuts

Process all ingredients in a blender until smooth, stopping to scrape down sides. Serve immediately. Garnish, if desired.
Makes: 5 cups.
Prep: 5 min.

Melissa Carafa
Broomall, Pennsylvania

Melissa recommends 2 cups of ice cream for thin milk shakes and 3 cups for thick ones. We went for rich and thick all the way using 1 cup milk and even took it a step further by freezing the banana slices.

Raspberry Punch

1   quart raspberry sherbet, slightly softened
2   cups orange juice, chilled
2   (2-liter) bottles lemon lime soft drink, chilled

Combine sherbet and orange juice in a punch bowl; stir in soft drink, breaking up sherbet. Serve immediately. **Makes:** about 15 cups.
Prep: 5 min.

Nichole Cohrs
Omaha, Nebraska

Nichole cautions that the sherbet doesn't need to melt completely. It takes the place of ice cubes and chills the punch. This beverage doesn't hold well, so reduce ingredient amounts by half if you're not serving a crowd.

Strawberry Cinnamon Sticks 'n' Dip

8   white bread slices
1   (8-ounce) container strawberry cream cheese
2   large eggs, lightly beaten
2   cups cinnamon-flavored lightly sweetened whole grain oat cereal squares, crushed*
Strawberry Dipping Sauce

Roll each slice of bread to ⅛-inch thickness, using a rolling pin. Spread 1 heaping tablespoon cream cheese evenly over each bread slice. Roll up, jellyroll fashion, starting at long end. Dip in egg, then roll in crushed cereal. Place on a lightly greased 15- x 10-inch jellyroll pan or baking sheet. Bake at 400° for 8 minutes or until crisp, turning once. Serve with Strawberry Dipping Sauce. **Makes:** 4 servings.
Prep: 22 min., **Cook:** 8 min.

*For testing purposes only, we used Quaker Oat Cinnamon Life Cereal.

Strawberry Dipping Sauce:
3   cups fresh strawberries, halved
⅓   cup sugar
1   teaspoon cornstarch
¼   teaspoon ground cinnamon

Process strawberries in a food processor or blender until smooth, stopping to scrape down sides.
Combine pureed strawberries and remaining ingredients in a medium saucepan. Cook over medium heat 5 minutes or until slightly thickened.
Makes: 1½ cups.
Prep: 10 min., **Cook:** 5 min.

Lisa Keys
Middlebury, Connecticut

Lisa browns these fun dippers in a skillet, but we found it easier to bake them in the oven until crisp.

Peanut Butter and
Banana Milk Shakes

"Apple Pie" Biscuits

Petite in size, these biscuits are ideal for the pint-size set. Our Test Kitchens liked these best when they were warm, but be sure to wait about 5 minutes before you bite into one so the filling won't burn you.

- 1   tablespoon granulated sugar
- ½   teaspoon ground cinnamon
- ½   cup apple pie filling, finely chopped
- 1   teaspoon brown sugar
- ⅛   teaspoon ground cinnamon
- 2   cups all-purpose baking mix *
- ½   cup granulated sugar
- ⅓   cup half-and-half
- 3½ tablespoons cream cheese, softened and divided
- Butter-flavored cooking spray

Stir together 1 tablespoon granulated sugar and ½ teaspoon cinnamon; set mixture aside.

Stir together pie filling and next 2 ingredients in a small bowl; set aside.

Combine baking mix and ½ cup sugar in a bowl; add half-and-half, stirring until dry ingredients are moistened.

Turn dough out onto a lightly floured surface. Pat or roll dough to ¼-inch thickness; cut with a 1½-inch round cutter, and place 20 on an ungreased baking sheet. Spoon about ½ teaspoon cream cheese onto center of each biscuit; spoon about ½ teaspoon pie filling mixture on top of cream cheese. Place remaining 20 biscuits over each topped biscuit, pressing sides to seal. Spray tops lightly with cooking spray; sprinkle with cinnamon-sugar mixture. **Bake** at 425° for 8 to 10 minutes or until biscuits are golden. Serve warm. **Makes:** 20 biscuits.

Prep: 33 min., **Cook:** 10 min.

* For testing purposes only, we used Bisquick Original All-Purpose Baking Mix.

Sue Charney
Palmyra, Virginia

Rolled Ham Biscuits

Serve these hearty spiral biscuits with honey mustard.

- 2   cups self-rising flour
- ½   cup chilled butter or margarine, cut into small pieces
- ½   cup milk
- 1   large egg
- ½   cup coarsely chopped ham
- ½   cup cream of chicken soup, undiluted
- 1   tablespoon chopped fresh cilantro

Place flour and butter in a food processor; process until crumbly. Add milk and egg; process just until a ball forms. Turn mixture out onto a lightly floured surface; knead lightly. Set aside.

Place ham, soup, and cilantro in processor; process until ham is finely chopped.

Roll or pat dough to form a 20- x 10-inch rectangle; spread ham mixture over dough. Roll up, jellyroll fashion, starting with long side. Cut into 1-inch slices. Arrange slices, cut side up, in a lightly greased 13- x 9-inch pan. Bake at 450° for 20 minutes or until golden. Serve warm. **Makes:** 20 biscuits.

Prep: 20 min., **Cook:** 20 min.

Tip: To easily cut dough into slices, use a sharp serrated knife, unwaxed dental floss, or string. Place a long piece of dental floss or string under dough 1 inch from end of roll. Cross ends of floss over top of roll; slowly pull the ends to cut through the dough.

Mary Jo Henrickson
Shelby, Michigan

Mary Jo serves these with a mustard sauce, but we liked the ease and flavor of prepared honey mustard.

Mama's Warm Square Doughnuts

Reminiscent of the famed warm beignets of New Orleans, these doughnuts contain a lot of sugar. Watch them closely as they fry so they won't get too brown.

3   tablespoons butter
1   cup granulated sugar
2   large eggs
1   teaspoon vanilla extract
3   cups all-purpose flour
4   teaspoons baking powder
½   teaspoon salt
¼   teaspoon ground nutmeg
⅔   cup half-and-half
Vegetable oil
Powdered sugar

Beat butter and granulated sugar at medium speed with an electric mixer; add eggs, 1 at a time, beating until blended after each addition. Stir in vanilla.

Stir together flour and next 3 ingredients; add to butter mixture, alternately with half-and-half, beginning and ending with flour mixture. Place dough in a bowl; cover and chill 2 hours.

Brigitte's children say these are the best doughnuts in the world. She lets them sprinkle their own powdered sugar on top, and they enjoy that, too.

Divide dough in half; turn dough out onto a lightly floured surface. Pat or roll to ¼-inch thickness; cut into 2-inch squares. Repeat procedure with remaining half of dough.

Pour oil to a depth of 2 inches in a Dutch oven; heat to 375°. Fry dough-nuts, in batches, 3 minutes or until puffed and golden brown, turning occasionally.

Drain doughnuts on paper towels; place on a serving platter, and sprinkle with powdered sugar. Serve immediately.

Makes: 3 dozen.

Prep: 16 min., **Cook:** 3 min. per batch, **Other:** 2 hrs.

Brigitte Grate
Del Rey Oaks, California

Triple Treats

These crispy doughnutlike treats get their name from having three tasty topping variations. After cooking, simply choose your favorite finishing touch, or try them all.

1½ cups all-purpose flour
⅓   cup sugar
1   teaspoon baking powder
½   teaspoon salt
¼   teaspoon ground cinnamon
½   cup milk
1   large egg
⅓   cup creamy peanut butter
1   teaspoon vanilla extract
Vegetable oil

Combine first 5 ingredients in a medium bowl; set aside. Combine milk and next 3 ingredients in a medium bowl with a wire whisk. Gradually add flour mixture, stirring well.

Pour oil to a depth of 1 inch in a large skillet; heat to 375°. Carefully drop batter by teaspoonfuls into hot oil; fry in batches 1 to 2 minutes or until golden, turning once. Drain on paper towels.

Makes: about 2 dozen.

Prep: 27 min., **Cook:** 10 min.

Variation 1: Roll cooked balls in 1 cup powdered sugar.

Variation 2: Combine 1 cup powdered sugar, 2 teaspoons strawberry jam, and 2 teaspoons milk. Dip each cooked ball into strawberry glaze, and drizzle with ½ cup melted white chocolate morsels.

Variation 3: Drizzle cooked balls with 1 cup melted peanut butter and milk chocolate chips. *

*For testing purposes only, we used Nestlé Toll House Peanut Butter and Milk Chocolate Morsel Mix.

Alice Franks
Belmont, North Carolina

Polka Dot Lemon Muffins

Golden raisins and sweetened dried cranberries create the chewy little polka dots in these tart muffins.

2   cups all-purpose flour
½   cup sugar
1   teaspoon baking powder
½   teaspoon salt
½   teaspoon baking soda
½   cup golden raisins
½   cup sweetened dried cranberries
¼   cup butter, melted
2   teaspoons grated lemon rind
¼   cup lemon juice

2   large eggs
1   (8-ounce) container lemon yogurt
1½   teaspoons vanilla extract

Combine first 5 ingredients in a medium bowl. Stir in raisins and cranberries; make a well in center of mixture.

Stir together butter and remaining ingredients; add to dry ingredients, stirring just until moistened. Spoon batter into greased or paper-lined muffin pans, filling two-thirds full. Bake at 400° for 18 minutes. Remove from pans immediately, and cool on wire racks. **Makes:** 16 muffins.
Prep: 12 min., **Cook:** 18 min.

Tip: Don't stir the batter too much; this makes muffins tough.

Geordyth Sullivan
Miami, Florida

Taste-of-the-Island Muffins

Macadamia nuts, coconut, and crushed pineapple jazz up these muffins.

2   cups all-purpose baking mix *
⅔   cup sugar
1   cup milk
1   large egg
1   (8-ounce) can crushed pineapple in juice, undrained
1   teaspoon vanilla extract
¼   teaspoon almond extract
⅛   teaspoon salt
½   cup chopped macadamia nuts
¼   cup sweetened flaked coconut

Combine baking mix and sugar in a large bowl; make a well in center of mixture.

Stir together milk and next 5 ingredients; add to dry ingredients, stirring just until moistened. Gently stir in macadamia nuts.

Spoon batter into paper-lined muffin pans, filling two-thirds full. Sprinkle evenly with coconut. Bake at 400° for 20 minutes or until golden. Remove from pans, and cool on wire racks.
Makes: 1 dozen.
Prep: 5 min., **Cook:** 20 min.

*For testing purposes only, we used Bisquick Original All-Purpose Baking Mix.

Becky Jewett
Irving, Texas

Becky prepares these muffins without sugar. We added some sugar to tenderize and sweeten them a little.

Spicy Pizza Muffins

With these quick muffins, it's now easier than ever to eat on the go. All the yummy flavors of pepperoni, cheese, tomato, and garlic are in this no-mess snack.

½ pound ground pork sausage
4 ounces fresh mushrooms, chopped
½ cup pepperoni slices, chopped
¼ cup chopped ripe olives
2⅓ cups all-purpose baking mix *
1 teaspoon fennel seeds (optional)
2 teaspoons dried Italian seasoning
1 teaspoon dried minced onion
¼ teaspoon garlic powder
3 large eggs, lightly beaten
¼ cup milk
¾ cup (3 ounces) shredded pizza cheese blend
1 (14.5-ounce) can diced tomatoes, drained

Cook first 4 ingredients in a large non-stick skillet over medium-high heat 5 minutes, stirring until sausage crumbles and is no longer pink. Drain.

Combine baking mix, fennel, if desired, and next 3 ingredients in a large bowl; make a well in center of mixture. Add sausage mixture, eggs, milk, cheese, and tomatoes, stirring just until moistened. Spoon batter into lightly greased muffin pans, filling three-fourths full.

Bake at 375° for 18 minutes or until lightly browned and muffin tops spring back when lightly touched. Remove from pans immediately. **Makes:** about 20 muffins.

Prep: 11 min., **Cook:** 23 min.

*For testing purposes only, we used Bisquick Original All-Purpose Baking Mix.

Zan Brock
Jasper, Alabama

Zan bakes this recipe in miniature muffin pans, but we liked the flavor so much we used regular pans to make more substantial servings.

Tropical-Treat Stuffed French Toast

12 slices honey white bread
1 (8-ounce) container pineapple cream cheese
¾ cup orange juice
1 cup lite coconut milk
1 tablespoon grated orange rind
4 large eggs
3 tablespoons sugar
1 tablespoon vanilla extract
1 teaspoon coconut extract
1 (8-ounce) can crushed pineapple in juice, undrained
½ cup orange juice
2 teaspoons cornstarch
1 teaspoon coconut extract

Spread each of 6 slices of bread with 2 tablespoons cream cheese; top with remaining bread slices. Place in a 15- x 10-inch baking dish; set aside.

Combine ¾ cup orange juice, coconut milk, orange rind, eggs, sugar, vanilla, and 1 teaspoon coconut extract; mix well. Pour mixture over bread. Cover and chill until most of liquid is absorbed, about 30 to 40 minutes.

Cover a large baking sheet with nonstick foil. Place bread on prepared pan (do not allow bread to touch). Bake at 400° for 30 to 35 minutes or until puffed and lightly browned.

While bread bakes, stir together crushed pineapple, ½ cup orange juice, cornstarch, and 1 teaspoon coconut extract. Bring to a boil; reduce heat, and simmer, stirring constantly, until thickened. Serve French toast topped with warm sauce.

Makes: 6 servings.

Prep: 20 min., **Cook:** 35 min., **Other:** 40 min.

Virginia C. Anthony
Boone, North Carolina

Bet these seem extra-special when **Virginia** serves them. She arranges the toast on warm plates before drizzling with the warm sauce.

Crusted French Toast With Warm Maple Syrup

A coating of cereal makes this French toast crunchy.

4   large eggs
2   teaspoons granulated sugar
½   teaspoon ground cinnamon
1   cup whipping cream
6   slices cinnamon raisin bread
2   cups coarsely crushed lightly
    sweetened whole grain oat
    cereal squares *
6   tablespoons butter, divided
⅓   cup powdered sugar
Maple syrup, warmed

Whisk together first 4 ingredients; pour into a shallow dish. Arrange 3 slices bread in egg mixture, turning to coat. Let stand 1 minute.

Dredge bread slices in cereal, making sure all sides are coated.

Melt 3 tablespoons butter in a large nonstick skillet over medium heat; add coated bread slices. Cook 4 minutes on each side or until lightly browned. Transfer to a serving platter; keep warm. Repeat procedure with remaining egg mixture, bread slices, cereal, and butter. Sprinkle evenly with powdered sugar. Serve with warm maple syrup. **Makes:** 3 servings.

Prep: 7 min., **Cook:** 16 min., **Other:** 2 min.

*For testing purposes only, we used Quaker Oat Life Cereal.

Elaine Sweet
Dallas, Texas

Elaine tops each serving of French toast with canned tropical fruit salad. We liked this breakfast so much we decided it could stand on its own without the fruit.

Pumpkin Pancake and Sausage Rolls With Lemon-Ginger Syrup

Serve sausage links on the side and, if you're pressed for time, substitute maple syrup instead of making lemon-ginger syrup.

15 brown-and-serve breakfast
    sausage links
1   teaspoon ground ginger, divided
2   tablespoons fresh lemon juice
1   cup light corn syrup
⅓   cup ginger ale
6   large eggs, separated
½   cup canned pumpkin
2   cups buttermilk
6   tablespoons butter, melted
2   cups all-purpose baking mix *
½   cup golden raisins (optional)

Prepare sausage links according to package directions. Cover and keep warm.

Combine ½ teaspoon ginger and next 3 ingredients in a small saucepan. Bring to a boil; remove from heat. Cover and keep warm.

Beat egg whites at high speed with an electric mixer until soft peaks form. Set egg white aside.

Beat egg yolks at high speed in a large bowl 2 minutes or until thick and pale. Stir in pumpkin, buttermilk, and butter.

Whisk together baking mix and remaining ½ teaspoon ginger in a medium bowl. Add to pumpkin mixture, and beat well; stir in raisins, if desired. Fold in beaten egg white.

Spoon about ⅓ cup batter for each pancake onto a hot, lightly greased griddle. Cook pancakes until tops are covered with bubbles and edges look cooked; turn and cook other side.

Place 1 sausage link in center of each pancake; roll up. Place pancakes, seam sides down, on a warm serving platter. Serve with syrup mixture. **Makes:** 15 pancake rolls.

Prep: 7 min., **Cook:** 16 min.

Tip: Placing the rolls seam side down helps keep the pancakes from unrolling.

*For testing purposes only, we used Bisquick Original All-Purpose Baking Mix.

Connie Emerson
Reno, Nevada

Dixie Griddle Cakes

Don't limit yourself to apple pie filling as a topping; try these moist cakes with cinnamon applesauce, fried apple rings, or escalloped apples.

1   (21-ounce) can apple pie filling
4   large eggs, lightly beaten
¾   cup canned mashed sweet potatoes
¼   cup butter, melted
1   tablespoon sugar
1   teaspoon apple pie spice
¼   cup milk
1   cup all-purpose baking mix *
¾   cup chopped pecans

Cook apple pie filling in a small saucepan over medium heat until warm, stirring occasionally. Cover and keep warm.

Combine eggs and next 6 ingredients in a medium bowl, stirring just until blended. Stir in pecans.

Pour about ¼ cup batter for each pancake onto a hot, lightly greased griddle. Cook pancakes until tops are covered with bubbles and edges look cooked; turn and cook other side. Serve immediately with warm apple pie filling.
Makes: 13 pancakes.
Prep: 6 min., **Cook:** 8 min.

*For testing purposes only, we used Bisquick Original All-Purpose Baking Mix.

Beverley Rossell
Morgantown, Indiana

Tropical Waffles With Pecan-Cream Cheese Butter

For a taste of paradise, try these tart pineapple waffles topped with cream cheese butter, toasted coconut, bananas, and maple syrup.

2   cups all-purpose baking mix *
2   large eggs, separated
1¼ cups buttermilk
1   cup crushed pineapple in juice, undrained
¼   cup butter, melted
1   teaspoon vanilla extract
Pecan-Cream Cheese Butter
½   cup sweetened flaked coconut, toasted
2   small bananas, sliced (about 2½ cups)
Maple syrup

Place baking mix in a large bowl, and make a well in center.
Combine egg yolks and next 4 ingredients, stirring well with a whisk; add to dry ingredients, stirring just until dry ingredients are moistened.

Beat egg whites at high speed with an electric mixer until stiff peaks form; fold into batter.

Cook in a preheated, oiled waffle iron until golden. Top with Pecan-Cream Cheese Butter, toasted coconut, banana, and maple syrup. **Makes:** 16 (4-inch) waffles.
Prep: 14 min., **Cook:** 7 min.

With this recipe, **Paula** is able to sneak a little fruit into her kids' diet at the first meal of the day.

Pecan-Cream Cheese Butter:
You'll want to make this butter again as a spread for bagels.

4   ounces cream cheese, softened
½   cup butter, softened
¼   cup firmly packed brown sugar
½   cup chopped pecans, toasted

Beat cream cheese and butter at medium speed with an electric mixer until creamy. Gradually add sugar, beating well. Stir in pecans. **Makes:** 1¼ cups.
Prep: 5 min.

Tip: To toast pecans in a skillet, cook on medium-high heat 3 minutes, stirring constantly, until toasted. To toast coconut, bake at 350° for 8 to 10 minutes.

*For testing purposes only, we used Bisquick Original All-Purpose Baking Mix.

Paula Mahagnoul
Faribault, Minnesota

New England
Harvest Waffles

New England Harvest Waffles

½ cup uncooked regular oats
1½ cups boiling water
1¼ cups all-purpose flour
½ cup yellow cornmeal
2 tablespoons wheat germ
2 tablespoons brown sugar
1 tablespoon granulated sugar
1 tablespoon baking powder
½ teaspoon salt
3 large eggs
1½ cups milk
½ cup raisins
½ cup butter, melted
Honey Butter

Place oats in a small bowl; cover with boiling water. Let stand 30 minutes until soft; drain well.

Combine flour and next 6 ingredients in a large bowl; stir well. In a small bowl, combine eggs and milk; add oats and raisins, and stir well. Add egg mixture to flour mixture, whisking until combined. Stir in melted butter.

Cook in a preheated, oiled waffle iron until golden. Serve immediately with Honey Butter. **Makes:** 16 (4-inch) waffles.
Prep: 14 min., **Cook:** 16 min., **Other:** 30 min.

Honey Butter:
½ cup butter, softened
¼ cup honey

Mix butter and honey in a small bowl until blended. Serve immediately, or store in refrigerator. **Makes:** ¾ cup.
Prep: 5 min.

Tip: To ensure everyone gets a hot waffle, place fresh-off-the-iron waffles on a baking sheet and keep in a 200° oven until serving time.

Kimberly K. Foster
West Simsbury, Connecticut

Kimberly says her children love to have "silly supper" where they have these breakfast waffles for dinner. She also makes this batter at night and chills it to be able to serve fresh waffles to her kids before school.

Waffle Toast With Orange Cream

If you don't have a Belgian waffle iron, you can substitute sliced white bread for the barbecue bread and use a regular waffle iron.

6 cups cinnamon-flavored lightly sweetened whole grain oat cereal squares, crushed*
1 cup sliced almonds
1 teaspoon ground cinnamon
6 large eggs, lightly beaten
2 cups orange juice
1½ teaspoons almond extract
¼ cup sugar
1 teaspoon salt
¼ teaspoon cornstarch
12 slices barbecue bread or Vienna bread
Orange Cream
Garnishes: orange slices, powdered sugar, maple syrup

Combine cereal, almonds, and cinnamon in a large shallow dish or pieplate; set mixture aside.

Whisk together eggs and next 5 ingredients. Pour egg mixture into a shallow dish or pieplate.

Soak bread slices in egg mixture for a few seconds on each side; dredge in cereal mixture. Cook in a preheated, oiled Belgian waffle iron until golden. Wipe waffle iron clean between batches. Serve with Orange Cream; garnish, if desired. **Makes:** 6 servings.
Prep: 8 min., **Cook:** 20 min.

Orange Cream:
1 cup whipping cream
3 tablespoons sugar
1 teaspoon orange rind
½ cup plain yogurt
¼ cup orange juice

Beat whipping cream until foamy; gradually add sugar, beating until soft peaks form. Fold in orange rind, yogurt, and orange juice. Cover and chill. **Makes:** 2¼ cups.
Prep: 5 min.

*For testing purposes only, we tested with Quaker Oat Cinnamon Life Cereal.

Martha Leverette
Lynchburg, Virginia

Chocolate Chip Scones

These chocolaty treats are ideal for breakfast, after-school snacks, or with a cup of coffee.

1   cup all-purpose baking mix *
3   tablespoons light brown sugar
½   teaspoon ground cinnamon
1   cup uncooked quick-cooking
     oats
½   cup semisweet chocolate
     morsels
1   large egg, lightly beaten
¼   cup milk

Combine baking mix, brown sugar, cinnamon, oats, and chocolate morsels in a large bowl. Whisk together egg and milk; add to dry ingredients, stirring until dry ingredients are moistened. (Dough will be sticky.)

Shape mixture into a 7-inch circle on a greased baking sheet. Cut into 8 wedges (do not separate).

Bake at 400° for 10 to 12 minutes or until lightly browned. **Makes:** 8 scones.
Prep: 11 min., **Cook:** 12 min.

*For testing purposes only, we used Bisquick Original All-Purpose Baking Mix.

Janet Flynn
Lawrenceville, Georgia

Chocolate Chip Scones

Orange Cheesecake Yum Yums

Your family will love the twist on this old favorite—orange cinnamon rolls with a wonderful white chocolate-cream cheese filling.

1 **(17.5-ounce) can refrigerated jumbo orange-flavored cinnamon sweet rolls with icing** ∗
¼ **cup cheesecake-flavored cream cheese, softened**
2 **ounces white chocolate baking bar, chopped and melted**

Carefully cut each sweet roll in half horizontally, removing top half; set rolls and icing aside.

Combine cream cheese and melted chocolate in a small bowl. Spoon 1 tablespoon cream cheese mixture into center of bottom half of each roll. Place top half of rolls over filling, pressing edges to seal. Place rolls on a lightly greased baking sheet.

Bake at 375° for 16 minutes or until lightly browned. Spread prepared orange icing over warm rolls. **Makes:** 5 servings.
Prep: 20 min., **Cook:** 16 min.

∗For testing purposes only, we used Pillsbury Grands! Orange Cinnamon Rolls with Icing.

Tip: Make sure there are no holes in the bottom half of each roll. Not only will you lose a lot of filling, but the filling will also burn on the pan.

Erin Ossewarde
Santa Barbara, California

Although leftovers are unlikely, **Erin** refrigerates the uneaten baked rolls for breakfast another day.

PB & Jammon Express Rolls

These warm spirals are filled with a strawberry spread and frosted with creamy peanut butter frosting. If strawberry isn't your favorite, substitute any other flavor fruit spread or preserves.

2¾ cups all-purpose baking mix ∗
⅔ **cup milk**
2 **tablespoons granulated sugar**
2 **tablespoons butter, melted**
1 **(10-ounce) jar seedless strawberry spread** ∗
1 **(8-ounce) package cream cheese, softened**
2 **tablespoons creamy peanut butter**
1 **cup powdered sugar**
1 **teaspoon vanilla extract**

Combine first 3 ingredients in a medium bowl, stirring until dry ingredients are moistened.

Turn dough out onto a lightly floured surface; knead 3 or 4 times. Roll or pat dough into a 15- x 9-inch rectangle. Brush dough evenly with melted butter. Spoon strawberry spread evenly over dough. Roll up, jellyroll fashion, starting at long end; press edges to seal. Gently cut into 12 (1¼-inch) slices using a serrated knife. Place rolls in lightly greased muffin pans. Bake at 375° for 23 to 25 minutes or until lightly browned.

Beat cream cheese and next 3 ingredients at medium speed with an electric mixer until fluffy. Spread over warm rolls. Serve warm. **Makes:** 12 servings.
Prep: 23 min., **Cook:** 25 min.

∗For testing purposes only, we used Bisquick Original All-Purpose Baking Mix and Polaner All-Fruit.

Tip: If you have leftover frosting, serve it with apple slices or graham crackers.

Jennifer Riley
Port Orange, Florida

Jennifer sent specific directions to "serve immediately with a glass of cold milk." We heartily concur.

Simply the Best Caramel Rolls

Simply the Best Caramel Rolls

Beating the biscuit mixture with an electric mixer for 2 minutes saves you time because it reduces the amount of time you have to spend kneading the dough.

1   (¼-ounce) envelope active dry
    yeast
⅔   cup warm water (100° to 110°)
2½ cups all-purpose baking mix ✳
2   tablespoons butter or
    margarine, melted
2   tablespoons granulated sugar
1½ teaspoons ground cinnamon
1   cup miniature marshmallows
½   cup firmly packed brown
    sugar
½   cup butter, melted
1   teaspoon molasses
¼   cup chopped pecans, toasted
    (optional)

Combine yeast and warm water in a large bowl; let stand 5 minutes. Add baking mix; beat 2 minutes at medium speed with an electric mixer.

Turn dough out onto a lightly floured surface, and knead until smooth (about 2 minutes). Roll into an 11-inch square (about ¼ inch thick), and spread with 2 tablespoons butter. Combine granulated sugar and cinnamon; sprinkle over butter. Roll up, jellyroll fashion. Cut into 9 slices.

Combine marshmallows and next 3 ingredients. Line a 9-inch square pan with nonstick aluminum foil. Spread marshmallow mixture in pan. Place rolls, cut side up, on mixture. Cover and let rise in a warm place (85°), free from drafts, 30 minutes or until doubled in bulk. Bake at 375° for 18 to 20 minutes or until lightly browned. Remove from oven; invert onto a large serving plate. Remove aluminum foil; sprinkle with pecans, if desired. **Makes:** 9 servings.
Prep: 28 min., **Cook:** 20 min., **Other:** 35 min.

✳For testing purposes only, we used Bisquick Original All-Purpose Baking Mix.

Tip: For perfectly round slices, place a long piece of unwaxed dental floss or string under dough about 1 inch from end of roll. Cross ends of floss over top of roll; slowly pull the ends to cut through the dough.

Eugenia Wychor
Shoreview, Minnesota

Full Meal Burger

These burgers earned their name because they have all the components of a full meal—meat, vegetables, and bread.

1½ pounds ground chuck
¼ cup shredded carrot
1 green onion, chopped
1 (2-ounce) jar diced pimiento, drained
¾ cup shredded sharp Cheddar cheese
1 teaspoon Worcestershire sauce
1 teaspoon salt
½ teaspoon pepper
1 (8-ounce) package shredded lettuce
⅓ cup Ranch-style dressing
6 (6-inch) pita rounds
12 slices ripe tomato (about 2 tomatoes)
Additional Ranch-style dressing

Combine first 8 ingredients. Shape into 6 (5- x 3½- x ¾-inch) oval patties. Grill patties, covered with grill lid, over medium-high heat (350° to 400°) 6 to 7 minutes on each side or until beef is no longer pink.

Combine lettuce and ⅓ cup dressing in a medium bowl.

Cut off 1 inch of bread from 1 side of each pita round, forming a pocket. Line each pita with 2 tomato slices and ½ cup lettuce mixture. Add burger. Drizzle with additional dressing, if desired. **Makes:** 6 servings.
Prep: 13 min., **Cook:** 14 min.

Note: These can also be prepared using the broiler. Broil 3 inches from heat 6 to 7 minutes on each side or until beef is no longer pink.

Fred G. Naifeh
Broken Arrow, Oklahoma

Form the patties into ovals as **Fred** does so they'll nestle nicely inside the pita.

Everybody's Favorite Sloppy Joes

Kids of all ages love this "messy" weeknight favorite.

1 pound ground beef
¼ cup diced onion
¼ cup diced green bell pepper
¼ cup diced celery
1 (8-ounce) can tomato sauce
¼ cup ketchup
1 tablespoon white vinegar
1 teaspoon sugar
1 teaspoon salt
1½ teaspoons Worcestershire sauce
⅛ teaspoon black pepper
6 sesame seed buns

Cook first 4 ingredients in a large skillet over medium-high heat, stirring until meat crumbles and is no longer pink. Drain well.

Add tomato sauce and next 6 ingredients; reduce heat to medium, and cook, uncovered, 10 minutes.

Serve on buns. **Makes:** 6 servings.
Prep: 6 min., **Cook:** 20 min.

Tip: We loved these served with pickles and shredded Cheddar cheese.

Matt Wallace
Fort Lauderdale, Florida

If you prefer a chunkier meat mixture, **Matt** recommends reducing the tomato sauce to ½ cup and adding ½ cup drained canned diced tomato.

Tex-Mex Chili Slaw Burgers

These big-boy burgers combine all the great flavors of chili, cheese, and corn chips with a spiced up slaw.

4   cups shredded cabbage (about ½ medium head)
1   cup shredded carrot (about 1 medium)
½   cup chopped green onions (about 3 green onions)
4   garlic cloves, chopped
1   (11-ounce) can yellow corn with red and green bell peppers, drained
1   cup salsa
3   tablespoons butter, cut into small pieces
1½ pounds ground chuck
1   tablespoon taco seasoning mix
1   tablespoon garlic powder
1   teaspoon ground red pepper
1   large egg
2   cups coarsely crushed corn chips
1   (15-ounce) can chili without beans
6   (1-ounce) slices processed American cheese
6   hamburger buns

Combine first 6 ingredients in a medium bowl. Place mixture on a large sheet of heavy-duty aluminum foil; dot with butter. Tightly fold in sides and ends of foil to form a packet.

Combine ground chuck and next 6 ingredients in a medium bowl. Shape mixture into 6 (5- x 1-inch) patties (mixture will be very moist).

Grill patties and slaw packet, covered with grill lid, over medium-high heat (350° to 400°) 8 minutes on each side or until beef is no longer pink. Top patties with cheese slices. Serve each patty on a bun topped evenly with slaw mixture. **Makes:** 6 servings.
Prep: 35 min., **Cook:** 16 min.

Tip: Be sure to make these patties at least 1-inch thick so they'll flip easily. Because the meat mixture is moist, thinner patties fall apart on the grill.

Mary Kay
New Llano, Louisiana

Mary uses Creole seasoning in these burgers, but we opted for taco seasoning to keep true to the Tex-Mex theme.

Cheesy Taco Cups With Green Cream

These soft taco bites are topped with a dollop of avocado cream; serve salsa on the side for the adults.

1   pound ground chuck
1   (1.25-ounce) envelope taco seasoning mix
1   (4.5-ounce) can chopped green chiles, drained
1   cup milk
½   cup all-purpose baking mix *
2   large eggs
1   cup shredded taco-blend cheese
Green Cream
Chopped tomato
Shredded lettuce

Cook ground beef in a large nonstick skillet, stirring until meat crumbles and is no longer pink. Drain excess fat. Stir in taco seasoning and green chiles; set mixture aside.

Combine milk, baking mix, and eggs; divide batter evenly among 18 lightly greased muffin pans, filling ⅓ full (batter will be thin). Spoon about 2 tablespoons beef mixture over batter in each muffin cup; sprinkle with cheese. Bake at 350° for 20 minutes or until browned. Top with Green Cream, chopped tomato, and shredded lettuce. **Makes:** 1½ dozen.
Prep: 14 min., **Cook:** 27 min.

Green Cream:
1   (8-ounce) container sour cream
1   medium avocado, peeled
1   garlic clove, chopped
1   tablespoon lime juice
¼   teaspoon salt

Combine all ingredients in a blender or food processor; process until smooth.
Makes: 2 cups.
Prep: 3 min.

*For testing purposes only, we used Bisquick Original All-Purpose Baking Mix.

Debra Brooks
Byron, Georgia

Mexi-Cups

Here's an updated variation of a taco that makes food fun for a kid's party. It's great as an appetizer for an adult party, too.

36 won ton wrappers (3½-inch squares)
1 pound ground beef
1 (1.25-ounce) envelope taco seasoning mix
⅔ cup water
1 cup (4 ounces) shredded sharp Cheddar cheese, divided
1 small tomato, chopped
1 (8-ounce) container sour cream
Garnish: fresh cilantro

Coat baking cups of 3 miniature muffin pans with cooking spray. Gently press 1 won ton wrapper into each muffin cup, allowing ends to extend above edges of cups. Bake at 350° for 10 minutes, rotating pans in oven after 5 minutes. Remove pans from oven; cool. Remove won ton cups from pans.

> **Lynda** proclaims these are a great alternative to tacos. The cups made from won ton wrappers are baked, not fried, and crunchy.

Meanwhile, cook meat in a large skillet over medium-high heat, stirring until meat crumbles and is no longer pink; drain. Return meat to pan over medium heat. Add taco seasoning mix and water; cook 3 minutes or until liquid is almost absorbed.

Sprinkle ½ cup cheese evenly into won ton cups; divide taco meat and remaining ½ cup cheese among won ton cups. Top each with tomato, and dollop with sour cream. Garnish, if desired. **Makes:** 3 dozen.

Prep: 26 min., **Cook:** 19 min.

Lynda Sanders
Trophy Club, Texas

Hot Ham and Cheese Snackwiches

This warm, creamy alternative to an everyday ham and cheese sandwich can be served as a meal or snack.

½ (8-ounce) package cream cheese, softened
1 tablespoon grated Parmesan cheese
1 tablespoon sour cream
1 teaspoon lemon juice
¼ teaspoon Old Bay seasoning
1 green onion, minced
12 white bread slices, crusts removed
12 ounces thinly sliced deli ham
¾ cup (3 ounces) shredded sharp Cheddar cheese

Combine first 6 ingredients in a medium bowl; beat with an electric mixer until combined.

Spread cream cheese mixture evenly over 6 bread slices; top each with 2 slices ham, 2 tablespoons Cheddar cheese, and a remaining bread slice. Place sandwiches on a baking sheet lined with nonstick aluminum foil. Bake at 350° for 15 minutes or until golden brown. Cut sandwiches into triangles or squares. Serve hot. **Makes:** 6 sandwiches.

Prep: 15 min., **Cook:** 15 min.

Sherry Little
Sherwood, Arkansas

> **Sherry** makes these sandwiches special for her family by forming each serving into a beggar's purse or individual pouch. We liked this concept but we streamlined the procedure by preparing individual sandwiches and cutting each one into quarters.

Surprise "Pots of Gold"

These comforting "pots of gold" perfume the house with a tantalizing aroma as they bake.

1½ cups diced ham
1 (10¾-ounce) can cream of
   mushroom soup, undiluted
2 teaspoons Dijon mustard
1 (3-ounce) package cream
   cheese, softened
½ cup milk
½ teaspoon garlic powder
⅛ teaspoon ground red pepper
1 (10-ounce) package frozen
   broccoli, cauliflower, and
   carrots in cheese sauce,
   thawed
½ cup butter, melted

⅛ teaspoon garlic powder
1 (16-ounce) package frozen
   phyllo pastry, thawed

Combine first 8 ingredients in a bowl;
set aside.

Combine melted butter and garlic powder
in a bowl.

Place 1 sheet of phyllo dough on a large
cutting board; brush with butter mixture.
(Keep remaining phyllo covered with a
damp cloth until ready to use.) Lay second sheet at an angle on top of first sheet;
brush with butter mixture. Continue with
3 more sheets of phyllo dough.

Spoon ¼ cup ham mixture in center of
phyllo sheets. Lift sides, twist, and
pinch tops. Repeat procedure with
remaining ham mixture, butter mixture,
and phyllo sheets.

Place "pots" 2 inches apart on a lightly
greased baking sheet. Bake at 375° for
15 minutes or until crisp and golden.
Makes: 8 servings.
Prep: 33 min., **Cook:** 15 min.

Tip: Try these with cooked chicken or
turkey as an alternative to ham.

Melissa Williams-Barbao
Oxford, Alabama

Bacon and Cheese Quesadillas With Tropical Fruit Salsa

These quick-and-easy quesadillas will have your kids screaming for more.

1 (15.25-ounce) can tropical fruit
   salad, undrained
⅓ cup diced red bell pepper
2 tablespoons chopped red onion
2 tablespoons chopped fresh mint
¼ teaspoon ground cumin
1 tablespoon lemon juice
1 tablespoon butter, melted
4 (8-inch) flour tortillas
1½ cups (6 ounces) Monterey Jack
   cheese or Monterey Jack
   cheese with peppers
4 fully cooked bacon slices,
   crumbled
2 tablespoons chopped peanuts
⅓ cup sour cream

Drain fruit salad, reserving 1 tablespoon
syrup. Discard remaining syrup.

Combine fruit salad, reserved syrup,
bell pepper, and next 4 ingredients in a
medium bowl. Set aside.

Spread butter evenly on 1 side of tortillas. Sprinkle cheese evenly on half of
unbuttered sides of tortillas; top with
bacon and peanuts. Fold tortillas in half.

Cook quesadillas, 2 at a time, in a large
skillet over medium heat 2 minutes on
each side or until tortillas are golden
and cheese melts. Cut into thirds; serve
with fruit salsa and sour cream. **Makes:**
4 servings.
Prep: 5 min., **Cook:** 8 min.

Tip: You can leave out the red onions, if
desired.

Gloria Bradley
Naperville, Illinois

Here's another great entry from **Gloria** who was a
Finalist and Brand Winner in the Simple and
Scrumptious Entrées category.

Lasagna Pizza

Don't stray too far from your silverware tray for this Italian pie. With lasagna noodles and a ricotta herb filling, you'll definitely want to keep your fork and knife handy.

4   uncooked lasagna noodles
2   links (8 ounces) sweet Italian sausage, casings removed
1   (4.5-ounce) jar sliced mushrooms, drained
1   (14-ounce) jar pizza sauce
1   (14.5-ounce) can petite diced tomatoes with mushrooms, drained
2   tablespoons sugar
1   (15-ounce) container ricotta cheese
1   large egg
2   tablespoons dried parsley flakes
½   teaspoon dried oregano
½   teaspoon garlic salt
¼   teaspoon pepper
½   (24-ounce) package refrigerated pizza crusts *
1½ cups (6 ounces) shredded mozzarella cheese, divided
¼   cup freshly shredded Parmesan cheese

Cook pasta in boiling salted water according to package directions. Drain. **Meanwhile,** cook sausage in a small skillet over medium-high heat 5 minutes, stirring until sausage crumbles and is no longer pink. Drain on paper towels.

Pat mushrooms dry with a paper towel. Combine mushrooms, pizza sauce, and next 2 ingredients in a medium bowl. Combine ricotta cheese and next 5 ingredients in a medium bowl.

Place pizza crust on a baking sheet. Spread 1 cup pizza sauce mixture evenly over crust. Sprinkle half of sausage over pizza sauce layer. Spoon half of ricotta mixture evenly over sausage layer. Arrange lasagna noodles evenly over ricotta layer, trimming edges of noodles to fit crust. Spoon 1 cup pizza sauce mixture evenly over noodles; sprinkle with 1 cup mozzarella cheese. Spoon remaining ricotta mixture evenly over mozzarella cheese. Sprinkle with remaining sausage, mozzarella cheese, and Parmesan cheese.

Transfer pizza directly onto oven rack. Bake at 400° for 20 to 25 minutes or until hot. **Makes:** 6 to 8 servings.
Prep: 16 min., **Cook:** 30 min.

*For testing purposes only, we used Mama Mary's Gourmet Pizza Crusts. You can find them in your grocer's dairy or deli department.

Mark East
Fort Lauderdale, Florida

Mark recommends cooking the pizzas directly on the oven rack to maximize crispness of the crust. The pizza's packed with lots of goodies, though, and may ooze in your oven. Place foil or a baking sheet on a lower rack to catch any drips.

Sausage Twirlybirds With Tilt-a-Whirl Sauce

These cheesy, full-of-flavor pastries are just as yummy without the sauce.

¾   pound ground hot or mild pork sausage
½   cup salsa con queso
1   (17.3-ounce) package frozen puff pastry sheets, thawed
Tilt-a-Whirl Sauce

Cook sausage in a large skillet, stirring until sausage crumbles and is no longer pink. Drain; return to skillet. Stir in salsa con queso. Set aside.

Roll each sheet of pastry to ⅛-inch thickness on a lightly floured surface. Cut with a 4½-inch round cutter. Spoon a heaping tablespoon sausage mixture in the center of each pastry circle. Bring up edges of each circle to center and twist to seal; place pastries on ungreased baking sheets.

Bake at 400° for 15 minutes or until golden. Serve with Tilt-a-Whirl Sauce.
Makes: 14 pastries.
Prep: 17 min., **Cook:** 20 min.

Tilt-a-Whirl Sauce:
¼   cup mayonnaise
2   tablespoons sweet-and-sour sauce
1   teaspoon prepared mustard

Combine all ingredients in a small bowl. Cover and chill. **Makes:** about ½ cup.
Prep: 3 min.

Tip: These are so versatile that you can serve them for breakfast, as a snack, or as an appetizer.

Rebecca E. Ellis
Roanoke, Virginia

Rebecca uses small round pretzels from snack mix to seal off the twisted top of each pastry. We found that the pastries stayed sealed without the addition of the pretzels.

Luau Pizza Pockets

Bite into these pockets, and you'll taste a big surprise: a tropical twist of pineapple, sausage, and cheese.

8   ounces ground pork sausage
3   cups all-purpose baking mix ✱
¾   cup water
1   (8-ounce) can tomato sauce
    with basil, garlic, and oregano
1   (6-ounce) can tomato paste
    with basil, garlic, and oregano
1   (8-ounce) can crushed
    pineapple in juice, drained
¾   cup (3 ounces) shredded
    mozzarella cheese
1   egg white, lightly beaten
3   tablespoons shredded Parmesan
    cheese

Cook sausage in a large skillet over medium-high heat, stirring until sausage crumbles and is no longer pink; drain.

Combine baking mix and water in a large bowl. Turn dough out onto a lightly floured surface; knead 3 or 4 times.

Divide dough into thirds; roll each portion into an 8-inch circle.

Combine tomato sauce and tomato paste; spread 1 tablespoon evenly over each circle, leaving a ½-inch border.

Combine sausage and pineapple; spoon about ½ cup over half of each circle. Sprinkle with mozzarella cheese. Fold dough over filling, pressing edges to seal; place on a lightly greased baking sheet. Brush tops with egg white. Sprinkle with Parmesan cheese.

Bake at 425° for 20 minutes or until golden brown. Cut into wedges to serve. Serve with remaining tomato sauce mixture. **Makes:** 3 servings.

Prep: 17 min., **Cook:** 25 min.

✱ For testing purposes only, we used Bisquick Original All-Purpose Baking Mix.

Tip: To save time, drain the pineapple and sausage together in a sieve.

Christopher Sweat
Atlanta, Georgia

Make-Your-Own Chicken Chalupas

2   pounds skinned and boned
    chicken breasts
1   (16-ounce) can diced tomatoes,
    undrained
1   (16-ounce) jar salsa
12 chalupa or tostada shells
Toppings: shredded lettuce, diced
    tomato, shredded Cheddar
    cheese, guacamole, sour cream

Place chicken in a 4- or 5-quart electric slow cooker. Combine tomatoes and salsa, and pour over chicken. Cook on HIGH 1 hour; reduce to LOW, and cook 4 hours. Cool slightly; shred chicken, and serve on shells with desired toppings. **Makes:** 12 chalupas.

Prep: 10 min., **Cook:** 5 hrs.

Tip: For a kid-friendly dish, use mild salsa.

Jenny Welsh
Keller, Texas

Living in Texas, **Jenny** is lucky to have chalupa shells available for this easy, slow-cooker meal. If you're unable to find this product, as we were, substitute tostada shells.

Taco Mac and Cheese

Taco Mac and Cheese

Bring a smile to little faces with this mac and cheese—a new kid favorite.

8   ounces uncooked elbow
     macaroni
1   pound ground pork sausage
1   (1¼-ounce) envelope taco
     seasoning mix
2   tablespoons butter or margarine
2   tablespoons all-purpose flour
2   cups milk
1   (8-ounce) package shredded
     Mexican taco cheese blend,
     divided
½   cup crushed tortilla chips
Salsa

Doug uses sausage in this meaty mac and cheese. We found it just as tasty using ground chuck.

Cook macaroni in boiling salted water according to package directions. Drain; keep warm.

Meanwhile, cook sausage in a large non-stick skillet over medium-high heat, stirring until sausage crumbles and is no longer pink; drain and return to skillet. Add taco seasoning, and cook according to seasoning package directions.

Melt butter in a large heavy saucepan over medium heat. Gradually whisk in flour until smooth; cook, whisking constantly, 1 minute. Gradually whisk in milk; cook, whisking constantly, 10 minutes or until thickened. Reserve ½ cup cheese for topping; stir in remaining cheese.

Combine cooked macaroni, sausage mixture, and cheese sauce. Spoon into a lightly greased 11- x 7-inch baking dish. Sprinkle with remaining ½ cup cheese and tortilla chips.

Bake at 350° for 5 minutes or until cheese melts. Serve with salsa. **Makes:** 6 servings.
Prep: 5 min., **Cook:** 31 min.

Doug Olsen
Morganton, Georgia

Chicken, Cheese, and Black Bean Enchiladas

Kids can load up the top of their enchilada with their favorite toppings.

2   tablespoons olive oil
2   teaspoons chili powder
1   teaspoon ground cumin, divided
1   pound skinned and boned chicken breasts, cut into bite-size pieces
1   (15-ounce) can black beans, rinsed and drained
1   cup salsa, divided
⅓   cup sliced green onions
½   (8-ounce) package cream cheese, cubed
¼   teaspoon salt
8   (10-inch) flour tortillas
1   (10-ounce) can diced tomatoes and green chiles, undrained
1   cup (4 ounces) shredded Monterey Jack cheese
4   fully cooked bacon slices, crumbled

Toppings: shredded lettuce, sour cream, sliced avocado, chopped tomato

Combine oil, chili powder, and ½ teaspoon cumin in a zip-top freezer bag; add chicken pieces, turning to coat.

Cook chicken in a large nonstick skillet over medium-high heat, stirring occasionally, 7 minutes or until chicken is done. Add beans, ½ cup salsa, and next 3 ingredients; cook until cream cheese is just melted.

Spoon ½ cup chicken mixture down center of each tortilla; roll up. Place tortillas, seam side down, in a lightly greased 13- x 9-inch baking dish.

Combine diced tomatoes, remaining ½ cup salsa, and remaining ½ teaspoon cumin in a small bowl; spoon over enchiladas. Cover and bake at 350° for 15 minutes. Uncover; sprinkle with cheese, and bake 5 more minutes or until cheese melts. Sprinkle with bacon. Serve with desired toppings. **Makes:** 8 servings.
Prep: 35 min., **Cook:** 27 min.

Tip: You can use your favorite variety of canned beans instead of black beans, if desired.

Gloria Bradley
Naperville, Illinois

Here's another great entry from **Gloria,** who was a Finalist and Brand Winner in the Simple and Scrumptious Entrées category.

Crunchy Chicken Nuggets With Peanut Dipping Sauce

Forget fried—these baked chicken nuggets are so crispy you'll never miss the skillet. Kids will love them with ketchup, barbecue sauce, honey mustard, and Ranch-style dressing, too.

1   cup all-purpose flour
1   teaspoon salt
1   teaspoon ground ginger
1   teaspoon pepper
1½ teaspoons garlic powder
3   large eggs
1   cup buttermilk
4   cups crushed lightly sweetened whole grain oat cereal squares*
3   cups crushed cornflakes cereal
2   pounds skinned and boned chicken breasts, cut into 1-inch pieces
Peanut Sauce

Combine first 5 ingredients in a shallow dish. Whisk together eggs and buttermilk in a shallow bowl. Combine crushed cereals in a shallow dish.

Dredge chicken, 1 piece at a time, in seasoned flour mixture; dip into egg mixture. Coat chicken pieces with cereal mixture. Place on lightly greased baking sheets.

Bake at 350° for 12 minutes on each side or until chicken is no longer pink. Serve with Peanut Sauce. **Makes:** 8 servings.
Prep: 30 min., **Cook:** 24 min.

*For testing purposes only, we used Quaker Oat Life Cereal.

Peanut Sauce:
1   tablespoon sesame oil
1   tablespoon olive oil
1   teaspoon minced garlic
1   teaspoon ground ginger
¼   teaspoon dried crushed red pepper
1   tablespoon rice wine vinegar
¼   cup firmly packed dark brown sugar
2   tablespoons soy sauce
½   cup chunky peanut butter
1   tablespoon honey
1   tablespoon lime juice

Heat sesame oil and olive oil in a small heavy saucepan over medium-low heat. Add garlic, ginger, and crushed pepper; cook 2 minutes. Whisk in vinegar and remaining ingredients. **Makes:** ¾ cup.
Prep: 2 min., **Cook:** 2 min.

Julie Biederman
Henderson, Nevada

Chicken Tacos With Homemade Tortillas and Salsa

It takes a little practice to make uniform tortillas, so don't give up. The end result is worth the effort. Although these tacos are authentic, you can always add a little cheese. Try a Mexican cheese such as queso blanco.

4   skinned and boned chicken breasts
3   cups water
1   tablespoon fajita seasoning *
½   cup firmly packed fresh cilantro leaves
1   small jalapeño pepper, halved crosswise and seeded
½   medium-size red onion, cut into wedges
1   (28-ounce) can diced tomatoes, undrained
1   teaspoon ground cumin
¼   teaspoon salt
2   cups instant corn masa mix *

Combine first 3 ingredients in a 2-quart saucepan. Bring to a boil; cover, reduce heat, and simmer 45 minutes. Remove chicken, reserving broth; cool chicken slightly. Shred chicken into bite-size pieces. Cover and cool completely.

Bring broth to a boil over high heat. Cook until reduced to 2 cups (about 7 minutes).

Meanwhile, process cilantro in a food processor until minced. Add jalapeño and onion; pulse until finely chopped.

Add tomatoes, cumin, and salt; process until smooth. Cover and set aside.

Pour broth through a wire-mesh strainer into a bowl, discarding solids. Cool completely.

Cut a 6-inch diameter circle from a large zip-top freezer bag; separate into 2 circles of plastic.

Lightly spoon masa mix into a dry measuring cup; level with a knife (do not pack). Place masa in a medium bowl. Gradually stir in about 1⅓ cups broth until masa is moistened. Finish mixing dough with hands. (Add more broth or masa as necessary to achieve an elastic dough—dough should not be dry and crumbly or sticky.)

Divide dough into 15 equal pieces. Roll pieces into balls; cover with a damp towel. Place 1 ball of dough between circles of plastic. (Dough will stick to tortilla press if not "sandwiched" between pieces of plastic.) Flatten dough in a tortilla press to about 6 inches in diameter. Carefully remove top piece of plastic from tortilla. Invert tortilla and plastic, tortilla side down, onto 1 hand; carefully peel away plastic with

other hand. Quickly place tortilla on a hot, ungreased well-seasoned cast-iron griddle or in a nonstick skillet; cook 30 seconds on each side. Remove to a plate. Repeat procedure with remaining dough. Stack tortillas as they are cooked; cover and keep warm until ready to fill.

Spoon about ¼ cup chicken in center of 1 tortilla. Top chicken with about 2 tablespoons salsa. Roll up tortilla. Place taco, seam side down, on a warm serving platter. Repeat procedure with remaining tortillas, chicken, and salsa. Serve immediately with additional salsa for dipping.
Makes: 15 tacos.
Prep: 32 min., **Cook:** 1 hr., 7 min.

*For testing purposes only, we used McCormick Gourmet Collection Blends Fajita Seasoning and Maseca Instant Masa Mix.

Tip: If desired, fold tortillas around filling instead of rolling up. Leftover salsa keeps well for several days in the refrigerator. Serve salsa with taco soup or chips.

Lori Sustaita
Longview, Texas

Tortilla Tips

Homemade tortillas are simple to make and well worth the effort. All you need to get started is masa harina, a tortilla press, a skillet, and these helpful hints.

- Thicker plastic from food storage bags is easier to work with than wax paper or plastic wrap when pressing out tortillas in the tortilla press. The thicker plastic is more durable, sticks to dough less, and is wrinkle-free.
- If your first attempts at pressing out the tortillas are less than desirable, the dough can be scraped from the plastic, re-rolled into balls, and pressed out again.
- Use a hot griddle or skillet to cook tortillas. If you have an electric one, set the thermostat at 425°.

Cereal-Encrusted Chicken and Sweet Potatoes

Your family will like these crunchy chicken fingers, and they'll be getting a full serving of vegetables to boot.

2 large sweet potatoes, peeled and cut into 1-inch cubes (4 cups)
½ cup honey mustard dressing, divided
½ teaspoon salt
¼ teaspoon garlic powder
¼ teaspoon freshly ground pepper
1 pound skinned and boned chicken tenders
2 cups lightly sweetened whole grain oat cereal squares ✱

Combine sweet potatoes and ¼ cup dressing in a large bowl, stirring until potatoes are coated. Place potatoes on a baking sheet covered with aluminum foil and coated with cooking spray.

Bake potatoes at 450° for 30 minutes; set aside.

Meanwhile, combine salt, garlic powder, and pepper; sprinkle over chicken. Toss chicken with remaining ¼ cup dressing in a large bowl until coated.

Place cereal in a large zip-top freezer bag. Finely crush cereal with a meat mallet or rolling pin. Add chicken to bag, a few pieces at a time. Seal bag, and shake to coat. Place chicken strips on a baking sheet covered with aluminum foil and coated with cooking spray.

Bake at 450° for 20 minutes, turning after 10 minutes. **Makes:** 4 servings.

Prep: 20 min., **Cook:** 30 min.

✱For testing purposes only, we used Quaker Oat Life Cereal.

Michael Trantham
Allen, Texas

"Oh-So-Easy" Layered Chicken Pot Pie

There's a surprise layer of pastry in the middle of this cobbler-type chicken pie.

4 cups chopped cooked chicken ✱
½ teaspoon poultry seasoning
1 (10¾-ounce) can cream of chicken soup, undiluted
1 (10¾-ounce) can cream of mushroom soup, undiluted
1 (14-ounce) can chicken broth
1 (12-ounce) can evaporated milk
½ (8-ounce) package cream cheese, softened
¼ teaspoon pepper
1 (15-ounce) package refrigerated piecrusts

Combine chicken and poultry seasoning in a bowl; set aside.

Combine cream of chicken soup and next 5 ingredients in a medium saucepan over medium heat. Bring to boil; boil 1 minute, stirring constantly. Reduce heat, and simmer 10 minutes.

Spoon half of chicken mixture into a lightly greased 13- x 9-inch baking dish; pour half of soup mixture over

Donna uses low-sodium soups in this pot pie. We used regular soups instead and omitted the salt.

chicken. Roll 1 piecrust into a 13-inch oval on a lightly floured surface; place over chicken, tucking edges in. Pierce crust with a fork. Bake at 425° for 20 minutes or until crust is browned.

Remove from oven. Repeat layers, ending with remaining crust. Pierce with fork; return to oven. Bake 20 more minutes or until crust is browned.

Makes: 8 servings.

Prep: 14 min., **Cook:** 51 min.

✱One large roasted chicken yields about 4 cups chopped meat.

Donna L. Williams
West Point, Georgia

Mom's Yummy Mini Chicken Tacos

Kids will love assembling their own supper, and they'll never guess the brown rice and refried beans are actually good for them. Shhh!

- 1 regular-size bag boil-in-bag brown rice
- 1 (8-ounce) jar taco sauce, divided
- 1 tablespoon taco seasoning mix
- 2 (6-ounce) packages refrigerated southwestern-seasoned chicken breast strips, chopped
- 1 (16-ounce) can refried beans
- 2 tablespoons sour cream
- 1 (18-count) package mini taco shells
- 4 to 6 (.75-ounce) American cheese strips *

Shredded lettuce

Sour cream (optional)

Cook rice according to package directions; drain and spoon into a medium saucepan. Stir in 1/3 cup taco sauce, taco seasoning mix, and chicken. Cook over low heat 3 to 5 minutes or until thoroughly heated. Cook refried beans in a small saucepan over low heat until thoroughly heated. Remove from heat; stir in 2 tablespoons sour cream.

Place taco shells on a baking sheet. Bake at 375° for 5 to 7 minutes or until shells are crispy.

Fill each taco shell with about 1 teaspoon bean mixture and 2½ tablespoons rice mixture; top each with 2 strips American cheese. Place filled taco shells on an aluminum foil-lined baking sheet. Bake at 375° for 1 to 2 minutes or until cheese melts. Place 3 tacos on lettuce-lined plates. Serve with remaining taco sauce and additional sour cream, if desired. **Makes:** 6 servings.

Prep: 21 min., **Cook:** 24 min.

*For testing purposes only, we used Kraft Rip-Ums peelable American cheese strips.

Cara Cresswell
Bentonia, Mississippi

Mom's Yummy Mini
Chicken Tacos

Plucky Chicken Nuggets With Tiger Sauce

Nothin' says Southern like fried chicken! And with a touch of filé powder, a seasoning used often in gumbo, it's even better. Serve this chicken nugget recipe to your family, and you'll give those famous fast-food chains a run for their money.

1 **cup buttermilk**
2 **large eggs, lightly beaten**
2 **tablespoons fresh lemon juice**
4 **cups self-rising flour**
1 **tablespoon paprika**
2 **teaspoons seasoned salt**
2 **teaspoons filé powder**
1½ **teaspoons onion powder**
1½ **teaspoons garlic powder**
1 **teaspoon ground red pepper**
1 **teaspoon ground black pepper**
7 **skinned and boned chicken breasts, cut into 2-inch pieces**
Canola oil
Tiger Sauce

Combine buttermilk, eggs, and lemon juice in a shallow dish. Combine flour and next 7 ingredients in a large zip-top freezer bag. Dip chicken in egg mixture. Add chicken to flour mixture; seal and shake until coated.

Pour oil to a depth of 1½ inches into a Dutch oven; heat to 370°. Fry chicken, in batches, 5 to 7 minutes or until golden. Drain on paper towels. Serve with Tiger Sauce. **Makes:** 6 to 8 servings.
Prep: 17 min., **Cook:** 18 min.

> We highly recommend the tasty Tiger Sauce, but if you're short on time, **Kathy** suggests barbecue sauce for dipping.

Tiger Sauce:
1 **cup mayonnaise**
¼ **cup ketchup**
3 **tablespoons Creole mustard**
1 **tablespoon Dijon mustard**
½ **teaspoon onion powder**
½ **teaspoon garlic powder**
½ **teaspoon hot sauce**

Combine all ingredients in a small bowl. Cover and chill until ready to serve.
Makes: 1⅓ cups.
Prep: 5 min.

Tip: Always be very careful when working with hot oil. Use long tongs to gently place chicken into hot oil.

Kathy Labat
Raceland, Louisiana

Clark's Mexican Pizza

Fresh cilantro livens up the flavor of this pizza.

9 **(10-inch) flour tortillas**
1 **(16-ounce) can refried beans**
¾ **cup sour cream**
¾ **cup chopped fresh cilantro**
3 **cups (12 ounces) shredded Mexican-blend cheese**
¾ **cup salsa**
¾ **cup chopped green onions**
1½ **teaspoons Mexican seasoning**

Place a tortilla on an aluminum foil-lined baking sheet; spread one-third of beans over tortilla. Spread ¼ cup sour cream in a thin layer over bean mixture. Sprinkle with ¼ cup chopped cilantro and ½ cup cheese. Place another tortilla over cheese, and press to seal. Spoon ¼ cup salsa over tortilla. Cover with ¼ cup green onions, and ½ cup cheese. Sprinkle with ½ teaspoon Mexican seasoning, and top with another tortilla. Wrap tightly in foil. Repeat procedure twice with remaining tortillas and ingredients.

Bake at 400° for 12 minutes. Unwrap foil; let pizzas cool 3 to 4 minutes before slicing. **Makes:** 3 (10-inch) pizzas.
Prep: 22 min., **Cook:** 12 min.

William Siler
Richmond, Kentucky

White Pizza Sticks

A white pizza (pizza bianca) uses sour cream or pesto sauce instead of traditional tomato sauce. This one caught our eye because it's cut into strips, and then dipped into pizza sauce, offering the best of both worlds.

2 cups all-purpose baking mix *
⅔ cup milk
1½ teaspoons dried Italian seasoning
1 (8-ounce) container sour cream
½ cup mayonnaise
¼ cup finely chopped onion
1 tablespoon dried parsley flakes
¼ cup shredded Parmesan cheese
½ teaspoon garlic powder
¼ teaspoon salt
¼ teaspoon pepper
1 (8-ounce) package shredded pizza cheese blend
Pizza sauce

Stir together first 3 ingredients in a bowl. Turn dough out onto a lightly floured surface; knead 12 times. Pat dough evenly into a lightly greased 13- x 9-inch pan.

Combine sour cream and next 7 ingredients; stir well. Spread sour cream mixture evenly over dough; sprinkle pizza cheese blend over sour cream mixture.

Bake at 400° for 25 minutes or until cheese is melted and bubbly.

Cut pizza lengthwise into 9 sticks; cut each stick in half crosswise. Serve with pizza sauce. **Makes:** 6 servings.

Prep: 12 min., **Cook:** 25 min.

*For testing purposes only, we used Bisquick Original All-Purpose Baking Mix.

Charleen Damron
Kodiak, Arkansas

Creamy-Crunchy Rice

Water chestnuts add crunch to this side dish while green chiles, Italian dressing, and Monterey Jack cheese boost the flavor.

1 cup uncooked long-grain rice
1½ cups water
1 cup chicken broth
1 (8-ounce) container sour cream
1 (4.5-ounce) can chopped green chiles
½ cup creamy Italian dressing
1 (8-ounce) can sliced water chestnuts, drained and chopped
4 cups (16 ounces) shredded Monterey Jack cheese

Prepare rice according to package directions using 1½ cups water and 1 cup chicken broth.

Meanwhile, stir together sour cream and next 4 ingredients; stir in rice. Pour rice mixture into a lightly greased 11- x 7-inch baking dish.

Bake at 350° for 30 minutes. **Makes:** 6 to 8 servings.

Prep: 8 min., **Cook:** 48 min.

Ann N. Walker
Madisonville, Kentucky

Ann also makes this cheesy side dish with reduced-fat sour cream, dressing, and cheese when she wants to trim fat and calories.

Pepperoni Pizza Rice

A clever concoction of rice, cheese, and pepperoni produces a dish with all the flavors of a pizza.

3   tablespoons olive oil
½   cup diced onion
1   garlic clove, minced
1   (8-ounce) can tomato sauce
2   cups water
1   teaspoon dried oregano
½   teaspoon salt
¼   teaspoon ground pepper
1   cup uncooked long-grain rice
1   (14.5-ounce) can petite diced tomatoes, drained
1   cup thick-sliced pepperoni, coarsely chopped
1½ cups (6 ounces) shredded mozzarella cheese, divided

Heat oil in a large saucepan over medium-high heat. Add onion and garlic; cook 3 minutes or until tender. Add tomato sauce and next 4 ingredients; bring to a boil. Add rice, diced tomatoes, and pepperoni; cover, reduce heat, and simmer 30 minutes or until liquid is absorbed and rice is cooked. Add 1 cup cheese; stir until melted. Top each serving evenly with remaining ½ cup cheese. **Makes:** 5 cups.
Prep: 12 min., **Cook:** 35 min.

Susi Edwards
Memphis, Tennessee

Spinach-Zucchini Pancakes

These pancakes will remind you of a slice of sweet zucchini bread—no need for syrup, just add a pat of butter for a different dinnertime side dish. And because they're sweet, you'll be able to sneak green vegetables into your kids' diet.

1   medium zucchini, sliced
1   cup fresh baby spinach
1   (8½-ounce) package corn muffin mix
1   teaspoon ground cinnamon
⅛   teaspoon salt
⅓   cup milk
¼   cup molasses
1   large egg, lightly beaten
1   tablespoon vegetable oil
1   teaspoon vanilla extract
Butter

Pulse zucchini and spinach in a food processor 10 to 12 times or until finely chopped.

Combine corn muffin mix, cinnamon, and salt in a large bowl.
Combine milk, molasses, egg, oil, and vanilla; add to dry ingredients with zucchini mixture, stirring mixture until combined.
Pour about ¼ cup batter for each pancake onto a hot, nonstick griddle or skillet. Cook pancakes 2 minutes or until tops are covered with bubbles and edges look cooked; turn and cook 2 more minutes. Serve hot with butter.
Makes: 12 pancakes.
Prep: 8 min., **Cook:** 12 min.

Note: These pancakes need to be turned carefully with a thin spatula, and it's essential to use a nonstick griddle or skillet to prevent sticking.

Rebecca Moreno
Birmingham, Alabama

Rebecca created this dish for her toddler who she says is a very picky eater. She reports that he loves it!

Malt-Shop Memories

Capture all the flavors of a chocolate "malted" in pretty little cupcakes.

1	cup all-purpose flour
¾	cup chocolate-flavored malted milk powder
½	cup granulated sugar
1½	teaspoons baking powder
½	teaspoon salt
2	large eggs, lightly beaten
½	cup butter, melted
½	cup water
1	teaspoon vanilla extract
¼	cup chopped unsalted dry-roasted peanuts
6	red maraschino cherries, halved
1	cup unsifted powdered sugar
1	tablespoon hot water
½	teaspoon vanilla extract
⅛	teaspoon salt

Whisk together first 5 ingredients in a medium bowl; make a well in center of mixture. Combine eggs and next 3 ingredients in a bowl; whisk well. Add to dry ingredients, stirring until smooth. Divide batter evenly among paper-lined muffin pans; sprinkle batter with peanuts.

Bake at 375° for 18 minutes or until a wooden pick inserted in center comes out clean. Top each cupcake with a cherry half, cut side down; cool in pan 10 minutes on a wire rack. Remove cupcakes from pan. Cool completely on a wire rack.

Combine powdered sugar and next 3 ingredients in a small bowl. Drizzle icing over cupcakes; let stand until icing is firm before serving. **Makes:** 12 cupcakes.

Prep: 20 min., **Cook:** 18 min.

Patricia Degenhart
Warner Robins, Georgia

Patricia sprinkles additional malted powder over the batter before baking the cupcakes, but we omitted this step for a milder malt flavor.

Fruit Cocktail Cake

Adults will love the crunch of coconut and walnuts in the glaze, while kids will go for the sweet, moist cake with fruit cocktail.

2	cups all-purpose flour
3	cups sugar, divided
2	teaspoons baking soda
1	(15.25-ounce) can fruit cocktail in heavy syrup, undrained
2	large eggs
2	teaspoons vanilla extract, divided
1	cup sweetened flaked coconut, divided
1	cup chopped walnuts, divided
½	cup butter or margarine
1	(5-ounce) can evaporated milk

Combine flour, 1½ cups sugar, and baking soda in a large bowl.

Combine fruit cocktail, eggs, and 1 teaspoon vanilla; add to dry ingredients, beating at medium speed with an electric mixer until combined. Stir in ½ cup coconut and ½ cup walnuts. Pour into a greased 13- x 9-inch pan. Bake at 350° for 30 to 33 minutes or until a wooden pick inserted in center comes out clean. Cool 15 minutes in pan on a wire rack.

Meanwhile, combine remaining 1½ cups sugar, butter, and evaporated milk in a small saucepan; cook over medium heat, stirring often, until sugar dissolves. Remove from heat; stir in remaining 1 teaspoon vanilla. Cool slightly.

Pour glaze over cake in pan while cake is warm; sprinkle with remaining coconut and walnuts. Serve warm or at room temperature. **Makes:** 12 to 15 servings.

Prep: 4 min., **Cook:** 33 min.

Note: Pouring the glaze on this cake while the cake is still warm allows the glaze to soak into the cake, giving it a moist texture and sweet flavor.

Pam Corder
Monroe, Louisiana

Peanut Butter Bars With White Chocolate Frosting

½ cup creamy peanut butter
¼ cup butter or margarine, softened
1 cup firmly packed light brown sugar
2 large eggs
1 teaspoon vanilla extract
1 cup uncooked quick-cooking oats
1 cup sifted self-rising flour
1 (11.5-ounce) package white chocolate morsels, divided
1 cup miniature marshmallows
½ cup coarsely chopped dry-roasted peanuts

Beat peanut butter and butter at medium speed with an electric mixer until creamy; gradually add sugar, beating until blended. Add eggs and vanilla, beating until blended.

Combine oats and flour; gradually add to peanut butter mixture, beating well. Stir in ¾ cup white chocolate morsels and marshmallows.

Press mixture into a greased 13- x 9-inch pan (crust will be very thin). Bake at 350° for 20 to 25 minutes or until edges begin to pull away from pan. Remove from oven; sprinkle with remaining white chocolate morsels. Let stand until morsels soften. Spread over bars; sprinkle with nuts. Cool completely. Cut into bars. **Makes:** 24 bars.

Prep: 15 min., **Cook:** 25 min.

Tip: Use plastic wrap to press mixture into a thin layer in pan.

Margie Tyler
Murfreesboro, Tennessee

Margie has a clever way to quickly frost these bar cookies. After she removes the pan from the oven, she sprinkles white chocolate morsels over the bars to soften and melt before spreading. Chopped peanuts add the finishing touch to the frosting.

Cereal Snacks

9 cups lightly sweetened whole grain oat cereal squares *
1 cup (6-ounce package) semisweet chocolate morsels
½ cup butter
¼ cup light corn syrup
2 cups creamy peanut butter
½ cup finely chopped peanuts

Place cereal and chocolate morsels in a large bowl.

Combine butter and corn syrup in a saucepan; cook over low heat until butter melts. Stir in peanut butter, and cook until mixture is smooth.

Pour peanut butter mixture over cereal and chocolate morsels. Mix well using the back of a large spoon to crunch the cereal into small pieces. Spread mixture into a lightly greased 13- x 9-inch pan; sprinkle with chopped peanuts, pressing into cereal mixture. Cover and chill at least 4 hours. Cut into bars. **Makes:** 36 bars.

Prep: 15 min., **Other:** 4 hrs.

*For testing purposes only, we used Quaker Oat Life Cereal.

Deb Rouse
Houston, Texas

Trail Mix Bars

This quick treat is perfect for lunch boxes or as an after-school snack.

¼ cup butter
2 (10.5-ounce) packages
  miniature marshmallows
6 cups cinnamon-flavored lightly
  sweetened whole grain oat
  cereal squares *
1 cup dried apricots, chopped
1 cup raisins
1 cup sliced almonds
1 cup mini candy-coated milk
  chocolate pieces

Melt butter in a Dutch oven over medium heat. Add marshmallows, stirring until melted; remove from heat. Stir in cereal and remaining ingredients until blended. Press mixture into a lightly greased 13- x 9-inch dish. Let cool completely. Cut into bars. **Makes:** 12 servings.
Prep: 12 min.

*For testing purposes only, we used Quaker Oat Cinnamon Life Cereal.

Sharon Palestino
Havertown, Pennsylvania

Crispy Fudge Nut Bars

Add a glass of cold milk, and these bars can double as breakfast on-the-run.

6 tablespoons butter or margarine
½ cup creamy peanut butter
1 cup (6-ounce package)
  semisweet chocolate morsels
1 (10.5-ounce) package miniature
  marshmallows
1 teaspoon vanilla extract
½ cup sweetened flaked coconut
½ cup raisins
1 cup chopped unsalted
  dry-roasted peanuts
4 cups crispy rice cereal

Melt butter in a large Dutch oven over medium-low heat. Stir in peanut butter until blended. Stir in morsels until blended; add marshmallows. Cook until smooth, stirring constantly. Remove from heat; stir in vanilla. Stir in coconut and next 3 ingredients until coated. Press cereal mixture into a lightly greased 13- x 9-inch pan. Let stand until firm. Cut into bars. **Makes:** 24 bars.
Prep: 10 min., **Cook:** 8 min.

Tip: To keep hands clean and achieve a smooth surface, place a sheet of wax paper over cereal mixture, and press mixture to smooth.

Elizabeth Kennett
Ellicott City, Maryland

Elizabeth says the great thing about this recipe is that kids can help make it. Very little cooking is involved.

James's Favorite Cookies

*The crisp, lacy texture of these cookies is irresistible. Don't be tempted to bake them for less
time to get chewy cookies—they won't hold together.*

3¾ cups uncooked regular oats,
   divided
1   cup unsalted butter, softened
1¼ cups firmly packed light brown
   sugar
¼   cup granulated sugar
2   large eggs
2   tablespoons milk
2   teaspoons vanilla extract

½   cup all-purpose flour
1   teaspoon baking soda
½   teaspoon salt
1¾ cups semisweet chocolate
   morsels
1   cup chopped pecans, toasted
1   cup crispy rice cereal
¾   cup butterscotch morsels

Pamela named these cookies
after her son. She created them by
using all his favorite ingredients.

Place 1 cup oats in a blender or food
processor; process until finely ground.
Set aside.

Beat butter at medium speed with an
electric mixer until creamy. Gradually
add sugars, beating well. Add eggs, 1 at
a time, beating well. Add milk and
vanilla; beat well.

Combine ground oats, flour, baking
soda, and salt; add to butter mixture,
and beat well. Add unprocessed oats;
beat well. Stir in chocolate morsels and
remaining ingredients.

Drop dough by tablespoonfuls onto
ungreased baking sheets. Bake at 350°
for 14 minutes. Cool on pans 1 minute.
Remove to wire racks to cool. **Makes:**
about 4 dozen.

Prep: 28 min., **Cook:** 14 min. per batch

Pamela Barnard
Ballwin, Missouri

Sputter Butters

Your family will go crazy over these gooey, peanut-buttery brownies.

1 (4-ounce) unsweetened chocolate baking bar, broken into pieces
1½ cups granulated sugar
½ cup butter, softened
2 large eggs
1 teaspoon vanilla extract
¼ cup chocolate syrup
1½ cups all-purpose flour
½ teaspoon baking soda
½ teaspoon salt
1 (8-ounce) package cream cheese, softened
¾ cup (7 ounces) creamy peanut butter
½ cup powdered sugar
16 miniature peanut butter cup candies, chopped (about 1 cup)
½ cup candy-coated peanut butter pieces
¼ cup chocolate syrup

Place chocolate pieces in a microwave-safe bowl. Microwave at HIGH 1½ minutes or until melted, stirring twice.
Beat granulated sugar and next 3 ingredients at medium speed with an electric mixer until creamy. Add melted chocolate and ¼ cup chocolate syrup; beat until blended. Gradually add flour, baking soda, and salt; beat well. Press into a greased 9-inch square pan. Bake at 350° for 25 to 28 minutes. Cool in pan on a wire rack.

Beat cream cheese, peanut butter, and powdered sugar until creamy. Spread mixture over cooled brownies; sprinkle with chopped peanut butter cups and candy-coated peanut butter pieces. **Drizzle** with ¼ cup chocolate syrup. Chill in refrigerator at least 45 minutes; cut into bars. **Makes:** 12 servings.
Prep: 9 min., **Cook:** 28 min., **Other:** 45 min.

Tip: For neatly cut bars, wipe off the knife after each slice.

Monica Banas
Astoria, New York

Crunchy Fudge Bars

You don't have to stick with dried cranberries. Try raisins or dried cherries in these crispy, crunchy treats.

2 cups (12-ounce package) semisweet chocolate morsels, divided
½ cup light corn syrup
6 tablespoons butter or margarine, divided
4 cups crispy rice cereal
1 (6-ounce) package cherry-flavored sweetened dried cranberries
1 cup sifted powdered sugar
2 tablespoons milk
½ teaspoon vanilla extract

Combine 1 cup chocolate morsels, corn syrup, and 2 tablespoons butter in a large microwave-safe bowl. Microwave at HIGH 1 minute; stir until morsels melt. Stir in cereal and cranberries. Press half of cereal mixture into a lightly greased 12- x 8-inch dish; chill.
Place remaining 1 cup morsels and remaining 4 tablespoons butter in a small microwave-safe bowl. Microwave at HIGH 1 minute, stirring until morsels melt. Stir in powdered sugar, milk, and vanilla until blended. Spread chocolate mixture over cereal mixture in dish. Firmly press remaining cereal mixture over chocolate mixture. Cover and chill 1 hour or until firm. Cut into bars.
Makes: 24 bars.
Prep: 20 min., **Cook:** 2 min., **Other:** 1 hr.

Tip: To keep hands clean and achieve a smooth surface, place a sheet of wax paper over cereal layers, and press layers to smooth.

Mary G. Knoblock
Omaha, Arkansas

Yummy Brownie Peanut Butter Bonbons

These brownie bites are filled with a creamy peanut butter mixture and drizzled with melted chocolate.

4   (1-ounce) unsweetened
    chocolate baking squares
¾   cup butter or margarine
2   cups granulated sugar
4   large eggs
1   teaspoon vanilla extract
1   cup all-purpose flour
1   (3-ounce) package cream
    cheese, softened
¾   cup chunky peanut butter
½   cup powdered sugar
2   tablespoons milk
1   teaspoon vanilla extract
1   cup (6-ounce package)
    semisweet chocolate morsels,
    divided

Combine unsweetened chocolate and butter in a large microwave-safe bowl. Microwave at HIGH 1 to 2 minutes or until melted; stir well. Stir in granulated sugar, eggs, and 1 teaspoon vanilla. Add flour; stir until well blended. Spoon batter into paper-lined miniature muffin pans, filling two-thirds full. Bake at 350° for 18 minutes. Remove brownies from pans; cool slightly on wire racks. Press an indentation into top of each brownie, using the tip of a spoon; cool brownies completely.

Beat cream cheese and next 4 ingredients at medium speed with an electric mixer until creamy; stir in ½ cup chocolate morsels. Spoon filling evenly into center of cooled brownies. Place remaining ½ cup chocolate morsels in a small zip-top freezer bag; seal.

Microwave at HIGH 30 seconds or until melted. Snip a tiny hole in 1 corner of bag, and drizzle chocolate over bonbons. **Makes:** 4 dozen.
Prep: 39 min., **Cook:** 20 min.

Dolores Vaccaro
Pueblo, Colorado

Butterscotch Cookies

Browning the butter lends a caramel flavor to the frosting of these cakelike cookies.

1½ cups butter, softened
1½ cups firmly packed light brown
    sugar
2   large eggs
1   teaspoon vanilla extract
2½ cups all-purpose flour
1   teaspoon baking soda
½   teaspoon baking powder
½   teaspoon salt
1   (8-ounce) container sour cream
1   cup butterscotch morsels
¾   cup butter
3   cups powdered sugar
2   teaspoons vanilla extract
¼   cup milk
Pecan halves (optional)

Beat 1½ cups butter at medium speed with an electric mixer until creamy; gradually add brown sugar, beating until blended. Add eggs and 1 teaspoon vanilla, beating until blended.

Combine flour, baking soda, baking powder, and salt; gradually add to butter mixture, beating well. Add sour cream, beating until blended. Stir in butterscotch morsels.

Drop dough by heaping teaspoonfuls onto ungreased baking sheets. Bake at 400° for 10 minutes. Cool 2 minutes on baking sheets; remove to wire racks to cool completely.

Melt ¾ cup butter in a saucepan over medium-low heat; cook 4 minutes or until butter is lightly browned. Pour butter into a large bowl; cool completely. Stir in powdered sugar and 2 teaspoons vanilla. Add milk, and stir until frosting is spreading consistency. Spread on cooled cookies; top each cookie with a pecan half, if desired. **Makes:** 5 dozen.
Prep: 32 min., **Cook:** 10 min. per batch

Candice Agnew
Butler, Missouri

Chocolate Grasshopper Brownie Cookies

If you can't find mint chocolate pieces, buy 2 (4.67-ounce) packages of chocolate mints and chop them.

1   cup butter, softened
¾   cup firmly packed light brown sugar
¾   cup granulated sugar
2   large eggs
1   teaspoon vanilla extract
2¼ cups all-purpose flour
1   teaspoon baking soda
¼   teaspoon salt
½   cup unsweetened cocoa
½   cup sliced almonds
2   cups (10-ounce package) mint chocolate pieces*

Beat butter at medium speed with an electric mixer until creamy; gradually add sugars, beating until blended. Add eggs and vanilla, beating until blended. **Combine** flour, baking soda, salt, and cocoa; gradually add to butter mixture, beating well. Stir in almonds and mint chocolate pieces.

Drop dough by rounded tablespoonfuls onto baking sheets lined with parchment paper. Bake at 350° for 10 to 12 minutes or until center of cookies are puffed. Cool 2 minutes on baking sheets; remove to wire racks to cool completely. **Makes:** 3 dozen.

Prep: 25 min., **Cook:** 12 min. per batch

*For testing purposes only, we used Andes mint chocolate pieces.

Karen L. Hildreth
Sarasota, Florida

Chocolate Grasshopper
Brownie Cookies

Chocolate-Studded Shamrocks

Kids enjoy making these cookies. They can roll the balls of dough, make the stems out of dough, and sprinkle the green sugar.

2½ cups all-purpose flour
1   teaspoon baking powder
1   cup butter, softened
⅔   cup sugar
2   teaspoons vanilla extract
2   large eggs
1   (12-ounce) package semisweet mini-morsels
¼   cup green decorator sugar crystals

Combine flour and baking powder, and set aside.

Beat butter at medium speed with an electric mixer until creamy; gradually add sugar, beating well. Add vanilla and eggs; beat well. Gradually add flour mixture to butter mixture, beating well. Stir in mini-morsels. Cover and chill 15 minutes or until firm.

For each shamrock, shape dough into 3 (¾-inch) balls, and place balls together to form a shamrock shape on an ungreased baking sheet. Roll a small amount of dough to form a stem. Sprinkle with green sugar. Repeat procedure with remaining dough and sugar. Bake at 375° for 8 to 10 minutes or until edges are golden. Cool on baking sheet 2 minutes. Remove to a wire rack to cool completely. **Makes:** 3 dozen.

Prep: 23 min., **Cook:** 10 min. per batch, **Other:** 17 min.

Lynne Breyer
Coconut Creek, Florida

Maw Gam's Bulgur-Oatmeal Cookies

Want to cut some white sugar out of your family's diet? Try these healthful cookies full of crunchy grains, seeds, and nuts. They're great crumbled over ice cream.

½   cup uncooked bulgur wheat
2   cups water
1½ cups honey
1   cup canola oil
2   large eggs
1   teaspoon vanilla extract
1   teaspoon butter extract
3   cups uncooked quick-cooking oats
1½ cups whole wheat flour
1   teaspoon ground cinnamon
1   teaspoon baking soda
1   teaspoon salt
2   cups raisins
1   cup roasted, salted sunflower seeds
1   cup chopped pecans

Place bulgur in a medium saucepan; add 2 cups water. Bring to a boil; cover, reduce heat, and simmer 15 minutes or until liquid is absorbed. Set aside.

Meanwhile, combine honey, oil, eggs, and flavorings in a large bowl. Stir together oats and next 4 ingredients; add to wet ingredients, stirring well. Stir in cooked bulgur, raisins, sunflower seeds, and pecans.

Drop by tablespoonfuls onto ungreased baking sheets. Bake at 375° for 12 minutes. Cool on baking sheets 1 minute. Remove to wire racks to cool completely. **Makes:** about 6 dozen.

Prep: 20 min., **Cook:** 12 min. per batch

Shelly prefers the thicker, insulated baking sheets for these cookies and bakes them up to 15 minutes. We used regular baking sheets and found 12 minutes to be perfect timing.

Note: You can store these cookies in an airtight container at room temperature for 2 days; in the refrigerator for 1 week; and in the freezer for 2 weeks.

Shelly Williams
Benton, Tennessee

Peanut Butter S'more Tarts

Roasted marshmallows crown a chocolate-topped creamy peanut butter filling in this re-creation of a fireside favorite.

½   cup creamy peanut butter
1   (3-ounce) package cream cheese, softened
½   cup powdered sugar
1   teaspoon vanilla extract
½   cup whipping cream
1   (4-ounce) package ready-made individual graham cracker crusts
1   cup (6-ounce package) semisweet chocolate morsels
⅓   cup whipping cream
6   tablespoons marshmallow cream
1   cup miniature marshmallows

Beat peanut butter and cream cheese at medium speed with an electric mixer until combined. Add powdered sugar and vanilla; beat until smooth.

In a separate bowl, beat ½ cup whipping cream at high speed until soft peaks form; fold into peanut butter mixture. Spoon mixture evenly into crusts; freeze 10 minutes.

Meanwhile, combine chocolate morsels and ⅓ cup whipping cream in a small microwave-safe bowl; microwave at HIGH 1 minute or until morsels are melted, stirring once. Cool slightly; spoon chocolate mixture evenly over peanut butter filling. Refrigerate at least 1 hour or until chocolate is set.

Spread 1 tablespoon marshmallow cream evenly over each tart; top with miniature marshmallows. Broil 3 inches from heat 30 seconds or until marshmallows are golden brown. **Makes:** 6 individual tarts.

Prep: 13 min., **Chill:** 1 hr., 10 min.

Note: If you have a kitchen or brûlée torch, you can use that instead of a broiler to toast the marshmallows.

Robert Gadsby
Great Falls, Montana

Peachy Pies

Soaked in a buttery, orange syrup, these tender little pies are plenty good served solo, but they're even better served with vanilla ice cream.

1   cup orange juice
¾   cup sugar
½   cup butter
1   (8-ounce) can refrigerated crescent rolls
1   (8.5-ounce) can peach slices in syrup, drained *

Combine first 3 ingredients in a medium saucepan over medium-high heat. Bring to a boil; reduce heat, and simmer 19 minutes or until thick and syrupy.

Meanwhile, unroll crescent roll dough, and separate into triangles. Place 1 peach slice in center of each triangle; fold dough over, and press edges to seal. Place pies in a lightly greased 11- x 7-inch baking dish. Bake at 375° for 15 minutes or until golden brown. Remove from oven; pour reduced sauce over pies. Return to oven; bake 3 more minutes or until sauce is bubbly.

Makes: 8 servings.

Prep: 9 min., **Cook:** 20 min.

*If ripe, fresh peaches are available, substitute 1 large peach, cut into 8 slices, for canned peaches.

Jennifer Cappleman
Lynn Haven, Florida

Jennifer bakes these pies with the sauce poured on top for the entire time. We poured the sauce on at the end of baking because we liked the pies with a golden brown pastry.

Rice Pudding

Rice Pudding

1 (4.6-ounce) package
cook-and-serve vanilla pudding *
3 cups milk
1½ cups cooked rice
½ cup raisins
½ teaspoon ground cinnamon

Prepare pudding according to package directions, using 3 cups milk. Remove from heat; stir in rice, raisins, and cinnamon. Serve warm, or cover and chill. **Makes:** 6 servings.
Prep: 1 min., **Cook:** 18 min.

*You can substitute 4 (3.5-ounce) packages prepared vanilla pudding in a pinch. Serve chilled.

Mike Hudson
Cedar Rapids, Iowa

Mike used boil-in-bag rice that can be prepared on the stovetop or in the microwave as the pudding cooks. Then both are stirred together with the raisins and cinnamon.

Awesome Banana Pudding Pie

Plan on spooning this creamy dessert into bowls instead of cutting it like a traditional pie.

½ cup butter, melted
1 (12-ounce) package vanilla wafers, crushed
2 small bananas (about 5½ ounces each), sliced
6 tablespoons caramel-flavored syrup, divided
½ (8-ounce) package cream cheese, softened
1½ cups milk, divided
2 (3.4-ounce) packages vanilla instant pudding mix
1 (8-ounce) container frozen whipped topping, thawed

Combine butter and vanilla wafer crumbs in a large bowl, stirring until thoroughly combined. Set aside ½ cup crumb mixture for top. Press remaining crumb mixture into bottom and up sides of an 8-inch square dish. Arrange banana slices over crust; drizzle with ¼ cup syrup.
Whisk together cream cheese and ¼ cup milk in a large bowl until smooth. Whisk in remaining 1¼ cups milk and pudding mix. Fold in whipped topping. Spoon pudding mixture over syrup; sprinkle with remaining crumb mixture, and drizzle with remaining 2 tablespoons caramel syrup. Cover and chill thoroughly. **Makes:** 8 servings.
Prep: 26 min., **Other:** 2½ hrs.

Paula Roche
Kingston, Tennessee

Paula uses banana cream pudding and cheesecake pudding when she makes this dessert. We substituted vanilla because it's easier to find.

Hot Fudge Sundae With Homemade Peanut Butter Ice Cream

Did we say this was just for kids? Not at all! Consider this peanut butter and fudge treat your reward after a hard day at work or home.

2   **cups half-and-half**
1½ cups heavy whipping cream
¼   **cup milk**
6   **egg yolks**
1   **cup sugar**
3   **tablespoons honey-roasted creamy peanut butter**
2   **teaspoons vanilla extract**
1   **(19.8-ounce) package fudge brownie mix**
1   **(9-ounce) package peanut butter cup candies** *
1   **(11.75-ounce) jar hot fudge topping**
½   **cup dry-roasted peanuts, coarsely chopped**
Frozen whipped topping, thawed

Combine first 3 ingredients in a large saucepan; cook over medium-low heat 8 minutes or until hot, stirring occasionally. **Beat** egg yolks and sugar at medium speed with an electric mixer until well blended. Whisk about one-fourth of hot cream mixture into eggs; add to remaining hot cream mixture, whisking constantly. Cook over medium-low heat, whisking constantly, 23 minutes or until a thermometer registers 180°. Remove from heat.

Gradually add peanut butter and vanilla, whisking until smooth. Cool. Pour cream mixture into a large metal bowl. Cover and chill 2 hours or until completely chilled.

Pour mixture into freezer container of a 2-quart ice cream maker. Freeze according to manufacturer's instructions. Spoon ice cream into an airtight container; freeze 8 hours or until firm.

Prepare brownie mix according to package directions in a 13- x 9-inch pan. Cool; cut into 12 squares.

Cut 8 peanut butter cup candies in half; set aside. Coarsely chop remaining peanut butter cup candies.

Place 1 brownie in each of 8 serving dishes. Spoon ½ cup peanut butter ice cream over each brownie. Microwave fudge topping at HIGH 30 seconds or until warm. Drizzle each serving with fudge topping. Sprinkle each serving evenly with chopped peanut butter cup candies and peanuts. Top each with whipped topping and 2 peanut butter candy halves. **Makes:** 8 servings.
Prep: 1 hr., 11 min., **Cook:** 1 hr., **Other:** 10 hrs.

*A 9-ounce package of peanut butter cup candies contains 6 (1.5-ounce) packages for a total of 12 regular-size candies.

Tip: Save remaining brownies, ice cream, fudge topping, peanut butter candies, and whipped topping for a later snack.

Deidre Towns
Conyers, Georgia

Peanut Butter Cookie Sundae

Let your kids help with this dessert; give them different cookie cutters to cut out cookies in fun shapes.

⅔   **cup creamy peanut butter**
½   **cup butter or margarine, softened**
¼   **cup molasses**
1   **large egg**
1   **cup sugar**
1   **cup all-purpose flour**
1   **teaspoon baking soda**
¼   **teaspoon salt**
2   **cups cinnamon-flavored lightly sweetened whole grain oat cereal squares, crushed** *
3   **tablespoons creamy peanut butter**

5   **cups vanilla ice cream**
1   **(16-ounce) jar hot fudge topping**
¼   **cup dry-roasted peanuts, finely chopped**

Combine first 5 ingredients; beat with an electric mixer at medium speed until well blended. Mix in flour, baking soda, and salt until combined. Stir in cereal; cover and chill 1 hour. Spread dough into a lightly greased 13- x 9-inch pan. Bake at 375° for 20 minutes; cool to room temperature. Cut into 15 squares. In a small bowl, mix peanut butter and ice cream until blended, about 30 seconds. Cover and freeze until firm.

To serve, microwave fudge topping at HIGH 30 seconds or until warm. Spread 1 tablespoon fudge topping on each dessert dish. Place 1 cookie square on topping; top with ice cream, and sprinkle with peanuts. **Makes:** 15 servings.
Prep: 7 min., **Cook:** 20 min., **Other:** 1 hr.

*For testing purposes only, we used Quaker Oat Cinnamon Life Cereal.

Alberta May
Kissimmee, Florida

Hot Fudge Sundae With Homemade
Peanut Butter Ice Cream

Rocky Road Pops

Kids will love to help make these frozen treats.

2½ cups chocolate milk
1 (3.9-ounce) package chocolate instant pudding mix
¾ cup miniature marshmallows
½ cup semisweet chocolate mini-morsels *
½ cup chopped unsalted peanuts, walnuts, or pecans
10 (3-ounce) paper cups
10 wooden craft sticks

Whisk together milk and pudding mix in a large bowl until smooth. Cover with plastic wrap, and chill 10 minutes.
Stir in marshmallows, chocolate morsels, and nuts. Spoon mixture evenly into paper cups; insert 1 craft stick into each. Freeze until firm. Carefully remove cups before serving.
Makes: 10 servings.
Prep: 10 min., **Other:** 2 hrs., 10 min.

*You can also use mini candy-coated milk chocolate pieces instead of the mini-morsels.

Rose Cruz
Roosevelt, Utah

Rose uses regular pudding mix, but we used instant to keep the preparation simple. Rose had a great idea to use chocolate milk in the chocolate pudding for double chocolate flavor.

Rocky Road Pops

Frozen Chocolate Peanut Butter-Banana Pops

Keep these pops, individually wrapped, in the freezer for a quick snack or dessert. Half a banana, a little peanut butter, and a dusting of peanuts makes for a pretty healthful kids' snack.

6   medium bananas, halved crosswise
12 wooden craft sticks
1½ tablespoons shortening
1   tablespoon light corn syrup
1   cup (6-ounce package) semisweet chocolate morsels
½   cup creamy peanut butter
¼   teaspoon salt
½   cup dry-roasted peanuts, chopped

Insert wooden sticks into bananas lengthwise; lay on a wax paper-lined 15- x 10-inch jellyroll pan.

Melt shortening in a medium saucepan over medium-low heat. Add corn syrup and chocolate morsels; cook 3 minutes or until chocolate melts. Add peanut butter and salt; stir until smooth. Reduce heat to low, and keep warm.

Dip each banana pop into chocolate sauce. Roll in chopped nuts; transfer to pan. Freeze at least 3 hours before serving. **Makes:** 12 pops.
Prep: 14 min., **Other:** 3 hrs.

Jean-Marie Gard
Concord, Massachusetts

Candy Caramel-Pineapple Dessert Pizza

Look for the apple dip in the produce section of the grocery store.

⅓   cup peanut butter and milk chocolate morsels
¼   cup dry-roasted peanuts
1   (16.3-ounce) can refrigerated jumbo biscuits *
½   (8-ounce) package cream cheese, softened
2   tablespoons light brown sugar
½   teaspoon vanilla extract
1   (8-ounce) can crushed pineapple in juice, well drained
2   tablespoons caramel apple dip *
¼   teaspoon ground cinnamon
Vanilla ice cream
Garnish: strawberries (optional)

Place morsels and peanuts in a blender or food processor. Pulse until finely chopped; set aside.

Separate biscuits, and place 3 inches apart on a lightly greased baking sheet. Press out each biscuit with fingers to form 3-inch circles.

Combine cream cheese, brown sugar, and vanilla; stir well. Spread cream cheese mixture on each biscuit.

Stir together crushed pineapple, caramel dip, and cinnamon. Spoon pineapple mixture over cream cheese mixture.

Bake at 375° for 17 minutes or until biscuits are browned. Remove from oven, and immediately sprinkle with reserved peanut mixture. Serve pizzas warm with ice cream. Garnish, if desired. **Makes:** 8 servings.
Prep: 18 min., **Cook:** 17 min.

*For testing purposes only, we used Pillsbury Grands! Original Flaky Biscuits and T. Marzetti's Old-Fashioned Caramel Apple Dip.

Gloria Bradley
Naperville, Illinois

Here's another entry from **Gloria** who was a Finalist and Brand Winner in the Simple and Scrumptious Entrées category.

Cookie Delight

If your kids don't like coconut, use regular chocolate chip or rainbow chip cookies instead of chocolate chip cookies with coconut, and omit the toasted coconut.

2   **cups half-and-half**
1   **(18-ounce) package chocolate chip cookies with coconut, divided**
1   **(16-ounce) container frozen whipped topping, thawed and divided**
1   **cup semisweet chocolate mini-morsels, divided**
½   **cup sweetened flaked coconut, toasted**

Pour half-and-half into a shallow dish; dip half of package of cookies in half-and-half for 4 or 5 seconds each. Layer

Randi's mother created this recipe so she and her brother could help make dessert when they were young. The tradition continues with Randi and her grandchildren.

cookies in an 8-inch square dish. Top with half of whipped topping; sprinkle with ½ cup morsels. Repeat layers once with remaining cookies, whipped topping, and morsels. Sprinkle evenly with toasted coconut. Cover and chill 8 hours. **Makes:** 8 servings.
Prep: 12 min., **Other:** 8 hrs.

Randi Blanscet
Fort Smith, Arkansas

German Chocolate Dessert Waffles With Whipped Cream Cheese Frosting

Can't coax the kids out of bed for breakfast? Try luring them with these waffles. We promise they'll love them. Make these special treats on the weekend when you have extra time to prepare them.

1   **(8-ounce) package cream cheese, softened**
¼   **cup sugar**
1   **(8-ounce) container frozen whipped topping, thawed**
¼   **cup chopped pecans**
¼   **cup sweetened flaked coconut**
1   **cup plus 2 tablespoons all-purpose flour**
½   **teaspoon baking powder**
½   **teaspoon baking soda**
¼   **teaspoon salt**
¼   **cup butter**
1   **(4-ounce) package German chocolate baking squares, divided**
2   **large eggs**
1   **teaspoon vanilla extract**
¾   **cup sugar**
1   **cup buttermilk**
2   **tablespoons butter**

Beat cream cheese and ¼ cup sugar at medium speed with an electric mixer until creamy. Add whipped topping; beat 3 more minutes. Cover and chill.
Combine pecans and coconut; place on a baking sheet. Bake at 325° for 7 minutes or until toasted, stirring occasionally. Cool completely.
Meanwhile, combine flour and next 3 ingredients; set aside.
Microwave ¼ cup butter and half of chocolate baking squares in a small microwave-safe bowl at HIGH 1½ minutes or until melted, stirring twice.
Beat eggs and vanilla at medium speed until foamy. Slowly add chocolate mixture, beating until combined. Add ¾ cup sugar and buttermilk, beating just until blended. Stir in flour mixture just until combined.
Cook in a preheated, oiled waffle iron until done.
Meanwhile, microwave remaining half of chocolate baking squares and 2

tablespoons butter in small microwave-safe bowl at HIGH 1½ minutes or until melted, stirring twice.
Top each waffle evenly with cream cheese mixture; sprinkle with coconut mixture, and drizzle with melted chocolate mixture. **Makes:** 11 (4-inch) waffles.
Prep: 20 min., **Cook:** 21 min.

Tip: It's best to use a regular waffle iron instead of a Belgian waffle iron when making this recipe. Be sure to spread the batter evenly when you pour it onto the waffle iron.

Emogene Bennett
Charlotte, North Carolina

Emogene uses a heart-shaped waffle iron, but we tested the recipe using the more standard square iron.

Stained Glass Cookies

Try making these beautiful cookie ornaments with your kids. This is one crafting project they're sure to enjoy! Ornaments harden as they cool.

3   tablespoons butter, softened
½   cup firmly packed light brown sugar
1   large egg
¼   cup molasses
2   tablespoons water
2   cups all-purpose flour
½   teaspoon ground cinnamon
½   teaspoon ground ginger
¼   teaspoon salt
¼   teaspoon ground nutmeg
1   (13-ounce) package assorted flavors roll candy*

Beat butter at medium speed with an electric mixer until creamy; gradually add sugar, beating well. Add egg, molasses, and water, beating until blended.

Combine flour and next 4 ingredients; gradually add to butter mixture, stirring until blended. Cover and chill dough 1 hour.

Meanwhile, separate candy by color. Crush candies, and set aside.

Roll heaping tablespoonfuls of dough into a 10-inch rope (about the thickness of a pencil) on a lightly floured surface. Place a 3-inch shaped cookie cutter on a baking sheet lined with nonstick aluminum foil. Carefully wrap rope around outer edge of cutter, connecting ends of rope to seal. Remove cutter. Repeat procedure with remaining dough. Sprinkle 2 tablespoons crushed candies by teaspoonfuls into center of each dough shape to fill. Punch a hole in the top of each ornament using a straw.

Bake at 375° for 7 minutes or just until candies melt. (Do not overbake.) Cool completely. Let stand 8 hours.

To hang, tie each ornament with a 12-inch piece of ribbon. **Makes:** 16 cookie ornaments.

Prep: 1 hr., 12 min., **Cook:** 7 min., **Other:** 9 hrs.

*For testing purposes only, we used LifeSavers Candy.

Tip: For best results, when working with each portion of dough, keep remaining dough chilled. This will make it easier to shape dough around cookie cutters. Simple cookie cutters such as hearts, circles, squares, diamonds, and stars work best, but whatever shape you use, make sure to fill its center to the top with crushed candies.

Margaret Heinrich
Oxford, Michigan

"Mousse" Tracks Tostadas

This sweet version of a tostada is a perfect weekend or rainy-day treat. Get your kids involved in pressing the tostadas and sprinkling their own serving with their favorite toppings. Be creative with the toppings—try a variety of sprinkles and candies instead of chocolate morsels.

8   cups lightly sweetened whole grain oat cereal squares *
1   cup firmly packed brown sugar
⅔   cup butter, melted
½   cup butter, softened
2   cups powdered sugar
3   tablespoons whipping cream
2   tablespoons chocolate syrup
1   (11.5-ounce) package milk chocolate morsels
2   cups (12-ounce package) semisweet chocolate morsels
2   cups coarsely chopped dry-roasted peanuts
2   cups miniature marshmallows

Process cereal in a food processor 5 or 6 times or until coarsely ground.

Transfer ground cereal to a medium bowl; add brown sugar and ⅔ cup melted butter. Stir until well combined. **Place** a 4-inch round biscuit cutter or cookie cutter on an ungreased baking sheet. Spoon ¼ cup cereal mixture into center of cutter; press well using the back of measuring cup or spoon. Remove cutter; repeat with remaining cereal mixture. Bake at 350° for 9 to 10 minutes or until crisp. Cool on baking sheets on a wire rack. **Meanwhile,** beat ½ cup softened butter at medium speed with an electric mixer until creamy. Add powdered sugar, whipping cream, and chocolate syrup; beat until well combined. **Spread** about 1 tablespoon chocolate "mousse" onto each cooled tostada shell.

Top evenly with morsels, peanuts, and marshmallows. Broil 5½ inches from heat 1 to 2 minutes or until marshmallows begin to brown. Cool slightly before serving. **Makes:** 20 tostadas.
Prep: 40 min., **Cook:** 22 min.

Variation: We also prepared this recipe omitting the chocolate "mousse." We spread each baked tostada with 1 tablespoon creamy peanut butter before topping with morsels, peanuts, and marshmallows. This variation got rave reviews.

＊For testing purposes only, we used Quaker Oat Life Cereal.

Linda Spranger
Farmington Hills, Michigan

Creamy Peanut Butter and Jelly Torte

If PB & J is one of your favorite combinations, you've got to try this creamy, upscale version of the classic duo.

1⅓ cups chocolate wafer crumbs
⅓   cup unsalted butter, melted
1½ cups whipping cream
2   cups creamy peanut butter
2   (8-ounce) packages cream cheese, softened
1½ cups sugar
2   teaspoons vanilla extract
⅔   cup seedless raspberry or strawberry jam or preserves
⅔   cup semisweet chocolate morsels
3½ tablespoons brewed coffee or water
¼   cup chopped dry-roasted peanuts

Stir together wafer crumbs and butter; press into bottom and up sides of a 9-inch springform pan. Set aside.
Beat whipping cream until soft peaks form; set aside.
Beat peanut butter and cream cheese at medium speed with an electric mixer until creamy; gradually add sugar,

Kathy uses light cream cheese in this recipe, but because of all the other rich ingredients in this torte, we decided to go with regular cream cheese.

beating well. Add vanilla; beat until smooth. Gently fold whipped cream into peanut butter mixture. Spoon a little more than half of peanut butter mixture into prepared crust. Carefully spread jam over mixture. Top with remaining peanut butter mixture. Cover and chill at least 1 hour.
Combine chocolate morsels and coffee in a heavy saucepan. Cook over low heat, stirring constantly, until chocolate melts. Cool slightly. Spread over torte; sprinkle with peanuts. Cover and chill 8 hours.
Makes: 12 servings.
Prep: 22 min., **Other:** 9 hrs.

Kathy Lee
Valley Center, California

Desserts

Choose sweet creations from our
reader favorites for the perfect ending
to a casual or elegant gathering.

The Gonzalez family came to the United States in 1966 with little more than the clothes on their backs and their Cuban heritage. Growing up on Cuban cuisine means that flan is the equivalent of apple pie for Jo Gonzalez-Hastings.

"My mother made traditional flan, which is a bit bland because it's made with only milk," says Jo. "When my mother—who is an *incredible* cook—came here, she started using condensed and evaporated milks and it made a huge difference." Jo went a step farther by adding cream cheese. "I make flan in several flavors, and they're all good."

A restaurateur and cookbook author, Jo says cooking is her real joy. She is so passionate about the food she grew up on that she now serves "nuevo Latino"—a blend of modern and traditional Cuban—in her Gulfport, Florida, restaurant. "Cuban food is a well-kept secret," she says. "I love nothing more than to get in my kitchen and experiment, giving a new twist to my family recipes."

Jo is the author of *The Habana Cafe Cookbook*, published in June 2004 by University Press of Florida. The cookbook includes many of the succulent dishes she serves regularly, including arroz con pollo, picadillo, and her specialty, lecon asado, a mouth-watering blend of roast pork, garlic, white wine, bay leaves, and grilled onions.

$11,000
Category & Brand
Winner!

PHILADELPHIA® Cream Cheese Brand Winner

Cream Cheese Flan

1½ **cups sugar, divided**
7 **egg yolks**
1 **(14-ounce) can sweetened condensed milk**
1 **(12-ounce) can evaporated milk**
¾ **cup milk**
1½ **teaspoons vanilla extract**
⅛ **teaspoon salt**
4 **egg whites**
1 **(8-ounce) package cream cheese, softened**

Cook 1 cup sugar in a medium saucepan over medium heat, stirring constantly, 5 minutes or until sugar melts and turns a light golden brown. Quickly pour hot caramelized sugar into a 2-quart flan dish. Using oven mitts, tilt dish to evenly coat bottom and sides. Let stand 5 minutes. (Sugar will harden.)

Whisk together egg yolks and next 5 ingredients in a large bowl.

Process egg whites, cream cheese, and remaining ½ cup sugar in blender until smooth. Stir egg white mixture into egg yolk mixture. Pour mixture through a wire-mesh strainer into a large bowl; pour custard over caramelized sugar.

Place dish in a large shallow pan. Add hot water to pan to a depth of one-third up sides of dish.

Bake at 350° for 1 hour and 45 minutes. Remove dish from water bath; cool completely on a wire rack. Cover and chill at least 3 hours.

Run a knife around edge of flan to loosen; invert onto a serving plate. Store in refrigerator. **Makes:** 6 to 8 servings.
Prep: 20 min., **Cook:** 1 hr., 50 min., **Other:** 3 hrs., 5 min.

Jo Gonzalez-Hastings
Gulfport, Florida

Jo's secret for a silky texture is straining the custard before pouring it into the baking dish. Head Judge Andria Hurst calls this "one of the richest, smoothest, creamiest confections I've ever had."

Cream Cheese Flan

"ooking is my therapy," says Lynda Sarkisian. "If I'm upset or depressed, I just cook it away. I've always loved to cook."

Desserts are Lynda's specialty and she's happy to share her prized recipes. "It makes me proud when someone likes what I cook well enough to ask for the recipe," she says. That sharing includes numerous past cooking contests. "Years ago, I used to contest quite a lot, but I got burned out with it for a while," she says. Reading about our first Cook-Off piqued Lynda's interest because she's a longtime fan of *Southern Living* recipes.

Lynda's three sons are grown up, but they look forward to coming home for the holidays and their mother's cooking. "My oldest son sends me a list of what he wants me to cook," she says. "It does a mother's heart good!"

$1,000 Finalist Winner! Sweet Potato Cake With Coconut Filling and Caramel Frosting

Vegetable cooking spray
All-purpose flour
1   cup butter, softened
3   cups sugar
6   large eggs, separated
1½ cups mashed cooked sweet potato
1   cup sour cream
1   tablespoon baking powder
1   teaspoon vanilla extract
½   teaspoon ground cinnamon
½   teaspoon ground ginger
¼   teaspoon salt
1   cup chopped pecans
3   cups all-purpose flour
Coconut Filling
Caramel Frosting

Coat 3 (9-inch) cakepans with cooking spray; dust lightly with flour. Set aside.
Beat butter and sugar at medium-high speed with an electric mixer until fluffy. Add egg yolks, 1 at a time, beating until blended after each addition. Beat in mashed sweet potatoes and next 6 ingredients, adding each ingredient one at a time. Add pecans and 3 cups flour, beating just until blended.
Beat egg whites in a separate bowl at high speed with an electric mixer until stiff peaks form; fold into batter. Spoon batter evenly into prepared pans.
Bake at 350° for 25 minutes or until wooden pick inserted in center comes out clean. Cool in pans on wire racks 10 minutes; remove from pans, and cool completely on wire racks.
Spread Coconut Filling evenly between cake layers. Gradually pour about ½ cup Caramel Frosting on top of cake, spreading over top and sides with a small spatula. Place cake in refrigerator, and chill remaining Caramel Frosting 45 minutes. Pour another ½ cup Caramel Frosting on cake, spreading over top and sides. Chill cake and frosting 15 minutes. Repeat procedure with remaining frosting, ½ cup at a time. Store cake in refrigerator. **Makes:** 12 servings.
Prep: 1 hr., **Cook:** 40 min., **Other:** 2 hrs.

Coconut Filling:
¼   cup sugar
2   tablespoons cornstarch
⅛   teaspoon salt
1   cup milk
1   large egg, lightly beaten
½   cup frozen grated coconut, thawed
1   teaspoon vanilla extract

Combine first 3 ingredients in a heavy 2-quart saucepan; gradually stir in milk, and cook, stirring constantly, over medium heat 3 minutes or until thickened.
Stir about one-fourth of hot milk mixture gradually into egg; add egg mixture to remaining hot milk mixture, stirring constantly. Return to a boil, and cook, stirring constantly, 1 minute or until thickened. Remove from heat; stir in coconut and vanilla. Place heavy-duty plastic wrap directly on warm filling. Cool completely; chill 1 hour.
Makes: about 1 cup.
Prep: 10 min., **Cook:** 5 min., **Other:** 1 hr.

Caramel Frosting:
2   (3-ounce) packages cream cheese, cut into cubes and softened
¾   cup whipping cream
2¼ cups sugar
⅔   cup water
9   tablespoons butter, cut into ½-inch cubes

Whisk together cream cheese and whipping cream in a small bowl until smooth. Set aside.
Cook sugar and ⅔ cup water in a heavy 3½-quart saucepan over medium-low heat, stirring constantly, 5 minutes or until sugar dissolves. Increase heat to high, and bring mixture to a boil without stirring. Using a pastry brush dipped in hot water, brush down any sugar crystals on sides of pan. Cook, without stirring, 10 minutes or just until syrup turns a deep amber color.
Whisk in butter gradually; gradually whisk in cream cheese mixture until smooth. Remove from heat; cool 10 minutes, whisking occasionally. **Makes:** 3 cups.
Prep: 10 min., **Cook:** 20 min., **Other:** 10 min.

Lynda Sarkisian
Seneca, South Carolina

Lynda spreads the soft Caramel Frosting on the cake a little bit at a time, chilling in between, to allow the frosting to set before adding more.

The Panama City *News Herald* sponsors an annual holiday recipe contest, so every year Jeremy Bazata puts on her thinking cap. Sometimes she wins a prize, sometimes she doesn't, but it's the inventive process that's the most fun.

"I'm an avid recipe experimenter and creator," says Jeremy. "It's part science, part art, and always an adventure. To create a tasty recipe that catches the eye and captures the imagination and taste buds is to reach the recipe summit."

An interior designer by day, Jeremy thinks nothing of spending the evening in her kitchen. "I don't have a family, but I'll often whip up a full dinner just for myself," she says. "After a long day, getting in the kitchen soothes my nerves."

Jeremy credits her culinary success to her mother's patience and encouragement. "I still have my first recipe book she gave me, *Betty Crocker's Cookbook for Boys and Girls,*" she says. "I brought it with me to the Cook-Off for good luck."

Layered Almond-Cream Cheese Bread Pudding With Amaretto Cream Sauce

SARA LEE® Brand Winner

Layered Almond-Cream Cheese Bread Pudding With Amaretto Cream Sauce

Vegetable cooking spray
1   (16-ounce) loaf honey white bread, sliced and divided
1   (8-ounce) package cream cheese, softened
9   large eggs, divided
¼   cup sugar
3   teaspoons vanilla extract, divided
1¼ cups almond filling*
1   cup butter, melted and divided
2½ cups half-and-half
Dash of salt
2   tablespoons almond filling*
2   tablespoons sugar
1   egg yolk
¼   cup slivered almonds
Amaretto Cream Sauce

Coat a 13- x 9-inch pan with cooking spray. Arrange 4½ bread slices in prepared pan, cutting slices as necessary to fit pan.

Beat cream cheese, 1 egg, ¼ cup sugar, and 1 teaspoon vanilla with an electric mixer until smooth. Spread half of cream cheese mixture over bread.

Whisk together 1¼ cups almond filling and ½ cup melted butter. Spread half of almond mixture over cream cheese mixture. Repeat layers once, using 4½ bread slices, remaining cream cheese mixture, and remaining almond mixture.

Cut remaining bread slices into 1-inch cubes; sprinkle over almond mixture.

Whisk together remaining 8 eggs, remaining 2 teaspoons vanilla, half-and-half, and salt; pour over bread cubes. Cover and chill 30 minutes or until most of egg mixture is absorbed.

Whisk together remaining ½ cup melted butter, 2 tablespoons almond filling, 2 tablespoons sugar, and egg yolk until blended. Drizzle evenly over bread pudding; sprinkle with almonds.

Bake at 325° for 1 hour or until set. Serve warm or chilled with Amaretto Cream Sauce. **Makes:** 12 servings.
Prep: 30 min., **Cook:** 1 hr., **Other:** 30 min.

Amaretto Cream Sauce:
½   cup amaretto liqueur
2   tablespoons cornstarch
1½ cups whipping cream
½   cup sugar

Combine amaretto and cornstarch, stirring until smooth.

Cook cream in a heavy saucepan over medium heat, stirring often, just until bubbles appear; gradually stir in amaretto mixture. Bring to a boil over medium heat, and boil, stirring constantly, 30 seconds. Remove from heat; stir in sugar, and let cool completely. **Makes:** about 2½ cups.
Prep: 5 min., **Cook:** 10 min.

*For testing purposes only, we used Solo Almond Filling.

Jeremy Bazata
Panama City, Florida

Jeremy alternates layers of bread pudding, cheesecake, and almond filling in a manner similar to assembling lasagna.

MILLSTONE® Brand Winner

Brownies Deluxe

1 cup butter
4 (1-ounce) squares **unsweetened** chocolate
¼ cup strong brewed French roast coffee
4 large eggs
2 cups sugar
1 teaspoon vanilla extract
1 cup all-purpose flour
2 cups (12-ounce package) semisweet chocolate morsels
1 cup chopped walnuts
Non-stick foil

Stir together butter, chocolate, and coffee in a heavy saucepan. Cook, stirring occasionally, over low heat until butter melts; cool slightly.

Beat eggs at high speed with an electric mixer. Gradually add sugar and vanilla, beating 3 minutes or until thick and pale. Add chocolate mixture, beating until blended. Gradually add flour, beating at low speed just until blended. Stir in chocolate morsels and walnuts. Pour into a 13- x 9-inch pan lined with aluminum foil.

Bake at 375° for 35 minutes or until set. **Cool** in pan on a wire rack. Lift foil with brownies out of pan. Cut brownies into squares. **Makes:** 24 brownies.
Prep: 20 min., **Cook:** 40 min.

Cynthia Brown
Wichita, Kansas

Cynthia uses a splash of coffee to add richness to these chocolate chip and walnut-studded brownies.

NESTLÉ TOLL HOUSE® Brand Winner

Shortbread Fudge Cake

1 cup butter, softened
2½ cups all-purpose flour, divided
1½ cups granulated sugar, divided
½ teaspoon salt
¾ cup coarsely chopped pecans
2 cups (12-ounce package) semisweet chocolate morsels
¾ cup butter
4 large eggs
2 teaspoons vanilla extract
Powdered sugar
Sweetened whipped cream or vanilla ice cream (optional)
Chocolate shavings (optional)

Beat 1 cup softened butter in a large mixing bowl at medium speed with an electric mixer until creamy.

Stir together 2 cups flour, ½ cup granulated sugar, and salt. Add to butter mixture, beating until crumbly. Stir in pecans.

Press dough into an ungreased 13- x 9-inch pan.

Bake at 350° for 25 minutes or until golden.

Microwave chocolate morsels and ¾ cup butter in a 2-quart glass bowl at HIGH 1½ minutes or until melted, stirring twice.

Whisk in eggs, vanilla, remaining 1 cup granulated sugar, and remaining ½ cup flour until smooth. Pour chocolate mixture over prepared crust.

Bake at 350° for 25 minutes or until set. (Do not overbake.) Cool completely in pan on a wire rack. Cut into 24 bars. Transfer bars to wax paper; dust with powdered sugar. Store bars in an airtight container. If desired, serve with whipped cream or ice cream, and sprinkle with chocolate shavings. **Makes:** 2 dozen.
Prep: 25 min., **Cook:** 50 min.

Amy Zitta
Starkville, Mississippi

Amy's creation is a combination of rich fudge pie and crisp shortbread cookies rather than a cake. Cake, pie, cookies—call it what you will. It's amazingly good.

Mango Upside-Down Gingerbread Cake

Topped with a dollop of sweetened whipped cream, this cake is very easy to make, and it's super moist warm from the oven.

⅔ cup fresh mango slices (about 1 large mango)
⅓ cup firmly packed dark brown sugar
½ cup unsalted butter, melted and divided
½ cup granulated sugar
1 large egg, lightly beaten
¼ cup molasses
1 cup all-purpose flour
1 teaspoon baking soda
1 teaspoon pumpkin pie spice
¼ teaspoon salt
½ cup water
1 cup whipping cream
1 teaspoon vanilla extract
3 tablespoons powdered sugar

Coat an 8-inch square pan with cooking spray. Arrange mango slices in 3 rows in pan. Sprinkle brown sugar over mango. Drizzle with ¼ cup melted butter; set aside.

In a medium bowl, stir together granulated sugar, egg, and molasses with a wooden spoon. Combine flour and next 3 ingredients; stir into molasses mixture. Add water and remaining ¼ cup melted butter; stir well.

Spoon batter over mango slices.

Bake at 350° for 35 to 40 minutes or until cake begins to pull away from sides of pan and center is set. Cool in pan on a wire rack 15 minutes.

Beat whipping cream and vanilla at high speed with an electric mixer until foamy; gradually add powdered sugar, beating until soft peaks form.

Serve sweetened whipped cream with warm cake. Store leftovers in refrigerator.
Makes: 9 servings.
Prep: 16 min., **Cook:** 40 min., **Other:** 15 min.

Tip: If fresh mango isn't in season, check the produce section for sliced mango in a jar.

Lisa Mosley
Beaumont, Texas

Chocolate Gingerbread With Warm Pear Sauce

Chocolate teams with gingerbread for an interesting flavor combo.

1 cup buttermilk
½ cup molasses
¾ teaspoon baking soda
2 cups all-purpose flour
½ teaspoon salt
½ teaspoon ground ginger
½ teaspoon ground cardamom
½ cup butter
1 (3-ounce) package cream cheese, softened
¾ cup granulated sugar
¼ cup firmly packed light brown sugar
1 large egg
1 (2-ounce) jar crystallized ginger, finely chopped
1 cup (6-ounce package) semisweet chocolate morsels
¼ cup butter
¼ cup firmly packed light brown sugar
2 (15¼-ounce) cans pear halves, drained and chopped

Whisk together first 3 ingredients in a small bowl; set aside.

Combine flour, salt, ginger, and cardamom; set aside.

Beat ½ cup butter and cream cheese at medium speed with an electric mixer until fluffy. Add granulated sugar and ¼ cup brown sugar; beat until creamy. Add egg, and beat until blended. Slowly add buttermilk mixture to butter mixture; beat 2 minutes. Stir flour mixture into butter mixture just until combined. Fold in crystallized ginger and chocolate morsels. Pour mixture into a lightly greased 9-inch square pan.

Bake at 350° for 53 minutes or until cake springs back when lightly touched in center. Cool completely in pan on a wire rack.

Melt ¼ cup butter in a large skillet over medium heat. Add ¼ cup brown sugar, stirring until sugar dissolves. Add pears; cook 5 minutes or until slightly thickened, stirring gently to coat. Serve warm sauce over cake.
Makes: 9 servings.
Prep: 17 min., **Cook:** 1 hr.

Kelly Walton
Severna Park, Maryland

Raisin and Pear Upside-Down Gingerbread Cake

Keep these ingredients on hand in the pantry for a throw-together, rustic dessert.

⅓ cup butter
¾ cup firmly packed brown sugar
1 (29-ounce) can pear halves, drained and sliced
½ cup raisins
⅓ cup walnuts, coarsely chopped
12 maraschino cherries, halved
1 (14.5-ounce) package gingerbread cake mix
1 cup water
1 large egg

Melt butter in a 12-inch cast-iron skillet over low heat. Sprinkle evenly with brown sugar. Arrange pear slices over sugar; top with raisins, walnuts, and cherries.

Stir together cake mix, water, and egg until moistened; pour over pears. Bake at 350° for 35 minutes or until a wooden pick inserted in center comes out clean.

Invert immediately onto a serving platter. Cool before serving. **Makes:** 8 to 10 servings.
Prep: 11 min., **Cook:** 35 min.

Tip: Make sure pears are well drained before arranging in skillet.

Betty Gilbert
Cape Coral, Florida

Betty used canned pears and a cake mix to make a quick, easy, and comforting homemade dessert.

$175,000 Cake

Starting with a cake mix makes a rich and gooey treat ready in no time.

1 (18.25-ounce) package devil's food cake mix
3 large eggs, divided
½ cup butter or margarine, melted
1 cup (6-ounce package) semisweet chocolate morsels
1 cup chopped pecans
1 (16-ounce) package powdered sugar, sifted
1 (8-ounce) package cream cheese, softened

Stir together cake mix, 1 egg, and melted butter until combined; press mixture into a greased 13- x 9-inch pan. Sprinkle evenly with chocolate morsels and chopped pecans.

Beverly gets 10 to 12 hearty servings out of this dessert, but it was so rich and satisfying, we opted for much smaller servings like a bar cookie.

Beat remaining 2 eggs, powdered sugar, and cream cheese at medium speed with an electric mixer until smooth; spoon over crust mixture in pan. Bake at 325° for 35 to 40 minutes or until golden and bubbly. Cool completely in pan on a wire rack; cut into squares.
Makes: 3 dozen.
Prep: 12 min., **Cook:** 40 min.

Tip: You can use a fine wire-mesh strainer to sift powdered sugar. Place a portion of powdered sugar at a time in strainer, and gently shake it back and forth.

Beverly Mays
Brazoria, Texas

Southern Heaven Chocolate-Praline Cake

This rich cake topped with gooey marshmallows, fudgy frosting, and praline-coated pecans is heaven on earth.

1½ cups butter, divided
1 cup firmly packed brown sugar
2 cups pecan halves
1 cup unsweetened cocoa, divided
4 large eggs, lightly beaten
2 cups granulated sugar
1½ cups all-purpose flour
Pinch of salt
1 teaspoon vanilla extract
2¾ cups miniature marshmallows (½ [10½-ounce] bag)
½ cup melted butter
½ cup milk
1 (16-ounce) package powdered sugar

Combine ½ cup butter and brown sugar in a medium saucepan over medium heat. Bring to a boil; boil 3 minutes, stirring constantly. Stir in pecans. Working rapidly, drop individual pecan halves onto wax paper; let stand until cooled and firm. Set aside 16 pecans for garnish; coarsely chop remaining pecans.

Melt 1 cup butter in a large saucepan over medium heat; stir in ½ cup cocoa until combined. Remove from heat; whisk in eggs and granulated sugar. Combine flour and salt; gradually stir into chocolate mixture. Stir in vanilla and chopped sugar-coated pecans. Pour batter into a greased 13- x 9-inch pan. Bake at 350° for 35 minutes or until a wooden pick inserted into center comes out clean. Remove from oven; immediately sprinkle marshmallows over hot cake.

Beat ½ cup melted butter, remaining ½ cup cocoa, and milk with an electric mixer at medium speed. Add powdered sugar; beat at low speed until smooth. Spread immediately over marshmallows. Garnish with reserved sugared pecans. Cool cake in pan on a wire rack. **Makes:** 16 servings.
Prep: 16 min., **Cook:** 35 min

David Onley
Cayce, South Carolina

David places the 16 sugar-coated pecans in four neat rows across the top of the cake so each serving gets a candied pecan half.

Bananas Foster Upside-Down Cake

Try this cake version of the famous New Orleans dessert. For the younger crowd, omit the crème de cacao and rum.

⅓ cup butter
1 cup firmly packed brown sugar
½ teaspoon ground cinnamon
3 ripe bananas
1 cup mashed ripe banana (about 2 large)
½ cup shortening
½ cup buttermilk
2 large eggs, lightly beaten
1 teaspoon vanilla extract
2¼ cups all-purpose flour
1⅓ cups granulated sugar
1 teaspoon baking powder
1 teaspoon baking soda
¾ teaspoon salt
3 tablespoons crème de cacao
⅓ cup rum
Vanilla ice cream (optional)
Whipped cream (optional)

Place butter in a 13- x 9-inch pan; place in a 350° oven for 5 minutes or just until melted. Remove from oven, and coat pan with cooking spray. Add brown sugar and cinnamon, stirring well. Spread mixture in pan.

Cut 3 bananas diagonally into ¼-inch-thick slices. Arrange slices on brown sugar mixture in 4 lengthwise rows; cover and set aside.

Combine mashed banana and next 4 ingredients in a large bowl; beat at medium speed with an electric mixer until blended. Combine flour and next 4 ingredients; add to mashed banana mixture, beating on low speed just until blended. Pour batter evenly over sliced banana in pan.

Bake at 350° for 35 to 40 minutes or until a wooden pick inserted in center comes out clean. Cool in pan 2 minutes; loosen cake from sides of pan with knife, and invert onto a large rectangular serving platter.

Drizzle crème de cacao over cake. Heat rum in a small saucepan just until simmering; ignite with a long match. Spoon rum over cake with a long-handled spoon. Serve warm cake with ice cream or whipped cream, if desired. **Makes:** 10 to 12 servings.
Prep: 23 min., **Cook:** 40 min.

Ruth A. Fay
Broken Arrow, Oklahoma

Grandpa's Chocolate-Rum Cake

Dark chocolate and rum are the predominant flavors in this dense and decadent cake. Because the flavors are so intense, you need only a thin slice to be perfectly satisfied. The cake slices well after chilling 1 hour, but plan to refrigerate it overnight before serving to allow the flavors to mellow.

1   cup butter, softened
2   cups sugar
4   large eggs
½   cup dark rum
2   cups all-purpose flour
1   cup unsweetened cocoa
1   teaspoon baking powder
1   teaspoon baking soda
½   teaspoon salt
⅛   teaspoon ground nutmeg
1   cup hot water
1   teaspoon almond extract
1   teaspoon vanilla extract
Mousse Frosting
Garnish: chocolate shavings

Beat butter at medium speed with an electric mixer until fluffy; gradually add sugar, beating well. Add eggs, 1 at a time, beating until blended after each addition. Add rum; beat until blended. **Combine** flour and next 5 ingredients; add to sugar mixture alternately with hot water, beginning and ending with flour mixture. Beat at low speed until blended after each addition; stir in flavorings. **Pour** batter into 2 greased and floured 9-inch round cakepans. **Bake** at 350° for 27 minutes (cake will not test quite done). Cool in pans on a wire rack 10 minutes; remove from pans, and cool completely on wire racks. **Spread** 1 cup Mousse Frosting between layers. Frost top and sides of cake with remaining frosting. Garnish, if desired. Cover and chill 8 hours. Store in refrigerator. **Makes:** 12 to 15 servings.
Prep: 16 min., **Cook:** 27 min., **Other:** 8 hrs., 10 min.

Mousse Frosting:
2   cups whipping cream
1   cup sifted powdered sugar
1   cup unsweetened cocoa
½   teaspoon almond extract
½   teaspoon vanilla extract
½   cup dark rum

Beat whipping cream until foamy; gradually add powdered sugar and next 3 ingredients, beating until blended. Add rum; beat until thick and smooth. **Makes:** 3¾ cups.
Prep: 7 min.

Juan Bostwick
Atlanta, Georgia

Mocha Coconut Cake With Mocha Frosting

Instead of butter or shortening, this cake batter uses vegetable oil and coconut milk as the fat to tenderize the cake. There's no creaming of fat involved, so it's quick to mix up.

2   cups all-purpose flour
2   cups sugar
¾   cup unsweetened cocoa
2   teaspoons baking soda
1   teaspoon baking powder
¼   teaspoon salt
1   cup strong brewed coffee
1   cup coconut milk
¼   cup vegetable oil
½   teaspoon vanilla extract
½   teaspoon coconut extract
2   large eggs, lightly beaten
4   cups white chocolate morsels
½   cup low-fat coffee yogurt
1   tablespoon strong brewed coffee
Garnish: chocolate shavings

Stir together first 6 ingredients in a large bowl. Stir together 1 cup coffee, coconut milk, oil, flavorings, and eggs; add to dry ingredients. Beat at medium speed with an electric mixer until blended. Pour batter into 2 greased and floured 9-inch round cakepans. **Bake** at 350° for 20 to 25 minutes or until a wooden pick inserted in center comes out clean. Cool in pans on wire racks 10 minutes; remove from pans, and cool on wire racks. **Microwave** white chocolate morsels in a large glass bowl at HIGH 1½ minutes or until melted, stirring twice. Add yogurt and 1 tablespoon coffee. Beat at medium speed 30 seconds or until spreading consistency. Spread frosting between layers and on top and sides of cake. Garnish, if desired. Store in refrigerator. **Makes:** 12 to 15 servings.
Prep: 14 min., **Cook:** 28 min.

Tip: Bake layers on the center oven rack, and stagger pans for even baking, being careful not to let pan sides touch. Make sure to use unsweetened coconut milk and not cream of coconut.

Jennifer Sweigert
Lynn Haven, Florida

Grandpa's Chocolate-
Rum Cake

"Over-the-Top" Chocolate Passion

Imagine all your favorite chocolate desserts—brownies, chocolate pudding cake, chocolate cake, chocolate chip cookies, and chocolate-dipped strawberries—all rolled or literally "stacked" into one bodacious dessert! Oh, and there's a fruit sauce, too. We thought the dessert was "over-the-top" without the sauce, so it can easily be omitted.

1   (18.25-ounce) package chocolate fudge cake mix
1   cup vegetable oil, divided
1⅓ cups water
3   large eggs
1   (19.8-ounce) package walnut brownie mix
2   large eggs
Butter-flavored vegetable cooking spray
3   tablespoons water
1   (18-ounce) package refrigerated ready-to-bake chocolate chip cookies (20 cookies)*
½   cup all-purpose flour
3   tablespoons unsweetened cocoa, divided
1   tablespoon butter-flavored shortening
⅓   cup granulated sugar
¼   cup milk
1½ teaspoons vanilla extract
½   cup firmly packed brown sugar
¾   cup boiling water
8   strawberries
1   (11.5-ounce) package milk chocolate morsels, divided
2   (16-ounce) cans ready-to-serve chocolate frosting
¼   cup powdered sugar
Strawberry Sauce (optional)

Beat cake mix, ½ cup oil, 1⅓ cups water, and 3 eggs at low speed with an electric mixer 1 minute, scraping bowl constantly. Pour batter into 2 (9-inch) round cakepans coated with butter-flavored cooking spray. Bake at 350° for 28 minutes or until a wooden pick inserted in center comes out clean. Cool in pans 10 minutes. Remove from pans, and cool completely on wire racks.

Stir together brownie mix, remaining ½ cup oil, 2 eggs, and 3 tablespoons water in a medium bowl until well blended. Spread in a 9-inch round cakepan coated with cooking spray. Bake at 350° for 35 minutes. Cool completely in pan; run a knife around pan to loosen.

Bake cookies according to package directions at 350° for 10 minutes. (Cookies will be soft.) Cool cookies on baking sheet 2 minutes before removing from baking sheet. Remove cookies to wire racks; cool completely.

Stir together flour and 1 tablespoon cocoa. Rub shortening and ⅓ cup sugar together in a medium bowl with back of a wooden spoon until blended. Gradually add milk, vanilla, and flour mixture, beating until smooth. Pour into a 9-inch round cakepan coated with cooking spray. **Stir** together ½ cup brown sugar and remaining 2 tablespoons cocoa until blended; sprinkle over batter. Carefully pour boiling water over sugar mixture. (Do not stir.) Bake at 350° for 40 minutes or until top looks thickened and set. Cool pudding cake completely in pan.

Rinse strawberries, and pat dry. Place 1 cup chocolate morsels in a small bowl. Microwave at HIGH 1 minute; stir until smooth. Carefully dip strawberries in chocolate to coat. Place on a large plate covered with wax paper. Chill until chocolate is firm.

Place brownie layer on a serving plate. Loosen edges of pudding cake with a narrow flexible spatula, and invert onto brownie layer. (Don't worry if pudding cake layer doesn't come out of pan in one piece. Carefully place pieces together in 1 layer on top of brownie layer. When the cake is assembled, this layer resembles frosting between the layers.)

Place 1 cake layer over pudding cake layer; press gently. Thinly spread cake layer with frosting. Place about 5 cookies in a single layer over frosting. Thinly spread bottoms of remaining cookies with frosting. Place cookies, frosted side down, on top of each other in even layers. (Do not allow cookies to extend beyond edges of cake layer. Trim cookies with scissors if necessary, so they do not extend beyond edges.) Spread top cookie layer with about ½ cup frosting (you should have a little more than 1 can of frosting left). Place remaining cake layer over frosting, pressing down gently. Thinly frost top of cake layer and sides of all layers with remaining frosting. Sprinkle remaining chocolate morsels on cake. Cover and chill at least 2 hours.

Before serving, sift powdered sugar over morsels. Arrange chocolate-covered strawberries on top of cake. Serve with Strawberry Sauce, if desired. Store cake in refrigerator. **Makes:** 16 servings.
Prep: 44 min., **Cook:** 1 hr., 55 min., **Other:** 2 hrs.

Note: For testing purposes only, we used Pillsbury Ready-to-Bake Chocolate Chip Cookies, Betty Crocker SuperMoist Chocolate Fudge Cake Mix, Betty Crocker Walnut Supreme Brownie Mix, and Betty Crocker Creamy Chocolate Frosting. If you use a different brand of brownie mix, make brownies by the "fudgelike" directions and bake according to times and temperatures for a 9-inch square pan.

Tip: Cake, brownie layer, cookies, and Strawberry Sauce can be made ahead. Assembled cake keeps well for several days and is better if chilled overnight.

*You can use homemade cookies. Just reduce baking time slightly so cookies will be soft. Cookies should be about 2¼ inches in diameter.

Strawberry Sauce:
2   cups orange juice
1½ cups unsifted powdered sugar
5   strawberries, thinly sliced

Gradually stir orange juice into powdered sugar in a medium bowl. Stir in strawberries. Cover and chill at least 1 hour. **Makes:** 2½ cups.
Prep: 3 min., **Other:** 1 hr.

Robyn Mekow
Summerville, South Carolina

4-Layer Dark Chocolate-Raspberry Cake

Looking for the perfect Valentine's Day dessert? Here's a delicious chocolate cake with a vibrant pink raspberry filling hidden inside.

2   cups sugar
1¾ cups all-purpose flour
¾   cup Dutch-process cocoa
1½ teaspoons baking powder
1½ teaspoons baking soda
1   teaspoon salt
2   large eggs
1   cup milk
½   cup vegetable oil
2   teaspoons vanilla extract
1   cup boiling water
Raspberry Filling
Dark Chocolate Frosting
Garnish: fresh raspberries

Combine first 6 ingredients in a large bowl, and make a well in center of mixture.

Stir together eggs and next 3 ingredients; add to dry ingredients. Beat at low speed with an electric mixer just until blended. Beat at medium speed 2 minutes. Stir in boiling water. Pour batter into 2 greased and floured 9-inch round cakepans.

Bake at 350° for 35 minutes or until cake begins to pull away from sides of pan and a wooden pick inserted in center of each layer comes out almost clean. Cool in pans on wire racks 10 minutes; remove from pans, and cool completely on wire racks.

Split layers horizontally. Spread Raspberry Filling evenly between layers. Spread Dark Chocolate Frosting on top and sides of cake. Garnish, if desired.
Makes: 12 to 15 servings.
Prep: 35 min., **Cook:** 35 min., **Other:** 10 min.

Raspberry Filling:
1   cup fresh raspberries
Milk
½   cup butter, softened
5   cups sifted powdered sugar

Process raspberries in a food processor until smooth, stopping once to scrape down sides. Pour puree through a fine wire-mesh strainer, pressing with the back of a spoon; discard seeds. Add enough milk to equal ½ cup.

Beat butter at medium speed with an electric mixer until fluffy. Gradually add powdered sugar alternately with raspberry mixture, beginning and ending with powdered sugar. Beat at low speed until blended after each addition.
Makes: 2⅔ cups.
Prep: 15 min.

Dark Chocolate Frosting:
6   tablespoons butter, softened
2⅔ cups sifted powdered sugar
½   cup Dutch-process cocoa
6   tablespoons milk
1   teaspoon vanilla extract

Beat butter at medium speed with an electric mixer until fluffy. Combine powdered sugar and cocoa; gradually add to butter alternately with milk and vanilla, beginning and ending with powdered sugar mixture. Beat at low speed until blended after each addition.
Makes: 2¼ cups.
Prep: 8 min.

Tip: To prevent a white dusting on your chocolate cake layers, dust cakepans with cocoa instead of flour.

Lauren Brumfield
Germantown, Tennessee

Decadent Chocolate-Lemon Ganache Cake

You'll find that the lemon isn't overpowering in this cake, but that it gives it a unique taste.

3   cups heavy whipping cream
2   teaspoons grated lemon rind
2   cups (12-ounce package) semisweet chocolate morsels
6   (1-ounce) unsweetened chocolate baking squares
1   tablespoon grated lemon rind
3⅓ cups cake flour
1   teaspoon baking powder
1   teaspoon baking soda
¼   teaspoon salt
1   cup unsalted butter, softened
2   cups sugar
4   large eggs
1   teaspoon vanilla extract
1⅔ cups lemon-flavored yogurt

Heat whipping cream and 2 teaspoons lemon rind in a large saucepan over medium-low heat until hot. Add morsels, and cook 5 minutes or until chocolate is melted, stirring constantly. Cool; cover and chill at least 5 hours.

Meanwhile, melt unsweetened chocolate and 1 tablespoon lemon rind in a small saucepan; let cool.

Stir together flour and next 3 ingredients; set aside.

Beat butter at medium speed with an electric mixer until creamy; gradually add sugar, and beat until light and fluffy. Add eggs, 1 at a time, beating just until blended; stir in vanilla. Add flour mixture alternately with yogurt, beginning and ending with flour mixture; stir in melted unsweetened chocolate mixture just until blended. Divide batter evenly among 3 lightly greased 9-inch round cakepans.

Bake at 350° for 25 minutes or until a wooden pick inserted in center comes out clean. Cool in pans on wire racks 10 minutes; remove from pans, and cool completely on wire racks.

Meanwhile, beat chilled whipping cream mixture at medium speed until stiff peaks form. (Be careful not to overbeat.)

Spread frosting between layers and on top and sides of cake. Store in refrigerator.

Makes: 12 to 15 servings.

Prep: 42 min., **Cook:** 32 min., **Other:** 5 hrs.

Corinne Portteus
Newark, California

Lemon Curd and Cream Cake

Lemon Curd (opposite page)
1   (18.25-ounce) lemon cake mix with pudding*
1¼ cups buttermilk
⅓   cup vegetable oil
1   tablespoon grated lemon rind
3   large eggs
¾   cup heavy whipping cream
3   tablespoons sugar
½   cup sour cream
⅔   cup hot water
⅓   cup sugar
⅓   cup fresh lemon juice (about 3 lemons)

Prepare Lemon Curd.

Beat cake mix and next 4 ingredients in a large bowl at low speed with an electric mixer until combined; increase speed to medium, and beat 2 minutes. Pour batter into 2 greased and floured 9-inch round cakepans. Bake at 350° for 30 minutes or until a wooden pick inserted in center comes out clean. Cool in pans on a wire rack 10 minutes; remove from pans, and cool completely on wire rack.

Beat whipping cream at high speed with an electric mixer until foamy; gradually add 3 tablespoons sugar, beating until soft peaks form. Gradually add sour cream, beating until mixture is spreading consistency. Chill at least 30 minutes.

Combine hot water, ⅓ cup sugar, and lemon juice in a small bowl, stirring until sugar is dissolved.

Place 1 cake layer on a cake plate; use a wooden pick to poke holes in cake ½-inch apart. Slowly pour half of sugar syrup mixture over cake layer until liquid is absorbed. Spread 1 cup Lemon Curd over layer. Top with remaining cake layer; use a wooden pick to poke holes in cake ½-inch apart. Pour remaining syrup over layer, and top with remaining Lemon Curd, leaving a 1½-inch border around edge of cake. Spread sour cream frosting on sides of cake, and on 1½-inch border around top edge of cake, leaving Lemon Curd visible. Chill at least 1 hour before serving. Store in refrigerator. **Makes:** 12 to 15 servings.

Prep: 25 min., **Cook:** 30 min., **Other:** 1 hr., 40 min.

*For testing purposes only, we used Betty Crocker SuperMoist Cake Mix.

Michelle dresses up a cake mix with the addition of buttermilk and grated lemon rind, then adds a homemade lemon curd and sour cream frosting. No one will ever believe this cake is not completely from scratch.

Lemon Curd:

- ¾ cup sugar
- ½ cup unsalted butter
- 1 tablespoon grated lemon rind
- ½ cup fresh lemon juice (about 4 lemons)
- 2 large eggs, lightly beaten

Combine first 4 ingredients in top of a double boiler. Cook over simmering water, stirring constantly, until butter melts. Gradually whisk about one-fourth of hot mixture into eggs, stirring constantly; add to remaining hot mixture.

Cook, stirring constantly, 8 minutes or until mixture thickens and coats back of a spoon. Remove from heat; cool. Cover and chill completely. **Makes:** 1⅔ cups.
Prep: 8 min., **Cook:** 10 min.

Michelle G. Davis
Cleveland, Tennessee

Decadent Lemon Cake

This cake takes a little time to prepare, but the end result is definitely worth it.

Lemon Filling
- 3½ cups cake flour
- 4 teaspoons baking powder
- ½ teaspoon salt
- 1 cup butter, softened
- 2 cups sugar, divided
- 1 teaspoon grated lemon rind
- 1 tablespoon fresh lemon juice
- 1 teaspoon vanilla extract
- 1 cup milk
- 7 egg whites
White Chocolate Frosting

Prepare Lemon Filling. Cover and chill at least 8 hours.

Combine flour, baking powder, and salt; set aside.

Beat butter at medium speed with an electric mixer until creamy. Gradually add 1¾ cups sugar, beating at medium speed until light and fluffy. Add lemon rind, lemon juice, and vanilla; beat well. Add flour mixture alternately with milk, beginning and ending with flour mixture. Beat at low speed just until blended after each addition.

Beat egg whites at medium speed with an electric mixer until foamy; gradually add remaining ¼ cup sugar, beating until stiff peaks form. Fold one-third of egg whites into batter. Gently fold in

remaining beaten egg whites just until blended. (Do not overmix.)

Pour batter into 3 greased and floured 9-inch round cakepans.

Bake at 350° for 18 to 22 minutes or until a wooden pick inserted in center comes out clean. Cool in pans on wire racks 10 minutes; remove from pans, and cool completely on wire racks.

Spread ¾ cup White Chocolate Frosting between each cake layer; carefully spread ½ cup Lemon Filling over White Chocolate Frosting between each cake layer. Spread remaining White Chocolate Frosting on top and sides of cake. Chill until ready to serve. Store in refrigerator. **Makes:** 12 to 15 servings.
Prep: 34 min., **Cook:** 22 min., **Other:** 8 hrs., 10 min.

Lemon Filling:

- 1 cup sugar
- ¼ cup cornstarch
- ¼ teaspoon salt
- 2 tablespoons butter
- 1 tablespoon grated lemon rind
- ½ cup fresh lemon juice
- 4 egg yolks, lightly beaten

Combine first 6 ingredients in top of a double boiler. Cook over simmering

water, stirring constantly, until butter melts. Gradually stir about one-fourth of hot mixture into egg yolks; add to remaining hot mixture, stirring constantly. Cook over simmering water, stirring constantly, until mixture thickens and coats back of a spoon (about 15 minutes). Remove from heat; cool. Cover and chill.
Makes: 1 cup.
Prep: 13 min., **Cook:** 17 min.

White Chocolate Frosting:

- 2½ (4-ounce) white chocolate baking bars
- 1½ (8-ounce) packages cream cheese, softened
- ½ cup butter, softened
- 2½ cups powdered sugar
- 1 tablespoon fresh lemon juice

Melt chocolate in top of a double boiler over simmering water until melted. Remove from heat; let cool.

Beat cream cheese and butter at medium speed with an electric mixer until creamy; gradually add powdered sugar, beating until smooth. Add juice and chocolate just until combined. **Makes:** 4¾ cups.
Prep: 14 min.

Marie Rizzio
Traverse City, Michigan

Lucky 7 Coconut-
Lemon Cake

Lucky 7 Coconut-Lemon Cake

Seven-Minute Icing and lemon lime soft drink double the luck in pleasing your crowd with this delicate cake filled with a tart lemon-coconut filling.

½ cup butter, softened
½ cup shortening
2 cups sugar
3 large eggs
2 cups all-purpose flour
2 teaspoons baking powder
1 teaspoon salt
1 cup buttermilk
¼ cup fresh lemon juice
¼ cup lemon lime soft drink
2 teaspoons vanilla extract
Clear Lemon Filling
Seven-Minute Icing
1 cup sweetened flaked coconut

Coat 3 (8-inch) round cakepans with cooking spray; line with wax paper. Set prepared pans aside.

Beat butter and shortening at medium speed with an electric mixer until fluffy; gradually add sugar, beating well. Add eggs, 1 at a time, beating until blended after each addition.

Combine flour, baking powder, and salt. Combine buttermilk and next 3 ingredients. Add flour mixture to butter mixture alternately with buttermilk mixture, beginning and ending with flour mixture. Beat at low speed until blended after each addition. Spoon batter into prepared pans.

Bake at 350° for 24 minutes or until a wooden pick inserted in center comes out clean. (Layers will be thin, about 1¼ inch thick.) Cool in pans on wire racks 10 minutes; remove from pans, and cool completely on wire racks.

Slice cake layers in half horizontally to make 6 layers. Place 1 cake layer, cut side up, on a cake plate. Spread with ⅓ cup Clear Lemon Filling. Place a second cake layer, cut side down, on top of filling; spread with 1 cup Seven-Minute Icing. Repeat procedure with remaining 4 layers, ending with icing on top. Frost sides of cake with remaining icing; sprinkle with 1 cup coconut. **Makes:** 8 to 10 servings.

Prep: 25 min., **Cook:** 24 min., **Other:** 10 min.

Note: For testing purposes only, we used 7-UP lemon lime soft drink. Add the soft drink to buttermilk just before using in recipe so it doesn't go flat.

Clear Lemon Filling:

6 tablespoons sugar
1½ tablespoons cornstarch
⅛ teaspoon salt
¼ cup water
1 tablespoon butter or margarine
1 tablespoon grated lemon rind
½ cup fresh lemon juice
½ cup sweetened flaked coconut

Whisk together first 3 ingredients in a medium saucepan; whisk in water until blended. Bring to a boil over medium heat; cook, whisking constantly, 2 minutes. Remove from heat; add butter, lemon rind, and lemon juice. Cook over medium heat, whisking constantly, 1 to 2 minutes or until slightly thickened. Remove from heat; stir in coconut. Place saucepan in a large bowl of ice water for about 5 minutes, whisking often until completely cool. **Makes:** 1 cup.

Prep: 8 min., **Cook:** 5 min., **Other:** 5 min.

Seven-Minute Icing:

1½ cups sugar
⅓ cup water
2 egg whites
1 tablespoon light corn syrup
⅛ teaspoon salt
2 teaspoons vanilla extract

Combine first 5 ingredients in top of a double boiler. Beat at low speed with a handheld electric mixer 30 seconds or just until blended.

Place over boiling water; beat constantly at high speed 7 minutes or until stiff peaks form. Remove from heat. Add vanilla; beat 2 minutes or until frosting is spreading consistency. **Makes:** 4½ cups.

Prep: 6 min., **Cook:** 8 min.

Claralita Davis
Central, South Carolina

Claralita uses lemon wedges to garnish around the bottom sides of the cake, and she tops the cake with a fresh mint sprig. Her recipe makes twice as much Clear Lemon Filling, and she serves the filling over vanilla ice cream alongside the cake. We thought the cake was delicious without the ice cream, so we cut the filling in half to eliminate leftovers.

Florida Keys Cake

Key lime cheesecake stands in as frosting between the layers on this decadent cake. It's important to use 10-inch cakepans to make this one-of-a-kind recipe. The cake received rave reviews from our taste-testing panel, and we all agreed the flavor and presentation warranted using specialty pans.

1 **(18.25-ounce) package white cake mix**
1 **cup buttermilk**
¼ **cup vegetable oil**
3 **large eggs**
⅓ **cup cream of coconut**
2 **cups sweetened flaked coconut, divided**
1 **cup sugar**
¼ **cup cornstarch**
4 **(8-ounce) packages cream cheese, softened**
3 **large eggs**
1 **(8-ounce) container sour cream**
½ **cup Key lime juice**
1 **(16-ounce) container ready-to-spread vanilla frosting**

Combine first 5 ingredients in a mixing bowl; beat at medium speed with an electric mixer 4 minutes. Stir in 1 cup coconut. Divide batter evenly between 2 lightly greased 10-inch round cakepans.

Bake at 350° for 25 minutes or until a wooden pick inserted in center comes out clean. Cool in pans 10 minutes on wire racks; remove from pans, and cool completely on wire racks.

Split cake layers in half horizontally to make 4 layers. Crumble 1 cake layer into fine crumbs. Toss cake crumbs with remaining 1 cup coconut; spread on a baking sheet. Bake at 350° for 10 minutes or until coconut is toasted. Set aside.

Combine sugar and cornstarch. Beat cream cheese at high speed with an electric mixer until creamy; gradually add sugar mixture, mixing well. Add eggs, 1 at a time, beating after each addition. Stir in sour cream and lime juice, blending well.

Place 1 cake layer, cut side up, in the bottom of a lightly greased 10-inch springform pan. Spoon ⅓ cheesecake batter over cake layer; repeat procedure with remaining cake layers and cheesecake batter. (See tip.)

Bake at 325° for 1 hour or until set. Cool completely in pan on a wire rack. Cover and chill at least 4 hours.

Run a knife around the edge of pan, releasing sides. Spread frosting over top and sides of cake. Pat reserved crumb mixture generously around sides and top of cake. Chill at least 1 hour before serving. Store in refrigerator. **Makes:** 16 servings.

Prep: 45 min., **Cook:** 1 hr., 35 min., **Other:** 5 hrs.

Tip: It may be necessary to use a foil collar around the springform pan to hold the cake and cheesecake mixture once it's layered in the springform pan. Cut a piece of aluminum foil long enough to fit around the 10-inch springform pan, allowing 1-inch overlap; starting from 1 long side, fold foil into thirds. Lightly grease 1 side of foil. Wrap foil around outside of pan, greased side against pan, allowing it to extend to 1½ inches above rim to form a collar; secure with string or masking tape. Bake as directed.

Donna Flynn
Wilmington, North Carolina

The textured coating on **Donna's** cake comes from a mixture of toasted coconut and cake crumbs.

Florida Keys Cake

Mom Edna's Old-Fashioned Jam Cake

Two rich glazes swirl together as they cascade from between mile-high moist cake layers studded with nuts and raisins. The first glaze is sweet and creamy; the second is caramel and silky with even more nuts and raisins. The Finishing Glaze is made similar to a caramel frosting; it's beaten but still flows easily.

1½ cups butter
2 cups sugar
1 cup seedless blackberry jam
6 large eggs
3 cups all-purpose flour
1 teaspoon baking soda
2 teaspoons ground cloves
2 teaspoons ground cinnamon
1 cup buttermilk
1½ cups chopped pecans
1 cup raisins
Finishing Glaze
Soaking Glaze

Line 4 (9-inch) round cakepans with wax paper; coat pans with cooking spray. Set aside.

Beat butter at medium speed with an electric mixer until creamy; gradually add sugar, beating well. Add jam, beating until blended. Add eggs, 1 at a time, beating until blended after each addition.

Combine flour and next 3 ingredients; add to butter mixture alternately with buttermilk, beginning and ending with flour mixture. Beat at low speed until blended after each addition. Stir in pecans and raisins. Spoon batter evenly into prepared pans.

Bake at 350° for 25 to 28 minutes or until a wooden pick inserted in center comes out clean. Cool in pans on wire racks 10 minutes; remove from pans, and cool on wire racks.

Prepare the Finishing Glaze. While the Finishing Glaze cools, prepare the Soaking Glaze.

Place 1 cake layer, upside down, on a cake plate. Prick layer with a small paring knife, making holes about ¼-inch apart. Spoon a scant ½ cup Soaking Glaze, about 2 tablespoons at a time, into

middle of cake layer. Spread glaze into cake in a circular motion after each addition, using a large spoon.

Spoon 1 cup Finishing Glaze onto cake layer, about ¼ cup at a time, using same procedure as for applying Soaking Glaze. (Finishing Glaze will overflow onto sides.)

Repeat procedure with remaining cake layers and glazes. Spoon remaining Finishing Glaze over top of cake allowing to flow down sides. Let cake stand until glaze becomes firm. **Makes:** 10 to 12 servings.
Prep: 28 min., **Cook:** 28 min.

Note: Cake can be prepared up to two days ahead, if desired.

Tip: If you want a clean cake plate, slip strips of wax paper (approximately 3 inches wide) between the edge of first cake layer and cake plate before applying glazes. Allow glazes to become firm, but not hard, before removing strips. However, we didn't mind the drips.

CeLina warns that this is not a recipe for the faint at heart, but it's well worth the extra effort. The cake has been a tradition in her family for more than 60 years. Her family prefers the cake when made a few days in advance, and she says it can also be frozen. We loved it freshly prepared, a few days later, and after freezing.

Finishing Glaze:
1 cup butter
3 cups sugar
1 cup buttermilk
1 teaspoon baking soda
1½ cups chopped pecans
½ cup raisins
½ cup seedless blackberry jam
2 teaspoons vanilla extract

Stir together first 7 ingredients in a 6-quart Dutch oven. Place over low heat, and cook, stirring often, 40 minutes. Using a pastry brush dipped in hot water, wash down any sugar crystals on sides of pan. Cook 15 more minutes, without stirring, until a candy thermometer registers 234° (soft ball stage). Remove from heat; add vanilla. (Do not stir.) Cool mixture to 110° (about 13 minutes). Stir glaze until mixture is thickened, but still flows easily. **Makes:** 4⅔ cups.
Prep: 8 min., **Cook:** 55 min., **Other:** 13 min.

Soaking Glaze:
2 cups sugar
⅔ cup milk

Stir together sugar and milk in a small saucepan. Place over medium-low heat. Bring to a simmer, stirring often. Cook 1 to 2 minutes or until sugar dissolves. **Makes:** 1¾ cups.
Prep: 1 min., **Cook:** 5 min.

CeLina C. Colvin
Ripley, Tennessee

Peach Cream Cake

A light dessert of fluffy sponge cake, this treat is layered with a smooth cream cheese filling and peach slices, then frosted with sweetened whipped cream.

6   egg whites
1   cup sugar, divided
6   egg yolks
¼   teaspoon grated lemon rind
¼   cup whipping cream
1   cup sifted cake flour
1   (24-ounce) jar refrigerated
     sliced peaches in light syrup,
     drained
Cream Cheese Filling
Whipped Cream Frosting

Beat egg whites in a large bowl at high speed with an electric mixer until foamy. Add ½ cup sugar, 1 tablespoon at a time, beating until soft peaks form. Set mixture aside.

Beat egg yolks and remaining ½ cup sugar at high speed with an electric mixer until thick and pale. Beat in lemon rind and whipping cream. Reduce speed to low, and beat in flour just until smooth. By hand, carefully fold in one-third of egg white mixture. Fold egg yolk mixture into remaining egg white mixture. Pour batter into 2 lightly greased and floured 8-inch round cakepans.

Bake at 350° for 13 minutes or until a wooden pick inserted in center comes out clean. Cool in pans on wire racks 10 minutes; remove from pans, and cool on wire racks.

Pat peach slices with a paper towel to remove excess moisture. Set aside 8 peach slices. Place 1 cake layer on a cake plate. Top cake layer with Cream Cheese Filling, spreading to edges. Arrange peach slices in spoke fashion on filling. Top peach slices with 1 cup Whipped Cream Frosting, spreading to edges. Top

frosting with remaining cake layer. Frost top and sides of cake with remaining Whipped Cream Frosting. Arrange reserved peach slices on top of cake. Chill until ready to serve. Store in refrigerator. **Makes:** 6 to 8 servings.
Prep: 25 min., **Cook:** 13 min.

Note: Substitute 2 cups of peeled fresh peach slices in season for the canned peaches.

Cream Cheese Filling:

1   envelope unflavored gelatin
¼   cup cold water
3   egg yolks
½   cup sugar
½   cup whipping cream
½   teaspoon grated lemon rind
1   (8-ounce) package cream
     cheese, cut into pieces and
     softened
2   tablespoons brandy
1   teaspoon vanilla extract

Sprinkle gelatin over cold water in a small bowl; stir and let stand 1 minute or until softened.

Meanwhile, combine egg yolks and next 3 ingredients in a 2-quart saucepan. Add gelatin mixture. Cook, whisking

constantly, over medium heat, 3 to 4 minutes or until gelatin dissolves and mixture thickens slightly. Remove from heat, and stir in cream cheese until smooth. Stir in brandy and vanilla. Cover and cool completely; chill thoroughly. Whisk filling until creamy before use. **Makes:** 2 cups.
Prep: 12 min., **Cook:** 5 min., **Other:** 30 min.

Tip: To quickly cool filling, set saucepan in a large bowl of ice water. Stir often for about 5 minutes or until completely cool.

Whipped Cream Frosting:

2   cups heavy whipping cream
⅓   cup powdered sugar
1   teaspoon vanilla extract

Place all ingredients in a medium bowl; beat at medium speed of an electric mixer until soft peaks form. **Makes:** 4 cups.
Prep: 4 min.

Tip: For best results when beating whipping cream, be sure the bowl and beaters are well chilled.

Sylvia Gibson
Tampa, Florida

Sylvia offers two good tips on slicing the cake: Refrigerate the cake until it's thoroughly chilled so it holds together well, and use a serrated knife to cut the cake. When she wants to change up the recipe a bit, Sylvia uses strawberries or apricots instead of peaches. She also uses this sponge cake recipe for strawberry shortcakes, and she serves the plain sponge cake with caramelized bananas and whipped cream.

Banana-Pecan Pound Cake
With Caramel Glaze

Banana-Pecan Pound Cake With Caramel Glaze

Studded with pecans, this extremely moist cake gets its punch of banana flavor from baby food rather than mashed fresh fruit.

1½ cups butter, softened
1 (8-ounce) package cream cheese, softened
3 cups granulated sugar
5 large eggs
2 (6-ounce) jars banana baby food
3½ cups all-purpose flour
½ teaspoon baking powder
¾ teaspoon vanilla extract
1⅔ cups chopped pecans
1 cup firmly packed light brown sugar
½ cup butter
¼ cup evaporated milk
2 tablespoons chopped pecans

Beat 1½ cups butter and cream cheese at medium speed with a heavy-duty stand mixer 6 minutes or until creamy. Gradually add granulated sugar, beating 2 to 3 minutes. Add eggs, 1 at a time, beating well after each addition. Stir in banana baby food.

Combine flour and baking powder; gradually add to butter mixture, beating at low speed just until blended after each addition. Stir in vanilla and 1⅔ cups pecans. Pour batter into a greased and floured 10-inch tube pan.

Bake at 350° for 1 hour and 40 minutes or until a long wooden pick or skewer inserted near center comes out clean. Cool in pan on a wire rack 10 to 15 minutes; remove from pan, and cool on wire rack.

Combine brown sugar, ½ cup butter, and evaporated milk in a small saucepan over medium heat; bring to a boil, and cook, stirring constantly, 3 minutes or until sugar dissolves. Stir in 2 tablespoons pecans; cool slightly. Serve glaze drizzled over cake or on the side. **Makes:** 12 to 16 servings.
Prep: 15 min., **Cook:** 1 hr., 40 min.

Note: With almost 10 cups of batter, this recipe makes a 4-inch-tall pound cake. If you don't own a heavy-duty stand mixer, make sure to use at least a 3½-quart bowl to prepare it. When choosing a pan for baking, use a 10-inch tubepan that's at least 4 inches tall. To test for doneness, it's necessary to use a long wooden pick or skewer to reach down to the bottom of the cake. The cake may appear done on the top and when tested with a toothpick, but still not be done deeper down in the center.

Shannen Tuten
Reedsburg, Wisconsin

Ginger-Pear Cake With Honey-Lemon Frosting

Don't let the amount of ground ginger in this recipe concern you. Surprisingly, it's not overwhelming and combines great with the pears.

2 cups all-purpose flour
1½ cups sugar
2 teaspoons baking soda
1 teaspoon salt
3 tablespoons ground ginger
¾ cup vegetable oil
2 large eggs, lightly beaten
⅓ cup milk
1½ teaspoons vanilla extract
3 cups fresh pears, coarsely grated
Honey-Lemon Frosting

Combine first 5 ingredients in a large bowl; stir well. Make a well in the center of flour mixture. Add oil, eggs, milk, and vanilla; stir just until combined. Stir in grated pears.

Pour batter into 2 greased and floured 9-inch round cakepans.

Bake at 350° for 40 minutes or until a wooden pick inserted in center comes out clean. Cool in pans on wire racks 10 minutes; remove from pans, and cool completely on wire racks.

Spread 1 cup Honey-Lemon Frosting between layers, and spread remaining Honey-Lemon Frosting on top and sides of cake. **Makes:** 10 servings.
Prep: 37 min., **Cook:** 40 min., **Other:** 10 min.

Rachel says this cake is also delicious when simply sprinkled with powdered sugar rather than frosted.

Honey-Lemon Frosting:
2 (8-ounce) packages cream cheese, softened
½ cup unsalted butter, softened
2 teaspoons vanilla extract
2 teaspoons grated lemon rind
2 cups powdered sugar
2 tablespoons honey

Beat first 4 ingredients at medium speed with an electric mixer until creamy. Gradually add powdered sugar, beating at low speed until blended. Beat at high speed until smooth. Add honey, beating just until blended. **Makes:** 3⅓ cups.
Prep: 13 min.

Rachel Rodriguez
Anchorage, Alaska

Creamy Peanut Butter Fudge Cake

Comfort doesn't get much better than this velvety-textured cake. The creamy peanut butter fudge frosting goes on hot and warms the whole cake. No surprise that it received our highest rating.

1   cup butter or margarine, softened
6   cups sugar, divided
1   (8-ounce) container sour cream
5   large eggs
3   cups self-rising flour
1   cup milk
1   teaspoon vanilla extract
1   (18-ounce) jar creamy peanut butter
1½ cups water

Coat 3 (8-inch) round cakepans with cooking spray. Line pans with wax paper. Coat wax paper with cooking spray. Set pans aside.

Beat butter at medium speed with an electric mixer until creamy; gradually add 3 cups sugar, beating well. Add sour cream; beat until light and creamy. Add eggs, 1 at a time, beating until blended after each addition.

Add flour alternately with milk, beginning and ending with flour. Beat mixture at low speed until blended after each addition. Stir in vanilla. Pour batter into prepared pans.

Bake at 350° for 27 to 30 minutes or until a wooden pick inserted in center comes out clean. Cool in pans on wire racks 10 minutes; remove from pans, and cool on wire racks.

When cake layers are completely cool, place peanut butter in a large mixing bowl. Place 1 cake layer on a cake plate.

Bring remaining 3 cups sugar and 1½ cups water to a boil over medium heat in a heavy 2-quart saucepan, stirring gently until sugar dissolves. Using a pastry brush dipped in hot water, wash down any sugar crystals on sides of pan. Cook, without stirring, until a candy thermometer registers 234° (soft ball stage). Pour over peanut butter, and beat with a wooden spoon until blended and mixture thickens just slightly.

Immediately pour about 1 cup frosting over cake layer, spreading almost to edges. Quickly repeat procedure with second and third layers of cake and frosting. Quickly frost sides of cake with remaining frosting. Let cake stand at least until frosting is firm before cutting. (Cake will remain warm inside for about 2 hours.) **Makes:** 16 servings.
Prep: 24 min., **Cook:** 30 min., **Other:** 1 hr., 20 min.

Tips: Work rapidly to frost cake. Frosting will harden quickly. Use a long thin spatula dipped in hot water to help spread frosting when it begins to become firm. An electric knife works best to cut the cake if serving while still warm.

Rita Barnhardt
Phenix City, Alabama

Mexican Chocolate Bundt Cake

1   (18.25-ounce) package devil's food cake mix
1   teaspoon ground cinnamon
1⅓ cups water
½   cup vegetable oil
3   large eggs
1   cup semisweet chocolate mini-morsels, divided
2   tablespoons butter
¼   cup firmly packed light brown sugar
3   tablespoons milk, divided
1   tablespoon vanilla extract
1   cup powdered sugar
1   tablespoon shortening
2   tablespoons sliced almonds, toasted

Combine first 5 ingredients in a large mixing bowl. Beat at medium speed with an electric mixer 2 minutes. Stir in ½ cup chocolate mini-morsels. Pour batter into a greased and floured 12-cup Bundt pan.

Bake at 350° for 33 to 35 minutes or until cake springs back when lightly touched. Cool in pan on a wire rack 10 minutes; remove cake from pan, and cool completely on wire rack.

Combine butter, brown sugar and 2 tablespoons milk in a heavy saucepan over medium-low heat, stirring constantly, until sugar is melted. Remove from heat; stir in vanilla. Gradually stir in powdered sugar; if necessary, add remaining 1 tablespoon milk, stirring to desired consistency. Drizzle glaze over cooled cake.

Microwave remaining ½ cup chocolate morsels and shortening in a small bowl on HIGH 30 seconds or until melted. Pour melted chocolate into a small zip-top freezer bag. Snip 1 corner of bag, and drizzle over brown sugar glaze. Sprinkle almonds on cake. **Makes:** 12 servings.
Prep: 20 min., **Cook:** 35 min., **Other:** 10 min.

Tip: For a thinner glaze, add more milk, 1 teaspoon at a time.

Mary Lou Cook
Welches, Oregon

Rather than using Mexican chocolate that's flavored with cinnamon, almonds, and vanilla, **Mary Lou** put convenience first. She added all these flavors to a devil's food cake mix.

Peanut Butter Cup Bundt Cake

The title says it all. This simple-to-make cake has all of the great flavors of peanut butter cup candy.

¾ cup creamy peanut butter
½ cup butter or margarine, softened
1 cup granulated sugar
½ cup firmly packed brown sugar
2 large eggs
2 cups all-purpose flour
2 teaspoons baking powder
⅔ cup milk
2 teaspoons vanilla extract
⅔ cup semisweet chocolate mini-morsels
Chocolate Glaze

Beat first 4 ingredients at medium speed with an electric mixer until well blended. Add eggs, 1 at a time, beating just until blended after each addition.

Combine flour and baking powder in a small bowl; add to butter mixture alternately with milk, beginning and ending with flour mixture. Beat at low speed until blended after each addition. Stir in vanilla and chocolate morsels. Pour batter into a greased and floured 10-inch Bundt pan.

Bake at 325° for 55 to 60 minutes or until a wooden pick inserted in center comes out clean. Cool in pan on a wire rack 15 minutes. Remove from pan; cool completely on wire rack. Drizzle Chocolate Glaze evenly over cooled cake; let stand 30 minutes or until set.
Makes: 12 to 16 servings.
Prep: 20 min., **Cook:** 1 hr., **Other:** 45 min.

Chocolate Glaze:
½ cup semisweet chocolate mini-morsels
2 tablespoons butter or margarine
1 tablespoon light corn syrup
1 tablespoon milk

Combine all ingredients in a 2-cup glass measuring cup. Microwave at HIGH 1½ minutes, stirring until smooth
Makes: ½ cup.
Prep: 3 min.

Debra Carter
Eureka Springs, Arkansas

Debra pours the hot glaze over the cooled cake, then lets the cake stand until the glaze is set.

Chocolate Cake in a Cup

These yummy little cakes ooze soft chocolate from the center when you spoon into them. Serve with a scoop of vanilla ice cream for a sinfully good dessert.

1 cup all-purpose flour
¾ cup unsweetened cocoa
1½ teaspoons baking powder
6 tablespoons butter or margarine, melted
⅔ cup granulated sugar
⅔ cup firmly packed light brown sugar
1 cup egg substitute
1½ teaspoons vanilla extract
¼ teaspoon almond extract
1 cup (6-ounce package) semisweet chocolate morsels

Sift together flour, cocoa, and baking powder in a medium bowl; set aside.
Whisk together butter and next 5 ingredients in a large bowl. Add dry ingredients; combine well. Spoon batter into 8 lightly greased 6-ounce custard cups or ramekins. Sprinkle each with 2 tablespoons morsels. Cover and chill at least 2 hours. Bake, uncovered, at 350° for 22 minutes. (Edges will be set and centers will be soft.) Let stand 5 minutes before serving. **Makes:** 8 servings.
Prep: 21 min., **Cook:** 22 min., **Other:** 2 hrs., 5 min.

Note: To eliminate the risk of salmonella contamination, this recipe uses egg substitute instead of real eggs because the cakes aren't in the oven long enough for eggs to cook thoroughly.

Wanda Bullock
Calvert City, Kentucky

Wanda has the right idea for a make-ahead dessert for eight. She chills the batter-filled custard cups until serving time. Then the cups are baked and everyone receives their own warm-from-the-oven molten chocolate cake.

Strawberry-Nut Pinwheel Shortcake

The combination of pecans and strawberries is delicious in this spiral version of shortcake. Try vanilla ice cream in place of whipped cream for a cool summer treat.

7   cups sliced strawberries
    (2 quarts whole)
1   cup granulated sugar
2¼ cups all-purpose flour
2¼ teaspoons baking powder
¾   teaspoon salt
¼   cup granulated sugar
¼   teaspoon ground cinnamon
¾   cup cold butter or margarine,
    cut into small pieces
⅔   cup milk
⅔   cup firmly packed brown sugar
2   tablespoons butter or
    margarine, melted
⅓   cup finely chopped pecans
1   cup heavy whipping cream
¼   cup sifted powdered sugar

Combine strawberries and 1 cup granulated sugar in a large bowl, tossing gently to coat. Let stand at room temperature 1 hour; toss gently. Cover and chill 1 to 2 hours.

Meanwhile, combine flour and next 4 ingredients in a large bowl; cut in ¾ cup butter with a pastry blender until mixture is crumbly. Add milk, stirring with a fork just until flour is moistened. Turn dough out onto a lightly floured surface, and knead 4 or 5 times.

Roll dough into a 12-inch square. Combine brown sugar and 2 tablespoons melted butter; sprinkle over dough, patting gently with fingers. Sprinkle with pecans. Roll up, jellyroll fashion; pinch seams and ends to seal.

Cut roll into 12 (1-inch) slices. Place slices, 1½ inches apart, on a lightly greased baking sheet. Bake at 425° for 15 minutes or until lightly browned. Remove pinwheels from oven, and cool on wire racks.

Beat whipping cream at medium speed with an electric mixer until foamy; gradually add powdered sugar, beating until soft peaks form.

Place 1 pinwheel on each serving plate; spoon strawberry mixture over pinwheels. Dollop shortcakes with whipped cream.
Makes: 12 servings.
Prep: 48 min., **Cook:** 15 min., **Other:** 3 hrs.

Janice Workman
Salem, Kentucky

La Petite Pineapple Cakes With Praline Sauce

One of our favorite things about this recipe was the wonderful texture produced by using a sweet corn muffin mix in the batter. Similar to northern Italian polenta cake, these individual cakes are moist, yet coarser than traditional cakes made with cake flour.

1   (8.5-ounce) package corn
    muffin mix
1   (20-ounce) can crushed
    pineapple in juice, drained and
    divided
1   large egg
½   cup milk
½   cup sweetened flaked coconut
2   tablespoons butter, melted
1   cup plus 2 tablespoons firmly
    packed brown sugar, divided
⅓   cup all-purpose flour
1   (2-ounce) package macadamia
    nut pieces
½   cup butter
1½ cups heavy whipping cream,
    divided
1   tablespoon granulated sugar

Combine corn muffin mix, ¾ cup pineapple, egg, milk, and coconut; stir just until blended.

Combine melted butter, 2 tablespoons brown sugar, flour, and macadamia nuts to form a streusel topping.

Spoon batter into 12 greased muffin pans, filling two-thirds full. Sprinkle streusel mixture evenly over batter. Bake at 350° for 22 to 25 minutes or until golden. Remove from pans, and cool on wire racks.

Meanwhile, combine ½ cup butter, 1 cup brown sugar, and ½ cup whipping cream in a small saucepan over medium heat. Bring to a boil; remove from heat, and add remaining ½ cup pineapple.

Combine remaining 1 cup whipping cream and 1 tablespoon granulated sugar in a medium bowl, and beat at medium-high speed with an electric mixer until soft peaks form.

Serve each individual cake with praline sauce and whipped cream. **Makes:** 12 servings.
Prep: 10 min., **Cook:** 32 min.

Christie Burns
Vilonia, Arkansas

When **Christie** wants to make these little cakes extra special, she garnishes them with macadamia nuts, toasted coconut, and pineapple.

**Strawberry-Nut
Pinwheel Shortcake**

Miniature Mascarpone-Mint Ganache Cakes

Creamy mint filling and smooth chocolate ganache blend with a moist chocolate cake for a special dessert that got top ratings from our taste-testing panel.

1   cup all-purpose flour
1   cup granulated sugar
½   cup unsweetened cocoa
1   teaspoon baking soda
¼   teaspoon salt
1   cup brewed coffee
½   cup butter
1   large egg
¼   cup butter, softened
½   cup mascarpone cheese
2   cups sifted powdered sugar
½   teaspoon peppermint extract
½   cup heavy whipping cream
¼   cup loosely packed fresh mint
    leaves
1¼ cups semisweet chocolate
    morsels
Powdered sugar
Garnish: mint leaves

Sift together flour, granulated sugar, cocoa, soda, and salt in a large bowl. Combine coffee and ½ cup butter in a small saucepan; cook over medium heat until butter melts. Gradually add coffee mixture to flour mixture, beating at medium speed with an electric mixer until combined. Add egg, and beat until blended.

Spoon batter evenly into 6 lightly greased jumbo muffin pans. Bake at 350° for 23 minutes or until a wooden pick inserted in center comes out clean. Cool in pans on a wire rack 20 minutes; run a knife around edges of each muffin pan to loosen cakes. Invert cakes onto a wire rack, and cool completely.

Beat ¼ cup butter and mascarpone cheese at medium speed until creamy; gradually add 2 cups powdered sugar and extract, beating until smooth.

Split cooled cakes in half horizontally. Spread cheese mixture between layers and on top and sides of each cake. Freeze cakes 15 minutes.

Meanwhile, combine cream and ¼ cup mint leaves in a 2-cup glass measuring cup. Microwave at HIGH 1 to 1½ minutes or until mixture boils. Pour mixture through a wire-mesh strainer into a small bowl, discarding mint. Add morsels, stirring until melted.

Pour ganache over cakes, coating tops and sides. Chill 1 hour or until set. Dust cakes with powdered sugar; garnish, if desired. Store in refrigerator. **Makes:** 6 servings.
Prep: 26 min., **Cook:** 26 min., **Other:** 1 hr., 15 min.

Note: If you don't already own a jumbo muffin pan, this recipe is worth the investment—which doesn't have to be much. Jumbo muffin pans are readily available in a variety of stores from discount super centers to specialty kitchen shops. In addition to creating an assortment of miniature cakes, you can use this pan to make wonderful jumbo bakery-style breakfast muffins. This recipe does not work in regular-size muffin pans.

Beth Royals
Richmond, Virginia

Frozen Chocolate-Caramel Cheesecakes

If you've been dreaming of a light and fluffy dessert, these billowy cheesecake pies with a caramel-toffee crunch will have you floating on cloud nine.

1   (8-ounce) package cream
    cheese, softened
1   (14-ounce) can sweetened
    condensed milk
2   cups (12-ounce package)
    semisweet chocolate morsels
1   (10-ounce) package almond
    toffee bits
2   (8-ounce) containers frozen
    whipped topping, thawed
¼   cup butter
1   cup chopped pecans
3   (6-ounce) ready-made graham
    cracker crusts
1   (12.25-ounce) jar caramel
    topping

Beat cream cheese at medium speed with an electric mixer until smooth. Add milk, beating until blended. Stir in chocolate morsels and toffee bits; fold in whipped topping.

Melt butter in a large nonstick skillet over medium-high heat. Add pecans; cook 5 minutes or until toasted, stirring constantly. Set aside.

Spread 1½ cups cream cheese mixture into each crust. Drizzle about 2 tablespoons caramel topping over each pie; sprinkle each pie with about 2 tablespoons toasted pecans. Spread remaining cream cheese mixture evenly over pecans. Drizzle remaining caramel topping over each pie; sprinkle with remaining toasted pecans. Cover and freeze 8 hours. **Makes:** 3 pies (8 servings each).
Prep: 15 min., **Cook:** 5 min., **Other:** 8 hrs.

Tip: You can substitute a chocolate graham cracker crust for the regular graham cracker crust.

Melissa Yarbrough
Paducah, Kentucky

Melissa lets the pies stand at room temperature a few minutes before serving so they are easier to slice.

Chocolate-Almond Cheesecake

Calling all chocoholics—this one's for you!

1½ cups chocolate wafer crumbs
3 tablespoons sugar
⅓ cup butter, melted
¼ cup finely chopped almonds
3 (8-ounce) packages cream cheese, softened
¾ cup sugar
2 tablespoons all-purpose flour
4 large eggs
2 cups (12-ounce package) semisweet chocolate morsels, melted
1 teaspoon almond extract
¾ cup sour cream
2 cups (12-ounce package) semisweet chocolate morsels
2 tablespoons shortening
Garnish: slivered almonds

Combine first 4 ingredients in a medium bowl; firmly press crumb mixture evenly into bottom and up sides of a lightly greased 9-inch springform pan. Bake at 350° for 10 minutes. Remove from oven; set aside.

Beat cream cheese at high speed with an electric mixer until creamy; gradually add ¾ cup sugar and flour, mixing well. Add eggs, 1 at a time, beating after each addition. Stir in melted chocolate and almond extract; beat until well blended. Stir in sour cream, blending well. Pour into prepared crust.

Bake at 350° for 15 minutes. Reduce temperature to 225°; bake 1 hour or until cheesecake is almost set. Turn oven off, and partially open door; leave cake in oven 1 hour. Remove from oven; cool to room temperature on a wire rack. Cover and chill at least 8 hours. Run a knife around edge of pan, and release sides.

Place chocolate morsels and shortening in top of a double boiler; place over simmering water, and cook until chocolate melts, stirring often. Spoon glaze over cheesecake. Garnish, if desired. Store in refrigerator. **Makes:** 12 servings.

Prep: 29 min., **Cook:** 1 hr., 25 min., **Other:** 9 hrs.

Tip: Dip knife into hot water for easier cutting.

Barbara Neri
Syracuse, New York

Double-Chocolate Cheesecake With Praline Nut Topping

While this cheesecake's crunchy praline topping may have initially caught your attention, it's the surprise inside you'll love—a touch of cinnamon in the crust and a wonderful chocolate swirl.

1½ cups graham cracker crumbs (about 12 crackers)
¼ cup granulated sugar
1½ teaspoons ground cinnamon
6 tablespoons butter, melted
4 (8-ounce) packages cream cheese, softened
1 cup granulated sugar
⅛ teaspoon salt
5 large eggs
1 (8-ounce) container sour cream
2 teaspoons vanilla extract
1 cup chopped white chocolate baking bars, melted
¼ teaspoon almond extract
1 cup (6-ounce package) semisweet chocolate morsels, melted
¾ cup firmly packed dark brown sugar
½ cup chopped pecans, toasted
¼ cup butter, melted

Stir together first 4 ingredients; press crumb mixture evenly into bottom and 1 inch up sides of a 9-inch springform pan. Set aside.

Beat cream cheese, 1 cup sugar, and salt at medium speed with an electric mixer until smooth. Add eggs, 1 at a time, beating just until blended after each addition. Add sour cream and vanilla, beating just until smooth.

Divide batter in half; fold white chocolate and almond extract into 1 portion. Pour into prepared crust. Fold semisweet chocolate into remaining half of batter. Drop chocolate batter evenly over white chocolate layer; gently swirl with a knife to create a marbled effect.

Bake at 325° for 1 hour and 10 minutes or until almost set. Remove pan from oven, and run a knife around edge of pan to loosen sides. Cool on a wire rack. **Combine** brown sugar, pecans, and butter in a small bowl. Sprinkle over cooled cheesecake. Cover and chill at least 8 hours. Store in refrigerator. **Makes:** 12 servings.

Prep: 32 min., **Cook:** 1 hr., 10 min., **Other:** 8 hrs.

Tip: A little swirling goes a long way. If you're looking for the perfect marbled effect, don't overwork your batter. Too much swirling will cause a muddy look rather than the distinct color contrast you're looking for.

Cindy Miller
China Grove, North Carolina

Triple-Layer Mint Cheesecake

Be sure to use real peppermint extract instead of imitation flavoring.

2   cups cream-filled chocolate
    sandwich cookie crumbs
    (about **22 cookies**)
¼   cup sugar
2   tablespoons butter or
    margarine, melted
4   (8-ounce) packages cream
    cheese, softened
1   cup sugar
4   large eggs
1   (8-ounce) container sour cream
1   teaspoon vanilla extract
1½ cups (12-ounce package)
    semisweet chocolate
    mini-morsels, divided
4   drops green liquid food coloring
½   teaspoon peppermint extract

Combine first 3 ingredients; stir well. Firmly press mixture into bottom and ½ inch up sides of a 9-inch springform pan. Bake at 325° for 12 minutes.

Beat cream cheese at medium speed with an electric mixer until creamy; gradually add 1 cup sugar, beating well. Add eggs, 1 at a time, beating after each addition and scraping sides and bottom as needed. Stir in sour cream and vanilla. Divide batter into thirds.

Microwave 1 cup mini-morsels at HIGH 1 minute or until melted and smooth; stir into one-third of cheesecake batter, stirring until combined. Add remaining mini-morsels to one-third of batter. Stir

Kelly garnishes this chocolate-mint cheesecake with fresh mint sprigs.

green food coloring and peppermint extract into remaining batter.

Pour melted chocolate batter into prepared crust; spoon mint batter gently over chocolate layer. Spoon chocolate morsel batter gently over mint layer. Bake at 325° for 1 hour and 5 minutes. Remove from oven; immediately run a knife around edge of pan, and release sides. Turn oven off, and partially open door; return cheesecake to oven, and cool in oven 45 minutes. Remove from oven; cool completely in pan on a wire rack. Cover and chill 8 hours or overnight. Store in refrigerator. **Makes:** 12 servings.

Prep: 45 min., **Cook:** 1 hr., 17 min., **Other:** 8 hrs., 45 min.

Kelly McLaughlin
Durham, North Carolina

Chocolate-Peanut Butter Cheesecake

Take this dessert to another level with a drizzle of chocolate or caramel sauce over each slice.

2   cups chocolate graham cracker
    crumbs (18 sheets crackers)
1   teaspoon sugar
⅓   cup butter, melted
1   cup (6-ounce package)
    semisweet chocolate morsels
5   (8-ounce) packages cream
    cheese, softened and divided
1   cup sugar, divided
5   large eggs
1   teaspoon vanilla extract
½   cup creamy peanut butter

Combine graham cracker crumbs, 1 teaspoon sugar, and butter; press mixture into bottom of a 9-inch springform pan.

Bake at 350° for 8 minutes. Remove from oven; set aside, and cool. Reduce oven temperature to 325°.

Melt morsels according to package directions; set aside.

Beat 3 packages cream cheese at medium speed with an electric mixer until smooth. Gradually add ½ cup sugar, beating until blended. Add 3 eggs, 1 at a time, beating well after each addition. Fold in melted chocolate and vanilla. Pour mixture into prepared pan; set aside.

Beat remaining 2 packages cream cheese at medium speed until smooth. Gradually add remaining ½ cup sugar, beating until blended. Add remaining

2 eggs, 1 at a time, beating well after each addition. Add peanut butter, beating just until combined. Carefully pour peanut butter mixture over chocolate mixture.

Bake at 325° for 1 hour or until center is almost set. Remove cheesecake from oven; cool on a wire rack. Cover and chill 8 hours or overnight. Gently run a knife around edge of pan, and release sides. Store in refrigerator. **Makes:** 12 servings.

Prep: 33 min., **Cook:** 1 hr., 8 min., **Other:** 8 hrs.

Lisa Coley
Elgin, South Carolina

**Triple-Layer Mint
Cheesecake**

Chocolate-Marbled White Chocolate Cheesecake

This black and white cheesecake has the perfect blend of creamy sweetness.

2   cups cream-filled chocolate
    sandwich cookie crumbs
    (about 22 cookies)
6   tablespoons butter, melted
1   cup white chocolate morsels
¾   cup semisweet chocolate
    morsels
3   (8-ounce) packages cream
    cheese, softened
1   cup sugar
3   large eggs
½   cup whipping cream
1½ teaspoons vanilla extract
Dash of salt

Combine cookie crumbs and butter in a medium bowl; press mixture into bottom and 1 inch up sides of a 9-inch springform pan. Set aside.

Place white chocolate morsels in top of a double boiler; bring water to a boil. Reduce heat to low; cook until chocolate melts, about 5 minutes. Pour into a small bowl; cool slightly.

Place semisweet morsels in top of a double boiler; bring water to a boil. Reduce heat to low; cook until chocolate melts, about 5 minutes. Pour into a small bowl; cool slightly.

Beat cream cheese at medium speed with an electric mixer until creamy; gradually add sugar, beating well. Add eggs, 1 at a time, beating until blended after each addition. Stir in whipping cream, vanilla, and salt.

Remove 1 cup batter; stir into melted semisweet chocolate until combined.

Stir melted white chocolate into remaining batter; pour batter into prepared crust.

Spoon reserved chocolate batter by rounded tablespoons onto white chocolate batter; swirl with knife to create a marbled effect.

Bake at 350° for 30 minutes. Reduce heat to 250°; bake 1 hour and 10 minutes or until cheesecake is almost set. Run a knife around edge of pan, and release sides. Cool completely in pan on a wire rack; cover and chill 8 hours. Store in refrigerator. **Makes:** 12 servings.
Prep: 14 min., **Cook:** 1 hr., 50 min.,
Other: 8 hrs.

Tip: If you don't have a double boiler, place the chocolate morsels in a microwave-safe bowl, and microwave at HIGH 1 minute, stirring once, until chocolate melts.

Drake Herrick
Lafayette, Louisiana

We used more cookie crumbs than **Drake** for a thicker chocolate crust. Although this cheesecake is ready to serve after chilling 8 hours, Drake says it's best to refrigerate overnight.

Milky Way Cheesecake

Because this velvety cake is laced with chewy, gooey caramel and chunky chocolate, it doesn't cut as neatly as smooth, creamy cheesecakes. But we promise you, no one will care once they taste it.

24 cream-filled chocolate sandwich
    cookies
⅓   cup butter, melted
4   (8-ounce) packages cream
    cheese, softened
1   (14-ounce) can sweetened
    condensed milk
2   cups (12-ounce package)
    semisweet chocolate morsels
4   eggs
1   teaspoon vanilla extract
1   (12-ounce) package semisweet
    chocolate chunks
18 fun-size chocolate-coated
    caramel and creamy nougat
    bars, chopped *

Process cookies in a food processor until finely crushed. With processor running, pour melted butter through food chute; pulse just until crumbs are moistened. Press crumb mixture into bottom and up sides of a 9-inch springform pan.

Beat cream cheese at medium speed with an electric mixer until creamy. Add condensed milk, beating until mixture is smooth.

Microwave chocolate morsels at HIGH 1 minute; stir until smooth. Add melted chocolate, eggs, and vanilla to cream cheese mixture, beating at low speed just until combined. Fold in chocolate chunks, then candy. Pour filling into prepared crust.

Bake at 300° for 55 minutes. Run a knife around edge of pan, and release sides. Cool completely on a wire rack. Cover and chill 8 hours. Store in refrigerator. **Makes:** 12 servings.
Prep: 35 min., **Cook:** 55 min.

★For testing purposes only, we used Milky Way Fun Size candy bars for the chocolate-coated caramel and creamy nougat bars.

John Duncan
Jasper, Indiana

Lemon Cheesecake With Warm Dried Cherry Sauce

This light lemon flavor pairs well with the bold taste of the cherry sauce.

1⅔ cups graham cracker crumbs
¼ cup sugar
¼ cup plus 2 tablespoons butter, melted
2 (8-ounce) packages cream cheese, softened
1½ tablespoons grated lemon rind
⅔ cup fresh lemon juice
2 teaspoons vanilla extract
½ cup sugar
½ teaspoon salt
6 large eggs
Warm Dried Cherry Sauce

Combine first 3 ingredients, mixing well. Press crumb mixture into bottom of a 9-inch springform pan.

Combine cream cheese, lemon rind, lemon juice, and vanilla; beat at high speed with an electric mixer until creamy. Gradually add ½ cup sugar and salt, beating well. Add eggs, 1 at a time, beating after each addition. Pour batter into prepared crust.

Bake at 325° for 50 minutes or until cheesecake is almost set. Turn oven off, and partially open door; leave cake in oven 1 hour. Remove from oven; run a knife around edge of pan, and release sides. Cool completely on a wire rack. Cover and chill at least 8 hours. Serve with Warm Dried Cherry Sauce. Store in refrigerator. **Makes:** 12 servings.
Prep: 20 min., **Cook:** 50 min., **Other:** 9 hrs.

Warm Dried Cherry Sauce:
1½ cups dried cherries
2 cups water
½ cup sugar
2½ tablespoons cornstarch
2½ tablespoons brandy

Combine all ingredients in a medium saucepan; stir well. Cook over medium heat 8 minutes or until thickened. Spoon sauce over cheesecake. **Makes:** 2 cups.
Prep: 3 min., **Cook:** 8 min.

Erin McCloskey
Venetia, Pennsylvania

Double-Lemon Raspberry Cheesecake

This lemon cheesecake gets extra zing from a creamy lemon sauce that's spooned over each serving.

1 cup vanilla wafer crumbs (22 wafers)
3 tablespoons sugar
½ teaspoon grated lemon rind
3 tablespoons butter, melted
3 (8-ounce) packages cream cheese, softened
1 cup sugar
3 tablespoons all-purpose flour
1 tablespoon grated lemon rind
2 tablespoons fresh lemon juice
½ teaspoon vanilla extract
3 large eggs
1 egg white
1 pint fresh raspberries
Lemon Sauce

Combine first 4 ingredients; press mixture into bottom of a 9-inch springform pan. Bake at 325° for 10 minutes. Remove from oven; set aside.

Beat cream cheese at medium speed with an electric mixer until smooth. Add sugar and next 4 ingredients, beating until blended. Add eggs and egg white, 1 at a time, beating well after each addition. Pour half of batter over cooled crust; top with raspberries, then remaining batter. Bake at 325° for 50 to 55 minutes or until almost set. Remove from oven; cool in pan on a wire rack 30 minutes. Cover and chill 8 hours. Serve with Lemon Sauce. Store in refrigerator. **Makes:** 12 servings.
Prep: 23 min., **Cook:** 1 hr., 5 min., **Other:** 8 hrs., 30 min..

Lemon Sauce:
¾ cup sugar
1½ teaspoons cornstarch
¼ cup butter, cut into small cubes
1 teaspoon grated lemon rind
3 tablespoons fresh lemon juice
1 large egg
2 egg yolks

Combine first 4 ingredients in top of a double boiler over simmering water. Cook, stirring constantly, 2 minutes or until sugar dissolves and butter melts.

Whisk together lemon juice and remaining ingredients in a small bowl; gradually add to butter mixture, whisking constantly. Cook 8 minutes or until thickened, whisking constantly. Pour into a small bowl; cover and chill. **Makes:** 1 cup.
Prep: 8 min., **Cook:** 10 min.

Dorothy Lacefield
Carrollton, Texas

When it comes to dessert, **Dorothy** knows how to do it right. She decorates the sides of this cheesecake with crushed store-bought lemon cookies, then garnishes the top of the cake with sweetened whipped cream, fresh raspberries, and lemon wedges.

White Chocolate-Hazelnut Crunch Cheesecake

So much goodness in one cake! White and semisweet chocolate, hazelnuts, and toffee bits to name a few. Satisfaction guaranteed with this mile-high cheesecake.

18 chocolate graham cracker sheets (2 cups crumbs)
½ cup chopped hazelnuts, toasted
¼ cup butter, melted
1 cup semisweet chocolate mini-morsels, melted
4 (8-ounce) packages cream cheese, softened
½ cup butter, softened
4 (4-ounce) packages white chocolate baking bars, melted
4 large eggs
1 egg yolk
1 (10-ounce) package almond toffee bits
¾ cup chopped hazelnuts, toasted
3 tablespoons hazelnut liqueur
1 tablespoon vanilla extract
¼ teaspoon ground nutmeg
1 (16-ounce) container sour cream

3 tablespoons sugar
1 tablespoon hazelnut liqueur
Sweetened whipped cream
Almond toffee bits
Chopped hazelnuts, toasted

Process graham crackers and ½ cup hazelnuts in a food processor until finely ground. Add melted butter; pulse 4 or 5 times or until blended. Press mixture into bottom and 1½ inches up sides of a 10-inch springform pan; freeze 15 minutes. Carefully spread melted mini-morsels over frozen crust. Freeze 15 minutes.

Meanwhile, beat cream cheese and softened butter at medium speed with an electric mixer just until smooth. Add melted white chocolate, beating just until blended.

Add eggs, 1 at a time, and yolk, beating just until blended after each addition. Stir in toffee bits and next 4 ingredients. Pour batter into prepared crust.

Bake at 325° for 1 hour and 15 minutes or until almost set.

Meanwhile, combine sour cream, sugar, and 1 tablespoon liqueur in a medium bowl. Remove cheesecake from oven; carefully spoon sour cream mixture evenly over cheesecake.

Bake 15 more minutes; remove from oven. Run a knife around edge of pan, and release sides. Cool completely on a wire rack. Cover and chill 8 hours. Serve with sweetened whipped cream, toffee bits, and hazelnuts. Store in refrigerator. **Makes:** 16 servings.

Prep: 41 min., **Cook:** 1 hr., 30 min., **Other:** 8 hrs., 30 min.

Tip: There are 8 cups of batter for this stately cheesecake. Once the sour cream mixture is added, the pan will be very full, so be careful when transferring to and from the oven.

Alberta Dunbar
San Diego, California

Lemon-Raspberry Cheesecake

Nikita uses frozen raspberries in this tart dessert, but we preferred the taste, texture, and appearance of the fresh berries.

1 cup graham cracker crumbs
5 tablespoons butter or margarine, melted
3 tablespoons sugar
3 (8-ounce) packages cream cheese, softened
1½ cups sugar
1 tablespoon grated lemon rind
¾ cup fresh lemon juice
2 teaspoons all-purpose flour
4 large eggs
1 pint fresh raspberries

Combine graham cracker crumbs, butter, and 3 tablespoons sugar. Press into bottom of an 8-inch springform pan; set aside.

Beat cream cheese at medium speed with an electric mixer until smooth. Add 1½ cups sugar and next 3 ingredients, beating until blended. Add eggs, 1 at a time, beating well after each addition.

Pour half of batter into prepared pan. Sprinkle with raspberries; pour remaining batter over raspberries. Bake at 325° for 1 hour and 30 minutes or until cheesecake is almost set. Turn oven off, and partially open door; leave cake in oven 1 hour. Remove from oven; run a knife around edge of pan, and release sides. Cool completely on a wire rack. Cover and chill 8 hours. Store in refrigerator. **Makes:** 10 servings.

Prep: 11 min., **Cook:** 1 hr., 30 min., **Other:** 9 hrs.

Nikita Chaffin
Atlanta, Georgia

White Chocolate-Hazelnut
Crunch Cheesecake

White Chocolate-Raspberry Cheesecake

Raspberry preserves and syrup combine to make a luscious, spreadable raspberry layer in this cheesecake.

1½ cups graham cracker crumbs
3   tablespoons sugar
½   cup butter, melted
2   cups (12-ounce package) white chocolate morsels
5   (8-ounce) packages cream cheese, softened
1   cup sugar
2   large eggs
1   tablespoon vanilla extract
⅔   cup raspberry preserves
2   tablespoons raspberry syrup*
Garnish: white chocolate curls*

Combine first 3 ingredients; press into bottom of a 9-inch springform pan. Bake at 350° for 8 minutes; cool slightly.
Place chocolate morsels in top of a double boiler; bring water to a boil. Reduce heat to low; cook, stirring constantly, until chocolate melts. Cool slightly.
Beat cream cheese at medium speed with an electric mixer until creamy; gradually add 1 cup sugar, beating well. Add eggs, 1 at a time, beating after each addition. Stir in vanilla. Add melted chocolate, beating well.
Combine raspberry preserves and raspberry syrup in a small bowl; stir well.
Spoon half of cream cheese batter into prepared crust; spread half of raspberry mixture over batter, leaving a ¾-inch border. Spoon remaining cream cheese batter around edges of pan, spreading towards the center. Cover remaining raspberry mixture and chill.
Bake at 350° for 50 minutes or until cheesecake is just set and slightly browned. Remove from oven; cool completely on a wire rack. Cover and chill at least 8 hours.
Run a knife around edge of pan, and release sides. Pour remaining raspberry mixture on top of cheesecake, leaving a 1-inch border. Garnish, if desired. Store in refrigerator. **Makes:** 12 servings.
Prep: 22 min., **Cook:** 58 min., **Other:** 8 hrs.

*If you can't find raspberry syrup in your grocery store, use ¾ cup raspberry preserves, and heat in microwave until preserves melt.

*To make curls out of white chocolate baking squares, pull a vegetable peeler along the narrow edge of each square.

Darlene Evans
Marshall, Texas

Piña Colada Cheesecake

With a creamy, soft-whipped texture and a touch of rum, this cheesecake takes on the characteristics of a frothy, cold piña colada. So pick up your fork, not your straw, and indulge in this tropical treat.

33   shortbread cookies (2 cups crumbs)
¼   cup butter, melted
4   (8-ounce) packages cream cheese, softened
1   cup sugar
3   large eggs
1   (10-ounce) can frozen piña colada mix concentrate, thawed
1   tablespoon coconut extract
2   (8-ounce) cans crushed pineapple in juice, drained and patted dry
Rum-Spiked Whipped Cream
1   cup coconut, toasted

Process shortbread cookies in a food processor until finely ground. Add butter; pulse 3 or 4 times or until blended. Press firmly into bottom of a 9-inch springform pan.
Beat cream cheese and sugar at medium speed with an electric mixer until smooth. Add eggs, 1 at a time, beating just until blended after each addition. Stir in piña colada mix and coconut extract. Pour into prepared crust.
Bake at 350° for 30 minutes. Turn oven off. Let cheesecake stand in oven, with door closed, 1 hour. Remove from oven, and run a knife around edge of pan, and release sides. Cool completely on a wire rack. Cover and chill at least 8 hours. Sprinkle pineapple evenly over cheesecake. Spread Rum-Spiked Whipped Cream over pineapple; sprinkle with coconut. Store in refrigerator. **Makes:** 12 servings.
Prep: 24 min., **Cook:** 30 min., **Other:** 9 hrs.

Rum-Spiked Whipped Cream:
1   cup heavy whipping cream
½   cup powdered sugar
2   tablespoons light rum
1   tablespoon coconut extract

Beat whipping cream at medium speed with an electric mixer until foamy; gradually add powdered sugar, rum, and coconut extract, beating until soft peaks form. **Makes:** 2½ cups.
Prep: 10 min.

Tip: The unusually short cook time is key to this dessert's frothy texture. It will not set up to be a firm cheesecake.

Jennifer H. Gentle
Birmingham, Alabama

Apple Pie Cheesecake With Warm Caramel Sauce

Just like eating a caramel apple . . . gourmet style.

18 honey graham cracker sheets
1 tablespoon sugar
½ teaspoon ground cinnamon
½ cup butter, melted
3 (8-ounce) packages cream
   cheese, softened
1 cup sugar
¾ teaspoon ground cinnamon
⅛ teaspoon ground nutmeg
3 large eggs
1 (8-ounce) container sour cream
½ teaspoon vanilla extract
1 (21-ounce) can apple pie filling
½ cup raisins
Caramel Sauce

Process graham crackers, 1 tablespoon sugar, and ½ teaspoon cinnamon in a food processor until finely ground. Add butter; pulse 4 or 5 times or until blended. Press mixture into bottom and 1 inch up sides of a 10-inch springform pan; set aside.

Beat cream cheese at medium speed with an electric mixer until smooth. Combine 1 cup sugar, ¾ teaspoon cinnamon, and nutmeg. Add to cream cheese, beating just until blended. **Add** eggs, 1 at a time, beating just until blended after each addition. Add sour cream and vanilla, beating just until blended. Pour half of batter into prepared crust.

Combine apple pie filling and raisins in a medium bowl; spoon evenly over cheesecake layer. Pour remaining half of cheesecake batter over fruit layer.

Bake at 325° for 1 hour and 15 minutes or until almost set. Remove from oven; run a knife around edge of pan, and release sides. Cool completely on a wire rack. Cover and chill 8 hours. Serve with warm Caramel Sauce. Store in refrigerator.
Makes: 16 servings.
Prep: 32 min., **Cook:** 1 hr., 15 min., **Other:** 8 hrs.

Caramel Sauce:
1 (14-ounce) package caramels
1 (5-ounce) can evaporated milk

Combine caramels and milk in a large saucepan; cook over medium-low heat until caramels are melted and smooth, stirring often. **Makes:** 1⅔ cups.
Prep: 5 min., **Cook:** 9 min.

Tip: Let caramel sauce cool 10 minutes before serving over your cheesecake to prevent melting.

Tip: Don't spoon too much apple filling in one area of your cheesecake batter because it will sink. To spread apple filling evenly over your cheesecake batter, dollop teaspoonfuls randomly over the batter, and then use your fingers to fan out the apples.

Sheryl Hall
Marriottsville, Maryland

Caramel Pecan Crunch Cheesecake

Dark brown sugar gives a wonderful caramel flavor and crunchy topping to this cheesecake.

1 cup graham cracker crumbs
¾ cup chopped pecans, toasted
¼ cup butter or margarine,
   melted
4 (8-ounce) packages cream
   cheese, softened
1 cup firmly packed dark brown
   sugar
¾ cup granulated sugar
4 large eggs
2 teaspoons vanilla extract
¼ cup firmly packed dark brown
   sugar
¼ cup chopped pecans, toasted

Combine graham cracker crumbs, ¾ cup pecans, and butter. Press into bottom of a 10-inch springform pan.
Beat cream cheese at medium speed with an electric mixer until smooth. Add

sugars, beating until blended. Add eggs, 1 at a time, beating well after each addition. Add vanilla, beating just until blended. Pour mixture into prepared pan. Bake at 325° for 55 minutes or until almost set. Turn oven off, and partially open door; leave cheesecake in oven 1 hour.

Remove cheesecake from oven; cool in pan on a wire rack 30 minutes. Cover and chill 8 hours. Run a knife around edges of pan, and release sides.

Sprinkle cake with ¼ cup brown sugar. Broil 5½ inches from heat 2 to 4 minutes or until sugar begins to melt. Sprinkle with ¼ cup pecans. Store in refrigerator. **Makes:** 16 servings.
Prep: 21 min., **Cook:** 59 min., **Other:** 9 hrs., 30 min.

Franki Hyde Martin
Pauline, South Carolina

Franki got coworkers to taste this cheesecake as she perfected it for the Cook-Off entry. They thought it was scrumptious and begged her to retest it every week. Franki tops each slice with a dollop of whipped cream and a couple of toasted pecan halves.

Caramel-Pumpkin Cheesecake With Gingersnap-Pecan Crust

With a yummy gingersnap cookie crust, this creamy pumpkin cheesecake is just what you need to wow your dinner guests during the autumn season.

12 crisp gingersnaps
1 cup all-purpose flour
⅔ cup chopped pecans
⅓ cup firmly packed light brown sugar
½ cup butter, softened
4 (8-ounce) packages cream cheese, softened
1⅔ cups granulated sugar
4 large eggs
1 cup canned unsweetened pumpkin
8 tablespoons whipping cream, divided
1 teaspoon pumpkin pie spice
1 teaspoon ground cinnamon
½ teaspoon ground allspice
3 tablespoons caramel topping

Process first 4 ingredients in a food processor until finely ground. Add butter; pulse 8 to 10 times or until blended. Press mixture into bottom and 1½ inches up sides of a 9-inch springform pan.

Bake at 350° for 20 minutes. Cool completely on a wire rack.

Beat cream cheese at medium speed with an electric mixer until smooth. Add granulated sugar, beating just until blended. Reserve ¾ cup cream cheese mixture for topping; cover and chill. Add eggs, 1 at a time, to remaining cream cheese mixture, beating just until blended after each addition.

Combine pumpkin, 5 tablespoons whipping cream, and next 3 ingredients; add to cream cheese mixture, beating just until blended. Pour batter into prepared crust.

Bake at 325° for 1 hour and 15 minutes. Turn oven off. Let cheesecake stand in oven, with door closed, 1 hour. Remove from oven, and run a knife around edge of pan, and release sides. Cool on a wire rack. Soften reserved cream cheese mixture; spread evenly over cheesecake. Drizzle caramel topping over cream cheese layer; gently swirl with a knife to create a marbled effect. Cover and chill 8 hours. Store in refrigerator. **Makes:** 12 servings.
Prep: 29 min., **Cook:** 1 hr., 35 min., **Other:** 9 hrs.

Tip: Make sure you don't cut into the cheesecake when swirling the caramel layer.

Lynn Podsiadlo
Alpharetta, Georgia

Pumpkin Cheesecake With Caramelized Pecan Topping

Perfect for an intimate get-together, this dessert serves up to 8 people.

1 cup graham cracker crumbs
¼ cup granulated sugar
¼ cup butter, melted
2 (8-ounce) packages cream cheese, softened
½ cup granulated sugar
½ cup canned pumpkin
1 teaspoon lemon juice
½ teaspoon vanilla extract
2 large eggs
½ teaspoon ground cinnamon
⅛ teaspoon ground nutmeg
⅛ teaspoon ground cloves
3 tablespoons butter, softened
⅓ cup firmly packed light brown sugar
⅓ cup chopped pecans

Stir together first 3 ingredients. Press crumb mixture into bottom and up sides of an 8-inch springform pan.

Bake crust at 325° for 8 minutes. Cool on a wire rack.

Beat cream cheese and next 4 ingredients at medium speed with an electric mixer until smooth. Add eggs, 1 at a time, beating until blended after each addition. Stir in cinnamon, nutmeg, and cloves. Pour mixture into prepared crust.

Bake at 325° for 40 minutes or until almost set. Remove cheesecake from oven; gently run a knife around edge of pan, and release sides. Cool completely on a wire rack. Cover and chill 8 hours.

Stir together 3 tablespoons butter, brown sugar, and pecans; spoon over top of cheesecake.

Broil 3 inches from heat for 3 minutes or until mixture begins to bubble. Let stand 10 minutes before serving. Store in refrigerator. **Makes:** 8 servings.
Prep: 15 min., **Cook:** 51 min., **Other:** 8 hrs., 10 min.

Tip: Use a straight-sided glass to press crumb mixture onto bottom and up sides of springform pan.

Deborah Fiedler
Pasadena, Maryland

Yummy Cappuccino Mocha Torte

With its "frothlike" chocolate mousse topping and a wonderful chocolate coffee fudge center, this dessert is just what the title says—yummy!

4   graham cracker sheets
½   cup chopped walnuts
½   cup slivered almonds
¼   cup granulated sugar
½   teaspoon salt
5   tablespoons unsalted butter, melted
2   cups whipping cream
4   (4-ounce) packages semisweet chocolate baking bars, finely chopped
½   cup unsalted butter, cut into pieces
2   tablespoons light corn syrup
3   (4-ounce) packages semisweet chocolate baking bars, finely chopped
6   tablespoons unsalted butter, cut into pieces
6   teaspoons instant coffee granules, divided
½   cup granulated sugar
3   tablespoons water
5   egg whites
1¾ cups whipping cream, divided
¼   cup powdered sugar
¼   teaspoon ground cinnamon

Process first 5 ingredients in a food processor until mixture becomes fine crumbs. Add 5 tablespoons melted butter; pulse 3 or 4 times or until combined. Firmly press crumb mixture into bottom and 1 inch up sides of a 10-inch springform pan.

Bake at 350° for 15 minutes. Cool completely on a wire rack.

Heat 2 cups whipping cream in a large saucepan over medium heat; bring to a simmer. Remove pan from heat, and add 16 ounces chocolate, stirring until chocolate melts. Add ½ cup butter and corn syrup, stirring until smooth. Pour fudge into prepared pan. Chill 1 hour or until firm.

Heat 12 ounces chocolate, 6 tablespoons butter, and 1 teaspoon coffee granules in a saucepan over low heat, stirring constantly, until chocolate is melted and smooth. Pour chocolate mixture into a small bowl. Set aside.

Bring ½ cup granulated sugar and 3 tablespoons water to a boil in a small heavy saucepan over medium heat, stirring constantly. Cook mixture 2 minutes or until a candy thermometer registers 240° (soft ball stage).

Meanwhile, beat egg whites at high speed with an electric mixer until soft peaks form. Gradually beat hot syrup into egg whites. Continue beating until medium-stiff peaks form, about 3 minutes. Fold in 1 cup reserved chocolate mixture. Spread cappuccino mixture evenly over fudge layer.

Combine ¼ cup whipping cream and remaining 5 teaspoons coffee granules in a large bowl, whisking until coffee dissolves. Add remaining 1½ cups whipping cream, powdered sugar, and cinnamon. Beat at high speed with an electric mixer until stiff peaks form. Fold in remaining ½ cup chocolate mixture. Reserve 2 cups mousse; spread remaining mousse evenly over cappuccino layer. Pipe reserved mousse around top of cake. Cover and chill 8 hours. Store in refrigerator. **Makes:** 16 servings.

Prep: 34 min., **Cook:** 34 min., **Other:** 9 hrs.

Tip: When preparing the mousse, the reserved chocolate will be a bit thick, causing a speckled look in the mousse mixture. For a fun touch, top this mousse layer with large chocolate curls.

Kory Murphy
Jacksonville, Florida

Pumpkin Praline Torte

Pumpkin Praline Torte

This cake can be sliced soon after preparing, but for best results, let it chill several hours.

- ¾ cup firmly packed brown sugar
- ⅓ cup butter
- 3 tablespoons whipping cream
- ¾ cup chopped pecans
- 1⅔ cups granulated sugar
- 1 cup vegetable oil
- 4 large eggs
- 1 (15-ounce) can unsweetened pumpkin
- ¼ teaspoon vanilla extract
- 2 cups all-purpose flour
- 2 teaspoons baking powder
- 1 teaspoon baking soda
- 1 teaspoon salt
- 2 teaspoons pumpkin pie spice
- 1¾ cups whipping cream
- ¼ cup powdered sugar, sifted
- ¼ teaspoon vanilla extract
- ¼ cup chopped pecans, toasted

Combine first 3 ingredients in a medium saucepan. Cook over medium heat 5 minutes, stirring constantly, or until sugar dissolves; pour evenly into 2 lightly greased 9-inch round cakepans. Sprinkle ¾ cup pecans evenly over brown sugar mixture in pans.

Beat granulated sugar and oil at medium speed with an electric mixer until smooth. Add eggs, 1 at a time, beating until blended. Add pumpkin and ¼ teaspoon vanilla, beating just until blended.

Combine flour and next 4 ingredients; add to pumpkin mixture, beating just until blended. Spoon over pecans in pans. Bake at 350° for 30 minutes or until a wooden pick inserted in center comes out clean. Cool in pans on wire racks 5 minutes. Carefully loosen cake from edges of pan (do not tear pecans from cake). Remove cake from pans, and cool completely on wire racks.

Beat 1¾ cups whipping cream at medium speed until frothy. Add powdered sugar and ¼ teaspoon vanilla; beat at medium-high speed until soft peaks form.

Place 1 cake layer, praline side up, on a cake plate. Spread half of whipped cream over cake layer; top with remaining cake layer, praline side up. Spread remaining whipped cream over cake layer. Sprinkle with ¼ cup toasted pecans. Cover and chill. Store in refrigerator. **Makes:** 12 to 15 servings.

Prep: 26 min., **Cook:** 35 min.

Candyce Rector
Hixson, Tennessee

Chocolate Kahlúa Macadamia Madness

Grated orange rind adds a citrus twist to this chocolate-espresso flavored torte, but feel free to leave it out, if you're a chocolate purist.

- 1½ cups semisweet chocolate morsels
- 1 cup unsalted butter
- 6 large eggs
- ¾ cup sugar
- ⅓ cup coffee liqueur
- 1 teaspoon vanilla extract
- 1½ cups unsweetened cocoa
- 1 teaspoon instant espresso granules *
- ½ teaspoon ground cinnamon
- 1 cup chopped macadamia nuts, toasted
- 1 teaspoon grated orange rind (optional)
- Ganache

Combine chocolate morsels and butter in a medium saucepan; cook over medium heat until melted, stirring often. Set aside; cool slightly.

Whisk together eggs and next 3 ingredients in a medium bowl. Add melted chocolate mixture, cocoa, and next 4 ingredients; stir until well combined. Pour into a lightly greased 9-inch springform pan. Bake at 350° for 40 minutes or until set. Cool on a wire rack 30 minutes. Cover and chill 1 hour.

Run a knife around edge of pan, and release sides. Spread top of cake with Ganache, allowing it to run down sides. Cover loosely, and chill 8 hours. Store in refrigerator. **Makes:** 12 servings.

Prep: 11 min., **Cook:** 45 min., **Other:** 9 hrs., 30 min.

*If you can't find instant espresso granules or desire a more subtle coffee flavor, substitute instant coffee granules for the instant espresso granules.

Ganache:

- ½ cup heavy whipping cream
- ¼ cup unsalted butter
- 1½ cups semisweet chocolate morsels
- 1 tablespoon coffee liqueur

Microwave cream and butter in a medium microwave-safe bowl at HIGH 1 minute or until hot. Add chocolate morsels and coffee liqueur, stirring until chocolate is melted. **Makes:** 1½ cups.

Prep: 5 min.

Robert Gadsby
Great Falls, Montana

Robert garnishes each slice of "madness" with a dollop of whipped cream and a sprinkle of ground cinnamon and grated orange rind.

Marbleized Flourless Chocolate Torte

1 (4-ounce) white chocolate
  baking bar, finely chopped
3 tablespoons butter
2 teaspoons almond extract
5 large eggs, divided
2 cups (12-ounce package)
  semisweet chocolate morsels
¼ cup butter
¾ cup strong brewed coffee
1 cup (6-ounce package)
  semisweet chocolate morsels
Praline Topping
Crème Chantilly

Place white chocolate and 3 tablespoons butter in top of a double boiler; bring water to a boil. Reduce heat to low; cook, stirring constantly, until melted and smooth. Stir in extract. Pour into a small bowl; cool. Beat in 1 egg with an electric mixer until smooth. Cover and chill.

Meanwhile, place 2 cups semisweet chocolate morsels, ¼ cup butter, and coffee in top of double boiler; bring water to a boil. Reduce heat to low; cook, stirring constantly, until melted and smooth. Remove from heat. Pour into a medium bowl, and cool. Beat in 4 eggs, 1 at a time, with an electric mixer until smooth. Cover and chill.

Pour semisweet chocolate mixture into a greased and aluminum foil-lined 8-inch springform pan. Drop white chocolate mixture by tablespoonfuls over semisweet chocolate layer; gently swirl with a knife.

Bake at 350° for 45 minutes or until torte begins to pull away from sides of pan. Cool completely in pan on a wire rack. Cover and chill 8 hours.

Cut a 24- x 1½-inch strip of wax paper. Set aside.

Place 1 cup chocolate morsels in top of double boiler; bring water to a boil. Reduce heat to low; cook, stirring constantly, until chocolate is melted. Remove from heat; cool 10 to 12 minutes or until mixture reaches 90°, stirring occasionally. Spread tempered chocolate in a very thin layer over wax paper strip. Wrap chocolate ribbon around sides of chilled cake, paper side out. Let stand 15 minutes or until chocolate ribbon is firm. Carefully remove wax paper.

Fold 1 cup Praline Topping into Crème Chantilly; serve with cake. Store torte and crème in refrigerator. **Makes:** 10 to 12 servings.
Prep: 27 min., **Cook:** 57 min., **Other:** 9 hrs.

Kudos to **Amy** for sharing this incredible dessert with us. A dollop of sweetened whipped cream dotted with crunchy almond pralines offers the perfect contrast of textures to the dense, fudgy torte.

Praline Topping:
1¼ cups chopped almonds
¾ cup sugar

Combine almonds and sugar in a small heavy saucepan. Cook over medium-low heat 19 minutes or until sugar is melted and mixture is golden brown, stirring constantly. Spoon mixture onto a lightly greased baking sheet; cool completely. Break into pieces. **Makes:** 2¾ cups.
Prep: 5 min., **Cook:** 19 min.

Crème Chantilly:
1 cup heavy whipping cream
1 tablespoon powdered sugar
1 teaspoon vanilla extract

Beat whipping cream at high speed with an electric mixer until foamy. Gradually add sugar, beating until soft peaks form. Fold in vanilla. **Makes:** 2 cups.
Prep: 5 min.

Tips: To decorate your cake with the chocolate ribbon, work with it one section at a time. Place ribbon, wax paper side down, on working surface as you carefully wrap one end of the ribbon around the cake. Use remaining praline mixture as a crunchy topping on ice cream sundaes, waffles, and pudding cups.

Amy Watts
Cedar Hill, Texas

Granny's Raisin Bran-Oat Cookies

Each bite of these buttery, thin lace cookies will take you back to the good old days of childhood, sitting on the porch, sipping milk, and dunking these melt-in-your-mouth treats.

1 cup butter or margarine, softened
1 cup firmly packed brown sugar
½ cup granulated sugar
2 large eggs
1 teaspoon vanilla extract
1½ cups all-purpose flour
1 cup uncooked quick-cooking oats
1 teaspoon baking soda
1 teaspoon ground cinnamon
1 cup wheat bran flakes cereal with raisins and granola *
1 cup cinnamon morsels

Beat butter at medium speed with an electric mixer until creamy; gradually add sugars, beating well. Add eggs and vanilla, beating until blended.

Combine flour and next 3 ingredients. Gradually add to butter mixture, stirring until blended. Stir in cereal and morsels. Cover and chill 2 hours.

Drop dough by rounded tablespoonfuls 2 inches apart onto lightly greased baking sheets.

Bake at 350° for 14 minutes or until golden. Cool on baking sheets 2 minutes. Remove to wire racks to cool. **Makes:** 4 dozen.

Prep: 18 min., **Cook:** 14 min. per batch, **Other:** 2 hrs.

*For testing purposes only, we used Raisin Bran Crunch cereal.

Tip: This dough is very soft. It's essential that you chill the dough before baking in order to work with the dough.

Sally Adkins
Holmes Beach, Florida

Sally often uses peanut butter morsels in these cookies instead of cinnamon morsels. We tried both and thought they were equally delicious.

Twice-as-Nice Raisin Oatmeal Cookies

Soft and chewy, yummy and comforting—oatmeal raisin cookies just the way Grandma makes 'em.

1 cup raisins
Boiling water
1 teaspoon butter
1 cup chopped pecans
1 cup shortening
½ cup firmly packed brown sugar
½ cup granulated sugar
2 large eggs
1 teaspoon vanilla extract
2 cups all-purpose flour
2 cups uncooked quick-cooking oats
1 teaspoon baking soda
1 teaspoon ground cinnamon
¼ teaspoon salt

Combine raisins and boiling water to cover in a small bowl. Let stand 5 minutes; drain, reserving 2 tablespoons liquid. Pat raisins dry with paper towels.

Melt butter in a medium nonstick skillet. Add pecans; cook over medium heat 5 minutes or until toasted, stirring constantly. Set aside.

Beat shortening at medium speed with an electric mixer until creamy; gradually add sugars, beating well. Add reserved raisin liquid, eggs, and vanilla, beating until blended.

Combine flour and next 4 ingredients. Gradually add to shortening mixture, stirring until blended. Stir in raisins and pecans. Drop dough by rounded teaspoonfuls 2 inches apart onto lightly greased baking sheets.

Bake at 350° for 11 minutes or until edges are lightly browned. Cool on baking sheets 2 minutes. Remove to wire racks to cool. **Makes:** 5 dozen.

Prep: 20 min., **Cook:** 11 min. per batch, **Other:** 7 min.

Tip: When making cookies, always place cookie dough on cool baking sheets. Using sheets that have just been in the oven can cause cookie dough to spread too much.

Mary Conrad
Devine, Texas

Chocoholic's Dream Torte

Chocoholic's Dream Torte

This rich dessert made with dark, fudgy brownies smothered in thick, creamy chocolate and pecans will make any chocolate lover beg for more.

1   (19.8-ounce) package fudge brownie mix
½   cup vegetable oil
¼   cup water
2   large eggs
1   cup (6-ounce package) semisweet chocolate morsels, divided
⅔   cup milk chocolate morsels
1   cup whipping cream
2   tablespoons unsalted butter
⅓   cup chopped pecans
1   teaspoon vanilla extract
Chocolate Mousse
Garnishes: whipped cream, chopped pecans

Combine first 4 ingredients in a large bowl; beat with a wooden spoon 2 minutes. Stir in ⅓ cup semisweet chocolate morsels. Spread batter into a greased 10-inch springform pan. Bake at 350° for 35 minutes or until a wooden pick inserted in center comes out clean. Cool completely in pan on a wire rack.

Combine remaining ⅔ cup semisweet morsels, milk chocolate morsels, and whipping cream in top of a double boiler; bring water to a boil. Reduce heat to low; cook until chocolate melts, stirring often. Remove from heat; stir in butter until melted. Stir in pecans and vanilla; pour mixture into a medium bowl. Place bowl in larger bowl filled with ice. Cool mixture, stirring constantly, 6 minutes or until mixture is cool and slightly thickened.

Pour chocolate-pecan mixture evenly over cooled brownie layer; cover and chill at least 1 hour.

Run a knife around edge of pan, and release sides. Spread Chocolate Mousse evenly over chocolate-pecan layer. Chill 30 minutes before serving. Garnish, if desired. Store in refrigerator. **Makes:** 10 to 12 servings.

Prep: 10 min., **Cook:** 35 min., **Other:** 1 hr., 30 min.

Chocolate Mousse:

1   (3-ounce) package cream cheese, softened
2   tablespoons unsalted butter, softened
¾   cup powdered sugar
¼   cup unsweetened cocoa
1   tablespoon milk
½   teaspoon vanilla extract
¾   cup whipping cream

Beat cream cheese and butter in a medium bowl at medium speed with an electric mixer until creamy. Add powdered sugar and next 3 ingredients; beat until light and smooth.

In a small bowl, beat whipping cream at medium speed with an electric mixer until stiff peaks form. Fold into cream cheese mixture until combined. **Makes:** 2 cups.

Prep: 10 min.

Note: The chocolate-pecan layer in this dessert will not firm up in the refrigerator; just make sure that it's well chilled before slicing.

Dorothy Lacefield
Carrollton, Texas

In addition to the whipped cream and chopped pecans, **Dorothy** also garnishes the sides of the torte with pecan halves.

Fudge Truffle Cookies

You'll be thrilled with the fudgy surprise tucked inside each cookie. And you'll even have some fudge leftover to serve as a second dessert.

2   cups (12-ounce package) semisweet chocolate morsels
1   (14-ounce) can sweetened condensed milk
2   tablespoons vanilla extract, divided
1   cup chopped walnuts
1   cup butter, softened
1   cup sugar
1   large egg
¼   teaspoon salt
2¼ cups all-purpose flour
¼   cup cocoa

Microwave chocolate morsels in a 2-quart glass bowl at MEDIUM (50% power) 2 minutes or until melted. Stir in condensed milk, 1 tablespoon vanilla, and walnuts. Spread mixture into a buttered 9-inch square pan. Cool completely. Cut fudge into ½-inch squares.

Beat butter at medium speed with an electric mixer until creamy; gradually add sugar, beating well. Add egg and remaining 1 tablespoon vanilla; beat well.

Combine salt, flour, and cocoa; gradually add to butter mixture, beating well.

Divide dough into 3 equal portions. Work with 1 portion at a time; keep remaining dough chilled.

Divide each portion into 12 pieces. Quickly press each piece of dough around a square of fudge; roll dough into a 1-inch ball. Place on ungreased baking sheets. Repeat process with remaining dough and fudge pieces. Reserve remaining fudge for another use.

Bake at 350° for 11 minutes. Cool completely on a wire rack. **Makes:** 3 dozen.

Prep: 37 min., **Cook:** 11 min. per batch

Tip: Be sure to keep dough you're not working with refrigerated. Chilling dough prevents it from becoming too soft to handle.

Cindy Eby
Jackson, Michigan

Grandma's Peanut Butter Fudge

Simple, basic ingredients best describe this creamy confection. We've provided several tips at the end of the recipe to make it foolproof.

⅓ cup creamy peanut butter
1 teaspoon vanilla extract
2 cups sugar
⅔ cup milk
2 tablespoons butter
⅛ teaspoon salt

Butter a 9-inch pieplate. Set aside.
Place peanut butter and vanilla in a medium bowl.
Combine sugar and next 3 ingredients in a 2-quart heavy saucepan. Bring to a boil over medium heat, stirring until butter melts. Using a pastry brush dipped in hot water, brush down any sugar crystals on sides of pan. Cook, without stirring, until a candy thermometer registers 235° (soft ball stage). Remove from heat, and let stand 5 minutes. Pour hot syrup over peanut butter mixture in bowl. (Do not scrape sides of pan.) Beat with a wooden spoon until smooth. Quickly pour into prepared pieplate. Cool completely. Cut candy into pieces. **Makes:** 1 pound.
Prep: 4 min., **Cook:** 15 min., **Other:** 5 min.

Tips: Grandma probably used the stage method to determine her candy's readiness, but a thermometer will give you more consistent results. Be sure to check that your thermometer works accurately and adjust accordingly if it doesn't. For example: if water boils at 212° on your thermometer, your thermometer works accurately. If it boils at 210°, cook this recipe to 233°; if the boiling point on your thermometer is 214°, cook this recipe to 237°. Be sure that the bulb of the candy thermometer is fully submerged in syrup but does not touch bottom of saucepan. Don't beat candy too long; it hardens quickly as it cools. Beating candy in a separate bowl helps prevent the grainy texture that results from accidentally scraping any crystals off sides of pan.

Lori Goding
Mascoutah, Illinois

Chocolate Cookies Crumbled

Looking for a chocolate fix? Give this creamy-crunchy cookie combo a try.

13 chocolate cream-filled chocolate sandwich cookies, crushed (1½ cups)
½ cup ready-to-spread chocolate frosting
2 cups milk
1 (3.9-ounce) package chocolate instant pudding
1 teaspoon cinnamon sugar or ⅛ teaspoon ground cinnamon*
½ teaspoon vanilla extract
¼ teaspoon salt
14 chocolate cream-filled chocolate sandwich cookies, coarsely chopped (2 cups)
⅓ cup chocolate syrup
1 (8-ounce) package cream cheese, softened
½ cup powdered sugar
1 (8-ounce) container frozen whipped topping, thawed
¼ cup chopped walnuts, toasted
¼ cup chocolate syrup

Combine 13 crushed cookies and frosting; spread in a 9-inch square dish. Freeze 15 minutes.
Combine milk, pudding, and next 3 ingredients in a large bowl; beat at medium speed with an electric mixer 2 minutes.
Spread half of pudding mixture over cookie layer in dish; sprinkle with 14 chopped cookies. Drizzle ⅓ cup chocolate syrup over chopped cookie layer. Carefully spread remaining half of pudding mixture in dish. Cover and chill 30 minutes.
Beat cream cheese and powdered sugar at medium speed with an electric mixer until creamy; fold in whipped topping. Spread cream cheese mixture over pudding layer. Sprinkle with walnuts, and drizzle with ¼ cup chocolate syrup. Cover and chill 8 hours. Store in refrigerator. **Makes:** 9 servings.
Prep: 29 min., **Other:** 8 hrs., 45 min.

*To make your own cinnamon sugar, combine ½ cup sugar and 1 tablespoon ground cinnamon.

Mary Beth Lenhart
Abilene, Kansas

This dessert is a staple in **Mary Beth's** kitchen because it's quick and easy to make, then it chills until serving time. Mary Beth says the dessert is even yummier if chilled overnight.

Chocolate and Strawberries From Heaven

Double-stuffed chocolate cookies, succulent strawberries, and rich vanilla pudding star in this celestial creation.

2　(18-ounce) packages double cream-filled chocolate sandwich cookies
1　(8-ounce) package cream cheese, softened
½　cup butter or margarine, softened
1　cup sifted powdered sugar
2　cups milk
2　(3.4-ounce) packages French vanilla instant pudding mix
1　(10-ounce) package almond toffee bits
1　(12-ounce) container frozen whipped topping, thawed
2　(16-ounce) containers fresh strawberries, stems removed

Process cookies from 1 package in food processor until finely crushed. Place remaining cookies in a large zip-top freezer bag; coarsely crush with a rolling pin. Set aside.

Beat cream cheese and butter at medium speed with an electric mixer until creamy. Reduce speed to low; gradually add powdered sugar, beating until smooth.

In a separate bowl, whisk together milk and pudding mix for 2 minutes. Stir pudding mixture into cream cheese mixture. Stir in coarsely crushed cookies and toffee bits. Fold in half of whipped topping; fold in remaining topping. Cover and chill.

Spread one-third of finely crushed cookie crumbs in a 4-quart trifle dish. Layer one-third of strawberries, stemmed side down, over crumbs. Carefully spoon half of pudding mixture over strawberries. Repeat layers with one-third of crumbs, one-third of strawberries, and remaining half of pudding mixture. Top with remaining crumbs and strawberries. Cover and chill at least 3 hours. Store in refrigerator. **Makes:** 16 servings.
Prep: 31 min., **Other:** 3 hrs.

Inga Graves Spinks
Greensboro, North Carolina

Sometimes **Inga** serves this dessert in individual glass bowls for wedding receptions, showers, or dinner parties.

Pineapple-Berry Burst Trifle

This trifle is a burst of color—tropical orange, strawberry red, ocean blue, and sunny yellow fruits.

1　quart fresh strawberries, quartered
½　cup sugar
1　(8-ounce) package cream cheese, softened
1　(18-ounce) jar apricot preserves, divided
1　tablespoon sugar
¼　teaspoon vanilla extract
⅛　teaspoon coconut extract (optional)
1　cup heavy whipping cream
1　(16-ounce) loaf pound cake, cut into 1½-inch cubes
Caramel Sauce
3　(20-ounce) cans crushed pineapple in juice, drained and divided
3　(4.4-ounce) packages fresh blueberries
Garnish: fresh mint leaves

Combine strawberries and ½ cup sugar in a large bowl, tossing gently to coat. Cover; let stand at room temperature 2 hours.

Meanwhile, beat cream cheese at medium speed with an electric mixer until smooth. Add ½ cup preserves, 1 tablespoon sugar, and flavorings, beating until blended. Gradually add 1 cup whipping cream, beating until blended.

Cook remaining ½ cup preserves in a small saucepan over medium heat 4 minutes or until melted, stirring constantly.

Arrange one-third of pound cake cubes in a 3-quart bowl or trifle bowl. Top with one-third each of cream cheese mixture, Caramel Sauce, pineapple, blueberries, and strawberry mixture. Repeat layers twice, ending with strawberry mixture. Drizzle with melted apricot preserves. Cover and chill 3 hours. Garnish, if desired. Store in refrigerator. **Makes:** 8 servings.
Prep: 33 min., **Cook:** 4 min., **Other:** 5 hrs.

Caramel Sauce:
½　cup butter
1　cup sugar
½　cup heavy whipping cream
2　teaspoons vanilla extract

Melt butter and sugar in a small heavy saucepan over medium heat, stirring constantly. Add whipping cream. Bring to a boil; cook 1 minute or until slightly thickened, stirring constantly. Stir in vanilla; remove from heat. Cool. **Makes:** 1¼ cups.
Prep: 1 min., **Cook:** 9 min.

Tip: Make sure you use a 3-quart bowl. This trifle is what it says: It's bursting with ingredients and won't fit in a smaller bowl.

Richard Moffitt
Marblehead, Massachusetts

"Tara" Misu

This Southern interpretation of a popular Italian dessert features the flavors of peaches, cream, and pralines.

1   (6-ounce) package dried
    peaches
¾   cup peach nectar
1   (8-ounce) container mascarpone
    cheese
1   cup heavy whipping cream
¼   cup powdered sugar
¾   cup granulated sugar
¼   cup water
¼   teaspoon cream of tartar
½   cup chopped pecans
2   (3-ounce) packages ladyfingers,
    split
½   cup peach nectar
½   cup peach schnapps
1   cup heavy whipping cream
2   tablespoons powdered sugar
Fresh peach slices (optional)

Combine dried peaches and ¾ cup peach nectar in a medium saucepan. Bring to a boil; cover, reduce heat, and simmer 20 minutes. Remove from heat, and let stand 10 minutes. Process cooled peaches and cooking liquid in a blender or food processor until smooth.

Combine mascarpone cheese and 1 cup whipping cream in a medium bowl; beat at medium speed with an electric mixer until smooth and thickened. Add ¼ cup powdered sugar and peach puree; mixing well. Set aside.

Combine ¾ cup granulated sugar, water, cream of tartar, and pecans in a heavy saucepan. Bring mixture to a boil; boil 5 minutes, without stirring (mixture will be the color of molasses). Immediately pour pecan mixture onto a lightly greased baking sheet; cool 20 minutes. Break cooled pralines into pieces; process in batches in food processor until mixture resembles coarse brown sugar. Set aside, reserving ¼ cup praline mixture for garnish.

Line bottom and sides of a lightly greased 9-inch springform pan with

Jean often makes the praline powder a day or two ahead and stores it in the refrigerator or freezer.

1½ packages ladyfingers, cut side in, forming a double layer on bottom of pan. Combine ½ cup peach nectar and peach schnapps in a small bowl; drizzle half of peach schnapps mixture over ladyfingers in bottom of pan. Sprinkle half of praline mixture over ladyfingers. Spoon mascarpone cheese mixture over praline layer; spread evenly. Sprinkle with remaining half of praline mixture. Top with remaining ½ package ladyfingers; drizzle with remaining peach schnapps mixture. Cover and chill 8 hours or overnight.

Beat 1 cup whipping cream and 2 tablespoons powdered sugar at high speed with an electric mixer until soft peaks form. Remove sides of springform pan; spread top evenly with sweetened whipped cream. Top with fresh peach slices, if desired, and reserved ¼ cup praline mixture. Store in refrigerator.
Makes: 10 to 12 servings.
Prep: 1 hr., 5 min., **Cook:** 27 min., **Other:** 8 hrs., 30 min.

Jean Russ
Atlanta, Georgia

Pear Crêpes With Chocolate

These creamy-filled crêpes with juicy pear and chocolate are great for dessert or for an extra-special brunch.

1   cup all-purpose flour
1¼ cups 1% low-fat milk
1   large egg
2   tablespoons sunflower oil
1   (8-ounce) package ⅓-less-fat cream cheese, softened
¼   cup light sour cream
2   tablespoons granulated sugar
¼   teaspoon almond extract
3   ripe Bosc pears, peeled, cored, and sliced
3   tablespoons lemon juice
5   (1-ounce) bittersweet chocolate baking squares, chopped
⅓   cup light corn syrup
2   tablespoons 1% low-fat milk
1   tablespoon granulated sugar
½   teaspoon vanilla extract
⅓   cup sifted powdered sugar
¼   cup ground almonds, toasted

Whisk together first 4 ingredients in a small bowl until smooth. Cover and chill 1 hour.

Beat cream cheese at medium speed with an electric mixer until creamy. Add sour cream, 2 tablespoons sugar, and almond extract; beat until combined. Cover and chill.

Sprinkle pear slices with lemon juice, set aside.

Combine chocolate and next 3 ingredients in a small saucepan over medium heat. Cook, stirring constantly, 5 minutes or until chocolate is melted. Stir in vanilla; set aside.

Coat a 6-inch crêpe pan or heavy skillet with cooking spray; place over medium heat until hot. Pour 3 tablespoons batter into pan; quickly tilt pan in all directions so batter covers bottom of pan. Cook 1 minute or until crêpe can be shaken loose from pan. Turn crêpe over, and cook 30 seconds. Place crêpe on a cloth towel to cool. Repeat procedure with remaining batter.

Spread 1 tablespoon cream cheese mixture over one-fourth of each crêpe; top with 3 or 4 pear slices. Fold crêpe in half, then in half again to form a triangular shape. Place filled crêpes on a lightly greased baking sheet; sprinkle evenly with powdered sugar. Bake at 400° for 6 minutes or until filling is melted.

To serve, divide crêpes among 6 plates; drizzle with chocolate sauce, and sprinkle with almonds. **Makes:** 6 servings.
Prep: 10 min., **Cook:** 30 min., **Other:** 1 hr.

Jenel Burkhardt
Harrison Township, Michigan

Pear Crêpes With Chocolate

Lemon-Mint Mousse Crêpes

1   envelope unflavored gelatin
¼   teaspoon grated lemon rind
¼   cup fresh lemon juice
½   cup whipping cream
½   cup white chocolate morsels
1   (3-ounce) package cream cheese, cubed
¼   cup honey
½   cup sour cream
8   (9-inch) refrigerated ready-to-use crêpes*
Lemon Sauce
Garnishes: fresh mint leaves, fresh raspberries, fresh blueberries

Sprinkle gelatin over lemon rind and lemon juice in a small saucepan; let stand 1 minute. Cook over low heat, stirring until gelatin dissolves (about 2 minutes). Add cream and next 3 ingredients. Cook, stirring constantly, over low heat until smooth. Remove from heat; stir in sour cream and lemon rind. Cool completely; chill thoroughly.

Spoon mousse mixture in center of crêpes. Fold crêpes in half, then in half again to form a triangular shape. Place 2 filled crêpes on each of 4 individual serving plates. Spoon warm Lemon Sauce over crêpes, and garnish, if desired. **Makes:** 4 servings.
Prep: 14 min., **Cook:** 3 min., **Other:** 2 hrs.

*For testing purposes only, we used Melissa's crêpes.

Tip: Be sure to grate the rind from the lemons first before squeezing the juice. Grate rind and squeeze juice for the mouse and Lemon Sauce all at once to save time.

Lemon Sauce:
¼   cup sugar
1   tablespoon cornstarch
¾   cup water
2   tablespoons butter
¼   teaspoon grated lemon rind
2   tablespoons fresh lemon juice

Whisk together sugar and cornstarch in a small saucepan. Whisk in water. Cook, whisking constantly, over medium heat 2 minutes or until thick and bubbly. Remove from heat; add butter, whisking until butter is melted. Whisk in lemon rind and lemon juice. **Makes:** 1 cup.
Prep: 3 min., **Cook:** 5 min.

Roxanne Chan
Albany, California

Roxanne adds ¼ teaspoon mint extract to both the crêpe filling and the Lemon Sauce. We preferred the dessert without the extract, but we kept the pretty mint leaves as a garnish. Fresh berries also add flavor and a shot of color.

Peach Rolls

Best served warm, these rolls are a cross between a dumpling and a cobbler. Fresh peaches are ideal, but you can make these rolls with frozen peaches year-round. Serve this dessert in bowls to hold all the sweet syrup.

4   medium peaches, peeled and coarsely chopped
1   tablespoon fresh lemon juice
½   teaspoon ground cinnamon
1½ cups all-purpose flour
½   teaspoon salt
2   teaspoons baking powder
¼   cup cold butter
1   tablespoon shortening
6   tablespoons milk
1   cup granulated sugar
1   cup firmly packed brown sugar
1½ cups water
Vanilla ice cream

Stir together peaches, lemon juice, and cinnamon; cover and set aside.
Stir together flour, salt, and baking powder in a large bowl; cut in butter and shortening with a pastry blender until mixture is crumbly. Gradually add milk, stirring just until moistened. Turn dough out onto a lightly floured surface, and knead lightly 3 or 4 times.
Roll dough into a 13- x 10-inch rectangle; spread peach mixture evenly over dough to within 1 inch of edges. Roll up dough, jellyroll fashion, starting at long side; pinch ends to seal. Cut into 8 slices. Place rolls in a greased 13- x 9-inch pan.

Combine sugars and water in a medium saucepan. Cook over medium heat, stirring constantly, 5 minutes or until sugars dissolve. Pour hot sugar mixture over rolls. Bake, uncovered, at 375° for 40 minutes or until lightly browned. Serve rolls and syrup warm with vanilla ice cream. **Makes:** 8 servings.
Prep: 44 min., **Cook:** 45 min.

Tip: To easily slice roll of dough, place a long piece of dental floss or string under dough 1½ inches from end of roll. Cross ends of dental floss over top of roll; slowly pull the ends to cut through the dough.

Valerie Salatino
Boynton Beach, Florida

Irish Sweet Scone

This loaf version of a scone is moist and most tender right out of the oven. Try some leftover slices toasted with butter and jam. Loaves freeze well.

6	cups all-purpose flour
2	cups sugar
2	tablespoons baking powder
2½	cups milk
2	large eggs
2	teaspoons vanilla extract
1	(18-ounce) container raisins
3	tablespoons butter, melted

Sift together first 3 ingredients into a large bowl.

Stir together milk, eggs, and vanilla; add to dry ingredients, stirring just until moistened. Stir in raisins Spoon batter evenly into 3 greased and floured 9- x 5-inch loafpans. Bake at 350° for 55 to 60 minutes or until golden. Remove from pans; brush loaves with melted butter. **Makes:** 3 loaves.

Prep: 12 min., **Cook:** 1 hr.

Eileen McGovern
Havertown, Pennsylvania

When **Eileen** is in the mood for chocolate, she omits the raisins and makes these loaves with a 12-ounce package of semisweet chocolate morsels.

Banana Butter Rum "I Scream" Open-Faced Sandwiches

When you're looking for something different for dessert, this recipe is the answer. Rum-glazed bananas and vanilla ice cream are served over homemade banana-pecan waffles. We highly recommend giving these waffles a try, but store-bought waffle bowls will work in a pinch.

2¼	cups all-purpose baking mix ✱
1	tablespoon granulated sugar
⅛	teaspoon ground nutmeg
2	ripe bananas, mashed (about 1 cup)
1	cup milk
1	large egg
2	tablespoons vegetable oil
¼	teaspoon vanilla extract
¼	cup chopped pecans
½	cup unsalted butter
1	cup firmly packed dark brown sugar
⅔	cup chopped pecans
6	bananas, cut in half lengthwise then crosswise
1	cup dark rum
1	teaspoon vanilla extract
	Vanilla ice cream

Combine first 3 ingredients in a medium bowl. Combine 2 mashed bananas and next 4 ingredients; add to dry ingredients, stirring with a wire whisk until moistened. Stir in ¼ cup pecans.

Cook in a preheated, oiled waffle iron until golden.

Meanwhile, melt butter in a large skillet over medium-high heat; add brown sugar and ⅔ cup pecans. Cook, stirring often, 3 minutes or until bubbly. Add 6 bananas; cook 3 minutes or until bananas are tender. Remove from heat.

Heat rum in a small saucepan over medium heat until warm (do not boil). Pour rum over banana mixture, and immediately ignite with a long match. Let flames die down. Return to heat; simmer 4 minutes or until sauce is thickened. Stir in vanilla.

To serve, place 2 banana slices on each waffle; top with vanilla ice cream. Drizzle 2 tablespoons rum mixture over ice cream. Serve immediately. **Makes:** 12 (4-inch) sandwiches.

Prep: 5 min., **Cook:** 18 min.

✱For testing purposes only, we used Bisquick Original All-Purpose Baking Mix.

Megan Creel
Austin, Texas

Megan saves time by preparing the waffles in advance (and even freezing them when necessary), then she reheats them in a toaster oven while she makes the sauce.

Creamy Lemon Ice Cream With Ginger Biscotti

You really get two delicious desserts out of one recipe here—the ice cream and cookies make a delightful duo, but each can also stand alone. If you want to cut corners when serving the two together, the biscotti are just as good plain and not dipped in white chocolate.

3¼ cups whipping cream, divided
1 (12-ounce) can evaporated milk
1 cup sugar
10 egg yolks, lightly beaten
¼ cup grated lemon rind (about 3 lemons)
¾ cup fresh lemon juice (about 4 lemons)
1 teaspoon lemon extract
Ginger Biscotti

Combine 2¼ cups whipping cream, evaporated milk, and sugar in a heavy saucepan over medium heat. Bring to a simmer, stirring occasionally; remove from heat. Gradually whisk about one-fourth of warm milk mixture into egg yolks; whisk into remaining hot mixture. Cook over low heat, stirring constantly, 5 to 7 minutes or until mixture coats the back of a spoon. Remove from heat; pour through a wire-mesh strainer into a large bowl. Stir in remaining 1 cup whipping cream, lemon rind, juice, and extract; cover and chill 1 hour.

Pour into freezer container of a 4-quart ice-cream maker. Freeze according to manufacturer's instructions. (Freezing instructions will vary among manufacturers.) Spoon ice cream into an airtight container, and freeze until firm. Serve with Ginger Biscotti. **Makes:** 8 servings.
Prep: 13 min., **Cook:** 22 min., **Other:** 4 hrs.

Ginger Biscotti:

1 (10¾-ounce) frozen pound cake, thawed and broken into pieces
¾ cup cinnamon-flavored lightly sweetened whole grain oat cereal squares *
½ cup whole almonds
¼ cup crystallized ginger
⅓ cup unsalted butter, melted
½ teaspoon ground ginger
½ teaspoon lemon extract
¾ cup white chocolate morsels
2 tablespoons milk
2 tablespoons dried lemon rind

Place cake pieces in a food processor; process until coarsely crumbled. Place crumbs in to a large bowl; set aside. Place cereal, almonds, and crystallized ginger in food processor; pulse 1 minute or until finely chopped (mixture will resemble sand). Stir into cake crumbs.

Stir butter, ground ginger, and lemon extract into crumb mixture until moistened. Shape rounded tablespoonfuls of dough into crescent shapes; place on greased baking sheets. Bake at 350° for 15 to 17 minutes or until lightly browned. Cool on baking sheets.

Microwave white chocolate morsels and milk at MEDIUM HIGH (70% power) 1 minute or until morsels melt; stir until smooth. Stir in lemon rind. Dip 1 end of each biscotti into chocolate mixture; place on wire racks until chocolate is firm. **Makes:** about 2 dozen.
Prep: 6 min., **Cook:** 17 min. per batch

*For testing purposes only, we used Quaker Oat Cinnamon Life cereal.

Corinne Portteus
Newark, California

Corinne showed her creative side when she used pound cake crumbs as the base for the biscotti.

**Creamy Lemon Ice Cream
With Ginger Biscotti**

Creamy French Vanilla Ice Cream

A silky smooth custard creates the base for this creamy frozen dessert.

4   large eggs
2   egg yolks
2   cups sugar
3   tablespoons cornstarch
½   teaspoon salt
5   cups milk
1   (16-ounce) bottle French vanilla-flavored liquid coffee creamer *
1   (14-ounce) can sweetened condensed milk
2   cups heavy whipping cream

Combine egg and egg yolks in a medium bowl; beat well with a whisk.

Whisk together sugar, cornstarch, and salt in a Dutch oven until blended.

Whisk in milk; bring to a simmer over medium heat, whisking constantly. Remove from heat. Gradually whisk about one-fourth of hot mixture into eggs; add to remaining hot mixture, whisking constantly. Cook over low heat 6 minutes or until thick. Remove from heat; whisk in coffee creamer, condensed milk, and cream. Cool completely; cover and chill thoroughly.

Pour mixture into freezer container of a 4-quart ice-cream maker, and freeze according to manufacturer's instructions. (Freezing instructions will vary among manufacturers.) Pack freezer with additional ice and rock salt, and let stand 1 hour before serving. **Makes:** 3 quarts.

Prep: 5 min., **Cook:** 24 min., **Other:** 3 hrs., 30 min.

*For testing purposes only, we used Coffee Mate liquid coffee creamer.

Tip: After processing in ice-cream maker, pour ice cream into a plastic container, and place in freezer to harden to desired consistency. It will take at least 3 hours to become firm, depending on the depth of container used.

Julie Black
Garland, Texas

Creamy Lemon Sherbet

Want to impress your guests? Try this refreshing yet easy dessert that's simple to make.

2   pasteurized egg yolks *
½   cup sugar
½   cup light corn syrup
1   (16-ounce) container whipping cream
2   teaspoons grated lemon rind
¼   cup fresh lemon juice
Garnish: fresh mint sprigs

Whisk together yolks and sugar in a large bowl until thick and pale. Whisk in syrup and next 3 ingredients; pour mixture into a freezer-safe container. Cover and freeze 4 hours or until almost firm.

Place mixture in a large mixing bowl; beat at medium speed with an electric mixer until creamy. Pour mixture into a 9-inch square pan; cover and freeze 8 hours or until firm. Garnish, if desired. **Makes:** 6 servings.

Prep: 9 min., **Other:** 12 hrs.

*For testing purposes only, we used Davidson's Pasteurized Shell Eggs.

Tip: Look for pasteurized shell eggs in foam cartons with the other eggs in large supermarkets and discount super centers. Pasteurized eggs are safe to eat raw and, therefore, eliminate the risk of salmonella contamination.

Erin Tsaconas
Honolulu, Hawaii

Citrus Cream Sorbet With Lemon Crunch Lace Cookies

Lookin' for a treat to cool down that summertime heat? Try this fun chiller—a creamy lemon sorbet and crisp pecan cookie.

½ cup orange juice
⅔ cup sugar
1 tablespoon grated lemon rind
2 tablespoons fresh lemon juice
⅛ teaspoon salt
1½ cups milk
½ cup heavy whipping cream
Lemon Crunch Lace Cookies
Garnishes: fresh berries, fresh mint sprigs

Combine first 5 ingredients in a large bowl, stirring until sugar dissolves. Add milk and whipping cream, stirring until well blended.

Pour cream mixture into freezer container of a 2-quart ice-cream maker, and freeze according to manufacturer's instructions. (Freezing instructions will vary among manufacturers.) Pack freezer with additional ice and rock salt, and let stand 1 hour before serving. Serve with Lemon Crunch Lace Cookies. Garnish, if desired. **Makes:** 3 cups.
Prep: 32 min., **Other:** 8 hrs.

Lemon Crunch Lace Cookies:
⅓ cup ground pecans
¼ cup sugar
¼ cup unsalted butter, melted
1 tablespoon milk
1½ teaspoons all-purpose flour
½ teaspoon grated lemon rind
½ teaspoon fresh lemon juice

Combine all ingredients in a small bowl. Drop batter by tablespoonfuls 5 inches apart onto nonstick aluminum foil-lined baking sheets.

Bake at 350° for 12 minutes or until dark caramel-colored. Cool on baking sheets 5 minutes. Working quickly, mold cookies into desired shapes. Cool completely on wire racks. **Makes:** 8 cookies.
Prep: 8 min., **Cook:** 12 min. per batch

Tip: These cookies will spread a lot when baking. Bake no more than 4 cookies on each baking sheet. When molding cookies, simply roll around a wooden spoon handle, shape into a cone, or mold around the outside of an inverted custard cup to form cookie bowls.

Lisa Keys
Middlebury, Connecticut

If you don't want to shape the cookies, **Lisa** says they can also be crumbled into crunchy bits and sprinkled over the sorbet.

Sweet Surprise

This great make-ahead dessert couldn't be easier.

9½ (4.25-ounce) vanilla ice cream with chocolate wafers ice cream sandwiches
1 (12-ounce) jar chocolate-coated caramel and creamy nougat bar-flavored ice cream topping*
1 (8-ounce) container frozen whipped topping, thawed
4 (2.1-ounce) chocolate-covered crispy peanut-buttery candy bars, crushed*

Arrange ice cream sandwiches in a single layer in a 13- x 9-inch pan. Pour ice cream topping over sandwiches. Spread whipped topping over ice cream topping. Sprinkle crushed candy bars over top. Cover and freeze at least 2 hours. **Makes:** 12 servings.
Prep: 9 min., **Other:** 2 hrs.

*For testing purpose only, we used Smucker's Milky Way Topping and Butterfinger candy bars.

Tip: Pound candy bars lightly with a rolling pin or meat mallet while still in their wrappers..

B. B. Watts
Brookhaven, Mississippi

B.B. knows how to please a crowd with very little effort from the cook.

Frozen Chocolate Ladyfinger Dessert

Fancy enough for company, this dessert is ready for the freezer in only 15 minutes.

1½ (3-ounce) packages ladyfingers
   (about 18)
1¼ cups miniature marshmallows
2   (5-ounce) cans fat-free
    evaporated milk
¾   cup semisweet chocolate
    morsels
1   teaspoon vanilla extract
1   (16-ounce) container frozen
    whipped topping, thawed
Garnish: chocolate curls

Split ladyfingers in half lengthwise. Line bottom and sides of a lightly greased 8-inch springform pan with ladyfingers, cut side in; set aside.

Combine marshmallows, milk, and chocolate morsels in a microwave-safe bowl; microwave at HIGH 3 minutes or until marshmallows and chocolate are melted, stirring occasionally. Stir in vanilla; cool completely. Fold whipped topping into cooled chocolate mixture; pour filling into prepared pan. Cover and freeze 8 hours. Carefully remove sides of pan. Garnish, if desired. **Makes:** 10 servings.

Prep: 12 min., **Cook:** 3 min., **Other:** 8 hrs.

Diane L. Fishman
Columbia, Maryland

Chocolate curls make an impressive garnish for this dessert, but **Diane** also uses semisweet chocolate morsels when she's pinched for time.

White Chocolate Cheesecake Bites

These sweet little bites are perfect for a crowd, and leftovers freeze well. But, the recipe can be easily cut in half to make 45. Instead of chocolate morsels, you can top each mini dessert with fresh raspberries, blueberries, or strawberries.

3   (8-ounce) packages cream
    cheese, softened
½   cup sugar
½   teaspoon vanilla extract
3   large eggs
8   ounces white chocolate baking
    squares, melted
6   (2.1-ounce) packages frozen
    mini phyllo pastry shells
1   cup (6-ounce package)
    semisweet chocolate morsels

Beat cream cheese at medium speed with an electric mixer until smooth. Add sugar and vanilla; beat until blended. Add eggs, 1 at a time, beating well after each addition. Stir in melted white chocolate.

If you forget to soften the cream cheese, **Dan** recommends microwaving it for 15 seconds to quickly soften it.

Place phyllo shells on baking sheets. Spoon 1 teaspoon filling into each shell (do not overfill). Sprinkle each with 3 or 4 chocolate morsels. Bake at 300° for 18 minutes or until set. Cool completely; chill until ready to serve. Store in refrigerator. **Makes:** 90 cheesecake bites.

Prep: 41 min., **Cook:** 18 min. per batch

Dan Sawyer
Anniston, Alabama

Lemon Meringue Cassata

"Cassata" is Italian for "in a case or chest." This tart and refreshing frozen dessert is encased in a loafpan until serving time when it's cut into multilayered slices. And, the wonderful thing about this dessert is you can cut a slice or two as you need it for a small family and keep the rest in the freezer for later. It's traditionally served at weddings or on special occasions.

Meringue
1   pint vanilla ice cream, softened
Lemon Curd
3   tablespoons grated lemon rind
1   pint lemon sorbet, softened
Garnishes: lemon rind curls, fresh
    mint leaves

Prepare Meringue.

Line a 9- x 5-inch loafpan with nonstick aluminum foil, allowing edges of foil to extend over sides of pan. Press foil smoothly into corners and along sides of pan. Spread ice cream in prepared pan. Freeze 30 minutes or until firm.

Meanwhile, prepare Lemon Curd. Pour curd over ice cream, spreading in a smooth layer. Freeze, uncovered, 1 hour or until firm.

Top frozen Lemon Curd with 1 meringue rectangle. Return cassata to freezer.

Stir lemon rind into lemon sorbet. Spread sorbet mixture in a smooth layer over meringue layer in pan. Top with remaining meringue layer. Gently press meringue slightly into sorbet mixture. Freeze, uncovered, 1 hour or until firm.

To serve, cut cassata into 8 slices. Garnish, if desired. Store, covered, in freezer. **Makes:** 8 servings.
Prep: 20 min., **Other:** 2 hrs., 30 min.

Tip: To quickly soften ice cream or sorbet: uncover container, and microwave at HIGH 20 seconds. Spoon into a medium bowl, and beat at low speed with an electric mixer until smooth.

Tip: An electric knife works especially well to slice through the different layers of this dessert.

Meringue:
4   egg whites
½   teaspoon cream of tartar
½   cup sugar

Cover a large baking sheet with parchment paper. Trace bottom of a 9- x 5-inch loafpan on paper twice. Turn paper over; secure with masking tape.

Beat egg whites and cream of tartar at high speed with an electric mixer until foamy. Add sugar, 1 tablespoon at a time, beating until stiff peaks form and sugar dissolves. Using a small spatula, spread half of meringue 1 inch thick on each drawn rectangle to completely fill rectangles. Bake at 250° for 1 hour and 15 minutes. Turn oven off, and let meringues stand in closed oven overnight. **Makes:** 2 (9- x 5- x 1-inch) meringues.
Prep: 10 min., **Cook:** 1 hr., 15 min., **Other:** 8 hrs.

Tip: Trace rectangles on side of parchment paper that curls up. When you turn the paper over, it will lie flat on the baking sheet without having to secure it with tape.

For tip-top flavor, **Marilyn** suggests that you splurge on premium vanilla ice cream and lemon sorbet.

Lemon Curd:
1½ cups sugar
⅓   cup cornstarch
¼   teaspoon salt
1½ cups water
¾   cup fresh lemon juice
4   egg yolks, lightly beaten
1   tablespoon grated lemon rind

Whisk together sugar, cornstarch, and salt in a medium saucepan. Stir in water. Bring to a boil over medium heat. Cook, whisking constantly, 1 minute; stir in lemon juice. Cook, whisking constantly, until mixture boils and thickens slightly. Remove from heat. Gradually stir about one-fourth of hot mixture into egg yolks; whisk into remaining hot mixture. Return to heat, and cook, whisking constantly, 3 minutes. Remove from heat. Stir in lemon rind. Cool completely. Cover and chill thoroughly.
Makes: 2½ cups.
Prep: 12 min., **Cook:** 8 min.

Tip: To quickly chill Lemon Curd, place saucepan in a large bowl of ice water for 5 minutes or until completely chilled, stirring often.

Marilyn Flowers
Downers Grove, Illinois

Piña Colada Cheese Chills

Our taste-testing panel was split on its preference for yogurt or sour cream. Yogurt gives a more tart flavor; sour cream, a creamy texture.

1 (20-ounce) can crushed
   pineapple in juice, undrained
1 envelope unflavored gelatin
¼ cup cream of coconut
2 cups low-fat vanilla yogurt or
   1 (16-ounce) container sour
   cream
½ (8-ounce) package cream
   cheese, softened
¼ teaspoon grated lemon rind
1 cup dried banana chips
Granola

Drain pineapple to measure ½ cup juice, reserving pineapple and remaining juice. Pour ½ cup juice into a small saucepan; sprinkle with gelatin. Let stand 5 minutes. Cook over low heat, stirring until gelatin dissolves (about 2 minutes).
Process reserved pineapple, remaining juice, gelatin mixture, cream of coconut, and next 3 ingredients in a blender until smooth.

Divide banana chips among 6 parfait glasses. Pour about 1 cup pineapple mixture over chips in each glass. Cover and chill thoroughly. Top parfaits with Granola just before serving. **Makes:** 6 servings.
Prep: 12 min., **Cook:** 2 min., **Other:** 2 hrs.

Granola:

This recipe doubles easily (bake time will be the same). Use as a topping for ice cream, yogurt, or fruit for a quick dessert. It's good with milk for breakfast or as a snack, too.

⅔ cup uncooked regular oats
¼ cup sweetened flaked coconut
¼ cup sliced almonds
1 tablespoon toasted wheat
   germ
3 tablespoons light brown sugar
2 tablespoons vegetable oil
1 teaspoon vanilla extract
Dash of salt

Combine first 5 ingredients in a medium bowl, stirring well. Whisk together oil, vanilla, and salt in a small bowl until blended. Pour over oat mixture, stirring until evenly moistened. Spread oat mixture in a 15- x 10-inch jellyroll pan lined with aluminum foil. Bake at 350° for 12 minutes, stirring after 10 minutes. Cool completely in pan. Stir well, and store in an airtight container. **Makes:** 1½ cups.
Prep: 4 min., **Cook:** 12 min.

Paula Mahagnoul
Faribault, Minnesota

When **Paula** needs to speed up the chilling process for this dessert, she places the parfaits in the freezer for 15 minutes, then refrigerates them until they're thoroughly chilled.

Apple Stack Dessert

Make this great dessert even greater, and serve it warm with vanilla ice cream.

14 sheets frozen phyllo pastry
1   (8-ounce) package cream
    cheese, softened
½   cup sugar
1½ teaspoons ground cinnamon
½   teaspoon ground nutmeg
1½ cups chopped Granny Smith
    apple (about 1 large)
1   teaspoon lemon juice
1   cup chopped dates
1   cup chopped pecans
¾   cup butter, melted
Sugar

Thaw phyllo pastry according to package directions.
Beat cream cheese at medium speed with an electric mixer until creamy; add ½ cup sugar, cinnamon, and nutmeg, and beat until smooth.
Toss apple with lemon juice. Stir in dates and pecans. Fold cream cheese mixture into apple mixture until combined.
Unfold phyllo pastry on a lightly floured surface. (Keep remaining sheets covered.) Stack 4 phyllo sheets on a baking sheet, brushing between each sheet with melted butter and sprinkling evenly with additional sugar. Carefully spread about one-third of apple mixture over phyllo, leaving a 1½-inch border around edges;

repeat procedure twice, ending with apple mixture.
Layer remaining 2 phyllo sheets, brushing with butter and sprinkling with sugar. Cut in half crosswise. Place 1 half on top of each other. Using a sharp knife, cut into 1-inch-wide strips. Place strips diagonally on top of apple mixture. (You may not need all the strips.) Fold over 1½-inch borders of pastry, pressing gently to seal.
Bake at 350° for 40 minutes or until golden. Serve warm. **Makes:** 20 to 24 servings.
Prep: 24 min., **Cook:** 40 min.

Rebecca B. Phipps
Winston-Salem, North Carolina

Umm...Chocolate Strawberry Delights

You'll have some of the white chocolate layer leftover to serve as a dip with fresh fruit or cubes of pound cake.

2   (15-ounce) packages
     refrigerated piecrusts
¼   cup evaporated milk
⅔   cup semisweet chocolate
     morsels
½   cup powdered sugar
1   teaspoon vanilla extract
1   cup white chocolate morsels
1   (8-ounce) package cream
     cheese, softened
⅓   cup granulated sugar
½   teaspoon almond extract
1   cup whipping cream
48   strawberries, stems removed
¼   cup red currant jelly, melted
½   cup sliced almonds

Roll each piecrust to ⅛-inch thickness on a lightly floured surface. Cut 12 circles out of each piecrust, using a 2½-inch round cutter. Press piecrust circles into ungreased miniature (1¾-inch) muffin pans; prick bottom and sides of piecrust with a fork.

Bake at 400° for 13 minutes or until golden brown. Cool in pans on wire racks 5 minutes. Remove from pans; cool completely on wire racks.

Meanwhile, combine milk and semisweet chocolate morsels in a microwave-safe bowl; microwave at HIGH 1 minute or until chocolate is melted. Add powdered sugar and vanilla, stirring until smooth. Set aside.

Place white chocolate morsels in a small microwave-safe bowl; microwave at HIGH 1 minute or until melted.

Beat cream cheese and granulated sugar at medium speed with an electric mixer until smooth; add white chocolate, beating until smooth. Stir in almond extract.

Beat whipping cream at high speed with an electric mixer until soft peaks form; fold into cream cheese mixture.

Spoon about ½ teaspoon semisweet chocolate mixture into bottom of each pastry shell; top with about 2 teaspoons white chocolate mixture. Place 1 strawberry, stemmed side down, onto white chocolate mixture, pressing down gently. Gently brush each strawberry with melted jelly; sprinkle evenly with almonds. Chill until ready to serve. Store in refrigerator. **Makes:** 4 dozen.
Prep: 58 min., **Cook:** 13 min.

Tip: You may need to add more milk, 1 teaspoon at a time, if semisweet chocolate mixture begins to firm up before you finish assembling the desserts.

Martha Macgowan
Sarasota, Florida

Sometimes **Martha** uses prepared strawberry glaze, found in the produce section of the grocery store, to coat the strawberries on each tartlet.

Caribbean Key Lime Pie

Coconut and a hint of spiced rum give a Caribbean twist to traditional Key lime pie.

1 cup sweetened flaked coconut
12 vanilla cream sandwich cookies, broken
¼ cup chopped macadamia nuts
5 tablespoons butter, melted
1 (8-ounce) package cream cheese, softened
1 (14-ounce) can sweetened condensed milk
3 egg yolks
½ cup fresh Key lime juice
½ teaspoon spiced rum (optional)
Sweetened whipped cream

Spread coconut in a shallow pan. Bake at 350° for 5 to 6 minutes, stirring occasionally, or until toasted. Set aside 2 tablespoons for topping.

Process cookies and macadamia nuts in a food processor until crushed. Add butter; process until moistened. Add remaining coconut, and pulse 2 or 3 times or just until combined. Press crumb mixture in bottom and up sides of a 9-inch pieplate. Freeze 15 minutes.

Beat cream cheese and condensed milk at medium speed with an electric mixer until creamy. Add egg yolks, 1 at a time, beating just until blended after each addition. Add lime juice and, if desired, spiced rum; beat just until blended. Pour filling into piecrust.

Bake at 350° for 25 minutes or until almost set. (Center of pie will firm when chilled.) Cool completely. Cover and refrigerate at least 4 hours or until thoroughly chilled. Dollop each serving with whipped cream, and sprinkle with reserved coconut. Store in refrigerator. **Makes:** 8 servings.
Prep: 58 min., **Cook:** 31 min., **Other:** 4 hrs., 15 min.

Catherine Sutrich
Oviedo, Florida

Catherine brings a taste of the Caribbean to a classic lime pie with the addition of coconut, macadamia nuts, and spiced rum. We recommend freshly squeezed Key lime juice, but bottled Key lime juice can be substituted; that reduces the prep time by about 40 minutes.

Chocolate-Caramel Dessert

Just close your eyes and you'll think you're eating a candy bar. Chock-full of goodies, this dessert's a winner with its creamy, smooth-textured cheesecake layer and crunchy pecans.

½ cup butter or margarine, softened
¾ cup sugar
1½ cups all-purpose flour
¼ teaspoon salt
4 (8-ounce) packages cream cheese, softened
⅔ cup sour cream
½ cup creamy peanut butter
1 (12.25-ounce) jar fat-free caramel topping, divided
3 large eggs
1 cup chopped pecans, toasted
1 (11.75-ounce) jar hot fudge topping
½ cup chocolate syrup

Beat butter at medium speed with an electric mixer until creamy; add sugar, beating well.

Combine flour and salt; add to butter mixture, beating until fine crumbs form. Press into bottom of a lightly greased 13- x 9-inch pan.

Bake at 375° for 10 minutes. Cool on a wire rack.

Beat cream cheese at medium speed until smooth. Add sour cream, peanut butter, and half of caramel topping, beating just until blended. Add eggs, 1 at a time, beating just until blended after each addition. Stir in pecans. Pour over prepared crust.

Spoon dollops of hot fudge topping evenly over cream cheese mixture. Swirl batter gently with a knife to create a marbled effect.

Bake at 325° for 45 minutes or until center is almost set. Cool on a wire rack. Cover and chill 8 hours. Cut into 18 squares. Spoon remaining caramel topping and chocolate syrup onto individual plates; top each with a square of dessert. **Makes:** 18 servings.
Prep: 16 min., **Cook:** 55 min., **Other:** 8 hrs.

Tip: Stir fudge topping in a small bowl before dolloping on cheesecake. This will help soften the mixture to easily swirl into cheesecake batter.

Nancy Loken
Sioux Falls, South Dakota

Caribbean Key Lime Pie

Ultra-Rich Molten Chocolate

This is the ultimate chocolate recipe. Once the crisp, sugary top of the dessert is broken, glorious liquid chocolate is unveiled. Spoon it into bowls, and top with ice cream.

1¼ cups graham cracker crumbs
3 tablespoons light brown sugar
⅓ cup coarsely chopped pecans
6 tablespoons unsalted butter, melted
1 cup whipping cream
2 cups (12-ounce package) semisweet chocolate morsels
½ cup unsalted butter
½ cup milk chocolate morsels
¾ cup granulated sugar
2 large eggs
½ cup all-purpose flour
16 assorted-filled chocolate pieces *
18 pecan halves

Combine first 4 ingredients. Press into bottom of a buttered 9-inch deep-dish pieplate. Bake at 350° for 8 minutes or until lightly browned; cool.

Bring whipping cream to a simmer in a medium saucepan over medium heat. Remove from heat; add semisweet morsels, stirring until smooth. Spread mixture over crust; cover and freeze 30 minutes.

Melt ½ cup butter in saucepan. Remove from heat; add milk chocolate morsels, stirring until smooth. Add granulated sugar, stirring until smooth. Add eggs, 1 at a time, beating just until blended. Stir in flour just until combined.

Cut each chocolate piece into 4 pieces; fold into milk chocolate mixture. Pour mixture over chilled chocolate crust; sprinkle with pecan halves.

Bake at 350° for 45 minutes or until outer edge is set. Remove from oven; cool slightly on a wire rack. Serve warm. **Makes:** 12 to 14 servings.

Prep: 20 min., **Cook:** 53 min., **Other:** 30 min.

*For testing purposes only, we used Nestlé Assorted Treasures.

Barbara Estabrook
Rhinelander, Wisconsin

Chocolate Cosmic Meringues

Got your head in the clouds dreamin' of a tropical getaway? When you taste this creamy pineapple pudding served over a cloud of meringue you won't be so far off from paradise!

4 egg whites
¼ teaspoon cream of tartar
1 cup sugar
1 cup chopped macadamia nuts, divided
Pineapple Filling
Chocolate Sauce

Beat egg whites and cream of tartar at high speed with an electric mixer until foamy. Gradually add sugar, beating until stiff peaks form. Fold in ¾ cup nuts.

Drop egg white mixture into 6 mounds on a large baking sheet lined with parchment paper. Make an indentation, using the back of a spoon, into the center of each meringue to form a 5-inch nest.

Bake at 225° for 1 hour. Turn oven off, and let stand in closed oven 8 hours.

Spoon Pineapple Filling evenly into center of each nest. Drizzle with Chocolate Sauce. Sprinkle with remaining ¼ cup nuts. Serve immediately. **Makes:** 6 servings.

Prep: 21 min., **Cook:** 1 hr., **Other:** 8 hrs.

Pineapple Filling:

1 (2.6-ounce) envelope whipped dairy topping
1 (3.4-ounce) vanilla instant pudding mix
1 (3-ounce) package cream cheese, softened
1 (8-ounce) can crushed pineapple in juice, well drained and chilled *
1 (6-ounce) container vanilla yogurt
3 frozen creamy coconut ice cream bars, cut into small chunks

Prepare dairy topping mix and pudding mix according to package directions.

Beat cream cheese at medium speed with an electric mixer until smooth. Fold in prepared dairy topping, pudding, pineapple, yogurt, and ice cream bars. **Makes:** 5 cups.

Prep: 12 min.

Chocolate Sauce:

¾ cup semisweet chocolate morsels
3 tablespoons pineapple juice
3 tablespoons sour cream

Combine chocolate morsels and juice in a small glass bowl. Microwave at HIGH 1 minute or until chocolate is melted, stirring once. Stir in sour cream until smooth. **Makes:** ⅔ cup.

Prep: 2 min., **Cook:** 1 min.

Tip: If you don't have a baking sheet that is at least 18 x 12 inches, use 2 baking sheets to accommodate the meringues.

*Save the juice from the crushed pineapple to use in the chocolate sauce.

Judy Quigley
Pawcatuck, Connecticut

Almond-Apple-Berry Cobbler With Vanilla-Brown Sugar Cream

Almond-Apple-Berry Cobbler With Vanilla-Brown Sugar Cream

Fresh berries make this a summertime favorite. The Vanilla-Brown Sugar Cream is wonderful in coffee.

¾ cup granulated sugar
2½ tablespoons almond paste, softened
1⅔ cups all-purpose baking mix ✶
1 cup milk
¼ cup unsalted butter
2 (21-ounce) cans apple pie filling
2 teaspoons grated lemon rind
1½ teaspoons vanilla extract
½ teaspoon almond extract
½ teaspoon apple pie spice
1 cup fresh raspberries or blackberries
⅔ cup all-purpose baking mix ✶
⅓ cup chopped almonds
¼ cup firmly packed brown sugar
2 tablespoons cold unsalted butter, cut into small pieces
Vanilla-Brown Sugar Cream

Beat together granulated sugar and almond paste at medium speed with an electric mixer until blended. Add 1⅔ cups baking mix. Gradually add milk, and beat until smooth. Pour batter into a lightly greased 13- x 9-inch baking dish.

Melt ¼ cup butter in a large saucepan over medium heat. Add pie filling and next 4 ingredients. Cook, stirring constantly, until heated. Stir in berries. Spoon filling evenly over batter.

Combine ⅔ cup baking mix, almonds, and brown sugar in a medium bowl. Cut in 2 tablespoons butter with a pastry blender until crumbly. Sprinkle streusel over filling.

Bake at 350° for 40 to 43 minutes or until bubbly. Serve warm with Vanilla-Brown Sugar Cream. **Makes:** 12 servings.
Prep: 18 min., **Cook:** 43 min.

Vanilla-Brown Sugar Cream:
1 cup whipping cream
¼ cup firmly packed brown sugar
2 teaspoons vanilla extract

Combine all ingredients. Beat at medium speed with an electric mixer until soft peaks form. **Makes:** 1¼ cups.
Prep: 5 min.

✶For testing purposes only, we used Bisquick Original All-Purpose Baking Mix.

Robert Gadsby
Great Falls, Montana

Miss Jeanne's Dutch Apple Pie

¾ cup sugar
1 teaspoon ground cinnamon
4 teaspoons quick-cooking tapioca, divided
2 pounds Granny Smith apples, sliced (about 6 cups)
¾ cup sugar
¾ cup all-purpose flour
½ cup cold butter, cut into small pieces
1 cup all-purpose flour
⅓ cup shortening
½ teaspoon salt
4 tablespoons ice water

Combine ¾ cup sugar, cinnamon, and 2 teaspoons tapioca in a large bowl, stirring well. Add apple slices; toss well. Set aside.
Combine ¾ cup sugar and ¾ cup flour in a bowl, stirring well. Cut in butter with a pastry blender until crumbly. Set aside.

Combine 1 cup flour, shortening, and salt with a pastry blender until crumbly. Sprinkle ice water, 1 tablespoon at a time, evenly over surface; stir with a fork just until dry ingredients are moistened. Shape pastry into a ball.
Roll pastry to ⅛-inch thickness on a lightly floured surface. Fit into a 9-inch pieplate; trim off excess pastry along edges. Fold edges under, and crimp. Sprinkle with remaining 2 teaspoons tapioca. Spoon apple mixture into crust, mounding in center. Sprinkle with butter mixture, covering apple mixture completely. Place on a baking sheet lined with aluminum foil.
Bake at 400° for 25 minutes. Shield pie from overbrowning by placing a square of aluminum foil lightly on pie. Bake 20 more minutes. Cool on a wire rack.
Makes: 8 servings.
Prep: 28 min., **Cook:** 45 min.

Tips: The shortening-flour mixture for the pastry should resemble small peas, not cornmeal, for maximum flakiness. Be careful not to work the pastry mixture for the piecrust anymore than absolutely necessary to "gather" it together into a ball or it will be dense, tough, and lose its flakiness. If your shortening is not cool, you can chill the shortening mixture *before* the water is added.

Jeanne Delp
Street, Maryland

Jeanne didn't roll out the pastry for this luscious pie, but we did because we preferred the fluted edge on a rolled pastry. Fluting helps to hold in all the juices.

Chocolate Chip-Buttermilk Custard Pie

This rich, decadent pie will quickly become a family favorite.

½ (15-ounce) package refrigerated piecrusts
½ cup butter, softened
1½ cups sugar
3½ tablespoons all-purpose flour
3 large eggs
¾ cup buttermilk
1 teaspoon vanilla extract
1½ cups semisweet chocolate morsels

Fit piecrust into a 9-inch deep-dish pieplate; fold edges under, and crimp. Bake at 400° for 6 minutes; cool crust on a wire rack. Reduce oven temperature to 350°.
Meanwhile, beat butter, sugar, and flour at medium speed with an electric mixer until blended. Add eggs, buttermilk, and vanilla; beat well. Fold in chocolate morsels. Pour into prepared crust.

Bake at 350° for 1 hour until just set and lightly browned. Cool completely before serving. **Makes:** 8 to 10 servings.
Prep: 5 min., **Cook:** 1 hr., 6 min.

Tip: Make this pie the day before you plan to serve it so it has plenty of time to cool.

Myrtle Jonson
Metter, Georgia

Granny's Pecan Cheesecake Pie

Sweet pecan pie and creamy cheesecake—a perfect pairing for a winning dessert.

1   (15-ounce) package refrigerated piecrusts
1   (8-ounce) package cream cheese, softened
4   large eggs, divided
½   cup sugar, divided
2   teaspoons vanilla extract, divided
¼   teaspoon salt
1¼ cups chopped pecans
1   cup light corn syrup

Unfold and stack 2 piecrusts; gently roll or press together. Fit into a 9-inch pieplate; fold edges under, and crimp.
Beat cream cheese, 1 egg, ¼ cup sugar, 1 teaspoon vanilla, and salt at medium speed with an electric mixer until smooth. Pour into piecrusts; sprinkle with pecans.
Whisk together remaining 3 eggs, remaining ¼ cup sugar, remaining 1 teaspoon vanilla, and corn syrup until combined; pour over pecans.

Bake at 350° for 55 minutes or until set. Cool completely. **Makes:** 8 servings.
Prep: 5 min., **Cook:** 55 min.

Karen Saum
Charlotte, North Carolina

Karen uses a single piecrust, but we doubled the crust on this ultra-rich, double-filled pie to make sure the filling doesn't leak into the bottom of the pieplate.

Death by Pecan

This buttery shortbreadlike crust forms a heavenly base for the rich and gooey pecan filling.

Death by Pecan Pastry
1   cup corn syrup
¾   cup sugar
3   large eggs, lightly beaten
3   tablespoons butter, melted
1   tablespoon brandy (optional)
1¼ teaspoons vanilla extract
¼   teaspoon salt
1   cup pecan pieces
1   cup pecan halves
Whipped cream (optional)
Vanilla ice cream (optional)

Prepare Death by Pecan Pastry.
Combine corn syrup and next 6 ingredients in a large bowl. Beat at medium speed with an electric mixer just until blended. Stir in pecan pieces. Pour into prepared Death by Pecan Pastry.

Arrange pecan halves on filling mixture. Bake at 325° for 1 hour or just until set, shielding edges of pie with aluminum foil, if necessary. If desired, serve warm with whipped cream or ice cream.
Makes: 6 to 8 servings.
Prep: 9 min., **Cook:** 1 hr.

Death by Pecan Pastry:
1   cup all-purpose flour
¾   cup ground pecans
¼   teaspoon salt
6   tablespoons cold butter, cut into small pieces
1   tablespoon white vinegar
1   egg yolk
1   tablespoon brandy (optional)
1   to 2 tablespoons cold water

Combine first 3 ingredients in a medium bowl; cut in butter with a pastry blender until mixture is crumbly.

Combine vinegar, egg yolk, and, if desired, brandy; sprinkle over dry ingredients. Stir with a fork. Add cold water, and stir just until dry ingredients are moistened. Shape dough into a ball; cover and chill 30 minutes.
Roll pastry to ⅛-inch thickness on a lightly floured surface. Place in a 9-inch pieplate coated with cooking spray; trim off excess pastry along edges. Fold edges under, and crimp. **Makes:** 1 (9-inch) pastry shell.
Prep: 16 min., **Other:** 30 min.

Irene Smith
Papillion, Nebraska

If you're serving a diehard pecan lover, **Irene** suggests offering butter pecan ice cream with the pie instead of vanilla.

Old-Fashioned Chocolate Pie

This quick pie has just enough meringue to balance the filling nicely, and you don't have extra egg yolks leftover.

½ (10-ounce) package frozen piecrusts ∗
2 egg whites
⅛ teaspoon cream of tartar
1¼ cups sugar, divided
3 tablespoons cocoa
2 tablespoons all-purpose flour
¼ teaspoon salt
2 egg yolks, lightly beaten
1 cup milk
½ cup butter
¼ cup semisweet chocolate morsels
1 teaspoon vanilla extract
¼ cup chopped pecans

Bake piecrust according to package directions. Cool on a wire rack.

Beat egg whites and cream of tartar at high speed with an electric mixer until foamy. Add ¼ cup sugar, 1 tablespoon at a time, beating until stiff peaks form and sugar dissolves. Set aside.

Whisk remaining 1 cup sugar and next 3 ingredients in a small bowl. Whisk together egg yolks and milk in a separate bowl.

Melt butter in a 2-quart heavy saucepan over medium heat. Add sugar mixture to melted butter, whisking until blended. Gradually whisk in milk mixture. Cook, whisking constantly, until mixture is thickened and bubbly.

Remove from heat. Add chocolate morsels and vanilla, stirring until chocolate is melted. Stir in pecans. Cover and keep warm.

Pour hot filling into piecrust. Spread meringue over hot filling, sealing to edge of pastry.

Bake at 375° for 12 minutes or until golden. Cool completely on a wire rack. Store in refrigerator. **Makes:** 8 servings. **Prep:** 9 min., **Cook:** 20 min.

∗For testing purposes only, we used Pillsbury Pet-Ritz frozen piecrust.

Tip: To avoid flattening out the meringue when you spread it on the filling, spoon meringue onto filling in large dollops; carefully connect the dollops with a light swirling motion.

Vickie Snow
Tuscaloosa, Alabama

Vickie makes a graham cracker crust for this pie, but we preferred a pastry crust.

Frozen Margarita Mousse Tarts

Salted pretzels form the crust for this light and refreshing dessert that mimics the flavors of the lime-flavored cocktail except for the tequila.

1   cup crushed salted pretzel
    sticks
¾   cup sugar
¼   cup butter, melted
⅓   cup orange juice
1   envelope unflavored gelatin
⅔   cup fresh lime juice (about
    5 limes)
1½ cups whipping cream
¼   teaspoon salt
1   cup sugar
Garnish: lime slices

Place paper baking cups in muffin pans. Combine first 3 ingredients in a medium bowl; stir well. Spoon tablespoonfuls of pretzel mixture into prepared pans, pressing to cover bottom of cups. Bake at 300° for 8 minutes. Remove from oven; cool slightly.

Meanwhile, place orange juice in a small microwave-safe bowl. Sprinkle with gelatin; stir and let stand 1 minute. Microwave orange juice mixture at HIGH 30 seconds or until gelatin dissolves; stir well. Stir in lime juice; cool to room temperature.

Combine whipping cream and salt in a medium bowl. Beat at medium speed with an electric mixer until foamy. Add sugar, 1 tablespoon at a time, beating until soft peaks form. Gradually fold in orange juice mixture until combined. **Fill** each muffin cup with ⅓ cup whipped cream mixture. Freeze 2 hours or until firm. Garnish with lime slices, if desired. **Makes:** 16 servings.
Prep: 3 min., **Cook:** 8 min., **Other:** 2 hrs.

Meryl Connelly
Essex Fells, New Jersey

Raspberry-Chocolate Tart

Cool, silky chocolate and juicy ripe berries, topped with sweetened whipped cream, in a buttery crumb crust—pure decadence!

1   (9-ounce) package chocolate
    wafers
½   cup butter, melted
½   cup heavy whipping cream
2   tablespoons light corn syrup
2   tablespoons butter
1   (10-ounce) package
    raspberry-flavored semisweet
    chocolate morsels
2   cups fresh raspberries
Sweetened whipped cream
Garnish: fresh raspberries

Process chocolate wafers in a food processor until finely crushed. With processor running, pour ½ cup melted butter through food chute; pulse just until crumbs are moistened. Press crumb mixture into a 9-inch tart pan. **Bake** at 350° for 8 minutes. Cool crust while preparing filling.

Combine ½ cup whipping cream, corn syrup, and 2 tablespoons butter in a small saucepan. Bring to a boil over medium heat, stirring constantly. Remove from heat; add chocolate morsels, stirring until smooth. Pour chocolate mixture into crust (crust will be warm). Cool 1 hour.

Arrange 2 cups raspberries, stemmed side down, in concentric circles on top of filling. Chill, uncovered, 1 hour or until firm. Serve with dollops of sweetened whipped cream. Garnish, if desired. Store in refrigerator. **Makes:** 8 servings.
Prep: 27 min., **Cook:** 11 min., **Other:** 2 hrs.

Judy Anderson
Albuquerque, New Mexico

If you don't own a tart pan, **Judy** says a 9-inch springform pan also works well for this dessert.

"Southern Joy" Peach and Praline Tart

A sweet and crumbly pâte sucrée (sugar pastry) lends a special cookielike flavor to this fruit tart. And the pecan mixture on top of the tart tastes like pralines, but it's actually soft and chewy—a yummy surprise.

¼ cup granulated sugar
¾ cup butter, softened
1 large egg
2 to 2¼ cups sifted cake flour
2 egg yolks
6 tablespoons granulated sugar
¼ cup butter, cut into pieces
1 tablespoon fresh lemon juice
⅔ cup coarsely chopped pecans
½ cup firmly packed light brown sugar
1 tablespoon dark corn syrup
1 teaspoon vanilla extract
2 cups sliced, peeled fresh peaches or 1 (16-ounce) package frozen peach slices, thawed (2 cups)
¼ cup peach preserves
Garnish: sweetened whipped cream

Process first 3 ingredients in a food processor until smooth. Add 2 cups cake flour. Process, adding additional flour, 1 tablespoon at a time, as necessary, until dough forms a ball. Shape dough into a 6-inch disk; wrap in wax paper, and chill 50 minutes or until firm but still malleable.

Coat a 10-inch tart pan with removable bottom and 1-inch sides with cooking spray. Remove wax paper from dough, and press into bottom and ½ inch up sides of prepared pan.

Bake at 350° for 35 minutes or until golden. Cool in pan on a wire rack 10 minutes; remove from pan, and cool completely. Remove to a serving platter.

Place egg yolks in a small bowl; whisk well. Combine 6 tablespoons granulated sugar, ¼ cup butter, and lemon juice in a small saucepan. Cook, whisking constantly, over medium-low heat until butter melts. Remove from heat. Gradually whisk about one-fourth of hot mixture into yolks; add to remaining hot mixture, whisking constantly. Place over medium-low heat; cook, whisking constantly, 2 to 3 minutes or just until thickened. Cover lemon curd; cool completely.

Combine pecans and next 3 ingredients in a medium skillet. Place over medium heat; cook, stirring constantly, until sugar melts and mixture is bubbly. Pour in a single layer onto wax paper; cool completely. Carefully remove wax paper, and break into small pieces.

Spread lemon curd in a thin layer over bottom of crust.

Drain peach slices well, and pat dry with a paper towel.

Place preserves in a medium bowl. Microwave at HIGH 20 seconds or just until warm; mash preserves with a fork. Add peach slices, stirring to glaze.

Arrange peach slices in a circular pattern on lemon curd. Gently brush any preserves remaining in bottom of bowl over peach slices. Top peach slices with praline mixture, mounding slightly in center of tart. Garnish, if desired. Serve immediately. Store in refrigerator.

Makes: 10 to 12 servings.
Prep: 30 min., **Cook:** 47 min., **Other:** 50 min.

Tip: Select firm, ripe fresh peaches. If using frozen peaches, be sure peaches are completely thawed and well drained. Soft, very ripe peaches produce an undesirable amount of juice on this tart, which interferes with the texture of the lemon curd. Carefully run a thin sharp knife between bottom of pan and pastry to release bottom of pan. Peach jam can be substituted for peach preserves.

Barbara Anne Belohovek
Huntington Beach, California

We enjoyed this fruit tart with whipped cream, but **Barbara Anne** often serves it with a scoop of vanilla ice cream.

Bartlett Delight

Bartlett Delight

Thinking about fixin' a traditional Southern cobbler? Well, put away that pan and get ready to make a galette—an absolutely wonderful pear crisp in traditional French form.

½ **cup firmly packed dark brown sugar**
½ **cup granulated sugar**
¼ **cup all-purpose flour**
1 **teaspoon ground cinnamon**
½ **teaspoon ground nutmeg**
4 **ripe Bartlett pears, peeled, cored, and thinly sliced (about 3½ cups)**
1 **tablespoon fresh lemon juice**
1 **teaspoon vanilla extract**
1 **(15-ounce) package refrigerated piecrusts**
⅓ **cup all-purpose flour**
¼ **cup firmly packed dark brown sugar**
¼ **teaspoon ground cinnamon**
2 **tablespoons cold butter, cut into small pieces**
1 **egg white, lightly beaten**
Sweetened whipped cream

Combine first 5 ingredients. Toss together pears, lemon juice, and vanilla in a large bowl. Add sugar mixture, tossing to coat.

Roll 1 piecrust to press out fold lines. Place piecrust on a nonstick aluminum foil-lined baking sheet. Spoon pear mixture in center of pastry, leaving a 3-inch border.

Combine ⅓ cup flour, ¼ cup brown sugar, and ¼ teaspoon cinnamon in a medium bowl; cut in butter with a pastry blender or fork until mixture is crumbly. Sprinkle over pear mixture. Lift pastry edges, and pull over pear mixture, fluting edges. Press edges gently to secure.

Roll remaining piecrust to press out fold lines; cut out leaves with a 2½-inch leaf-shaped cutter. Arrange leaves over pear mixture; brush with egg white.

Bake at 425° for 10 minutes. Reduce heat to 350°; bake 35 more minutes or until golden and bubbly. Let stand 20 minutes before serving. Serve with sweetened whipped cream. **Makes:** 8 servings.

Prep: 36 min., **Cook:** 45 min., **Other:** 20 min.

Tip: If you don't have leaf-shaped cutters, any shaped cutters will work. Your piecrust will slip down during baking, so make sure it's fitted snug up over your pear mixture before baking.

Cindy Cable
Carencro, Louisiana

Tarte à la Bouille

This delicious Cajun pie consists of a twice-cooked custard in a shortbreadlike crust. You can serve it slightly warm, but we preferred it chilled. It slices better chilled.

1½ cups sugar
⅓ cup cornstarch
¼ teaspoon salt
5 large eggs
6 cups milk
1 (5-ounce) can evaporated milk
¼ cup half-and-half
2 tablespoons butter
2 teaspoons vanilla extract
1 cup butter, softened
¾ cup sugar
2 cups all-purpose flour, divided
1 teaspoon vanilla extract
1 teaspoon fresh lemon juice
½ teaspoon baking powder
¼ teaspoon salt
Butter-flavored vegetable cooking spray

Whisk together first 3 ingredients in a large Dutch oven. Whisk in eggs, milks, and half-and-half. Add 2 tablespoons butter; place over medium heat. Cook, whisking rapidly and constantly, 18 minutes or until mixture thickens and coats the back of a spoon. (Do not boil.) Remove from heat; stir in 2 teaspoons vanilla. Set aside to cool.

Meanwhile, beat 1 cup butter and ¾ cup sugar at medium speed with an electric mixer until creamy. Reduce speed to low, and beat in 1 cup flour and next 4 ingredients. By hand, stir in remaining 1 cup flour until mixture forms a ball. Divide dough in half. Place half of dough between 2 sheets of floured wax paper. Roll dough into an 11-inch circle. Carefully peel off top piece of wax paper, and invert dough into a 9-inch deep-dish pieplate coated with cooking spray. Repeat rolling procedure with remaining half of dough. Carefully remove top piece of wax paper, and cut dough into ½-inch-wide strips.

Set Dutch oven containing custard in a large bowl of ice water. Stir for about 3 minutes or until mixture is completely cooled. Pour 4⅓ cups custard into bottom crust, reserving and chilling remaining custard for other uses. Immediately, arrange dough strips in a lattice pattern on top of pie. Seal strips to bottom crust. Bake at 350° for 45 minutes. Cool completely. Store in refrigerator. **Makes:** 8 servings.
Prep: 1 hr., 22 min., **Cook:** 1 hr., 3 min.

Note: You'll have half of the custard leftover. When chilled, it makes a delicious soft custard or a sauce to serve over fresh fruit. You can spike it with rum or bourbon or make a second recipe of the crust and bake 2 tarts. For best results, if you decide to make a second tart, do not double the crust in one bowl, but prepare it as 2 separate recipes.

Marian George
Fayetteville, Arkansas

How to Create a Prizewinning Recipe

Our judges and Test Kitchens' experts know
what makes a great *Southern Living* recipe. They
offer this seasoned advice that can help
your recipe stand out in the crowd.

Top 10
tips for a
prizewinning recipe

1 PUMP UP THE FLAVOR. Taste is our top priority—one bite has to make us want more. Experiment with ingredients to tweak your recipe up to the highest level possible. Include any helpful tips so that our Test Kitchens get the same results that you do.

2 LOOK FOR A FRESH TWIST. We love recipes that put a new spin on an old favorite. Head Judge Andria Hurst describes the winning Southern-Fried Stuffed Chicken as "a Southern icon turned into an elegant knife-and-fork food." With all its ingredients and gravy, Susan Rotter's chicken keeps its skin on to fry up crispy, like traditional fried chicken.

3 BE CREATIVE. Your recipe must be original. This means that it's your idea and has never been published or publicized. If you use a published recipe to start with, you must make significant changes to call it your own.

4 DO YOUR HOMEWORK. Is your recipe appropriate for this contest? Look at several past issues of the magazine to study the types of foods we usually feature. *Southern Living* recipes are more likely to be grits or fried chicken than steak tartare or paté de foie gras. Study past winning Cook-Off recipes to see what sets them apart.

5 MAKE IT LOOK GOOD. Presentation counts with a magazine known for beautiful photos. A dish that gets oohs and aahs on sight has a good chance to rise to the top. Consider whether a garnish or side dish will enhance the eye appeal of your recipe. Be sure to add your garnish to the ingredient list and recipe instructions.

DOES YOUR RECIPE HAVE WHAT IT TAKES TO WIN?

Southern Living Foods Editors list the following as the most vital features of an outstanding recipe. An entry that scores high on all five points stands a good chance of winning.

- Taste
- Originality
- Ease of preparation
- Presentation (visual appeal)
- Use of eligible sponsor products

We also give extra points to recipes that have broadly available ingredients. A hard-to-find or very expensive ingredient could keep a great-tasting recipe from winning. It also helps to use familiar standard appliances and equipment.

many good recipes. Make sure that every item used in the method is included in the ingredient list in the order used and with exact quantities.

8 **PUT IT TO THE TEST.** Errors and omissions are most likely to occur in the frenzy of a last-minute rush. Give yourself time to test your written entry. Ask someone who is unfamiliar with it to prepare the dish to be sure it works perfectly. Don't coach the cook; let her work on her own from your written recipe.

6 **KEEP IT SIMPLE.** We consider the time and procedures a recipe requires, and we may fail those that don't live up to expectations after hours of work. That doesn't mean you have to skimp—our grand prize recipe has a lengthy ingredient list, but assembly and cooking is relatively easy, and the payoff is first-rate. We adore a recipe that's quick and easy yet tastes and looks terrific.

9 **ENTER THE RIGHT CATEGORY.** We won't move an entry from one category to another to give it a better chance, so choose well. Some recipes fit more than one category. Susan Rotter capitalized on a Southern connection to enter her fried chicken in *Taste of the South*—a good choice, since she won the category and the grand prize. You can enter the same recipe in more than one category; each submission must be printed on a separate entry or sheet of paper.

7 **FOLLOW RULES TO THE LETTER.** Any error or omission in your written recipe will disqualify it. Check off each requirement on the entry form. For example, don't think that pretty stationery will impress the judges—the rules call for recipes to be submitted online or on an 8½" x 11" piece of plain white paper, and nothing else will do. Check that you have included oven temperature and cooking times, omissions that disqualified

10 **MAKE IT ACCESSIBLE.** Recipe ingredients should be readily available at mainstream stores nationwide. Find a common substitute for any ingredient that's unusually expensive, limited to a particular region, or so obscure that you have to order it from a gourmet catalog.

How to get the judges' attention

Attention to detail can make your recipe stand out in a crowded field. Try these suggestions to give your entry extra pizzazz that grabs the spotlight.

• THINK OF A CATCHY NAME.

A clever title may win your entry a second glance. Ruth Kendrick had this in mind with Spicy Tex-Mex Chicken Cobbler, anticipating that 'cobbler' would pique our interest in an entrée. A mouthwatering title such as Melt-in-Your-Mouth Braised and Barbecued Chicken sounds so good, who wouldn't want to taste it?

• RIDE A HOT TREND.

Check out culinary magazines and fashionable restaurants to get an idea of what's hot in the food world. Our 2003 finalists reflect the current wave of Asian and Southwestern flavors as well as adventurous use of exotic spices and herbs. (See *Top 10 Food Trends in Our 2003 Cook-Off,* page 18.)

• MAKE THE MOST OF SPONSOR PRODUCTS.

Your recipe can use as many sponsor products as you like, but it must have at least one. If you can give a sponsor product a starring role, so much the better. Cash prizes are awarded to recipes that make the best use of each sponsor product.

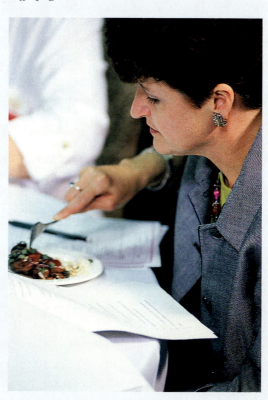

• ENTER AS OFTEN AS YOU LIKE.

Multiple entries increase the chances that you'll hit upon the right recipe for the right category. Several of our finalists hit the jackpot with a single entry, while others sent in several.

Index